four sisters of hofei

ANNPING CHIN

four sisters of hofei

ANNPING CHIN

BLOOMSBURY

Excerpts from *The Book of Songs,* translated by Arthur Waley, reprinted with permission of Grove/Atlantic, Inc. Copyright 1937 by Arthur Waley.

Excerpts from *Anthology of Chinese Literature: From the Earliest Times to the Fourteenth Century,* edited by Cyril Birch, reprinted with permission of Grove/Atlantic, Inc. Copyright 1965 by Grove Press, Inc.

Excerpts from *The Selected Poetry of Rainer Maria Rilke* by Rainer Maria Rilke, translated by Stephen Mitchell, reprinted with permission of Random House, Inc. Copyright 1982 by Stephen Mitchell.

Excerpts from *Peach Blossom Fish* by Chang Ch'ung-ho, translated by Hans W. Frankel with Ian Boyden and Edward Morris, reprinted with permission of Crab Quill Press. Copyright 1999 by Hans W. Frankel

First published in Great Britain 2003

Bloomsbury Publishing Plc, 38 Soho Square, London W1D 3HB

A CIP catalogue record for this book is available from the British Library

ISBN 07475 5477 3

10 9 8 7 6 5 4 3 2 1

Printed in Great Britain by Clays ltd, St Ives plc

To Jonathan

Contents

Acknowledgments *xi*

The Chang Family *xiii*

Prologue *xvii*

Chapter 1: *The Wedding* 1

Chapter 2: *Birth* 9

Chapter 3: *Reasons for Moving* 17

Chapter 4: *The Hofei Spirit* 23

Chapter 5: *Grandmother* 38

Chapter 6: *Mother* 60

Chapter 7: *Father* 73

Chapter 8: *The School* 98

Chapter 9: *Nurse-Nannies* 111

Chapter 10: *Yuan-ho* 125

Chapter 11: *Yun-ho* 155

Chapter 12: *Chao-ho* 185

Chapter 13: *Ch'ung-ho* 242

A Note on Sources 271

Notes 273

Bibliography 293

Index 301

Acknowledgments

My deepest gratitude goes to Chang Ch'ung-ho for her time and attention, and for all that she has taught me over the years. She has tried to answer all my queries at whatever hour of the day and has shared with me her knowledge of calligraphy and of *k'un-ch'ü* opera. Because of her, I wanted to get things right.

The other three Chang sisters, Yuan-ho, Yun-ho, and Chao-ho, and their brothers Ting-ho, Yü-ho, and Huan-ho have also been generous and patient. They shared with me all they could think of—diaries, letters, books, family journals, poems, photos, and what they remembered about things past—in order to help me get things right. Thanks are also due to Yuan-ho's daughter Ling Hung, who showed me her adoptive mother Ling Hai-hsia's unpublished memoir, and to Chao-ho's granddaughter Shen Hung for sending me her grandparents' photo.

Over the years, I have also benefited from the help of Sherman Cochran, Vivienne Shue, Bai Qianshen, Xia Chuntao, Peter Carroll, and Chen Hsiao-ch'iang. They have either pointed to sources crucial for my work or have tried to help me locate sources that were difficult to find.

When I was in Hofei, Weng Fei from the Anhwei Chinese Academy of Social Sciences gave me important leads; and two local historians, Cheng Rufeng and Ma Qi, and a cousin of the Chang sisters, Chang Hsi-ho, accompanied me to the Chang ancestral home, thirty miles west of the city. Traces of the old world were still visible on the grounds of the two family compounds: a pair of *wu-t'ung* trees, which were gifts from the Empress Dowager Tz'u-hsi to the sisters' great-grandfather Chang Shu-sheng for helping the Ch'ing government to put down the Taiping rebels in the 1860s; a partially burned-out storehouse; a two-story building that young ladies in the family had once used as their retreat. I want to thank them for taking me there.

Andrew Wylie and Zoe Pagnamenta were enthusiastic about the project from the beginning. Their encouragement always came at the right moment. Nan Graham and Sarah McGrath at Scribner gave me a lot of time to work on this book and did much to make it clearer and better. Janet Fletcher was shrewd and thorough in her copyediting.

My son, Yar, rescued me from many computer crises. My daughter, Mei, gave a thoughtful reading to an earlier version. My husband, Jonathan Spence, read many drafts and thought through everything with me. In this long course, he remained the person who understood me best and what I tried to say. And even when he was most helpful, he let me be. He had an art that only those with true compassion and civility could attain. To him this book is dedicated.

MARCH 22, 2002
WEST HAVEN, CONNECTICUT

The Chang Family

Chao-ho, Yun-ho, and Yuan-ho with their two younger brothers and
their first tutor, Miss Wan, in 1916.

CHANG SHU-SHENG: great-grandfather.

CHANG HUA-KUEI: grandfather, oldest son of Chang Shu-sheng

CHANG WU-LING: Chang Hua-kuei's only son and father of the four
Chang sisters.

LU YING: Chang Wu-ling's first wife and mother of the four Chang sisters.
She also had five sons with Chang Wu-ling.

WEI CHÜN-I: Chang Wu-ling's second wife and stepmother to the Chang sisters.

CHANG YUAN-HO: oldest sister.

CHANG YUN-HO: second sister.

CHANG CHAO-HO: third sister.

CHANG CH'UNG-HO: fourth sister.

CHANG TSUNG-HO: oldest brother.

CHANG YIN-HO: second brother.

CHANG TING-HO: third brother.

CHANG YÜ-HO: fourth brother,

CHANG HUAN-HO: fifth brother.

CHANG NING-HO: son of Chang Wu-ling and Wei Chün-i; the sisters' half-brother

Brothers-in-Law

KU CH'UAN-CHIEH: husband of oldest sister, Yuan-ho.

CHOU YU-KUANG: husband of second sister, Yun-ho.

SHEN TS'UNG-WEN: husband of third sister, Chao-ho.

HANS FRANKEL: husband of fourth sister, Ch'ung-ho.

In that river, far this side of Stygia,
The mere flowing of the water is gayety,
Flashing and flashing in the sun.

—WALLACE STEVENS,
"THE RIVER OF RIVERS IN CONNECTICUT"

THIS BOOK IS ABOUT four Chinese sisters and their family. Born between 1907 and 1914, the Chang sisters are all alive. Together they are able to recall the shape and practice of the old Chinese society and the people who inhabited that world. It was the sisters' great-grandfather who brought fame and fortune to the family and gave the Changs a respectable position in their community when in the 1860s he helped the imperial army defeat the Taiping rebels in a long and destructive civil war. The book starts in the nineteenth century with the story of this man and ends in the present as his four great-granddaughters reflect on the century they lived through—the huge shifts in social customs and private expectations, wars against foreigners and civil wars, and those things that endured despite life's inconstancy.

The writing of this book began by chance. The youngest of the Chang sisters, Ch'ung-ho, was having dinner with us at our house. I had met Ch'ung-ho a few times before; she and her husband, Hans Frankel, had been my husband's teachers at Yale in the 1960s. I revered her and was also a little afraid of her. Ch'ung-ho had a reputation because of her learning. Men and women deferred to her on matters of art and calligraphy and on the history of Chinese opera; they also sought her help on textual problems, which could be anything from reading and dating the colophons on a painting, to unpacking the allusions in a classical poem, to deciphering the emperor's handwriting on an eighteenth-century palace memorial. Elderly scholars would stop by the house where she lived north of New Haven if they were traveling through New England. Younger ones— those who were brought up on modern education and had read only a handful of poems from the *Classic of Odes* and ten or twenty biographies in the Han dynasty histories—could gauge her only by the way the elderly scholars regarded her. We were simply too handicapped to appreciate what she knew.

The mood that evening was particularly convivial. My mother was with us, and I think that we had either fish or shrimp for dinner. The confluence of these things set Ch'ung-ho off with tales of the grandaunt who adopted her when she was eight months old. The grandaunt had been a lay Buddhist and a vegetarian. On many occasions, she had saved live fish and shrimps from the frying pan, instructing her servants to buy them at the market and then return them to the stream. Cooks from local restaurants, when they recognized these servants at the stream, would wait at some distance with baskets and nets for what later would become their menu. Ch'ung-ho's storytelling was delightful, but I suspect only her husband and I could catch most of what she said. My husband understood only standard Chinese. My mom was hard of hearing. Ch'ung-ho's Chinese had a Hofei lilt, and she spoke softly.

In the months that followed, I visited Ch'ung-ho several times. We were comfortable with each other. I liked to listen to her speak and the fun of deciphering everything she said, including her many wordplays and puns. If I got stuck, she seemed to enjoy explaining to me why she thought a turn of phrase or a matching couplet was particularly clever. This was how our friendship began. But why, in the end, did I want to write about her family? And why should I write a contemporary family history when I had known for a long time that I would be content just to read and write about the works of Chinese philosophers from more than two millennia ago?

I know that Ch'ung-ho's learning—the fact that it is both flexible and precise, and makes her scintillate—was one reason for my initial pursuit. Scholars and philosophers since Confucius' time have been trying to put into words their love for learning and their anxiety about not learning enough. They debated why one should learn, how to learn, and whether there were steps to follow. They wrote treatises on such questions and had their disciples record what they said. The subject of learning was something I had been interested in since my graduate studies. With Ch'ung-ho, I could actually ask her: How did she acquire her learning and how did she begin? Who gave her the opportunities and who encouraged her? Who were her teachers? What were her parents like? Were her brothers and sisters as accomplished as she? Did the end of imperial rule and the views and politics of the 1920s and 1930s change the way the Chinese learned?

I also wanted to know more about Ch'ung-ho's grandaunt. Since she was a widow for a long time and lived a sequestered life, leaving her private quarters only for short periods, once or twice a year, I wondered how she was able to run her household and manage her enormous landholdings. Who helped her and how did she keep an eye on those who helped her? Did anyone take advantage of her situation as a childless widow? I also wanted to understand her charity, and her belief in doing whatever she could for those she loved, before leaving them to their own resources and to chance. I came to realize later that this was also the belief of Ch'ung-ho's parents, which would eventually help me to make sense of her sisters, of their characters and their lives' trajectories.

Then there were Ch'ung-ho's sisters. When I heard that she had three just as I had three, I could not resist the idea of going to see them. Ch'ung-ho told me that her father had moved the family from their home in Hofei to Shanghai and then to Soochow, and that after her grandaunt adopted her and took her back to Hofei, she saw her brothers and sisters only on short visits, once or twice a year, before she went home to Soochow at the age of sixteen. I met Ch'ung-ho's second and third sisters, Yun-ho and Chao-ho, next. They lived in Peking.

It was a sultry July morning in 1996, and it took me a long time to find Yun-ho's apartment on Walking Stick Lane. Nothing Ch'ung-ho had told me beforehand could have prepared me for Yun-ho. She had just come home from the hospital. A chronic heart ailment had nearly taken her life a month earlier, but I would not have known this from her voice or movement. Yun-ho was all volume and vim. She spoke in trills, sharing a bountiful store of family tales. She also acted out the parts and relived the emotions. From her, I learned about their parents, the children's wet nurses and nurse-nannies, and a huge spectrum of minor characters—relatives, friends, servants, and tutors—who had moved in and out of the Chang household in Soochow.

Next to Yun-ho, her sister Chao-ho, who joined us on this occasion, seemed shy and inarticulate. She was the most famous of the sisters because of her marriage to a very fine and extremely popular novelist, Shen Ts'ung-wen. It was Shen Ts'ung-wen who had fanned public interest in his wife by suggesting that he might have tucked a few scenes from his marriage into his fiction. In 1949, Shen became the target of a literary persecution. When the Communist critics pressured him to produce literature more suitable to their vision, he stopped writing. When he was rehabilitated in the 1980s, his old works resurfaced. And as new editions of his writings appeared in bookstores, there was renewed interest in Chao-ho. But Chao-ho hardly seemed like someone accustomed to fame, especially with Yun-ho in the room. Although she would respond when asked a question, and even occasionally would banter with her sister, on the whole she was content to let Yun-ho dominate the conversation. I figured that this was how it had always been between these two sisters. When, later in the afternoon, Yun-ho reluctantly retreated to her bedroom, Chao-ho chose to stay up with me to chat. She managed to fill in a lot about herself and her family while her sister napped, but she never seemed to abandon her reserve and her slightly stiff demeanor. I returned to these two sisters several times after this visit, in the summer of 1996 and then a year later, seeing them separately in their homes. Chao-ho seemed frail in 1997. Yun-ho was as indefatigable as before, only she seemed unwilling to let me go. We talked about my next visit, knowing, of course, that this reunion could be our last.

The oldest sister, Yuan-ho, was the last one I visited. I saw her several times in Oakland, California, where she was living at the time, and then when she moved to Connecticut, where she now resides with her daughter. Yuan-ho was as buoyant as Yun-ho, but in other ways she was Yun-ho's opposite. While Yun-ho was candid and opinionated, Yuan-ho offered a lot of information and many stories about their family but no strong views and very little about herself. She was the most enigmatic of the four sisters and someone I could only begin to understand through her sisters.

In addition to the hours and hours spent talking with the Chang sisters and three of their brothers who are still alive, I had access to Yun-ho's diary from the 1980s, her brother Tsung-ho's diary from the 1920s and 1930s, the letters Chao-ho and her husband had exchanged over a forty-year period, and the siblings' writings in a family journal called *Shui*, or "Water," which Yun-ho has edited for five years with Chao-ho. (Since my last visit to Peking, Yun-ho has also published three books of essays about her family, many of which overlap with her oral accounts and the pieces collected in *Shui*.) These sources are the anchor of my book. They also inspired me to make further excursions into a host of related topics: the history of their native place, Hofei; the exploits and hopes of their great-grandfather Chang Shu-sheng; Shanghai politics and culture in the 1920s and 1930s; the school founded by their father; women's education in the republican period; wartime China under occupation; the art of calligraphy; and the history of the southern-style opera, *k'un-ch'ü*, in which the sisters all had extensive training and stage experience.

The first half of this book is organized around the Changs' native place, their ancestors, and the guardians of the sisters' early life, a group that included the children's mother, father, and nurse-nannies, and the grandaunt who became Ch'ung-ho's adoptive grandmother. The grandaunt was a learned woman of extraordinary inner resources. In the eyes of those who knew her or merely heard about her, her conduct was the measure of propriety. The sisters' mother was like the grandaunt. She died when they and their five brothers were still very young but remained perfect in the children's imagination and a beneficent specter in their lives. Their father was a wealthy landowner. He never did very much with his life, but he had a large way of looking at the world. He gave his children every educational opportunity and poured generous sums of family money into a school for women, which he founded in Soochow.

The nurse-nannies were mostly widows from the Hofei countryside, who had to rely on themselves to support their families after their husbands had died. These were women with no education but with firm opinions about modern institutions and modern ways, women who knew attachments and despair but also how to make mirth.

The early chapters in this book can stand on their own, but they are also meant to point to those things that could have helped to shape the lives of these sisters: the opportunities given to their great-grandfather, for instance, and what he made of them; their father's decision to pick up his family and leave for Shanghai; and their mother's early death—in other words, things that had to do with both calculated moves and chance, hard work and native temperament, the influence of the times and of other people, the presence of ancient ghosts and of the modern spirit.

The second half of the book is about the sisters themselves. Instead of writing four chronological biographies, I followed a practice in *k'un-ch'ü* performance, which is to showcase only one or two scenes in, say, a fifty-four-scene drama. So for each sister, I concentrated on the story that is most consequential to her and that at the same time can take us far into Chinese culture and social history.

Yuan-ho's tale is that of the wife of a professional *k'un-ch'ü* actor, a man who in fact had quit the stage when the two first met. At the time, a union between a gentry woman and an actor, even a former actor, was considered unsound because an actor was lowly in the Chinese social arrangement. Yuan-ho's love for the stage and for *k'un-ch'ü* theater must have influenced her decision to marry this man. So while her marriage fulfilled these private yearnings, it also introduced problems so secret and unsettling that Yuan-ho, even now, will not talk about them.

Yun-ho's story is that of a perpetual scrapper—a woman born with a hero's sensibilities and an old warrior's toughness. Yet despite her forceful character, Yun-ho managed to survive the most violent political storms under Communist rule with hardly any emotional wound or physical injury.

Chao-ho's life was also linked to that of her husband, the novelist Shen Ts'ung-wen. Because they wrote to each other often and their letters were not destroyed in the wars or during the Cultural Revolution, we have an intimate account of a modern marriage through correspondence. Also, because Shen was an uncommon writer, his letters caught many elusive things in life and relationships—dreams, longings, feelings of powerlessness or disconnection.

The book ends with Ch'ung-ho, as it should, for it was my friendship with her that began this pursuit. The last chapter is my attempt to understand how she acquired a scholar's confidence and a scholar's way of working and how she translated skills and scholarship into art. My journey into the history of calligraphy and the aesthetics of opera performance throughout this book has one goal: to make sense of a conversation the two of us had long ago about the idea of "being suspended," which Ch'ung-ho called *ling-k'ung*. A good calligrapher has it in the wrist, she said. A good *k'un-ch'ü* performer has it in her gesturing. And a good poet is able to express it in words.

FOUR SISTERS
OF HOFEI

Chapter 1

THE WEDDING

WHEN LU YING OF YANG-CHOU married Chang Wu-ling of Hofei in 1906, her dowry procession stretched along ten streets, from Ssu-k'ai-lou to Lung-men-hsiang. It had taken Lu Ying's mother ten years to get things ready for this occasion, and when it was all over she died of exhaustion.

A grandmother in the family remembered Lu Ying on her wedding day, particularly the shock of meeting her eyes as her pearl-beaded veil came off. They were phoenix eyes with a phoenix glow, which foretold a life that would quickly be spent. Lu Ying died sixteen years later, after fourteen pregnancies and nine children.

In China's pre-republican society, a bride of Lu Ying's stature was something of a mystery. She spent a good part of her wedding day in a sedan chair, her face concealed. She appeared before her guests only toward the end of the ceremony, when she left the ancestral hall, in which she had paid obeisance to her husband's forebears, and was led to her nuptial chamber. Even then she remained demure and seemed reluctant to part with her maiden life and with her own family. Unlike modern brides who wave to their guests and smile for the camera, a bride in the old society seemed always on the verge of tears. She leaned on her escorts for support as she made her way deliberately into the nuptial room. Since it was not customary for the bride's side of the family to be present at the wedding, her escorts were relatives of the groom's family. They were married women deemed lucky because of the number of male children they had borne.

The bride had only one sure ally on her wedding day. This ally was not a relative or a best friend, but a bridesmaid her parents had hired to give her protection. The bridesmaid was, by training, a professional talker; she said clever things and was able to churn out propitious jingles. She was a foil for the bride, and her chatter was the shield she created for her young mistress at the time it was most needed. Before the wedding, the bride would have had a cloistered existence in the women's quarters, and so it was natural that she should be reticent. She was not used to being viewed, much less to being the object of everyone's curiosity. And she was nervous in her anticipation of the wedding night and of her life ahead, which she had to face on her own.

The women in the Chang household would talk about Lu Ying's wedding long after she was gone. They remembered the ditty the bridesmaid sang after Lu Ying and her husband were seated on their nuptial bed and the women guests had scattered coins and nuts all around the room to encourage fertility:

> *A little stick, red and glossy,*
> *I shall use to lift the bride's veil.*
> *If it lands on her bed,*
> *She shall have a house full of children.*
> *If it drops on the ground,*
> *She shall be buying land and fields.*

Lu Ying had come all the way from Yang-chou, a vibrant commercial city by the Grand Canal. Her dowry traveled more than a hundred miles down the Yangtze, across the Kiangsu border to Wuhu in Anhwei province, and another eighty miles along the tributaries and by land before it reached Hofei. We don't know how many men guarded the bride's entourage, or whether these men were sent from Hofei or hired by the Lu family in Yang-chou. We also don't know whether bandits along the way had given them trouble. The precious cargo that accompanied them was like spots on a leopard, the Chinese would say, making them an easy target for predators.

The Changs' home province, Anhwei, had never been a safe place to travel in. Frequent flooding of the Yellow and the Huai Rivers, alternating with drought and plagues of locusts, had created severe poverty and an unstable environment in the north, in an area called Huai-pei. The people of Huai-pei did very little to prepare themselves for disasters or to try to change their circumstances. They would move to cities south of the Yangtze when things were bad and return home when conditions eased a little. They continued this pattern of life throughout much of the Ch'ing dynasty. The local gazetteers described them as weak and violent, lazy and contentious: "too lazy even to weed after they've sown their seeds and to prepare for irrigation works in case of flood and drought," yet "quick to congregate and compete for small gains." The people of other parts of Anhwei and of the neighboring Chekiang and Kiangsu provinces referred to them as troublemakers. To them, the people of Huai-pei seemed to be everywhere, and wherever they went, they were either pillaging or in need— bandits or beggars.

During the nineteenth century, parts of Shantung and Honan provinces and much of Anhwei were ravaged by the Nien bandits from Huai-pei. The Nien were at first involved in ordinary crimes: murder, plunder, extortion, kidnapping, and smuggling. In the 1850s, their activities escalated into a major insurrection against the state. In 1868, the Ch'ing government, with the help of the local Anhwei army, brought the Nien rebels under control, but banditry continued to be a way of life for some. As a result, most of the well-to-do families in rural Anhwei employed their own braves and protected their living quarters with walls and moats. Life was relatively safe within, but outside, brigands could descend, demanding money, goods, or a fee for safe passage; they could also seize victims and exact a ransom from their family. Even as recently as sixty years ago, when gentry women or their young daughters wanted to visit relatives ten or twenty miles away, they usually traveled on foot, not in sedan chairs, and they dressed simply, to look as if they were one family with the men hired to protect them.

The period from 1905 to 1910 was difficult for nearly all the people of Anhwei, not just those of Huai-pei, and 1906, the year of Wu-ling's marriage, was a particularly bad year. Flood, drought, windstorm, and locusts arrived in turn. As many as forty counties suffered some form of natural disaster, and flooding visited over two-thirds of the province. Hunger drove people to robbery and looting. In the city of Hui-chou, for instance, peasants, working in groups, raided local grain shops. The most serious incidents, however, were reported around Wuhu: in April, a band of desperadoes foraged a shipment of rice as it was coming across the border from the east; and in November, thousands of starving peasants stormed into the residential compounds of the local gentry, taking food and whatever else they could get their hands on.

Lu Ying and her family were traveling through Wuhu around the time of these incidents. The journey must have been very difficult and dangerous. What is puzzling is that the marriage should have taken place at all. Why did the Chang family want to go to the trouble of having Wu-ling marry a woman from Yang-chou when for over forty years they had been pairing their sons and daughters with the children of the Lius, T'angs, Chous, and Lis in their own county? Yang-chou was not only two hundred miles away and in a different province, but the people there spoke a different dialect. And why would the Lus agree to such an arrangement? They knew that to transport a dowry of a size appropriate for the match across such a long distance would be extremely risky.

We know that Chang Wu-ling's grandfather, Chang Shu-sheng, had also married a woman from a Lu family. And we know that Lu Ying's family was originally from Hofei; her family moved to Yang-chou sometime during the Ch'ing dynasty. It is possible that the two Lu families were related. There is, however, another explanation. According to the women of the Chang family, Lu Ying was not an ordinary woman. At the age of twenty-one, she was already known for her intelligence, her managerial skills, and her sense of appropriateness. Her older sister, less attractive and dull by comparison, was passed over as a possible marriage partner for Wu-ling.

In the old world, it was not only the bride's family that lost sleep thinking about their child's impending marriage; the groom's family, too, had their worries—about handing over the household responsibilities to a near stranger and about "the question of progeny," that is, whether the new daughter-in-law could produce sons. In the case of the Changs, the elders had to give extra consideration to Wu-ling's marriage because he was the heir to the primary descent line. Wu-ling's grandfather, Chang Shu-sheng, had eight younger brothers. Together they formed the nine branches of the Chang clan. Wu-ling was the heir to Chang Shu-sheng's branch. Even though he was adopted from the fifth branch, within the lineage organization he was considered the grandson of Chang Shu-sheng, and a descendent of the senior branch, the day he entered their door. His adoptive father, the oldest of Chang Shu-sheng's three sons, had no children with his principal wife and only a daughter with his concubine. He died at forty-nine, when Wu-ling was only eight. Wu-ling's adoptive mother was naturally anxious for him to begin producing heirs early, which also meant that his wife would have to be able to look after him—he was only seventeen at the time of his wedding—and to help him manage his enormous landholdings. Moreover, in 1906, the families of Chang Shu-sheng's sons were still living together; the men had all died sometime before, but their wives and concubines—five widows in all—were alive. Chang Wu-ling's wife would have to look after them as well, plus a large staff of accountants, nursemaids, servants, cooks, gatekeepers, and gardeners.

It was the custom in Hofei for the bride to be older than the groom. Lu Ying was four years older than her husband. Their two families were compatible in money and status, and her dowry reflected the seriousness with which her parents had treated her marriage. The women in the Chang family recalled that nothing was amiss in this abundant load: gold, silver, pearl, and jade, all the luxurious goods and household items imaginable; even the dustpan had a silver chain dangling from it. The servants also received lavish amounts of gift money from the bride's family when Lu Ying's brothers came to call three days after the wedding ceremony. By all accounts, Lu Ying's parents outdid themselves from beginning to end. Their splendid display of generosity seems to have pleased everyone in the groom's family. One could say that Lu Ying's grand send-off was her parents' last attempt to look after her. It was their way of making sure that she would begin her new life under the most favorable circumstances.

In the Chang family history, Lu Ying remains an elusive figure. She was the anchor of the household, an example for all, yet no one could describe her precisely. Her children could recall the feel of the house when she was alive; they say that she was the sole maker of its climate—harmonious and calm, without a trace of discontent. They remember the mood she created but not her person, not her words or her features, nothing exact. Lu Ying was what the eighteenth-century historian Chang Hsüeh-ch'eng would have called a "quiet woman." Her strength lay in her refraining, a holding back out of propriety and a reining in for balance and equilibrium. "[Quietness] is the finest appellation that can be given to a woman," Chang declared, "because it implies learning."

During Chang Hsüeh-ch'eng's time, it was fashionable for men of letters to encourage women to write poetry and to help them have their works published. Chang called these men "shameless hypocrites" and their protégées "women of activity," and he characterized their venture as a grand delusion, men deluding women and women deluding themselves. The men were hypocrites, he wrote, because they disguised lust as appreciation. "The intentions are unspeakable. Alas! They think that they are praising a woman for her talent when the rest of the world knows that it's sympathy born out of lust." The women they spur on are "busy scribbling away even though what they say has no range, no more than a woman's 'private sorrows in spring and fall' and the sentiments of 'flowers flourish and fade.'" The women Chang Hsüeh-ch'eng respected were the "quiet women," women who knew when to desist.

The earliest reference to the "quiet woman" is found in the *Classic of Odes*, an anthology of poetry from two and half millennia ago. The first stanza of Ode 42 in "Airs of the State" reads:

> *Lovely is the quiet woman.*
> *She was to await me at a corner of the wall.*
> *Loving and not seeing her,*
> *Scratch my head, pace up and down.*

For centuries, commentators could not even agree on the character of this woman, whether she was virtuous or not. The poem says that the woman waits by the city wall. One commentator explains that she waits and does not appear to her lover because she feels that she is not ready: "She must wait until she is cultivated before letting herself become his wife." Another insists that the poem "describes a tryst" and that the woman must be morally lax because no respectable woman would wait by the city wall for a man. Over time the first reading became orthodox, and by Chang Hsüeh-ch'eng's day, the idea of a quiet woman had lost all its ambiguity.

Chang believed that the tradition of the quiet woman began more than twenty-five hundred years ago, in the Chou dynasty, when women worked as court historians and ritualists. Such women were restrained in speech and writing because what they said had to be fit for diplomacy. Reticence was, therefore, a reflection of their learning and proof of their integrity. But as rulers ceased appointing women to offices and as women withdrew more and more into the domestic world, few people understood what the ancients meant by learning for women, and even fewer appreciated the power of reticence. Chang wrote that any woman of his own time who showed some refinement and quickness and had some knowledge of literature considered herself an expert. She flashed her abilities and wore them like makeup, unaware that women once had their own learning and that this learning was rooted in the practice of rites. In Chang's view, these women took their limited talents too seriously, not realizing that writing poetry was no substitute for the profession women once had.

Perhaps Chang Hsüeh-ch'eng exaggerated the power of early Chinese women, but what he said about their learning is compelling. He believed that learning for women was once sacred and demanding because it was the learning of ritualists and historians. Over the centuries, this quiet and rigorous learning had fallen into obscurity with the multiplication of loud women and their loud display of small talents. When women abandoned their learning, Chang wrote, they lost the art of life. That art, which is both moral and aesthetic, could perhaps be described as some strange resistance in "the cataract of death" *and* in the flood of life—a "throwing backward on itself." The idea is as old as the *Classic of Changes,* yet it remains difficult to define and defend. Chang Hsüeh-ch'eng suggested an approach: "One must use women of the past such as T'ai-jen and T'ai-ssu to render the fullness of its hidden virtues." T'ai-jen was the mother, and T'ai-ssu the wife, of King Wen, founder of the ancient Chou state and the most illustrious of all kings. The two women were the subject of several poems in the *Classic of Odes.* T'ai-jen "had great dignity," one poem says, and was loving to her own mother-in-law. T'ai-ssu, her daughter-in-law, "carried on her fine tone, /

Bearing a multitude of sons." T'ai-ssu was also "retiring and virtuous," and when she was young, her reticence made the prince anxious: "Day and night the prince sought her. / Sought her and could not get her." She cultivates herself in quietness, we are told, and "will not show herself."

Confucians have always known how to relate the stories of T'ai-jen and T'ai-ssu to the life of King Wen. It was under their influence, it seemed, that King Wen "did what was right without instruction" and "walked on the path of benevolence without admonition." Perhaps Lu Ying had a similar effect on her husband and children. She loved her mother-in-law, and her four daughters inherited her "fine tone." She also had five good sons and her husband's character was immaculate. But these were obvious measures of her worth. There had to be more.

The year after Lu Ying was married, a woman named Ch'iu Chin was executed in the neighboring Chekiang province in connection with the assassination of the Manchu governor of Anhwei. Ch'iu Chin had been a model of reckless behavior. She left her husband and two children in 1904 to go to Japan, to get away from China—"to scrub off the old mud," she wrote. In Japan, she learned to make bombs, had herself photographed in Western male attire, and drew crowds of Chinese students to her lectures. Ch'iu Chin was a woman of fire and charisma. By 1906, she was back in China, helping her cousin Hsü Hsi-lin stockpile ammunition and recruit young men to fight their revolution. When Hsü shot and killed the governor, Ch'iu Chin was implicated. Authorities claimed that she was simultaneously planning an uprising in Shao-hsing. After a mock trial, she was beheaded. One could argue, as some did, that she got what was coming to her. But many Chinese were moved by her violent death, and they made her a martyr. Her collected poems were published a few months after her execution, and a second edition soon followed.

Lu Ying must have read about Ch'iu Chin. She could have even read her writings. What did she think of this woman and her unsparing indictment of the Chinese family, of her own family and her husband's family, and of the awful business of getting married to a stranger who might turn out to be "an animal"? Ch'iu Chin once wrote: "When it's time to get married and move to the new house, they hire the bride a sedan chair all decked out with multicolored embroidery, but sitting shut up inside it one can barely breathe. And once you get there, whatever your husband is like, as long as he's a family man they will tell you you were blessed in a previous existence and are being rewarded in this one. If he turns out no good, they will tell you it's 'retribution for that earlier existence' or 'the aura was all wrong.'"

The wedding Ch'iu Chin had described could have been Lu Ying's. Lu Ying left no hint that hers was at all like it. And what of the argument that whether a woman gets a good husband or a bad one she should accept it as her karmic destiny? Ch'iu Chin regarded it with contempt. Did Lu Ying make much of it? After all the Chinese applied the gist of this argument to many situations, and to men as well as women. Did Lu Ying share in Ch'iu Chin's anguish? Was she at all touched by her and by her death?

Chapter 2

BIRTH

THE SUMMER CH'IU CHIN DIED, Lu Ying was heavy with child. Yuan-ho was born at the end of 1907, the year after her parents married. Lu Ying's mother-in-law was happy beyond words even though her grandchild was a girl. She herself had been barren—"a basket without fruit," as the *Classic of Changes* called such women. Her only son was adopted, and her husband's other child, a daughter, had been born to a concubine. In 1907, Yuan-ho's grandmother was already in her late fifties and was "nearly going mad from wanting children." She would say that "a boy is good, but a girl is also nice." She figured that if a woman could have a girl she could also have a boy, and so she welcomed all. Before she died, she was blessed with six more grandchildren, three girls and three boys. But Yuan-ho remained the apple of her eye.

As soon as her wet nurse left, Yuan-ho was moved into her grandmother's room. Every day the two would breakfast and lunch together upstairs, in their private wing, apart from the rest of the family. Perhaps because of this, Yuan-ho's brothers and sisters always regarded her as something of an enigma. Not only was she more beautiful than they, she was more poised and assured. While their grandmother was living, she alone was exempt from scolding and punishment. Her parents refrained so as not to upset the old grandmother, and the servants were careful not to antagonize Yuan-ho even when she provoked them. Yuan-ho recalls one exception. One afternoon, she and her wet nurse were sitting on the edge of their bed, and for no reason at all, Yuan-ho slapped the woman's hand. Her wet nurse slapped back. The game became a contest of willfulness between an adult and a child, a servant and her young mistress. Then Yuan-ho jumped down from the bed and declared that she was going upstairs to tell her grandmother. Her wet nurse did nothing to stop her, and Yuan-ho did not carry out her threat.

Yuan-ho remembers her wet nurse because she was not weaned until she was five. The wet nurse's family name was Wan; she had a rectangular face, fair skin, and perfect teeth. A woman of few words and much gravity, she was Yuan-ho's "mom," and that was how Yuan-ho addressed her. This woman was the anchor of the nursery as she sat on a low stool, watching her child play. Yuan-ho had unusual toys, some of which were imported from the West: an iron butterfly whose wings flapped and made a *geda-geda* sound when it was pulled; a windup train that went around and around on a kidney-shaped track. In between playing with her toys, Yuan-ho would rush to her "mom," stand between her legs, and drink from her breasts. Oddly, being treated as precious did not deter her from acquiring practical skills later on or seeking self-reliance. It may have made her more conscious of how she looked or how others looked at her, but Yuan-ho was not a delicate flower.

When Yuan-ho was seven, her wet nurse went home to the Hofei country-side, where she contracted a serious illness and soon died. Among the well-to-do families in Anhwei, when a child was weaned, it was customary to replace her wet nurse with a *kan-kan*. A *kan-kan* looked after the child during the day and shared her bed at night; she disciplined her when she strayed and comforted her when she was ill. She was the child's nurse and nanny. She was also her protector and constant companion. Often she was someone who was already in the family ser-vice, someone who had demonstrated loyalty and good sense—in other words, a reliable woman, as in the case of Ch'en Kan-kan, Yuan-ho's nurse-nanny.

Ch'en Kan-kan had been the personal servant of Yuan-ho's grandmother for many years. She remembered Lu Ying as a bride. In fact, after her young mas-ter and mistress's ceremony, she had staged a mock wedding with two other women servants, using the streamers and candies left over from the festivities. Ch'en Kan-kan, decked in her master's hat and socks, played the part of the bridegroom, with the other two cast as bride and bridesmaid. The three tried to give an accurate reenactment, as their audience had witnessed the real thing only a few days before. The bridesmaid scattered peanuts and walnuts dyed red and green along the bridal path. She escorted the bride out of the sedan chair, lend-ing her support throughout each act, first in the ancestral hall and then in the wedding chamber. But just as the newlyweds were exchanging nuptial cups, the old mistress woke from her afternoon nap. She called to Ch'en Kan-kan to help her up, bringing the play to a sudden halt.

Ch'en Kan-kan was already a mother of four children, three sons and a daughter, when she arrived in the Chang household. The Changs chose their servants from the Hofei countryside or from the nearby counties of Ts'ao-hsien, Shu-ch'eng, Wu-wei, or Lu-chiang. They felt more at home with servants who spoke their dialect, cooked local dishes, and observed similar customs. Ch'en Kan-kan was from Wu-wei county, about sixty miles southeast of Hofei. She was considered a woman of "perfect happiness" (*ch'üan-fu*); not only did she have three sons but her husband was still living.

Nearly all the *kan-kan* came to the Chang family as young widows in their twenties or early thirties. Peasant women often had to rely on themselves when their husbands died. Many preferred working as household servants. This way, they were able to apply their skills immediately, whether by cooking, sewing, cleaning, or tending to the old and young, and to live in a relatively safe environment. In some cases a stable household could also offer a woman a home, where she could foster attachments and create a family separate from her own. And here is the irony: A woman leaves her young children to the care of relatives so that she can provide for them. She ends up spending nearly the rest of her life in her employer's house, "staying ten years and sometimes decades," looking after his mother, his wife, and his children before she returns home to die. Meanwhile, her children have grown up and often have died before her. Whatever love she had, she gave to someone else.

Ch'en Kan-kan was not a widow, but since her husband could not adequately support his family of six from farming, she took to the road and found employment with the Changs. We do not know how often Ch'en Kan-kan visited her own family in Wu-wei county. From Yuan-ho's account, up to the time she went away to college, her nurse-nanny never left her side, moving with the Chang family first to Shanghai and then to Soochow, when she could have stayed in Hofei, working in a household closer to home. Ch'en Kan-kan never told Yuan-ho why she'd made this choice—whether it was a financial decision or an emotional one. Nurse-nannies, according to the Chang children, were not prone to analysis. They did what was necessary. Yuan-ho gave an example—a story Ch'en Kan-kan had told about herself. Ch'en Kan-kan said that she delivered her last baby alone, leaning against a doorway with a sturdy broom in her hands. The baby was her fifth, and it was a girl. As soon as she had given birth, Ch'en Kan-kan picked up the placenta and pressed it against the baby's face. The baby was dead within minutes, and the mother "went on with life as if this child had never existed." Ch'en Kan-kan betrayed no emotion and no sense of regret when she recounted this scene from her life, adding that "it had been a lean year, the baby could not have survived, and so it was better for her to be reincarnated in a family that had more to offer her."

Women like Ch'en Kan-kan are "as strong as nature is strong." They manage to move beyond self-pity and blame even when a person or an event might occasion remembrance of some past sorrow. Ch'en Kan-kan was probably among the women in the delivery room the day Lu Ying's second child was born. It was another daughter.

Yun-ho, as Lu Ying's second child was named, came into this world silently, in the predawn hours of a late July morning in 1909, with three coils of umbilical cord wrapped tightly around her neck. The midwife tried every technique she knew to shock her into life—slapping, dunking her in cold and then hot water, and finally artificial resuscitation, "a new gimmick at the time." Nothing worked. The women in the room were ready to give up, saying that heaven did not intend this child to live. The grandmother, however, refused to go along. Sitting in her round-backed, mother-of-pearl-inlaid sandalwood chair, she looked like the Buddha, though without his repose. One minute she was begging, the next she was commanding the women there to bring the baby back to life. The rest of the story, Yun-ho herself would reconstruct years later from what others had remembered about that day:

There was a fat woman in the room, who loved smoking. She said to my grandmother, "Let me light a water pipe and smoke that child to life." No one believed that she could do it. Everything else had failed, and so why should the fat woman work miracles? Besides, no one had ever heard that tobacco smoke had life-giving powers. Everyone was skeptical but no one dared to reject her offer. Right away, one woman went to fetch a water pipe, and another started rolling paper spills. Soon a large packet of quality cut tobacco arrived. The fat woman immediately went to work.

The midwife carefully held the baby, her arms stretched out in front of her, while the fat woman smoked tobacco pinch after pinch, blowing every puff onto the baby's face. Another hour went by. One heard only the sound of smoking in the room.

The fat woman quietly counted to herself the number of pinches she had consumed—it must have been over fifty. She was glutted with nicotine, yet she felt tired. Sweat had streamed down to her heels. The midwife was even more worn out. Others around them were busy wiping the moisture off their foreheads. On this sweltering day, no one dreamt of using a fan, for fear of causing even the slightest draft in the room. . . . The women looked at my aged grandmother, hoping that she would change her mind. Grandma sat in her sandalwood chair, her eyes wide open and her hunchback straightened by the weight of this crisis. She made no gesture. . . .

When the clock struck twelve, Grandma shut her eyes. She was a Buddhist. Her mouth wanted to chant the Buddha's name but couldn't because the delivery room was unclean. She knew she was losing the battle. She also knew that as soon as she admitted defeat the women in the room would abandon their struggle.

Finally the midwife put the baby down on her bright-colored apron, her arms giving out altogether. She said to my grandmother, "Old Mistress, it's already been a hundred pinches. Old Mistress, why don't you go and get some rest." As she talked, the baby tumbled from her apron into a washbowl on the ground. . . .

With tears welling up in her eyes, my grandmother replied, "Give her eight more pinches of puff, and then I'll get some rest." Grandma always carried with her a string of prayer beads. The hundred and eight beads on the string signified the completion of a virtuous deed. The fat woman had no choice but to smoke some more, now aiming her puffs at the washbowl. She had never known that smoking could be so disagreeable. A few more puffs, she thought to herself, and she would never touch the stuff again. Thus resolved, she executed the final stage of her task briskly and neatly. One pinch, two pinches, three pinches . . . time glided by.

Grandma got up from her chair. She paused to steady herself before walking toward the washbowl. "My little granddaughter is finished," she said, "so at least let me have a look at her—after all, she is still my descendent." As she was bidding farewell to me through the thick curtain of smoke, she noticed that my nose was twitching, my mouth was trying to make a sound, and I was trying to raise my arm.

Yun-ho does not remember her wet nurse's name, only the shape of her nose and eyes. She claims that except for her wet nurse and the cooks in the kitchen no one was particularly fond of her before she was three. She cried late at night and cried before the cock crowed, a humorless, scrawny little thing, but she had the adoration of her wet nurse, which, at that age, was enough. Her wet nurse, she says, loved her like the lad in a Hofei folk song who was smitten with his young bride:

> From the top floor of my cousin's home,
> From the top floor of my cousin's home,

I flung open the windows,
And that's how I saw her.
Her face was powdered white,
Her teeth like shiny rice,
Flat her shoes,
Bright the stitchings,
Red, red her robe.
Returning to my home, I ask my mom,
Let's sell our house,
And sell our land,
Have her come and marry me.
I am scared hot water might burn her,
I am scared cold water might chill her.
If I carry her on my shoulder,
I might drop her.
If I cradle her in my mouth,
I might bite her.
If I burn incense,
I might jinx her.
But if I don't burn incense,
The Bodhisattva might forsake her.

This wet nurse left when Yun-ho was three and a half, just after the New Year celebration. She was sent home because of an accident, for which Yun-ho even now feels responsible. As Yun-ho remembers it, it all began on New Year's Eve. That night her wet nurse told her how mice conducted their weddings: Peasant girls are usually married on the eighth day of the twelfth lunar month, but mice marry off their daughters on New Year's Eve. The mouse groom, looking smart in his new riding jacket, leads the procession from his tiny white horse. Behind him come tens of cases of wedding dowry all in a row and eight robust mice in waistcoats, carrying a festooned chair. In the chair sits the bride, stylishly coiffured and holding in her hands a red kerchief. The band played, gongs and drums sounded, and Yun-ho was spellbound. Her wet nurse then decorated cakes and sweet buns with velvet flowers and placed them on top of a tall armoire. She told Yun-ho that these were gifts for the newlyweds. Days later, when Yun-ho had long forgotten their game, her wet nurse went to collect the gifts meant for the mice in her story. The stool on which she was standing tipped over, and she broke a leg. She went home a few days later, and no one knew what became of her.

* * *

When Yun-ho's younger sister, Chao-ho, was born, the servants in the house said that her mother wept. She was the third child, also the third daughter. Even the old grandmother was indifferent. To make things worse, Lu Ying had a son by the next year, but he died as soon as he was born. For months after, the family was in mourning. Chao-ho brought them no joy because she was born at the wrong time. She claimed that unlike her sisters she was a child of no significance. No one fussed over her and no one watched her closely. On account of this, she says, she gained a sturdy constitution and had lots of time on her own, with more freedom than her sisters to do what children liked to do.

Chao-ho does not recall her wet nurse at all, only the feeling of missing her after she was gone. The cooks taught her a way to get rid of her blues. They said that she would feel better if she sang,

> *Hurry on there*
> *and hurry on back.*
> *Save me from worrying,*
> *worrying about you.*

So every day, Chao-ho sat on her little stool, chanting this ditty again and again.

The year after their baby son died, Lu Ying's husband decided to move their home to Shanghai, where they rented a two-story house in the French Concession. It was around this time that Lu Ying found herself pregnant again, and the auguries were good. A distant relative from a prominent Hofei family, the Lis, was certain that Lu Ying was to have a boy and the boy would survive. She should know. She was a woman who had produced only sons. Before the baby was due, this relative—who was the same age as Lu Ying—dispatched to the expectant mother two emissaries bearing gifts of gold and silver. She wanted to rub some of her luck on Lu Ying and to show the Changs she could make good her prediction. It was decided that when the boy was born, he was to be adopted in name by the Li family. And since the Lis were not going to take the baby away, it would be done amicably and in good taste; moreover, the formality would draw the two families even closer. So among the gifts was a gold lock—a pendant—to suggest that the Lis had the baby forever fastened to them. The emissaries took a room in a nearby hotel to wait for the good news. On the day Ch'ung-ho was born, Lu Ying was silent, and no congratulations could be heard in the delivery room. The two women sent by the Lis left quietly with the gifts that had been intended for the newborn.

Ch'ung-ho's first wet nurse was named Kao. She was married to an opium addict, and being around the toxic smoke desiccated her. So Ch'ung-ho was always crying for more milk. One night, mother and child were alone downstairs. Both were crying and both were beyond consolation—Ch'ung-ho from hunger and Lu Ying from tiredness and perhaps from wanting a son. Ch'ung-ho was eight months old. Upstairs, her grandaunt was listening. The next day, she asked Lu Ying if she could formally adopt the baby, taking her home to Hofei and looking after her as if she were her own granddaughter. Lu Ying said yes.

Ch'ung-ho's adoptive grandmother had been widowed long before. She had a daughter and a granddaughter, but both were dead by the time Ch'ung-ho was born. Many in the family thought that she took Ch'ung-ho in because she needed company. Ch'ung-ho, however, believed that her adoptive grandmother acted out of love and compassion for her mother. Before the decision became final, the grandaunt wanted to visit a fortune-teller to find out whether her fate and Ch'ung-ho's fate tallied. She had already lost a daughter and a granddaughter. She needed some indication from the gods, some sign from Heaven to tell her that it was suitable for her to bring up this child, that she would not ruin Ch'ung-ho's chance for life if their destinies were joined. But Lu Ying said to her elderly relative: "Ch'ung-ho has her own destiny. What's hers is hers alone." So it was with her mother's assurance that Ch'ung-ho began her own journey, apart from her family, in Hofei.

Chapter 3

REASONS FOR MOVING

IT WAS IN THE EARLY MONTHS OF 1912 that Chang Wu-ling decided to abandon Hofei for Shanghai. He took with him all three families of his branch, which included his wife and three baby daughters, his half-sister, five elderly widows, and several cousins, plus his daughters' wet nurses, a fleet of servants, and trunks full of possessions.

From the sheer number of dependents that accompanied him on this journey it would not appear that Wu-ling went to Shanghai to seek adventure or glamour. Even though his financial circumstances could have afforded him a very agreeable life there, it would not be the same as living in Hofei, where the Changs had been enjoying the amenities of being affluent and prominent ever since Chang Shu-sheng, Wu-ling's grandfather, helped the Ch'ing government to win the wars against the Taiping and Nien rebels in the 1860s. Nor did Chang Wu-ling go to Shanghai to become an activist, although the city could have offered many opportunities in radical or reform politics. In Hofei, he had studied with tutors at home and so was nowhere near a public school or a military academy, where revolutionaries liked to gather and do their recruiting. In fact, in the five years Wu-ling was in Shanghai, he never joined any political organization, never published anything. Why then did he choose to leave Hofei? Was he anticipating the dark days ahead in Anhwei?

For most people of Anhwei, the first decade of the twentieth century was without benefaction or protection. Tax collecting had run amok, partly due to the debts the Ch'ing government had incurred through losing out to the foreigners. Between 1905 and 1907, for example, Anhwei was remitting over one million taels of silver to Peking annually just to help pay for the Boxer indemnities. This did not include the province's contributions toward military expenditures or the money the Ch'ing government spent on modernizing schools and constructing roads, railroads, and other public works, which added up to another 450,000 taels each year.

Traditionally, the most significant portion of government revenue came from land tax. During the 1850s, to raise money to fight the Taiping rebels, officials in Peking introduced a transit tax called *likin*. Goods such as tea, tobacco, liquor, medicine, rice, and porcelain all carried *likin* duties. Because *likin* was often collected before the goods were sold, abuse was rampant; it was possible for an item to be taxed several times at several *likin* stations while it was in transit. By the 1900s, *likin* goods in Anhwei might be taxed more than thirty times before they reached their destination. And many other commercial taxes were instituted around this time. There were levies on opening up a shop; on land deeds and broker's fees; on school grounds and reed lands; on cows, horses, pigs, sheep, and bodyguards; on cotton prints, husks, and chaff. "Everything has a tax," someone wrote, "fuel, soy, vinegar, every chicken, duck, and shrimp, all of our daily staples—nothing is exempted."

The combination of relentless taxing and violent weather forced some people in Anhwei to lawlessness and others to collective action. In 1906, the shops in Wuhu went on strike. In 1908, the shops in Hsü county went on strike. In 1909, an angry mob in Su-chou* vandalized a branch office of the Salt Commission, and when local officials still would not reduce their salt tax, they attacked the office again.

In the five years prior to the fall of the Ch'ing, there were also at least ten large-scale rice raids in Anhwei. Yet peasants rioting out of despair did not seem as threatening to the Manchu rulers as the gatherings of men and women with education and some means, who met in schools and private homes to discuss assassination plans or ways to infiltrate the military. The earliest of such gatherings in Anhwei took place in the river-shore treaty ports of An-ch'ing and Wuhu, where antiforeign sentiment had been strong. These were political rallies with specific agendas, usually directed against foreign incursions, British and Italian businessmen buying into the rights of Anhwei coal mines, for instance, or Russia's occupation of the three eastern provinces. But after 1904, patriotic activities in Anhwei became increasingly anti-Manchu and increasingly secretive.

---

*This is not the Soochow in Kiangsu province but the one in Anhwei.

Even before Sun Yat-sen founded the T'ung-meng-hui (Revolutionary Alliance) in 1905, the Anhwei radicals had formed their own revolutionary associations. The Anhwei Patriotic Society met for the first time on May 17, 1903, in a local library in An-ch'ing. The Shanghai paper *Su-pao* reports:

> Over three hundred people, two hundred of them students from the Anhwei Advanced Level School, the Military Preparatory Academy and T'ung-ch'eng Public School, are gathered here to hear the Anhwei patriots speak. Outside the rain is pouring. The building is small. Not everyone could get in. People are standing by the entrance, trying to catch what the speakers are saying.

In his keynote speech, Ch'en Tu-hsiu, the principal organizer, warned that a national crisis was at hand. Unless Chinese of his generation were willing to work together to reverse their country's physical and moral conditions, he said, they were all going to end up as slaves, like oxen and horses or worse. Two years after this gathering, in 1905, members of an Anhwei revolutionary association tried to assassinate five Ch'ing government officials in the Peking Railway Station. The plan was botched: the bomb intended for these five men exploded ahead of time, killing the would-be assassin and causing only minor injuries to three of the officials. Then, in 1907, several young officers in the police academy at An-ch'ing shot and killed the Manchu governor of Anhwei when he was there on a visit. The insurrection was swiftly put down, but it must have shaken up Manchu officials everywhere.

When the Ch'ing dynasty finally collapsed, it looked as if it was the result of a concerted effort, carefully coordinated among the provinces, between the revolutionaries and the army, with the tacit approval of the provincial assemblies. How it really happened is more difficult to piece together. On October 10, 1911, a small group of revolutionaries in the city of Wuchang launched an uprising the day after the local police stumbled upon their headquarter. By the next day, six divisions of the Ch'ing New Army stationed nearby had decided to throw in their lot. By the end of October, the New Army regiments in five provinces had mutinied. By early November, two provinces bordering Anhwei had seceded. On November 8, 1911, the Anhwei provincial assembly formally declared its independence from the Ch'ing government.

The revolution added a new level of confusion in Anhwei. On the day Anhwei declared its independence, a revolutionary leader, with the support of the provincial assembly, forced the governor of Anhwei—someone who had been appointed by the Ch'ing court—to surrender his official seal. But within three days, the new governor lost his mandate. Merchants closed shops, and people in the provincial capital, An-ch'ing, gathered around his office building, demanding his resignation, all because he ordered the officials and military personnel in his province to cut off their queues. The people invited their old governor back and restored him to power, not because they liked him, but because they knew what to expect from him and also because he let them keep their queues.

The old governor did not last long either. Within two days, an Anhwei military division stormed into the provincial capital and began emptying the arsenal and treasury. The governor sought safety in a Catholic church and eventually made his way out of the city. The tug-of-war between the revolutionary forces and the various independent and pro-Ch'ing factions continued into 1913, well after the last emperor, P'u-i, had abdicated. Warlords took charge of Anhwei politics in the ensuing decade while life in the province descended further into dullness and gloom.

Wu-ling, however, could not have foreseen this when he decided to leave home. No one could have known in the spring of 1912 how the forces of history would play themselves out. There had just been a revolution. The emperor had stepped down, but might regain power. Men with private ambitions were beginning to dig in, but it was too early to guess what they would bring to pass. Wu-ling left no record of what he thought in those years, but from what we know of his views later in life, it appears that he would have welcomed this change even though it meant a plunge into the unknown, possibly with catastrophic consequences. He was by nature slow to act. Yet he made two or three big moves in his life, and they usually followed the collapse of an old order. An upheaval in the outside world could give him a jump-start. So when the Ch'ing dynasty fell, he packed up his family and went to Shanghai.

He was also leaving behind many problems within his clan. Like many families that had grown too big and too comfortable, the Changs during Wu-ling's time were plagued with slovenliness and depravity. It is possible that in 1912 Chang Wu-ling was moving his family away from these influences. He could have stayed and tried to change things at home, but he was only twenty-three at the time, a youngster in the clan's hierarchy. Besides, he was not the sort of man who believed that he should lecture anyone or that lectures on moral conduct could change human behavior.

If Chang Wu-ling was trying to find a good environment for his children to grow up in, why did he choose Shanghai, a city that made no secret of its unbridled money making and pleasure seeking, a city that had grown callous at the sight of human misery? Shanghai in the second decade of the twentieth century was at once morally corrosive and energized. It got its charge from trafficking goods and ideas among conflicting standards and competing claims. And so it was possible for a city glutted with guidebooks on prostitutes also to have the most progressive schools for women. Pornography and revolutionary materials were often displayed in the same bookshop, because Shanghai entrepreneurs regarded all things as equal. Winners in contests of the most beautiful and talented courtesans were accorded titles traditionally given to successful candidates in the civil service examinations. Such ambiguities had been around for a long time, probably ever since the city had been turned into a treaty port in the 1840s and carved up into three relatively independent entities: the Chinese City, the International Settlement, and the French Concession. And of those who were reared in this climate, some became unscrupulous or hollow, and others, morally strong and alert.

From the 1890s to 1910, as scholars and publicists began to recognize the press as the quickest and most immediate way of disseminating knowledge and raising political awareness, they came to Shanghai to publish their journals and newspapers. They were drawn to the possibilities of this city and all its resources. The most progressive papers in those two decades were all founded in Shanghai. For those who dared to challenge the limits of permissibility, the foreign settlements also offered some protection from government retaliation. *Su-pao* was an important test case at the time. The newspaper was located in the International Settlement, and so when the Ch'ing government demanded the paper be closed and its writers arrested for publishing seditious material, it was the governing body of the International Settlement that handled the arrest, the trial, and the incarceration of the six defendants. Within two years, all but one, who died in prison, were released.

Chang Wu-ling came under the influence of the press early in his life. We don't know which of the papers published in Shanghai he read, but in the first decade of the twentieth century, there were at least fifteen papers and journals being circulated in Anhwei and several Shanghai papers were reaching the provinces through subscription. His children later would recall that while they were growing up in the 1920s their father subscribed to at least twenty papers—"national papers and local papers, he read everything."

The founder of the *Anhwei Vernacular Paper*—the famous radical Ch'en Tu-hsiu—explained in his first issue what it was like to live in Anhwei in 1904 and not have any papers to read.

If a person were to stay home three hundred and sixty days a year with no papers to read, it would be like sleeping in a drum. This would be true for a first-rate scholar; how much more so for a merchant or a craftsman. He wouldn't know about anything that happened outside of his district, not even cataclysmic events. For instance, in 1900, after the foreign soldiers had already occupied Peking, here in Anhwei, the people from Hui-chou and Yin-chou still claimed that the Boxers were scoring major victories everywhere. If there were vernacular papers at the time, then we could have gotten real news from outside, and we would not have gone so far as uttering this type of nonsense.

For most people who lived in the provinces, the press served a practical purpose. It brought good news and bad; it told them whether there was a war on and who had the upper hand, whether bandits were on the rise and where it might be safe to hide. The press also introduced new categories of knowledge and new ways of organizing and utilizing knowledge. On the whole it gave the reader a sense of proportion—where he stood in relation to the rest of the world and how to measure what he knew against what others knew. It allowed a person awareness, which did not usually lead to activism but often prepared him for change.

The press was probably a conduit in Chang Wu-ling's decision to uproot his family and head for Shanghai. Life had become listless in Hofei, and he wanted to start anew. Shanghai possessed the energy and quickness Hofei lacked. It was a world so much bigger because of what it contained and the room it still had left. The combination of admiration for foreigners and foreign things and deep resentment of their presence also gave this city an edgy disposition, which some, especially the young, found attractive.

Chang Wu-ling was able to make this move because he had the money to do so; he chose to make it because he had absorbed from his family worries about the larger world and the belief that change could be good. At the time, he could not have known the full implications of his action; that it would determine the fate of his children—the friends and education they would have, the books they would read, the types of music and theater they would enjoy, the careers they would choose, and the extent of their empathy. The move meant that all of Wu-ling's children, those born before 1912 and those born after, would follow a course utterly different from that of their cousins in the other eight branches. Even Ch'ung-ho, who had come back to the city of Hofei from Shanghai with her adoptive grandmother, was able to have a life quite separate from that of her cousins, who grew up in the Changs' ancestral home in West Hofei. Wu-ling's children, therefore, never took part in their native community and never had to submit themselves to its rules and rulings. Yet aspects of that world would remain staples in their lives: memories of their ancestors and what their father carried with him when he left home—something we can call the Hofei spirit.

Chapter 4

THE HOFEI SPIRIT

THE CHANGS HAD NOT ALWAYS lived in Hofei. An early ancestor had moved there from Kiangsi, a province just to the south, sometime during the fifteenth or sixteenth century. A spirit tablet of this man had been sittting on the family altar for generations, but memories of the older home had long disappeared. Three out of the four Chang sisters grew up in Soochow, yet they all considered themselves "natives of Hofei": they spoke Hofei dialect, had Hofei nurse-nannies, and could all recall details of that world, even though they had only heard about it from other people.

Hofei sits in the middle of Anhwei province, between the Huai and the Yangtze Rivers.* The military first recognized its strategic importance twenty-seven hundred years ago. Then, Hofei straddled two rival kingdoms and so naturally became the venue of their seesaw struggles. Merchants and traders soon followed the soldiers, seeing that profits could be made from trafficking goods there. They dealt in arms and grain when there was a war, and in timber, hides, and exotic food when respite set in. Throughout Chinese history, Hofei would find herself in the same circumstances many times, especially in periods when

---

*Hofei here refers to Hofei county, which is not to be confused with Hofei city. Until early in the twentieth century, it was one of five counties under the jurisdiction of Lu-chou prefecture. When the republican government abolished the prefecture (*chou*) as an administrative unit, the prefectural capital of Lu-chou was renamed Hofei city. The Changs were originally from Hofei county. In the 1870s, the great-grandfather of the Chang sisters also built a lavish residence in the prefectural capital.

China was divided, such as the end of the second century and the beginning of the tenth century.

Early texts traced Hofei's ancestry to the ancient kingdom of Ch'u. In the Chinese imagination, the world of Ch'u suggests color and darkness, playful madness, and a love for the irrational. The philosopher Chuang Tzu, the poet Ch'ü Yuan, and the patron of scholars, Liu An, all contributed to its mystery and splendor. Yet Hofei did not come into its own until the second half of the nineteenth century. A new type of elite had emerged after the imperial army had foiled the Taiping and the Nien rebels. Most did not have the credentials of the traditional gentry—no extensive schooling in Confucian thought and no degrees to prove their erudition. Yet it was these men that gave Hofei the kind of respectability it had not known before. Wu-ling's ancestors belonged to this group.

Before the 1850s, the Changs could call themselves only low gentry. They owned a modest plot of land, and very occasionally a member of the family would pass the county examination, which helped the family to maintain a scholarly status in the eyes of the community. Wu-ling's great-grandfather had a local literary degree, but of his nine children, only his oldest, Wu-ling's grandfather Shu-sheng, achieved the same distinction. Had there not been a civil war, Chang Shu-sheng probably would have sat for the next round of examinations at the provincial level and his brothers at the county (or entry) level, doing what most men in China for over a thousand years had been doing, if they had the means: getting themselves certified for civil service.

The Taiping and Nien uprisings in the mid-nineteenth century changed all this. Four of the Chang brothers fought with the government troops under the leadership of another Hofei man, Li Hung-chang, who went on to become China's foremost statesman and a close advisor to the Manchu rulers. When the last rebel group was suppressed, one Chang brother was dead, killed in action, while the other three were generously rewarded and swiftly posted to other government jobs. Of the brothers, Chang Shu-sheng was the most widely acknowledged for his achievements. His sterling performance as a battalion commander was backed by Li Hung-chang, whose recommendations already carried a lot of influence in Peking. The Manchu court conferred on Chang the title Cho-yung Brave (*Cho-yung-pa-tu-lu*) and posted him as their judicial commissioner in Chihli province. This was followed by a succession of high-level appointments, as governor-general of grain transport; governor-general of Kwangsi, Kiangsu, and Anhwei; of Kwangtung and Kwangsi, and finally acting governor-general of Chihli.

Chang Shu-sheng's rise to power was not unique among the Hofei men who took part in the Taiping conflict. Four of his neighbors—a peddler, a roving gang leader, and two desperately poor farmers—followed similar career tracks. Merit in war gave them titles and good jobs, while spoils of war helped them to amass huge personal fortunes, tens of thousands of *mu* of land in Hofei and prime properties in cities south of the Yangtze. Though barely literate, these men, after they had attained money and power, learned to behave like upper gentry and conduct business like upper gentry. They gave their genealogies a complete makeover; they hired professionals to help them collect books, antiques, paintings, and calligraphy.

The same men also poured money into repairing and building schools and examination halls. The West Hofei Academy was established around this time with the money Chang Shu-sheng and his neighbors donated. In addition to education, the new Hofei elite supported many other local projects: poor relief and charitable estates; road and bridge repair; the construction of ponds, dams, and dikes; and the restoration of temples, shrines, and ancient relics. Because most of them were away on official assignments in other provinces much of the time, they could make only material contributions: money, land, and objects such as tables and chairs for the examination halls and religious implements and musical instruments for the temples. The other types of responsibilities, such as settling local disputes, supervising public works, and organizing famine relief, which were normally expected of the gentry, they had to leave to their family and relatives, and to the less important gentry there.

On the whole, in Hofei the newcomers to gentry status did what good gentry had done for many centuries, keeping an eye on regional affairs, looking after the interests of their home areas, and helping to finance numerous community projects. In temperament and style, however, they were noticeably different. Compared with their predecessors, these newcomers seemed more flexible and adventurous, more likely to break rules, and less afraid of change and unfamiliar ways; they were also tougher and more decisive, equally comfortable with administering a province and fighting on the battlefield, and less likely to back down in a conflict; finally, they had seen more and experienced more and so had more interests and wider concerns than the local gentlemen and were more capable of handling big problems. They preferred action, trying things out for themselves, and had little patience for theories.

Take Liu Ming-ch'uan, Chang Shu-sheng's compeer during the suppression campaigns. In the 1850s, when the Taiping rebels were moving violently across Anhwei, all fired up by the vision of a Christian kingdom in China, Liu was raising his own hell in the western corner of Hofei county, near Ta-ch'ien Mountain. In 1854 he killed a man, a thug who had been extorting money from his widowed mother, and became an outlaw himself. Two years after he went on the run, the Ch'ing authorities set fire to his family's four-room house, and that night, his mother hanged herself from a cassia tree. This tragedy spurred Liu to commit even more serious crimes. He recruited smugglers and stragglers and formed his own roving band. They stayed together in a fortified camp at the foot of Ta-ch'ien Mountain and lived off resources extorted from the local community. Finally, in 1858, the prefect in neighboring Liu-an county lured him into a trap. If there had not been a war, Liu would have been dead that year, at the age of twenty-two, executed as a common criminal. But the prefect saw some usefulness in him and struck a bargain: Liu would be allowed to live if he threw himself in with the government forces. The way local historians described this episode is like a page from a knight-errant romance:

> The prefect appreciated Liu's chivalrous nature and thought him promising, and so persuaded him to work with the Ch'ing army, saying that he should offer his undying service to the Ch'ing court as atonement for his crimes. Liu, deeply moved by the prefect's kindness, decided to join the Ch'ing camp. Thereupon he went home to organize the local militia.

Liu Ming-ch'uan probably had no choice in the matter if he wanted to save his neck. But once he made up his mind to work for the Ch'ing government, he never switched sides. The same cannot be said of many other men in similar circumstances. In the 1850s, during the period when the Taiping army was conducting an aggressive campaign in Anhwei, many small towns and villages in the Hofei area and in northern Anhwei began to fortify their communities with earthen walls, some eleven feet tall, with trenches dug around them. The local Nien bandits saw this as an opportunity: they could take the walled area as their base and draw an income from the residents' land taxes. To persuade a community to come to their side, the Nien leaders might apply force or they might try to influence the commander of the local militia and negotiate a peaceful takeover. But if the government troops came and drove out the Nien, the community would swing around again and return to being the subjects of the Ch'ing court. Between 1853 to 1863, it was not unusual for a city, a town, or a village to switch sides several times. The leaders of the local militia and of the gentry played a crucial role under these uncertain conditions. Some sparred with the Nien and the Taipings with only their own interests in mind; others worried about the safety of their communities and acted as they saw fit. According to Hofei folklore, sometime in 1858, before Liu surrendered to the Ch'ing, he and several strongmen from West Hofei got together to discuss the possibility of joining forces with the Taipings. During the meeting a violent wind snapped the flagpole that was to fly the rebel flag. An old schoolteacher at the meeting interpreted this as a bad omen. So they all went home that night, ready to confront the Taipings in the morning.

Liu Ming-ch'uan's career took off as soon as he was put on the battlefield. He scored several victories against the Nien rebels in 1859, and by the year's end was made a first captain (*tu-ssu*). Fighting was what Liu knew best. For years he had been fighting the Ch'ing authorities, the Taipings, the Nien, other hoodlums, and even other militia corps. Li Hung-chang once described the kind of life his Hofei generals had led before they joined the regular army: "When the enemies came, they helped one another; when the enemies left, they fought one another." Even women fitted their lives into this rhythm. The local history tells us that whenever Liu Ming-ch'uan's camp was under attack, Liu's wife could be seen busily loading the ammunition.

Liu Ming-ch'uan's real break came in 1861. That year, Tseng Kuo-fan, the commander-in-chief of the anti-Taiping forces, persuaded Li Hung-chang to organize the Anhwei Army, whose main task was to help the Ch'ing government secure Shanghai in case of an enemy assault. Tseng had high regard for Li, who had studied with Tseng when he was a student in Peking and had served on Tseng's personal staff; Tseng also knew that Li was experienced in working with the local militia in his native Hofei. Soon after he received his command, Li Hung-chang enlisted Liu Ming-ch'uan's Ming Battalion as one of the thirteen that made up the original Anhwei or Huai Army. It seems unlikely that the two had known each other well before 1861. They had little in common and could not have traveled in the same social circles. Li had earned the highest civil degree and was a compiler at the imperial Hanlin Academy; Liu had only on occasion attended a village school and was nicknamed "the hood." But family background and education did not interest Li Hung-chang when he was considering someone for employment. He always said that the world needed "more talented men, not more Hanlin scholars."

As a military commander, Li Hung-chang followed his own way. He demanded loyalty and courage from those he had promoted, and he did not like to be disappointed; in return, he let these men fight the enemy as they saw fit and hoard as much spoils as they liked. Li's style suited Liu Ming-ch'uan. By the end of the Taiping war, Liu held the rank of baron of the first class, and he had hoarded enough silver to buy tens of thousands of acres of land—he was handsomely rewarded because Li Hung-chang's own reputation had profited from his service. If Liu had retired to his estate permanently then, he would not have been different from most of the enterprising heroes of the past, and his relation with Li Hung-chang could have been seen as purely one of convenience. But as it happened, his public career did not conclude with the suppression of the Nien in 1868. In fact, Liu Ming-ch'uan is best remembered today as Taiwan's first governor—the man who, after having blocked the French from invading Taiwan in 1884, introduced economic and educational reform on the island, and laid the foundation of a vast communication network that included railroads, telegraph, and a modern postal service.

Li Hung-chang once remarked that the battalion commanders in his Huai Army "rose to fame at the same time and swiftly" and so must have had "talents," and that they should not be compared with "the self-promoting, cliquish type," because these men "worry about their country in the same way they worry about their family and regard matters far away as something near at hand." But how did this come about? How did a rabble-rouser like Liu Ming-ch'uan come to worry about the broader questions regarding his country? How did he make the transition from knight-errant to statesman, from perpetual scrapper to enlightened reformer? Chang Shu-sheng's life might offer some clues. Chang "rose to fame" together with Liu. He exhibited talents on the battlefield and had the same instinct and foresight about China's future, and the same drive as Liu. But he was another kind of Hofei man, someone with more gravity, less charm, and probably little flair. Chang also made a lot of money because of the Taiping war but was too preoccupied with work to enjoy any of it. Liu had at least eight concubines; Chang had one, an ugly one given to him late in life by a wealthy friend.

Through his great-granddaughters and a tomb inscription, we know something about Chang Shu-sheng's own family. His father, Yin-ku, was a tough and principled man. In the 1840s and 1850s, when it was common for local leaders around Hofei to broker deals with rebel forces, Chang Yin-ku refused to do so. At the same time, he knew that he could not rely on the government troops for protection, so he organized a local detachment, fortified his own base, and did whatever he could to safeguard the areas around him. He waited out this volatile period and told the people in his village to do the same. No threats or gainful prospects ever swayed him from his purpose. In this way his oldest son was like him.

Chang Shu-sheng's wife was another steely figure in the Chang family history. When the Taiping soldiers first came to the Changs' ancestral home in West Hofei, it was this woman who faced them down. The men had gone to hide in the nearby mountains because they would have been killed if they stayed. (The Taipings spared no men from the gentry class when they captured a town or moved into a village but would let the women go.) According to Ch'ung-ho, who heard this story from her adoptive grandmother, Chang Shu-sheng also had put his wife in charge of his youngest brother, who was only five at the time and so too young to take flight with the rest of the family. When the Taipings arrived, they searched through the family compound, poking everywhere with their spears. The five-year-old had been carefully concealed and told not to make a sound no matter what happened. When the soldiers were gone, the boy was found bleeding from a neck wound but still alive. Madame Chang placed a piece of skin from a freshly killed chicken on the wound to stop the bleeding. The boy was saved. There is no way of knowing if all the details of this story are true, but they suggest a capable and sturdy woman, a right match for Chang Shu-sheng.

Chang Shu-sheng did not leave any personal writings behind, no letters or poems or even tomb inscriptions for friends or colleagues. In fact, nearly all the writings we have of Chang Shu-sheng are memorials—letters and reports he sent to the emperor. These are official documents, written in a formal language, yet they surprise us with just how much they tell about his thought and action, his bearing and temperament, and how he made distinctions and apportioned weight. Because this man had, for many years, fought for his own survival and for the survival of his neighbors and the Ch'ing dynasty, he possessed a greater sense of urgency than his contemporaries about the problems his country was facing. He felt that the dangers were real and immediate, and that they could threaten China's existence. But Chang Shu-sheng was not a pessimist: he worked without stop, trying to find solutions for these problems. His daughter-in-law, Ch'ung-ho's adoptive grandmother, accompanied him to Kwangsi and Kwangtung in the early 1880s, when he was posted there as governor-general. She was a young woman then, married for only a few years to Chang Shu-sheng's middle son. Her father-in-law impressed her deeply: "Even though he had a good confidential secretary, he always insisted on reviewing every letter and document delivered to him from the Transmission Office before he passed them on to his confidential secretary. So he was always swamped with work." His secretary took care of many things for him, matters that he could not attend to personally, and often his letters would be in his secretary's handwriting. But the instructions came from Chang Shu-sheng, and he would always have a first glance at all his correspondence so that he would not be misled or misinformed.

Chang Shu-sheng's work took up nearly all his waking hours, and summers in South China were taxing. The weather was hot and moist; mosquitoes were everywhere and always thirsty. They stuck to skin and thin gowns, and they swarmed around you and above you. Chang slapped as he read, his palms stained with blood. He also had a habit of eating sugared rice dumplings as he worked, correcting the drafts of his secretaries with red ink. Occasionally he would dip the dumplings into the wet inkstone instead of the sugar bowl, and his beard would be streaked in red.

Chang Shu-sheng's collected memorials show us the nature and range of the problems he had to consider. Most were questions that needed his immediate attention: collection of land and commercial tax; border and coastal defense; local banditry; funding for the construction of steamboats, arsenals, and schools; recommendations of meritorious officials. Others had to do with local habits and practices, which Chang felt needed redress. Then there were the more fundamental issues: educational reform, the Ch'ing government's policy toward foreigners in China and foreign nations, and a more effective approach to Western technology and Western knowledge. His writings on these problems tell us that he disliked inflexibility but favored expediency only if it did not deviate from propriety. He wrote:

I have made this observation about men of the past and of the present. Those who are sincere and truthful, pure and prudent—in other words, men who carefully guard their character from corruption—often end up holding on to old theories, unable to adapt themselves to change. These men are so impractical and obstinate that they simply cannot take on any responsibilities.

Chang contrasted the "pure and prudent," the "impractical and obstinate," with another type, "men who are sloppy in character but have considerable talents and ability, men who are anxious to succeed and pushy to make a score":

When knocked together to get something done, they have loads of energy and are willing to do a lot of running around. One can trust them with short assignments, but if you give them a succession of serious responsibilities, they are bound to transgress important principles and bring ruin to our country.

Ideally the two categories, men of learning and men of action, should not exist separately because, as Chang Shu-sheng pointed out, a person learns in order to put his knowledge into action and his action should always be an extension of his knowledge. He felt that there was universal agreement on this principle but only the Westerners understood how it worked. He told the emperor Kuang-hsü:

[Westerners] have a firm and unbending disposition. But they do not engage in discussions of moral principles and human nature. When they investigate the nature of things and extend their knowledge, their mind tries to understand every bit of what they are studying. After they had investigated the nature of things, they knew how to make weapons. From making weapons, they went on to train armies. There was nothing they did not learn and no one that they did not learn from. Henceforth they would win every contest, every war, and do whatever they liked and go as far as they liked.

Chang Shu-sheng noticed that as Western men "investigated the nature of things" (*ko-wu*) and "extended their knowledge" (*chih-chih*), their endeavors led them to wealth and power, not a deeper moral understanding. This was different from the Confucians. Confucian thinkers had been exploring the possibilities of "investigating the nature of things" and "the extension of knowledge" since the eleventh century, and in the end they all came to the same conclusion, that learning took a person back to himself, to self-understanding and self-reform. Chang was brought up on the books and commentaries these thinkers had written, but now, having witnessed what the Western nations had accomplished, he wondered whether there could be a different type of learning. It was plain to him that both the Chinese and the Westerner applied themselves to the quest for knowledge, yet one ended up sequestered in a makeshift dwelling brooding about his spirituality and inner virtue, and the other found himself conquering the world. The distinction between them was not fabricated and not an illusion, as some had claimed. This was one message he wanted to convey to the emperor. His other message was the urgency of the situation. The Western nations had gotten so powerful that Britain and France regarded China as "merely another province." He wrote: "Having tucked their troops and steamships, guns and cannons under their arms, they crossed the ocean, heading east. All of these countries eye China like an aggressive cockerel."

Chang realized that his government had tried to respond to this situation. "We constructed naval yards to build ships, and we established agencies to simplify red tape. We are trying in every way to achieve efficiency." Yet, he observed, "after many years, China still lags behind, completely unable to compete with the West on the same level." He believed that this was because the Chinese had gotten only a "semblance" of Western learning. With only a semblance, China could not "create a path for herself"—she could not "march forth on her own." In order to have a grasp of Western learning, Chang felt, students should begin early with a Western-style education. "Those who did not acquire Western learning from a proper school have only appropriated its skin and hair, its branches and knots; they know what is so but not why it is so."

Ultimately, Chang Shu-sheng would help to build one such school in Kwang-tung province. Construction began in January 1882. A year later, when it was completed, he sent a report to the emperor. The school had four parallel rows of buildings, twenty-two dormitory rooms, bathrooms, privies, kitchens, a watch-tower, and a teahouse. Altogether the cost was 16,470 taels of silver. He wrote:

> We have already decided on the school regulations. We are going to hire from the Fukien academies teachers in Western languages, linguistics, and mathematics to teach here first. Once the students have made some progress, we are going to ask Western experts to take over the instruction. Books and all the necessary equipment have already been purchased. As soon as the students are selected, classes can begin.

In this memorial, Chang Shu-sheng again emphasized the importance of Western learning, suggesting that it might be superior to the traditional Chinese education. "Western learning is broad yet precise; it teaches one to be discerning yet reflective. By itself, it can enlighten the mind. And when you try to get to the root of it, it is none other than seeking [knowledge] collectively, in a critical and practical manner. It is not jostling each other in empty rhetoric." He returned to the subject of "the investigation of things" and "the extension of knowledge" to make an even finer distinction between China and the West:

> When investigating things, the Chinese search for the noumenal princi-ples in them while the Westerners seek [an understanding] of the actual facts. In areas of technology and applied science, the Chinese employ arti-sans while the Westerners dispatch their professionals. Those who look for principles tend to sit around and discuss metaphysics. It is easy for them to be drawn to idle talk. Those who hire artisans to do the technol-ogy pursue their work only with a sketchy knowledge of things. It is rare for them to comprehend how things are made.

In conclusion, the governor-general called for a fresh understanding of what Western learning was all about: "It concerns itself with practical questions in contemporary society." He believed that when Western learning "is not vulgar-ized or trivialized," and when the Chinese "have thoroughly comprehended Western affairs and Western technology," then they "can look forward to a time when true talents will flourish [in their country]."

In his discussions, Chang Shu-sheng distinguished Western learning from some of its untoward outcomes. He also noted the difference between the spirit of the Europeans and their conduct: the Europeans were "practical" and "resolute by nature," yet their behavior toward China was "predatory." Having made this observation, he offered some practical advice: The Chinese had nothing to gain from imitating the West, but they needed to understand the source of its power. Westerners were greedy and aggressive, so China had to strengthen herself first, in order to reason the Western nations out of their offensive intent. By this he meant that to be in a position to reason, one had to be physically strong—an absurd idea, since it undermined the power of reason, but something China simply had to accept in the 1880s.

Just how well China had to perform in a test of strength in order to be taken seriously by the West was a question Chang Shu-sheng faced in 1883. That year the French were stepping up their activities in northern Vietnam and were moving their troops closer to the Chinese border, near Kwangsi province, where Chang was the governor-general. Chang had been writing to Emperor Kuang-hsü about the goings-on along the frontier, urging him to be ready with a plan in case the French were going to make mischief. By early 1884, a showdown was imminent. Chang favored war because the secret reports his scouts had been sending him from the Kwangsi border had convinced him that China had a good chance of winning if she acted quickly and decisively. Reactions in the capital were mixed. A group of young conservatives, called the Purists, also wanted war. But these officials, with little experience in diplomacy and practical administration, were calling for war on principle, seeing the clash as a moral contest. Li Hung-chang, on the other hand, was pushing for a peaceful settlement with the French, arguing that the Chinese navy was not ready for a major confrontation with a European power.

This was not the first time Chang Shu-sheng disagreed with his old commander. As the two got older and undertook greater responsibilities, their differences became more evident. Li Hung-chang, by reputation, was too quick to bend to practical necessity and too easily co-opted by the empress dowager Tz'u-hsi and her circle of supporters. Chang's conduct, on the other hand, was never contested while he lived.* It is true that he was not well known like Li and so was not under close scrutiny. It is also true that Li often had to resort to shifty devices and underhanded maneuvers because of the nature and range of his enterprises. Still, their styles were different, and so were their modes of thinking and tones of thought. One was capable of chicanery and the other was not.

Chang's communications with the throne on the French question brought

---

*The criticisms he received in Communist historiography were mainly through his association with Li Hung-chang.

no result. In early 1884, illness forced him to resign as governor-general, but he asked to remain as military commander of Kwangtung. The Ch'ing government dispatched a leader from the Purist Party to take his place and to begin preparing for war. In the meantime Li Hung-chang botched his negotiation with the French, who thought that the Chinese government was acting in bad faith when, in fact, Li had not been honest with his superiors about the terms of the agreement.

The war finally broke out on August 23, 1884, in Foochow harbor. The French navy opened fire, and within fifteen minutes, they sank or badly damaged all but two of the Chinese wooden ships. By the afternoon, they also laid waste to the Foochow naval yard. The Chinese commander was among the first to flee. Prior to this confrontation, the Ch'ing court had asked officials from the coastal provinces to send reinforcements. Kwangtung responded with ships and troops. But Li Hung-chang, the commander of the northern port, answered that he had no ships to spare, and that even if he had he would not be so foolish as to divert them to Foochow just to have them destroyed.

It is unclear who decided to send the fleets from Kwangtung, the new governor-general or Chang Shu-sheng. That August, Chang knew he was dying. He continued to write to Peking and seemed more anxious in these letters. Either the problems had grown or he noticed more: army officers showing no discipline, senior officials expecting gratuities from their own staff, and people behaving like rogues. His last letter to the throne is moving. It was dictated to his confidential secretary on October 26, the day he died. Chang wrote: "Ever since my previous memorial, I have been seeking treatments everywhere. The medicine is not working. The more I worry about my illness, the deeper my gratitude toward Your Majesty's kindness." Chang told his emperor that he came from "a military background, among the poor and simple," and that "it was the sagely rulers who plucked him from the common lot" and entrusted him with important responsibilities. He went on: "But now as Your Majesty and the empress dowager are distressed over the increasing foreign hostilities and the disturbances along the coast, I am heading toward my grave—just another horse, another dog, filling the ditch. I am going ahead now with no chance again to repay your kindness."

Even as he was going, Chang Shu-sheng returned one last time to those matters that were most pressing to him:

> In the last decades, the Russians have been encroaching on us from the north; the Japanese are spying on us in the East China Sea; the British are planning their move into Yunnan and Tibet from India and Burma, while

the French are coveting Yunnan and Kwangtung from the west, by way of Hanoi and the coastal regions. We gaze in astonishment at these repeated incidents, and the situation has become more and more difficult to control. [We are shocked,] but we still carry on as usual. We still insist on dressing in our caps and gowns when fighting a fire and bowing ceremoniously when trying to rescue someone from drowning. If this is what we do, how are we meant to save anyone or anything from disaster? In recent years scholars are beginning to understand the ways of diplomacy, and they are talking about using Western technology to defend our coastal regions. There is, at least, universal agreement on this.

When Westerners establish their countries, they start at the beginning and move to the end. They are not as advanced as we are in ritual practice and moral education, yet they have attained wealth and power gradually. This is because they have a command of both the substance and function [of their learning]. They nurture talents in their schools; they discuss government in their parliaments. Rulers and people are of one entity; above and below share the same mind and sentiments. They work on what is real and practical and avoid the abstract.

Chang Shu-sheng wanted the court to know that technology alone was not enough to prepare China for any major confrontation with the West. When the French shifted their target from Foochow to Taiwan in October 1884, the Ch'ing government was again at a loss about what to do. So China seemed to have learned nothing from her humiliating experiences—she was merely gazing "in astonishment at these repeated incidents." Chang Shu-sheng believed that to compete with the West, the Chinese, like their opponents, had to "start at the beginning and move to the end." As he put it, "If you cannot tune a lute, then you have to change its strings." Other men at the time made similar arguments, but they were writing for an audience while Chang Shu-sheng was writing to the emperor. Toward the end of his letter, he said:

It is crucial that we do not vacillate and make a mess of things, and that we do not debate in the abstract and ruin our efforts. If only we could adapt unceasingly to change, then in time we could be more assured about the future of our country. When this happens, the day I die is the day I am born.

We read Chang Shu-sheng's passionate appeal with irony because we cannot believe that he died with hope. In the same letter, he told the emperor that he had been up all night—this last night of his life—brooding about Foochow and about Taiwan: "Even though I am saying farewell to the world, it is hard for me to rest in peace."

Years earlier, when the Hunan-born scholar and general Tseng Kuo-fan was sent to Shantung to suppress the Nien, he had a chance to work closely with the battalion commanders of the Huai Army. He observed that these Hofei men "possessed an excitable energy and high spirits but no trace of anxiety." He wrote:

> Consequently I became very concerned. I feared that they were not able to take on the Nien bandits. [The philosopher] Chuang Tzu said, "Two armies facing each other, the pessimistic one is going to win." [The T'ang strategist] Lu Chung-lien wrote, "The one who is anxious and diligent is bound for success. The one who is relaxed and is having fun is bound for failure." Mencius also said, "We survive through worrying about adversity and perish in ease and comfort." Later that year I became ill and was relieved of my military duties. The Grand Secretary from Hofei, Li Hung-chang, [having succeeded me,] was able to get rid of the Nien altogether, using the Huai Army. Thus the spirit of the Huai Army must have been ardent.

The success of the Huai Army came as a surprise to Tseng Kuo-fan because according to Confucian and Taoist wisdom this simply could not have happened. That the army did succeed forced him to reevaluate his position. He wrote:

> I myself have always been partial to the view that emphasizes the importance of "having anxiety," which goes to show that I have only known one thing but not the other. But now I realize that my views had been slanted and also that any theory, no matter how superior, cannot cover all grounds; that each has in it what is appropriate.

Tseng Kuo-fan, in these remarks, expressed an ambivalence he shared with some of the best minds of his generation. He looked upon men like Liu Ming-ch'uan and Chang Shu-sheng with a "questioning and admiring gaze." These fighters, he thought, managed to win wars and rise above the crowd purely on the strength of their "ardent spirit." But he, like most Chinese, was brought up with the assumption that there was virtue in having anxiety—anxiety about one's moral descent, about the skiddy road ahead, about not doing one's best and not doing enough for others; anxiety about being unprepared, about having too much luck or too little humility. Older than Confucius, the assumption delineates the Chinese spirit—guarded and passive, perhaps, to critics and outsiders, but an essential and activating principle in the way the Chinese approach a problem and live their lives. So although Tseng Kuo-fan was impressed with what force and energy alone could accomplish, he was reluctant to part with this assumption. He posited no theory, having convinced himself that the two, venturing ahead and holding back, need not contradict one another.

Tseng's understanding of the Hofei spirit needs refining because we find in men like Chang Shu-sheng a strong "trace of anxiety" in addition to sheer energy. Chang was anxious to go forward, yet wary about getting it wrong; but he always had enough pluck to risk a change. He told others that he made his name and fortune in soldiering, that he was not a scholar. Yet his analysis of China and the West—precise and smart, avoiding any abstract discussion and dogmas—exemplifies that of the best scholars.

By Wu-ling's time, very few people in the Chang household remembered Chang Shu-sheng. Two or three old servants who had fought the Taipings with him could describe what he was like, and also Ch'ung-ho's adoptive grandmother, the general's daughter-in-law, who had gone to Kwangtung with him in the 1880s. So it was primarily this woman, and through her, Ch'ung-ho, who had been keeping his memory alive in the family. Their return to their Hofei home was also important. Chang Shu-sheng's shrine was placed there, in the residential compound. As a child, Ch'ung-ho had, on occasion, climbed on top of his altar, tucking her small body behind the ancestor tablets as she enjoyed a game of hide-and-seek with a friend.

Chapter 5

GRANDMOTHER

C H'UNG-HO'S GRANDMOTHER was glad to come home from Shanghai. The *Book of Lieh Tzu* says, "There is travel *and* travel." "There is travel to contemplate sights or travel to contemplate the way things change." But then there is also "perfect travel," which is "to find sufficiency in ourselves." It was this perfect travel that the elderly lady was seeking when she took her adopted granddaughter and returned to Hofei.

The grandmother was originally from an East Hofei family and later married a West Hofei man. Ch'ung-ho has never known her grandmother's given name. In those days, it was considered disrespectful for youngsters to ask their elder relatives' names. It was, however, perfectly all right to refer to one's male ancestor by his posthumous name—his honorary title—if the throne had given him one, as was the case for Chang Shu-sheng. In the same way it was possible for children and grandchildren to know their elders' religious names. Therefore, even as a child, Ch'ung-ho learned that her grandmother's Buddhist name was Shih-hsiu, which means "knowing" and "cultivating."

Shih-hsiu's father was Li Hung-chang's fourth brother, Li Yun-chang. Historians rarely mention Yun-chang because he never held any office and, unlike his oldest brother and fifth brother, known for their spendthrift ways and their abuse of family power, Yun-chang did not have anything in the way of gossip or fictional history to contribute to their accounts. A serious illness left him blind, probably in his late teens. But he remembered well the colors and forms of things, distance and depth, and his earlier reading of the classics. Shih-hsiu told

Ch'ung-ho that her father would pace around the family estate, planning in his head a garden or a new addition to the family quarters, and then instruct a draftsman to reproduce on paper the design he had in mind.

We also learn from Li Hung-chang's "Family Letters" that Yun-chang was not only the household manager and the anchor of the family, while his brothers came and went, but was also the guardian of their children during their absence. Li Hung-chang urged his oldest son to discuss with his fourth uncle all matters, particularly any questions he might have regarding his studies, adding that he was never to disobey this uncle's instructions. Yun-chang had two wives and never took a concubine. His first wife died soon after they were married. With his second wife, a woman from the Ning family, Yun-chang fathered eighteen children, of whom four sons and seven daughters lived to maturity. More than anything else, he wanted his descendants to be properly educated. His daughter recalled just how difficult it had been for their tutors to survive his scrutiny. He could tell who was a good teacher and who was not by his children's performance; and he did not need his eyesight to verify the accuracy of their recitation, since he had long ago committed their texts to memory. At one point Yun-chang had his sons "study on their own" because he could not find suitable tutors for them—which probably meant that he took over the teaching himself.

Ch'ung-ho's grandmother was very fond of her own tutor, and he of her. But after she was married, it was no longer possible for her to see him again as it was considered improper for a married gentry woman to be in the company of men who were not from her own family or her husband's family. Her family made an exception during one of her visits, arranging for her to have a glimpse of him from a distance. She told her adopted granddaughter years later that although she could hardly make out his face from where she was standing, she found herself crying.

Shih-hsiu was Li Yun-chang's fourth daughter. We don't know anything about her older sisters; the sixth, seventh, and eighth sisters, however, were frequent visitors at her Hofei home. Ch'ung-ho remembered Shih-hsiu as a better and more serious scholar than her younger sisters. She could not offer any precise evidence, but as a child she could tell that this was so from her grandmother's demeanor and speech, from the books her grandmother read, and from the education she gave her.

Shih-hsiu also had a remarkable older brother, Li Ching-shih, who showed much promise as a young man but lived only to age forty. Li Hung-chang was partial to this nephew. In one letter he writes: "Among my nephews, this child is the most decent and the most mature. He has inherited the finest elements in our family." Li Hung-chang also shared with Ching-shih his more radical ideas about how to reform Chinese society—ideas that he does not seem to have shared with his own children. In one letter to his nephew he writes: "The more competitive the world has become, the less applicable our ancient principles will be." These "ancient principles" were the principles underlying familial relations, which, in his view, had nothing to do with a person's relation to his country. The burden of the family, he added, diminishes the strength of the state and works against those efforts that are meant to prepare a country for the modern world. At the end of this letter, Li Hung-chang tells his nephew never to forget that in the future only the "fittest" people will survive. Since we do not have Ching-shih's reply, we can only speculate about the level of his awareness. From the tone of this letter, it seems that Li Hung-chang was writing to someone who was attuned to his ideas, and so there was no protracted argument or explanation.

Shih-hsiu could not have participated in such discussions. In those days a young woman did not concern herself with national affairs, and even if she did, it had to remain a very private matter. But Shih-hsiu was Li Hung-chang's niece and Chang Shu-sheng's daughter-in-law. She grew up in one political family and then married into another, and so must have had her own views, especially when her country was faced with a crisis. In the 1880s, when her uncle and her father-in-law clashed on the question of whether or not China should take a more aggressive position against the French in Vietnam, she and her husband were actually living with Chang Shu-sheng in South China. At the time, she, too, felt that China should go to war with France. Although she and her father-in-law often ate at the same table, it is unlikely that he shared with her any classified information he might have had about the fighting in northern Vietnam. What Ch'ung-ho's grandmother remembered from those days was the old general hunched over the piles of documents he was reviewing in the sweltering Kwangtung nights. She was persuaded in her loyalty to him by what she witnessed—a knowledge that had little to do with those questions that concerned policymakers and politicians.

Shih-hsiu always lived by the rules the old society imposed on her and all gentry women, yet she was willing to adjust those rules in matters that concerned her granddaughter. Ch'ung-ho described her grandmother as someone who possessed a liberal disposition, but this needs qualification. Shih-hsiu was liberal in the context of her own situation. She was liberal also in the sense that she "refused to be dogmatic or obstinate," as Confucius had once said about himself. She did not arrange a marriage for her granddaughter, although that was the normal practice in China up to the 1930s. And she did not force her to become a Buddhist like herself; she did not even insist Ch'ung-ho follow a vegetarian diet.

In other ways, however, Shih-hsiu was conservative—conservative in her choice of Ch'ung-ho's tutors and in questions of propriety. She looked for tutors who could give her granddaughter a rigorous education in the classical texts, and she was willing to pay them generously for it. The teacher who stayed the longest, Chu Mo-ch'ing, was an archaeologist by training. He was paid three hundred silver dollars a year, a large sum, considering the fact that a household servant at the time earned around twenty dollars a year.* With his salary, Mr. Chu was able to support a family of five plus his own parents. He left his wife and children in their native Shantung province at first, but when he realized that his stint might last a few years, he moved them to Hofei, just a few streets down from the Chang residence. Besides keeping a close watch on Ch'ung-ho's education, Shih-hsiu also saw to it that the girl knew the rules and ways of appropriate behavior. Shih-hsiu, for instance, did not tolerate a lazy posture, whether one was standing, sitting, or walking. And as a child, Ch'ung-ho was taught to be respectful in the presence of adults and never to interrupt their conversation.

Shih-hsiu rarely talked about her daughter or that daughter's own child, although it was their deaths that deepened her compassion toward all living things. Every dead frog or bird in the garden called for a prayer. Shih-hsiu would chant quietly to herself in Sanskrit those words that she believed had the power to send the deceased to the blessed Pure Land. It is unlikely that she began this type of practice in her parents' home, before she was married. The Li family had always been guarded about Buddhism, averting not only its teachings but also those practices that might lead one to its path. In a letter to Shih-hsiu's father, Li Yun-chang, Li Hung-chang enumerated habits and excesses that might be harmful to one's health, and he warned his brother specifically against "consuming too much meat," lest this weaken the body's defense system. But, he added, this did not mean that one should give up eating meat altogether. He observed that during his own time, "more and more people were promoting vegetarian diets and gathering together solely for the purpose of eating vegetarian meals together"—a trend he regarded as dangerous because, if one were not careful, one could veer toward the Buddhist way. His worry betrayed a deep anxiety some Confucian gentry had about Buddhism, that it was more harmful than any physical disease. Toward the end of his letter, he told Shih-hsiu's father

---

*The average income of an urban middle school teacher in the 1920s was about 450 silver dollars a year.

"to be cautious in matters of belief and not to be deluded into following the Buddha."

Given these circumstances, it seemed unlikely that Shih-hsiu would have had any contact with Buddhism while she was under her father's tutelage. She was probably introduced to it after her marriage. Her husband, Chang Hua-chen, had a collection of Buddhist literature, which he kept in his private library, along with the novels and poetry he loved. The two could have studied the sutras together, discussing the opaque passages or even debating their readings. Sharing scholarly interests was one of the pleasures gentry men and women enjoyed when they found themselves in a companionable marriage. The Sung dynasty poet Li Ch'ing-chao wrote an intimate account of the many evenings she and her husband spent together, examining a bronze tripod or a work of calligraphy, repairing an old book they had just purchased, or copying onto paper a rare edition they had borrowed from a friend.

We don't know just how devout Shih-hsiu's husband was—or whether his religion, like other interests in his life, was merely something that helped him pass the time. Chang Hua-chen is an enigmatic figure in the Chang family history. He was a disappointment to his parents and possibly to his wife because he never really did anything. After failing the lowest examination in the prefectural capital, he dutifully followed the rites prescribed for the unsuccessful candidates: he traveled the last twenty kilometers of his journey home on foot, entered his parents' house by the side door, and prostrated himself before the ancestors' tablets, asking for forgiveness. He never tried the examination again and never wanted to talk about it. His family left him alone, probably because his older brother Hua-kuei was already showing great promise.

Hua-kuei earned his provincial degree in 1884, possibly just before Hua-chen sat for the lower exam, and then the metropolitan degree six years later, thus fulfilling his parents' and his ancestors' highest expectations. Next to him, his two younger brothers seemed unremarkable. Ch'ung-ho recalls only one story about Hua-chen. This was a strange story with some critical gaps and an incredible ending. Once, while he was traveling downstream on the Yangtze River, Hua-chen's boat capsized. He either swam or kept afloat on a piece of driftwood for several miles before he reached land, and he was unconscious when peasants from a nearby village found him. His family had already presumed Hua-chen dead when a letter from him arrived, telling them where he was and how he had survived the accident. They claimed that he owed his life to his faith and to the Buddha's deep compassion.

Shih-hsiu's spiritual awakening was unlike her husband's, which would not have happened had there not been a miracle. Hers was born of suffering and was muddled up with guilt. Shih-hsiu blamed her previous lives for having caused the premature deaths of her daughter and her granddaughter. Her past crimes could never be known, but the tragedies in her present life persuaded her that they had to have happened. Shih-hsiu sought redemption by loving all living things and doing her best to keep them alive, be they beggars at her gate or rats in her own granary. She never tried to proselytize. At times, however, her acts of kindness could seem absurd. On birthdays and Buddhist holidays, she would instruct the servants to buy baskets of live fish and shrimps from the peddlers at the market so as to let them go in a stream just outside the city's eastern gate. The stream would take the fish and shrimps to a nearby canal, where cooks from local restaurants would be waiting for their catch of the day. The servants probably never told their old mistress that she had been deceived regularly in what she considered a benevolent act. Ch'ung-ho also kept quiet about these things. Once, Shih-hsiu sent a servant to buy from a peddler all the wild ducks he had in his basket so that she could have them set free. When the servant came home with the wild ducks, he told his mistress that one of them was dying. Shih-hsiu instructed him to have it buried after it died. Later, when Ch'ung-ho asked the same servant where he had buried the duck, the servant replied, "in the Five Viscera Temple," which of course meant that he had it for supper.

Shih-hsiu's conduct follows a pattern that is as old as the one described in the ancient Confucian texts. Confucius' follower Mencius, from the fourth century B.C.E., told the story of how a wise minister was duped into believing that the fish he had asked his gamekeeper to set free was back "in its own element," when in fact the gamekeeper had cooked and eaten it. In Mencius' view, the minister was merely deceived by what the gamekeeper told him and by what seemed reasonable at the time; the incident could not have taken anything away from the minister's intent and action. In other words, what happened to the fish was inconsequential to the minister's character, which had to be good because he wanted to save the fish. Mencius' argument could also apply to Shih-hsiu. One might say that Shih-hsiu did her best for the fish and fowls, but once they were set free, their fate depended on chance.

When Ch'ung-ho was living with her grandmother, two nuns came to Hofei regularly to see them, one from Nanking and the other from Yang-chou. The nun from Yang-chou was originally an indentured servant, a *ya-tou*, in the Chang family. When Shih-hsiu's daughter married, the *ya-tou* went with her as part of the dowry. Once the *ya-tou* was in her new home, her mistress's husband—Shih-hsiu's son-in-law—took a fancy to her and wanted her to be his concubine. When she understood this, the *ya-tou* shaved her head and became a nun. She was beautiful and intelligent, and yet there was no other way out for her. If she became a concubine, her life could only end tragically. The principal wife, in this case her mistress, would hate her, and even Shih-hsiu would reject her, since it was natural for a mother to protect her daughter. But Pao-hsing—this was her Buddhist name—did not go that route. Instead, she came back to Hofei, a nun. Shih-hsiu soon "found" her a temple in Yang-chou, which probably meant that she endowed one for her. With this arrangement, Pao-hsing had not only a place to go but a family of sorts, with her own disciples to teach and care for.

Whenever Pao-hsing came to visit, she still addressed Ch'ung-ho's grandmother as "Old Mistress," even though she had long ago left this world for another where such appellations did not exist. When Ch'ung-ho first knew her, she was already in her forties, and even at that age, with her tonsured head, she was beautiful. She would pay her respects to Shih-hsiu at least once a year, and each time she would bring presents: for Ch'ung-ho, mica lanterns made in the shapes of rabbits or fish; for Shih-hsiu, rouge and powder so that she could give them to her relatives in Hofei, and toothbrushes made with bamboo handles and palm fiber, as Buddhists did not brush their teeth with animal bristles.

Ch'ung-ho's grandmother always employed women who either had been *ya-tou* when they were girls or else had been widowed when they were still young. She thought that these women were just like her, born to a life of misfortune. They all abstained from eating meat and they all prayed to the Buddha every day. Their ritual became a form of commiseration, although one was the mistress of the house while the others were hired to serve her. Ch'ung-ho remembered a Big Sister Ho (*ho-ta-chieh*) and a Second Sister Ju-i (*ju-i-erh-chieh*), whose hair had already turned white when she knew them. Both women had their own small temples to retire to, but while their mistress was alive they chose to delay becoming full-fledged nuns. They did light chores around the house, which would not have been possible if they had taken the tonsure, because Shih-hsiu would not have allowed religious women to do servants' work.

Ch'ung-ho also remembers an old Buddhist layman, who would light the incense in the formal prayer hall, which was in a building separate from the living quarters. He had a queue and always used flint stones, never matches, to start a fire. Ch'ung-ho says he was scared of matches, of their quick energy and of what he thought might be demonic power. Every day, after he finished his chores in the Chang household, he would wander around the neighborhood with a basket, picking up all the trash he could find—a responsibility Ch'ung-ho's grandmother had assigned him. When dusk fell, one could see him standing alone by the pavilion in the back garden, burning the gathered-up pieces.

Not only desperate women showed up at Shih-hsiu's door but also handi-capped children whose families simply were not able to care for them. One such child was a blind girl whose Buddhist name was Ch'ang-sheng. She was two or maybe three years old when Ch'ung-ho's nurse-nanny, Chung-ma, found her in front of the Chang ancestral hall. It was a cold winter night, and someone had covered her with dry leaves. Chung-ma told others later that she knew this child was uncommon when she first saw her: her big ears and square face portended good omens, and her body seemed to emit a warm energy even though she had been lying in the freezing cold for hours. As soon as the child was inside the house, the servants bathed her and shaved her head, making sure they had deloused her thoroughly before taking her to their mistress. With her hair gone, Ch'ang-sheng looked even more astonishing: her face was luminous like the Buddha's. Ch'ung-ho's grandmother recognized her special aura right away, and when the child seemed stronger, she put her under the care of a nun. From that day until her benefactor's death, Ch'ang-sheng's needs were fully provided for: rice, clothes, and money would arrive regularly at the temple for her upkeep.

Ch'ang-sheng grew up to be a woman of many talents. When she was still a young girl, her abbess taught her to chant the sutras. While she was learning, Ch'ang-sheng always tried to remember the precise place where her teacher would pause and turn the page. Later on, she would punctuate her chanting in the same way. With the unseen text in front of her, she would stop to turn each page at the place where one would have done so if one were actually reading it. Ch'ang-sheng also learned to sing Buddhist hymns and to play the vertical *hsiao* flute. When she sang, Ch'ung-ho says, she would tap her hands and feet in a rhythm, and she would tell her friend what instruments they were meant to rep-resent. When she got older, she would perform for a fee during birthday cele-brations and funerals, thus bringing back an income for her temple. After Ch'ung-ho's grandmother died, this income became more important to Ch'ang-sheng, since she no longer had outside support.

Ch'ung-ho remembers other handicapped children her grandmother helped by finding them a home or some means of making a living: a blind girl who was sent to work in a brush factory and a deaf girl who was placed in a nearby tem-ple to tend the nuns' vegetable garden. Ch'ung-ho says: "I think people knew that if their babies were born with the fates clearly against them, my grand-mother would do her best to sustain them and to find a way out for them. Thus many left their babies in our courtyard."

Shih-hsiu lived over half her life as a widow, and much of that time with nei-ther parents-in-law to care for nor her own descendants to fret over, since they died young. She chose not to be under the same roof as other branches of the

Chang clan, although they lived not far away, in West Hofei, and would visit her from time to time. She managed her own financial matters with the help of her estate manager and his assistants, and she lived by a simple Buddhist tenet. She was sensitive to the living impulse in things and was generous in her compassion. One would imagine that the gods would spare such a woman. They didn't. Time and again, they tested her will, her patience, and her judgment.

When Shih-hsiu's husband, Chang Hua-chen, died, his only concubine decided to starve herself to death. Even at the end of the nineteenth century, most Chinese would have considered her suicide a moral action. Such women were called *lieh-nu*, "women who died for their principles." A *lieh-nu* would have her own spirit tablet among her husband's ancestors, and her name was often recorded in the local history. It did not matter if she had been a concubine. And as she lay dying, even the officials nearby had to come and prostrate themselves before her to show their respect.

This particular concubine had no past. No one now remembers how she was acquired, whether Hua-chen was sweet on her or whether he purchased her so that she could give him a son. It was not at all uncommon for a man of his social position to have a concubine or two; his father had one and so did his older brother. Hua-chen's concubine did not bear him any sons, not even a daughter. When he was gone, she had no one. But she knew that if she were to die a righteous death, at least she would have a position among the dead. Once she made up her mind, no one could stop her, and no one tried. Even the principal wife, Shih-hsiu, who considered life sacred, surrendered to social rules, putting them above her faith. When the family realized that Hua-chen's concubine was determined to die, they stopped giving her water, and they did everything they could to help her die.

Hua-chen's concubine was one kind of chaste widow. Shih-hsiu, Hua-chen's wife, was another. She did not hurry to end life, and she did not seek to gain a reputation on the strength of a single act. She simply lived until she died, facing each day essentially alone.

Sometimes Shih-hsiu would discuss with Ch'ung-ho's nurse-nanny, Chung-ma, how she would like a certain matter handled and then entrust her with carrying out the details. Chung-ma was a countrywoman with no schooling, yet in the more important matters, say, those pertaining to propriety, she was completely in tune with her mistress. She knew her mistress's intent but would act on it her own way, and Shih-hsiu almost never questioned her.

Shih-hsiu went to bed each evening around eight and would be up at three while it was still dark outside. Ch'ung-ho says that while growing up she always slept in a room behind her grandmother's, sharing a bed with her nurse-nanny, who also rose at that early hour with Shih-hsiu. Ch'ung-ho's grandmother would recite poetry or chant passages from the classical texts while Chung-ma combed her hair. Sometimes the two women would chat or discuss the shape of the day. After she was dressed, Shih-hsiu would always go to her private Buddhist prayer hall, just in front of her own room, to do her morning studies. In this room, she kept her sutras in a stack. Some of them, such as the Lotus Sutra, had several volumes, and each day she would read one volume, while sitting in the lotus position. She prayed alone and pursued her studies alone, except when her Buddhist sister—she addressed her as "Buddhist brother"— Tao-ming-shih, the nun from Nanking, came to visit. Only then did she have a companion in learning. Between five and six, she would always have a light snack of thin rice gruel with walnuts and crystallized sugar before returning to finish her morning studies at seven. She would come back to her prayer hall again after three to do her afternoon studies, in a shorter session than her morning ones.

On most mornings, Shih-hsiu took Ch'ung-ho for a walk in the "small flower garden" behind the family compounds. Apricot, pear, and pomegranate trees grew there next to a pavilion. Sometimes on these walks Shih-hsiu would tell Ch'ung-ho a story from early Chinese history or an event in the Chang family history; sometimes she asked Ch'ung-ho about her studies; but often they just strolled. When they came back, they breakfasted together, but at separate tables, Ch'ung-ho at her small table and her grandmother at her larger, vegetarian one. Ch'ung-ho loved the pungent smell that came from her grandmother's table. Fermented bean curd and wheat gluten always seemed more enticing than her own food, and occasionally her grandmother would share some of her crusty rice soaked in fermented bean curd sauce. Shih-hsiu kept two kitchens in her Hofei residence, a regular kitchen and a vegetarian kitchen. Not only the cooking was kept separate but also pots and pans, china and chopsticks. And when she traveled—to visit Ch'ung-ho's family in Soochow, her seventh sister in Shanghai, or her Buddhist sister in Nanking, which was about once or twice a year—she always brought her own cook, a vegetarian himself, and her own cooking utensils.

The business part of Shih-hsiu's day began around eight each morning when Ch'ung-ho left for the two-story family library to study with her tutor. Shih-hsiu had two groups of employees, those who took care of her household and those who looked after her land. Her domestic men servants included two gate-keepers, two cooks, one man to carry the water and another to collect and burn trash, one man to serve guests tea, and still another just to prepare calligraphy ink for Ch'ung-ho, plus the help Shih-hsiu hired for her accountant, her estate manager, and the tutors. Among the women servants, besides Big Sister Ho, Second Sister Ju-i, Chung-ma, a younger nurse-nanny who assisted Chung-ma, the washerwomen, and the cleaning women, there were four or five seamstresses. Shih-hsiu was always dressed in cotton. Ch'ung-ho had several sets of nice clothes in silk or velvet for special occasions. The rest of the time, she, too, wore cotton. The seamstresses had lived in the family for decades; for their former mistresses, it would have taken them a month to make a set of clothes, to do the fancy borders and embroideries, but now their work was made much easier. "It's a cinch to stitch something together," they would say. "A set a day, like sewing clothes for ghosts."

The Chang family's city estate was one block long and one block wide, enclosed in a wall tall enough to stop any fire coming from the streets. The estate had three aligned areas, separated by two long pathways. The middle area was divided into five residential compounds, or *chin*, each with its own courtyard, formal sitting area, and living quarters as well as its own front and side doors. The first two *chin* served as the corridor to the outside world. There, the servants would park the guests' sedan chairs, brew tea in a side room, and then serve it in the reception hall. Male guests on extended visits could stay in one of the two rooms on either side of the reception hall. The three remaining *chin* were reserved for Chang Shu-sheng's three sons and their families. Ch'ung-ho's parents had started their family in the fourth compound, behind Shih-hsiu's, but ever since they moved away in 1912, it had remained empty—except for foxes and rats and, some would say, ancient ghosts. The fifth compound was also vacant, as the descendents of Chang Shu-sheng's third son also chose to make their permanent home elsewhere, in Wuhu, where they had most of their landholdings. The fourth and fifth compounds were open only when members of those two branches came back for a visit. The rest of the time, the place took on a deserted appearance. Servants used the rooms for storage, and Ch'ung-ho used them for adventuring.

The area to the right of the residential compounds served many purposes. It had the two kitchens: the larger, main kitchen was next to the first compound, while the vegetarian kitchen was next to Shih-hsiu's living quarters in the third compound. Behind the kitchens, kindling, cut grass, and coal stood in neat piles. The servants and their children liked to gather in the big kitchen after their meals, to hear stories told or chanted. Among the servants were a few who had been to the south with Chang Shu-sheng. One old man had come to the Changs when he was thirteen. He had seen the Taiping soldiers, their hair hanging down to their shoulders. In those days, in order to survive, he said, one had to be able to climb over city walls and lie in a pile of corpses.

The servants all lived on the premises, some with their families. They were not grouped together in one area, but tended to reside close to their work. So the cooks lived near their kitchens, the seamstresses near their mistress. Big Sister Ho and Second Sister Ju-i lived inside the third compound across from their mistress's private prayer hall, while the menservants, responsible for water and fuel, lived in the back, behind the residential compounds.

The buildings to the left of the residential compound were all temples of sorts: a shrine to the family's most illustrious ancestor, Chang Shu-sheng; a library that paid homage to Confucius, whose altar and spirit tablet were on the first floor; and a formal Buddha prayer hall. We don't know if someone had planned it like this, or if the space just grew over time into a sacred ground. One can imagine Shih-hsiu feeling at home in it, because the men honored in the three sanctuaries were the ones she admired most.

Ch'ung-ho remembers clearly Chang Shu-sheng's shrine and the family library; she played in one and studied in the other. When you walked toward Chang Shu-sheng's shrine from the street, you would pass the courtyard flanked by two *yü-lan* magnolia trees; then, as you climbed the five steps and approached his altar, you would see a row of his battalion flags on the left and two coffins on the right, one for each of the two elderly ladies in the house—Ch'ung-ho's grandmother and Chang Shu-sheng's very old concubine. In the back, to the right of Chang Shu-sheng's altar and spirit tablet, there was a small door that led to the two-story library. The first floor of the library doubled as schoolhouse and teachers' residence. The tutors taught the Chang children in the front rooms, slept in the back rooms, and had their three meals in front of Confucius' altar. The actual library was on the second floor. The courtyard in front of the library had a kidney-shaped garden terrace. Parasol trees and flowering crab apple and plum trees grew there along with osmanthus, hydrangeas, and fragrant orchids.

The Hofei residence was only a small portion of the Chang family estates. According to Ch'ung-ho, the Changs had so much land that their holdings were never measured by their physical size, in the fractions of an acre the Chinese called *mu*. They had properties in the Anhwei countryside around Hofei and Wuhu, and also real estate in several major cities south of the Yangtze. So instead of calculating their wealth in units of *mu*, they would say how many thousand units of seeds were planted on their land each year.* They also hired many caretakers to help them manage their estates. Ch'ung-ho remembered

---

*Each unit is *dan*, which is about 133.3 lbs.

well how the caretakers were organized and what their responsibilities were because after her grandmother died she too had to employ such men to look after the land she had inherited. She said that her grandmother had always had the same estate manager, or *kuan-chia*. His name was Liu Chieh-p'ing. Under him there were two assessors, or *ch'ao-feng*, who in turn relied on the information given to them by their four assistants, their *pao-hsiang*. The assistants did most of the legwork; they went from county to county, investigating the situation of each tenant, which meant the condition of his land, the quality of the soil, the weather patterns, and whether there were any special circumstances that might have affected his harvest that year. They would report their findings to the assessors, who, on the basis of this information, would decide how much rent their employer should demand from each tenant. The assessors sent their recommendations to the estate manager, who would summarize them for the landowner, in this case Ch'ung-ho's grandmother.

As the estate manager, Liu Chieh-p'ing carried other responsibilities. Ch'ung-ho's grandmother had him draft most of her business letters. He would come to the ancestral hall in Shih-hsiu's residential compound in the morning, dressed in his formal, long gown. She would instruct him on how she would like the letters to be written, and he would listen, without ever taking any notes. Later in the day he would return with the drafts, and she would review them and make her corrections. No one knew much about Liu Chieh-p'ing. He had his own place on the Chang estate and his own manservant. He was also an opium addict. Ch'ung-ho's grandmother saw him every day, yet she would not have had any sure way of knowing whether he or her other employees had done their work conscientiously, or whether they had been honest with her—in other words, whether the rent she was collecting was too much or not enough. Ch'ung-ho believed that since her grandmother rarely questioned the figures sent to her, it was possible that some of her assessors and their assistants had been fleecing both ends to benefit themselves.

Shih-hsiu did not seem to care whether her employees were stealing from her. She was by nature a generous woman and someone with a keen sense of propriety, and so would never count pennies with those who worked for her. Besides, this was the Chang style. Her husband's younger brother, when he was a young man, once told a servant who sometimes acted as a purchasing agent for the family, "You would be a son-of-a-bitch if you didn't make a profit for yourself."

In other matters, however, especially Ch'ung-ho's education, she was watchful. As her father had for his children, Shih-hsiu sought out good scholars to teach her granddaughter and let them go if they proved unsatisfactory. The

tutors would come by way of recommendations. Shih-hsiu would never interview the tutors and would never attend any of her granddaughter's lessons; in
fact she never had a face-to-face meeting with any of them because she still followed the etiquette prescribed for gentry women in pre-revolutionary China.
Yet without direct contact or personal observation, she was able to gauge their
skills through Ch'ung-ho's progress. On days when they had some time
together, Shih-hsiu would ask her granddaughter to recite a chapter from the
Mencius, or she'd ask her to explain the significance of a story told in one of the
Han histories, the *Records of the Grand Historian* or the *History of the Former
Han.* She would also read over Ch'ung-ho's schoolwork after it had been
reviewed by her tutor, so that she could also evaluate his performance through
his comments and corrections.

Shih-hsiu was, in fact, her granddaughter's first teacher. Ch'ung-ho learned
to recite poetry almost as soon as she was able to talk, and before the age of six,
she was reading and writing simple characters and had memorized the first two
primers, the "Trimetrical Classic" and the "Tetrametrical Classic." From six until
sixteen, she had several tutors, one of whom was even a provincial-degree
holder. The best among them was the archaeologist from Shantung province,
Mr. Chu Mo-ch'ing, who stayed for five years, from the time Ch'ung-ho was
eleven until she left Hofei at sixteen.

Ch'ung-ho would spend most of her day with her tutor, from eight in the
morning until five, with an hour's break for lunch. Aside from important holidays, there was only half a day of rest every ten days. What did she study that
required so many uninterrupted hours each day and nearly all year long for ten
years? Mainly the Han histories, the *Tso Commentary,* the *Classic of Odes,* T'ang
and Sung poetry, and the Four Books: the *Analects,* the *Mencius,* the *Doctrine of
the Mean,* and the *Great Learning.** Ch'ung-ho first learned to punctuate what
she was reading, as all classical texts were unpunctuated. Her tutors would correct her mistakes in punctuation, but they rarely expounded the meaning of the
text she was studying. There was no need, because "understanding comes with
repeated reading and from knowing where to break and where to come to a full
stop." As she got older, Ch'ung-ho also learned to write matching sentences and
classical poetry and prose.

She had all her lessons downstairs in the family library. Books were stored
upstairs, but hardly anyone ventured there, except for her. She occasionally stole
up there to play among the dusty furniture and the thousands of volumes of

---

*These four texts and their commentaries were the basis for the civil service examinations
from the fourteenth century until the examinations were abolished in 1905.

history, essays, and poetry, many of them rare editions. Ch'ung-ho remembers that the library also held hundreds of the bulky woodblocks used in printing. She thought that her own grandfather, Chang Hua-kuei, not her adoptive grandfather, was probably responsible for putting the library together, because he was most interested in collecting.

Before Chang Hua-kuei received his official assignment in Szechwan, he lived for the most part in Peking. His own father, Chang Shu-sheng, at the time was either fighting wars or on administrative duty in the provinces. Shu-sheng needed Huai-kuei to tell him the mood in the capital, who was in and who was out, or what the imperial court was saying about the Japanese or the French, so that he would not blunder when faced with a crisis. While in Peking, working as his father's informant, Hua-kuei found time to assemble a large collection of books, paintings, and ancient bronzes. And when he was posted to Szechwan, a province known for its woodblock carving, he had all seventy-five chapters of Yao Nai's *Anthology of Ancient-style Writings* engraved on wooden blocks, which became his most precious possession.* Once, on a journey home from Szechwan, Hua-kuei hired several boats to carry the blocks for this heavy book. And so for a few days in the year 1896, travelers on the Yangtze could see boats heavy with chapters of Yao Nai's anthology bobbing up and down on the river, heading east, replete with navigators and escorts. Such was the extent of Hua-kuei's obsession. The blocks all arrived safely. But not long after, their owner died, and then for years they sat in a corner of his library, unnoticed and unloved, until a careless descendent began to sell them, a few blocks at a time, to whoever happened along.

The seventeenth-century writer Chang Tai once described how thirty thousand *chüan* (volumes) of books had disappeared overnight from his family's library.

> After my father died and before I could get back, my uncles, my younger brothers, the houseguests, the gardeners, the carpenters, and even the men and women servants, in other words, all the people living at home at the time, made a clean sweep of the library. So the collection, which was the cumulative effort of three generations, was gone in a day.

---

*The prose and verse represented in this hefty compendium span nearly two thousand years. The collection was very popular during the nineteenth century, which explains why Chang Hua-kuei wanted his own woodblocks of all seventy-five chapters. But there was another reason. The compiler, Yao Nai (1732–1815), was an Anhwei man from T'ung-ch'eng county, which was about sixty miles south of Hofei.

Twenty years later, Chang Tai's own collection, again tens of thousands of *chüan*, was also gone in a day, seized by local soldiers during the last days of the Ming dynasty and used as fuel for the winter. Most of the books in Chang Hua-kuei's library, not just the woodblocks, suffered a similar fate. Some were sold for quick profit and others lost through the circumstances of war. Nearly all the treasured possessions in the Chang family—antique furniture and bronzes, paintings and porcelain—vanished in this way. Ch'ung-ho said that when she was a child her family was already in decline: her father's generation produced no grand figures, not even an official. But she added, "a camel starved to death is still bigger than a horse."*

> So even though the family was not what it used to be, there was still plenty to go around, and we were still able to live in the style we were accustomed to. However, that too came to an end. One could blame it on the Japanese and the civil war, but the family also brought this upon itself.

Ch'ung-ho explained how this happened in her own branch. Two years after she was adopted, the ninth branch of the clan approached Shih-hsiu, asking her to take in one of their children, an eleven-year-old boy. The gesture seemed generous. They were offering Shih-hsiu and her deceased husband an heir, which the couple had failed to produce. There was, however, another motive. Members of the ninth branch wanted to plant one of their own in the main branch because they knew that this child could expect a walloping sum, mostly in land, after Shih-hsiu died. Shih-hsiu never wanted to adopt a son—she already had Ch'ung-ho as her companion and was content—but as often happened to widows in traditional Chinese society, she at the end had to yield to the pressure her husband's relatives put on her. Thus, since the boy was now formally Shih-hsiu's adopted son, while Ch'ung-ho was her adopted grand-daughter, in generational terms the boy was Ch'ung-ho's father, although only nine years older than she was.

From the beginning Shih-hsiu knew she had made a mistake. This boy, shoved upon her against her wishes, did not show any interest in his studies. His own father had hired a tutor for him, and like Ch'ung-ho, he spent much of the day in the downstairs library, reading classical texts with that tutor. But his heart was wild, and he was by nature lazy. So even though he was under constant

---

*Ch'ung-ho was quoting Granny Liu, who said this about the Chia family in *Story of the Stone*, the eighteenth-century novel by Ts'ao Hsüeh-ch'in. Granny Liu was a clodhopper and clown but also a sharp observer of what life was like among the wealthy and powerful.

supervision, he learned very little. By the time he was in his late teens, he found ways to elude both his tutor and his adoptive mother. It was also around this time that he developed a fondness for gambling and for visiting the brothels. He never gave up these habits, so that even after he was married, he kept a separate residence for his private pleasures—a servant posted near the door to keep watch.

Shih-hsiu probably knew about her adopted son's secret goings-on. But there was little she could do about what had already been decided for her. She had to accept the fact that this man was her deceased husband's sole heir and the inheritance was his to squander. She also realized that her adopted son was not going to share any part of it with her adopted granddaughter, despite the fact that the two were father and daughter through their relationship to her. Thus she specified in her will that the land, which she had originally intended for her own daughter and her descendants, be given to Ch'ung-ho as her portion of the inheritance. It was a discreet move, and the rest of the family did not seem resentful. To this day, Ch'ung-ho still holds the deeds to these properties. She says that these deeds, whether real or illusory, gave her hope and a sense of independence; that even during the most despairing period of the Sino-Japanese War, she was able to dream and to plan the life she wanted to live, on her own land, once the enemies were gone. Perhaps her grandmother had foreseen all this, so she did her best to prepare her granddaughter for the day when Ch'ung-ho no longer could depend on her.

Ch'ung-ho recalls many such instances in which her grandmother demonstrated her skills as head of the family, often steering them without a hitch through situations that could have become hostile or embarrassing. Shih-hsiu had tact, but what impressed others most in these situations was her compassion and her sense of fairness. When her adopted son married, his bride turned out to be the daughter of a concubine. Normally this was an awkward situation for both families because no one was certain of what sort of etiquette should be accorded to a mother who happened to be a concubine. Most people looked down on concubines, regardless of their age, and concubines were usually poor, so that even if they wanted to give the semblance of respectability they would not be able to afford it. Shih-hsiu helped the bride's mother solve all these problems. She persuaded her adopted son's own father from the ninth branch to contribute a hefty sum toward the dowry fund. The wedding was celebrated with much fanfare, and everyone in the family, from relatives to servants, was under instruction not to address the bride's mother as "Elderly Concubine-Wife" (*lao-i-t'ai-t'ai*).

Shih-hsiu also helped to resolve conflicts among the women in the Chang clan. She listened to grievances and complaints, daughters-in-law against mothers-in-law, sisters-in-law against each other, and one branch against another branch. She tried to find a fair solution or a way out for them. Sometimes, as in the case of daughter-in-law being mistreated by her mother-in-law, there was little Shih-hsiu could do except try to console her. When two young widows from her husband's younger brother's family decided to divide their joint holdings and set up separate households, Shih-hsiu was witness and arbiter. Ch'ung-ho recalls:

It was a formal occasion. Grandmother and I journeyed to Wuhu—this was about halfway between Hofei and Shanghai—where the Chang family had some property and where the two widows were residing at the time. I was then eleven or twelve. The event took place in the family's private Buddhist prayer hall. There were only five of us there, Grandmother, the two widows, my nurse-nanny Chung-ma, and me. No man was around. I have no idea how the land or the house was parceled out, but I do remember how the boxes of gold and precious jewels were divided between the two widows. Chung-ma did the actual dividing, since it was unthinkable for a gentry woman like my grandmother to handle the gold and the jewels herself. So Grandmother watched while Chung-ma first apportioned the gold bars and the gold leaves, and then the jewels and the pearls by the bowlful—a bowl for this widow, a bowl for that widow. The whole thing was carried out so casually, one for this side and one for that side, a bowl here and a bowl there, pearls scattered on the floor and trapped between the cracks.

I remember that the widows were particularly anxious about one small chest of jewelry. The description of its contents filled a whole account book. I had a glimpse inside the account book. I remember that the eight columns on each page were further divided into thirty-two grids and each grid had an item written in it. Grandmother quickly flipped through the book and said to the two widows that since they shared the same son they should make the contents of this chest a joint gift to their only child. She then had the servants take the chest back to China Bank, which was just across the street. The two widows had nothing to say.

These two women were daughters-in-law of Chang Shu-sheng's third son, Hua-tou. Ch'ung-ho explains how they became the mothers of the same child:

The older of the two was from a wealthy family, the Weis of Wuhu. She was betrothed to Chang Hua-tou's older son when she was a girl. As it turned out, her betrothed died years before they were to marry. She was only thirteen at the time, but the parents from both families decided that the girl was his widow and should remain his widow, which meant that she was to observe the moral standards pertaining to widows and never marry again. It was totally absurd. And this wasn't the end of it. The parents waited until she reached a marriageable age and the younger daughter-in-law produced a son, and then they arranged to have her wedded, adopting a son and becoming a widow all on the same day. So in the morning, she married my dead uncle's spirit tablet in a bride's dress. A few hours later, she put on another set of clothes and formally adopted her sister-in-law's baby so that her deceased husband would not be without a descendant. By the end of a day she donned hemp and was made to mourn like a woman who had just lost her beloved.

This widow remained a sad and lonely figure in the family. Her sister-in-law never shared her son with her. In fact, this sister-in-law, following her elders' example, continued to pursue an unnatural course when she was in a position to influence her own son's marriage. She tried to force her son to divorce his wife soon after his wife had borne the family two sons; she even put pressure on relatives and servants to bear witness against her daughter-in-law. One nurse-nanny, who refused to go along with her scheme, said to her old mistress: "You are a widow. I am also a widow. You have only one son. I too have only one son. You can bring yourself to do this, but I can't."

There were many widows in the Chang family history. They were all chaste. Whether they were mistresses of the house, concubines, or servants, they chose not to remarry after their husbands died. Their choice was coerced, some would say, the result of a thoroughgoing and protracted effort in late imperial China to gull women into believing that chastity was their first principle and that without it they could not hope to respect themselves or influence their children or anyone else. Men had a hand in it, and so did women. But as the Chang family history attests, chastity and integrity were not the same, because among chaste widows there were many variations. A chaste widow might be perverse, forcing her own daughter into widowhood, even though her daughter had never known her husband or a married life. Or she might abandon all sense of propriety in trying to hold on to her son at any cost. Chastity was not in itself a moral condition; it merely set the rules by which Chinese widows had to live their lives. Some regarded living the life of a chaste widow as a test—an unreasonable test that, after long suffering, separated the strong from the weak, the strong and affable from the strong and inflexible, the truly virtuous from those who only had the semblance of being virtuous. But unlike most such tests, this one did not have to be a lonely journey for the woman, especially if she was a mother, or if she was someone like Shih-hsiu who understood "perfect travel."

Shih-hsiu rarely left her living quarters, yet she was active in a world well beyond her immediate family circle. She remained close to her natal family, and was revered within her husband's clan and within the Hofei community. Beggars who had never seen her would cup their hands and bow when they passed by her gate. The people of Hofei knew about her because they could always depend on her support for famine relief, bridge and road repairs, and the upkeep of their temples and shrines. She was probably uncommon in the roster of chaste widows as well as in the roster of philanthropists. She benefited others but sought no recognition and claimed no merit. Her religious devotion and her family learning—what the Chinese called *chia-hsüeh*—could help explain why her awareness extended beyond what her experiences allowed, why she cared about universal suffering, and why it was not enough for her just to have compassion. However, there must have been other factors: the strength of her inborn nature, perhaps, and her quiet reclusion. The Confucian thinker Hsün Tzu wrote: "Only the deepest inwardness allows integrity to take form." Hsün Tzu also said this, of the person who has attained perfect inner power, or *chih-te*: "Though silent, he is understood; though bestowing no special favors, he is a warm presence to other people. Though never angry, he inspires awe." Shih-hsiu fit this description, but that she had integrity does not mean that she had also found her peace. She worried about Ch'ung-ho's health. She worried even more about her adopted son's idleness and depravity. And when she died in 1930, at the age of seventy, Ch'ung-ho says, the cause was a bleeding ulcer.

When her grandmother died, Ch'ung-ho was sixteen. For weeks, Ch'ung-ho had noticed her growing weaker. During those last days, her grandmother asked her to recite her favorite passages from Ssu-ma Ch'ien's *Records of the Grand Historian* to give her solace. When she breathed her last, Ch'ung-ho was at her bedside. Crying was not allowed, not until the formal services, lest it throw the household into disorder at a time when everyone needed to concentrate on preparations for the funeral. So Ch'ung-ho watched quietly as the servants bathed her grandmother, dressed her in Buddhist burial clothes, and placed her in the coffin. Then the lid came down, and the coffin was nailed shut. At that moment Ch'ung-ho fainted. A serious illness followed, but by the time the funeral rituals began, she had recovered.

Shih-hsiu's death was mourned formally for forty-nine days in the family ancestral hall. The Chinese referred to such rites as "doing the sevens." The family engaged seven Buddhist monks to come every seventh day until the seventh seven, to "quell the burning mouths" of the hungry ghosts (*fang-yen-k'ou*). They chanted sutras and did penance, and they burned petitions and spirit money, all to ensure that the soul would have a safe journey in the spirit world. On certain seventh days, these seven monks were joined in their performance by one or three or five groups of seven monks. The extras were funeral gifts from relatives or friends.

The most elaborate and important of these rites took place during the last three days, inside Chang Shu-sheng's shrine, before Shih-hsiu's coffin was removed from home. Relatives and friends came throughout those three days to pay their respects. And as they arrived, the musicians at the gate sounded their trumpets, to announce their presence and also to signal the chief woman mourner, who sat in a room behind the ceremonial hall, to begin her wailing. The chief woman mourner was a daughter-in-law of the family, but since sustained funeral wailing might sap too much energy from the mourner, the family sometimes hired a sturdy peasant woman to help her out. The hired woman would cry when males arrived with their condolences, and the chief woman mourner would save her crying for the females.

This system made sense: because males were not allowed in the inner room to console the mourner, it did not really matter who was crying in the back, as long as the sound added to an atmosphere of sadness and despair. Perhaps for this reason, the family would try to hire a woman with a tragic past to do the crying, someone to whom such emotions came naturally. The Changs paid well, one silver dollar, for her work. When Ch'ung-ho's natal grandmother, not her adoptive grandmother, died in Shanghai, her mother was with child, and so a woman was hired to do most of the wailing. This woman had a strong voice and a hefty appetite, probably from not having enough to eat most of her life; the family offered her plenty of meat, vegetable, and rice, so that she could replenish her energy. Ch'ung-ho, who was a very young child then, remembered watching this wailer with total fascination, as she moved between crying and eating, and sometimes did both at the same time.

Things were different at the funeral of her adoptive grandmother. Ch'ung-ho's hair was cut short, and she was dressed in a boy's mourning clothes to look like Shih-hsiu's grandson since Shih-hsiu's own grandson from her adopted son was only five at the time and too young to take part in the formal ritual. Ch'ung-ho remembered the funeral procession to be very long. Along the roadside to the family graveyard in West Hofei county, friends, acquaintances, and people who had benefited from Shih-hsiu's good works set up altars. The procession moved slowly, stopping at each altar to acknowledge the respect being paid to the deceased. It took hours for Shih-hsiu's body to leave the city of Hofei. Ch'ung-ho sat in a sedan chair with her grandmother's spirit tablet in her arms. Although she was merely playing the part of being the grandson, in the spirit's mind she had always been the true heir.

Chapter 6

MOTHER

Lu Ying, around 1916, in Shanghai.

CH'UNG-HO LEFT HER FAMILY when she was eight months old, and by the time she came home for good at the age of sixteen, her mother had been dead for nine years. Ch'ung-ho recalls only vaguely the day her adoptive grandmother learned of her mother's death: "A telegram arrived from Soochow. After reading it, Grandmother sat motionless for a while. She then noticed that I was wearing a floral print shirt. She asked my nurse-nanny to turn the shirt inside out so that a plain-color lining showed."

The last time Ch'ung-ho saw her mother was in the spring of 1920, when she was six. It was at the end of her annual visit with her family. Her mother went to the Soochow railway station to see her off. Just as the train was leaving the platform, she asked Ch'ung-ho's nurse-nanny to lift the girl up so that she could have one more glimpse of her through the window. Of that year, Ch'ung-ho's second sister, Yun-ho, wrote: "It was the perfect year of my life. I was eleven at the time. There were nine children in the family, four girls and five boys in that order, ages one to thirteen. My parents were both living." The next year, their mother died. For Lu Ying's children, this marked the close of the perfect happiness, which, they say, had begun three years before, when their mother found a house on Shou-ning Lane in Soochow and decided to rent it for the family.

It was Lu Ying who wanted to move to Soochow. She and Wu-ling lived in Shanghai for five years and had four more children there. During that period, they had two thefts, and they changed houses three times. She figured that it was safer to live in Soochow, and there they would be able to afford a larger house with a bigger garden for their growing family. Once Wu-ling went along with her decision, Lu Ying, who was the more resourceful and energetic of the two, took charge of finding the right home for them. The fact that she had just had a baby and was pregnant with another did not faze her. Two servants accompanied her to Soochow, and for several days Lu Ying went house hunting in a sedan chair.

The house Lu Ying chose had many amenities: a room for each of her children and their nurse-nannies and plenty of space for guests, servants, and storage. But its most attractive feature was the gardens attached to the house. Lu Ying was entranced with the pretty pavilions and cool ponds on her plot, and the two *yü-lan* magnolias in shades of white and blue. She also liked the fact that she and her husband each could have a study. Lu Ying's was the smaller of the two. She spent most of her early mornings there, practicing calligraphy and doing the accounts. On the wall of her study there was a horizontal board. Of the four characters inscribed on it, her daughters today remember only two, *lan* (orchid) and *shih* (room). In front of her desk was a row of glass windows, which faced a miniature mountain and two banana trees. Across the garden was her husband's study. His study had French windows and a door that led into the garden. Lu Ying and Wu-ling could actually gaze at each other from their separate studies; sometimes Wu-ling would walk across the garden to his wife's side, and the two would chat with the window between them.

Wu-ling rarely demonstrated his affection, but his children knew that he loved their mother. They realized this even more deeply after their mother was gone and their father married again and became more anxious and less sure of himself with his second wife. Their stepmother was strong-willed and needed appeasement. Their mother had been strong-willed, too, but their father did not fret in her presence, and he never seemed weak by comparison.

None of Lu Ying's children could describe her features precisely—the size of her hands, the shape of her ears, or whether her arms were soft or bony. They believe that she must have unbound her feet long before, when she was a young lady in Yang-chou or right after she married, because she walked steadily, not in a swaying gait. Lu Ying preferred muted colors, light shades in spring and summer, and dark shades in fall and winter; she avoided black because it portended misfortune. She wore trousers at home, and skirts on top of trousers when she went out, and always with a silk or cotton jacket. Her clothes were all made by Shanghai seamstresses, so they followed Shanghai fashion—collars moving up or down, fabrics in floral or checker prints. The only photo her children have of her was taken in a studio; it shows her standing in front of a dramatic sea view, with crags looming in the distance and waves lashing against the rocks. They have reproduced this photo many times, but the details of her have not been lost: perfectly arched brows and witty eyes, averted from the camera; also a strong chin and a generous mouth with a full lower lip. Her dress was Edwardian, probably ten years behind the fashion in Europe. Her children say that this was the only time they saw their mother in Western clothes. Lu Ying probably rented the outfit from the studio to play up to the occasion of being photographed. An evening bag dangles from her left hand, while her right hand lifts her full skirt just slightly to reveal the tip of her shoe. Her hat has been the subject of much discussion in the family because it is elaborate and big, and the ornamental flowers are piled up high around the broad brim. (A grandson that Lu Ying could not have known asked his father years later whether his grandmother had sold steamed rice cakes. Her hat, he remarked, looked just like the ones the rice cake peddlers wore on the streets of Chungking.)

Lu Ying was a woman of uncommonly good sense, and maybe this was the reason she believed in fox spirits. Many Chinese women in traditional society shared the belief. They did not see it as a reflection of ignorance or something at odds with their religious practices. Shih-hsiu had a fox spirit altar in her Buddhist chapel. Lu Ying had one in the house; twice a month she made offerings of eggs, cakes, and dried fruits to the fox spirits. An aunt in her mother's family claimed fox spirits lived in the storage room above her, and Lu Ying learned from this woman that foxes could give protection to a house if the human dwellers respected their privacy. A daughter-in-law in the fox family was said to be the liaison between the two worlds, and if there had been a breach of propriety, she would appear in the aunt's room in the form of a woman, asking her to tell her family to show more restraint. One New Year's Eve, the fox-woman apparently brought cakes, dried fruits, jujubes, and gift money for the aunt's newborn. Lu Ying's aunt accepted the sweets but not the money, realizing that the fox must have stolen it from another family. On this occasion, the fox sat by this woman's bedside, and the two chatted like old friends.

Other than strange stories like these, Lu Ying told her children very little about her own family. Her children remember having visited their mother's home in Yang-chou. A photograph of them sitting in a row in front of their mother's childhood house still exists. But none of them knew their maternal grandparents because both had died by the time they came along. The children give conflicting accounts of what kind of work their grandfather had done or how he had acquired his wealth. Some claim that he was a merchant, while others insist that he was an official working in the Salt Commission. Had her parents been alive while her own children were growing up, Lu Ying probably would have returned home more often, and we would have been able to learn more about them. Yun-ho recalls a Hofei song that describes the ambiguous relationship a married woman had with her own family in traditional Chinese society:

> Big moon, small moon,
> It's best to meet our young lady when it's shady and cool.
> Brother sees her,
> Holds a parasol to welcome her in.
> Mother sees her,
> Two rows of tears come tumbling down.
> Sister-in-law sees her,
> Hides in her room
> And refuses to come out.
> "Sister-in-law, sister-in-law,
> Please come out.
> I won't eat your food or drink your wine.
> Just call me your little sister,
> And I will be on my way."
> Sister-in-law walks her to the gate,
> Lifts her silk skirt,
> And bows three times.
> Mother walks her to the family graves,
> Lifts her silk skirt,

And wipes her tears.
Brother walks to the willow bank,
Asks her when she will be coming home again.
"Time and again,
If Mom and Dad are alive,
But if they are gone,
Never again,
*Not until the iron trees are in bloom."**

We know that Lu Ying was strongly attached to her brothers. It was to them she would go for advice whenever she was put in charge of delicate matters that involved the well-being of the Chang clan. Lu Ying knew that any misstep on her part might lead to bad feelings among relatives, which could not be easily mended. When the descendents of Chang Shu-sheng decided to go their separate ways, the widows of Chang Shu-sheng's three sons entrusted Lu Ying with the task of dividing their joint holdings. Lu Ying was barely thirty at the time and had only a daughter-in-law status.

The Chang family holdings included tens of thousands of acres of land and many commercial ventures, plus paintings, antiques, books, and caches of gold ingots, gold leaves, and jewelry. To work out something that would satisfy all parties was extremely difficult. It was a daunting task just to divide the land, because to do it equitably the arbiter would have to balance the quantity of the land against its location and the quality of the soil. Lu Ying worked with her older brother on the technical questions, but the overall principles she followed reflected her judgment. She thought that since her husband was adopted into the first branch and the second branch was also without a direct heir, the best properties in their joint holdings should go to the youngest branch, the only branch that could claim to be Chang Shu-sheng's true descendents. The three elderly widows applauded the fairness of her decision.

On the same occasion, Lu Ying had to handle another question, which was just as touchy. The widows all wanted a large amount of cash as part of their settlement, to help them cover the expenses they would need to set up their separate households. The Changs did not have that kind of money in the bank; most of their assets were in land and urban real estate, and to liquidate some of them for cash would take time and could not be done easily. At the end, Lu Ying decided to sell a large portion of the gold ingots the Chang family had put in

---

*Iron trees (*tieh-shu*) are never in bloom.

their bank safe-deposit box. Gold was highly speculative at the time because the world was at war, and it happened that gold was selling at a high price when Lu Ying was desperate for cash. But it was still a gamble. From all accounts, she acted without first asking for her mother-in-law's consent. In fact, most of the family did not know how she was able to produce so much cash on such short notice. A few months later, gold prices tumbled, and Lu Ying bought back most of the gold she had sold. She and Chao-ho's nurse-nanny, Chu Kan-kan, quietly returned the bags of ingots to the bank. Lu Ying's daughters, who later learned about this incident from Chu Kan-kan, liked the idea that their mother was decisive and willing to take risks. They also acknowledged that luck was on her side.

Lu Ying trusted all the nurse-nannies in her family. She relied on these women to take care of her children's needs and to discipline them when they misbehaved. But she also depended on them for special tasks, especially those that required discretion. She knew all the nurse-nannies well. She understood their strengths and talents and how to put them to use. Chu Kan-kan, for instance, was a serious woman, strict with children and dogged in her principles; she kept things to herself. So Lu Ying gave her the responsibility of looking after her room and assisting her with her toilette every morning. Although these were menial jobs, they allowed Chu Kan-kan to be alone with her mistress at least an hour a day, and often Lu Ying would divulge what was on her mind.

Yun-ho's nurse-nanny, Tou Kan-kan, on the other hand, was someone who was fiercely loyal but partial to a fault. She was also a good cook. Lu Ying put her in charge of preparing her breakfast, which she had privately with her husband every morning, and of taking care of her during her month of confinement after childbirth. Since Lu Ying had a child nearly every year, Tou Kan-kan's service was always in demand. Yun-ho claimed that her nurse-nanny was a wizard in the kitchen: "Her chicken soup was divine, and so were her potted chicken and fish, and her salted ducks and gizzards." Lu Ying herself did not follow the traditional custom of "entering the kitchen three days after her wedding, and personally preparing soups and stews for her mother-in-law," but she was skilled at making pastries and Hofei delicacies: tender pancakes, crispy rice cakes, chive pockets, and shepherd's purse dumplings. Tou Kan-kan learned these dishes from her, and would supplement Lu Ying's private meals with some of her own specialties.

There was also Kao Kan-kan, who was born with unusual intelligence. She knew how to solve numerical problems even though she had never learned arithmetic. Lu Ying would read out a question printed in the local newspaper— How many chickens and how many rabbits are in a cage if there are altogether *x* number of heads and *y* number of legs?—and Kao Kan-kan would be the first to give the answer. She had her own way of conceptualizing the problem and seeing the solution, which always amazed Lu Ying's children. Kao Kan-kan also had an extraordinary memory, which proved to be extremely useful to Lu Ying, who was in charge of sending gifts to relatives and family friends on their birthdays and on major holidays.

Gift giving among the Chinese gentry was a refined art. There were rules and protocols, but in order for it to work—or in order for it to give pleasure—the gift had to reflect the sender's taste and her awareness of the recipient's age, status, and temperament. Gifts for an elderly person, for instance, would usually include a plate of steamed buns shaped like "peaches of immortality," a bowl of longevity noodles, a string of firecrackers, a pouch of quality cut tobacco, a crock of rice wine, two tins of top-grade green tea, and a large joint of smoked ham. This part was easy. But the sender also had to enclose two extra presents intended only for the recipient, and this required thought and specialized knowledge. Lu Ying had both, but she also depended on Kao Kan-kan's memory so that she did not leave anyone out or send the same present to someone twice in a row. Kao Kan-kan was illiterate, but even without keeping a written record she never muddled up one relative with another, and she never forgot anyone who was on her mental list; she simply did not make mistakes.

All the nurse-nannies did their best for Lu Ying. They said that they were merely reciprocating her generosity to them. Lu Ying always welcomed relatives of her children's nurse-nannies to her home, and she allowed all women servants to have their children stay with them if this was what they wanted. For a while, Chu Kan-kan, Tou Kan-kan, and Ch'en Kan-kan each had either a son or a grandson with her. Then there was Kao Kan-kan's daughter and a maid's daughter called Chü-chih, both of whom grew up with Lu Ying's own daughters.

Three years before she died, Lu Ying began teaching all the nurse-nannies to read. Whether she was repaying their devotion to her and her children or acting on some higher principle we cannot be sure, but by the next year she had enlisted her daughters' help, and her private literacy campaign was well on its way. Yun-ho writes:

> The smartest and the most conscientious student was Chu Kan-kan, my younger sister Chao-ho's nurse-nanny. Every morning as she combed my mother's hair, my mother would teach her to recognize anywhere from ten to twenty characters. My nurse-nanny, Tou Kan-kan, was my student, but she was an underachiever. Whenever someone asked her, "How many words do you recognize?" she would reply, "Of words big as watermelons,

I could read a bushel." This, of course, brought great shame to me, who was her instructor.

Lu Ying also taught her own daughters to read before they were five. Yun-ho faintly remembers having stubbornly resisted her mother's initial efforts "to enlighten" her. Then one day after she tried to steal out of the nursery during a lesson, her mother spanked her. Humiliated and sad, she cried herself to sleep, and that night she wet her bed. By the next morning, she was ready to learn her characters. She claimed that within weeks she was able to catch up with her younger sister. Everyone in the family said that when she peed on her bed that night, she got rid of her muddleheadedness.

With the exception of this episode, Lu Ying and her husband never physically punished their daughters. When a child misbehaved, they would tell her to stand in a small back room alone, to reflect on what she had done. And when she felt regret and was ready to apologize, she was let out. From the children's point of view years later, this form of discipline was, on the whole, inconsequential. First of all, it did not apply to the oldest, Yuan-ho, who, being the grandmother's favorite child, was exempt from any type of punishment while the grandmother was alive. Chao-ho was also exempt because she was too young to stand in a dark room alone. Finally there was Yun-ho, who simply could not be disciplined because she, at that age, never felt any remorse and so would never apologize for her action even when it meant that she might have to spend a long time in the back room. Meanwhile, her nurse-nanny, Tou Kan-kan, would be on her knees, howling and pleading with her mistress to let her little Yun-ho out. Yun-ho said, "Tou Kan-kan was so sad and so relentless in her sadness when I was in trouble that I believe she suffered more on these occasions than when she lost her own husband."

When the Changs were still living in Shanghai, their daughters were not allowed outside their garden walls. The heavy gate was always chained when the children were playing in the courtyard; a gatekeeper was never more than a few steps away. It was Wu-ling's mother's idea to have her granddaughters confined at home. For at least a thousand years, gentry girls and women had spent most of their lives in their family compounds. In the early twentieth century, this practice was beginning to change. When Wu-ling proposed that he send his daughters to a modern-style grammar school, he pointed out that several of their girl cousins were already attending schools in Shanghai. His mother was not impressed. She said: " How could you let your daughters suffer! At school they only have cold food to eat. Cold food is bad for their health." Wu-ling did not argue any further, and Lu Ying also went along with her mother-in-law's decision. They did this in order not to upset her, not because her argument had persuaded them. Yet even after the grandmother died, the girls continued to study with tutors at home. This was at Lu Ying's insistence; she did not want to disobey her mother-in-law's wish even after the old woman was dead.

The Chang sisters' paternal grandmother was quite different from the grandaunt who adopted Ch'ung-ho. She had very little education, and even though she was a Buddhist, she only chanted the Buddha's name. Unlike her sister-in-law Shih-hsiu, she could not read sutras. Yuan-ho said: "Grandaunt had learning and cultivation, and her world reached far beyond her courtyard and her family. But Grandmother was bound to her home, and so was the extent of her empathy." Nonetheless, this grandmother, in the eyes of her immediate family, was an amiable woman—gentle, devout, and very loving. Her family never interfered with how she did things; they never questioned whether her ways made sense or whether they brought any benefits. She was the grandmother, the old matriarch. And it never occurred to her that she should be answerable to anyone other than the Buddha and her ancestors. Her family accepted this. They also complied with her demands because these were so few and her intentions were always good.

This grandmother loved her daughter-in-law. Every time Lu Ying was in labor, she would also be busy at work, paying obeisance to the four directions on her prayer mat until the baby was born. This was an act of empathy, and also the only way she knew how to beseech the Buddha and all the benevolent spirits to grant the mother and her child a safe passage. A bad leg made the effort strenuous, so by the time the baby was born, the grandmother was usually exhausted.

Lu Ying also had great affection for her mother-in-law. This, however, did not mean that she attended to her mother-in-law's needs around the clock as daughters-in-law were expected to do in traditional Chinese society. Lu Ying loved Peking opera when she was living in Shanghai, and on evenings when a great actor—Mei Lan-fang or Shang Hsiao-yun—was in town, she liked to sneak out to the theater and enjoy a performance in her private box. Chu Kan-kan, holding a very young Chao-ho in her arms, usually went with her. And when her mother-in-law asked where Lu Ying was, the family would reply, Downstairs, washing her feet. Eventually this excuse became a euphemism. Everyone knew what Lu Ying was up to when she was "washing her feet." The old matriarch never tried to find out for herself whether the others were telling the truth about her daughter-in-law. She had difficulty getting downstairs, but even if she hadn't had a bad leg, she would not have wanted to find out.

The year her mother-in-law turned seventy, Lu Ying orchestrated a grand birthday party for her. Months ahead she sent servants to Ching-te in Kiangsi province, a place that for centuries had produced the best porcelain in China, to purchase hundreds of long-life bowls, dishes, and spoons. These were for the guests to take home after the celebration, part of an Anhwei custom called "passing on the long life." Lu Ying also hired women who were skilled at tying red ribbon flowers and balls. Yuan-ho recalled just how exciting it was for her and her sisters to watch these women work. On the day of the party, every door was festooned with flowers and streamers, and a children's troupe called the *hsiao-ming-t'ang* performed. All little boys under the age of twelve, the members could sing and dance; they could also play the horn, the flute, and the drum. Their master was usually an opera performer from Soochow who was long retired from the stage and needed to continue to work in order to get by. Although these men could barely make a living, they took their teaching seriously, hoping that one of their boys, one day, might be good enough for the opera troupes. For Yuan-ho's grandmother, the little boys sang arias from a southern-style opera called *k'un-ch'ü*.

By the next year the Chang clan gathered in Wu-ling's house again, this time to mourn his mother's death. White ribbon flowers replaced red, and the family wore cotton and hemp instead of silk. The atmosphere was solemn, but no one was overcome with grief because the old matron had lived to be seventy-one, which in the eyes of her children was cause for rejoicing. The deceased was dressed in the burial clothes she herself had gotten ready more than a decade before. (She had slept in them one New Year's Eve, to formally establish that they belonged to her.) Her coffin was completed around the same time her burial clothes were made. Its material was yellow, *nan-mu* cedar, the best money could buy for a coffin. The family had it stored in a funeral home in Shanghai. Every year an employee of the undertaker would apply an extra coat of lacquer to the coffin. When its owner died, a final layer was added and the coffin was taken back to her family for the funeral and burial.

Yuan-ho said that before her father's branch of the clan divided their holdings, her mother took charge of the birthdays, weddings, and funerals for all three families. "This was in addition to her daily responsibilities," Yuan-ho continued, "not to forget, of course, that my mom was carrying a child in her womb nearly all the time." Just prior to her grandmother's funeral, a young aunt of Yuan-ho's from the third family died. Soon after this relative was buried, Lu Ying was planning again, for the marriage of her husband's half sister.

Wu-ling's half sister was the daughter his father had with a concubine. No one in the family, however, treated her like the daughter of a concubine. This woman was feisty and self-assured, and a favorite among Wu-ling's children. When she was of marrying age, Lu Ying and Wu-ling gave a lot of thought to her betrothal. They wanted her to marry well, preferably with an educated man from a good family. In the end they made an arrangement that few daughters of concubines would have dreamt of: the groom was a distant relative and a man of good character; he was also a graduate of St. John's University in Shanghai.

Lu Ying also wanted her sister-in-law to leave the Changs in style. So for years she had been assembling her sister-in-law's dowry: twelve place settings of silver bowls, plates, wine goblets, chopsticks, and spoons of various sizes; embroidered garments and jewelry; shoes and bedding; big and small leather cases; a rosewood bed and furniture; plus two red lacquer chamber pots. Weeks before the event, servants in the house were busy wrapping jujubes, longans, and peanuts in twos, first in gold paper, then in red and green. The dowry was organized into different clusters, each covered with a red cotton mesh that the servants had woven. On the day of the wedding, the bride kowtowed to her ancestors and bid farewell to her mother. Her brother then carried her on his back to the horse-drawn carriage, which by this time had replaced the sedan chair. At this point it was customary for the bride to cry, but Wu-ling's sister did not shed a tear. She said that she did not want any sentimental outpouring to ruin her freshly applied rouge. The musicians were playing a popular tune on their Western horns. The bride hummed along as she climbed into her carriage.

Lu Ying died in 1921, in the ninth lunar month. Her daughters believe that work and duty killed their mother. Yet work and duty must have given pleasure to women like Lu Ying, who had made them into an art. The actual illness that took Lu Ying's life began with an abscessed tooth. Lu Ying took the train to Shanghai from Soochow to have the tooth pulled. When she returned, her infection had gotten worse—the poison was filtering into her bloodstream. She was also nine months pregnant at the time, with her tenth baby. Yun-ho remembered seeing her mother sitting by the garden pond, crying, and her father trying to comfort her. A doctor trained in Western medicine was brought in. He recommended terminating the pregnancy. Lu Ying had no choice but to let him induce labor. She gave birth to a baby girl. Yun-ho said:

> This baby girl was our youngest sister, but when she was born, no one paid any attention to her. Our nurse-nannies hated her. They thought it was because of her that our mother was dying. Chao-ho was very young at the time, so my older sister and I and our companion, who was Kao Kan-kan's daughter, took care of her. We tried to feed her, but she wouldn't eat. After a while, her mouth spurted blood. We told our nurse-nannies about this. They took her and dumped her in the garbage pile even though she was still breathing. The three of us were so upset. We cried, "Little sister, little

sister!" They threw her away while there was still some life left in her. My mom's youngest daughter lived only for four or five days, yet I always felt that she had an existence—that she had been my sister.

Lu Ying followed her baby daughter a few days later. Before she died, she bequeathed to each of the nine nurse-nannies in her service two hundred silver dollars from her private account. She asked that the rest of her dowry be sent back to Yang-chou to be divided among the relatives of her natal family. She left her own children neither money nor possessions. She believed strongly that her dowry did not belong to the Changs, that even her children had no claim to it. Besides, she felt that her children were too young to know what to do with money; an inheritance, she thought, could only encourage them to rely on family resources and not on themselves for support. Lu Ying's arrangements were deliberate. The money she gave to the nurse-nannies was her way of acknowledging what they had already done for her children. It was also her way of assuring herself that she was not leaving her children to the mercies of others or to the arbitrariness of fate. Lu Ying knew that even without her there the nurse-nannies would protect her children and look after their interests.

As Lu Ying was dying, her children all gathered around her. They had been crying, and the room was in confusion. Her husband was sitting in a corner. Her older brother was somewhere nearby. Yun-ho later wrote:

> My brothers, sisters, and I were all kneeling beside her. My head was next to her pillow. Mom was very thin but still very handsome. I remembered what my grandmother had told us about her as a bride: "The glow in her eyes astonished all the guests there." But now these eyes were shut. She would never open them again to see her children. As these thoughts rushed through my head, I realized that there were tears rolling down her temples and sides of her ears. I stopped crying and gazed at her even more closely. I knew she could hear us. I knew she was still alive. She was crying because she knew she was leaving this world. When I understood this, I felt we shouldn't cry anymore to make her even sadder. So I screamed: "Stop crying! Mom is still alive. Mom is crying." But the wailing in the room became even louder. Someone picked me up and shoved me toward my father. I held myself tight against him. He seemed so lost. His body was trembling.

Suddenly a gentle calm descended upon them; everyone was quiet. Lu Ying drew her last breath, but her face still showed consciousness. Someone passed incense around. Lu Ying's children clasped their hands and began murmuring a

Buddhist prayer, *"Nan-wu Amitabha"*—"I have faith in the Amitabha." The prayer was their hope that their mother was on her way to the Western Paradise, where the Amitabha Buddha had created for the faithful their last stop before salvation. Lu Ying was not a Buddhist. Her family uttered the prayer in order to allow themselves peace. That night, Yun-ho curled up in her baby brother's cradle and slept.

Yuan-ho recalled that after their mother had been washed and dressed in burial clothes, and placed in her coffin, she and her sisters leaned against the wooden box and wept. They called out her name and begged her to come back. Their father was sitting nearby, unable to offer them any consolation. His eyes were fixed on her, and that day he would not let the servants shut the coffin lid.

Their mother remained at home for another forty-nine days. After the monks performed "doing the seven" seven times to quell her burning mouth and soul, her body was sent back to Anhwei for burial. Lu Ying probably would have preferred to stay in Soochow. She had a world there, and because she was its maker, the spirit of the place always belonged to her. In his essay "A Deed of Sale for My Hill," the seventeenth-century novelist and playwright Li Yü wrote about this idea. He claimed that all the great hills and mountains had their rightful owners—those who once lived there and gave the place a spirit and a distinction inseparable from their character and their making of the place. Li Yü himself was forced to sell his beloved home on Mount I, and in his essay he addresses the man who now holds the deed to his hill. He tells the new owner: "I have received from you the string of copper coins in payment for the physical substance of the hill, its rocks and trees. But you will have to wait before you can obtain the spirit of the place and change its name." Li Yü then makes this suggestion:

> If you wish to "change the dynasty," then there is an easy solution open to you. Quickly climb up to the high point and compose a rhapsody. Make a tour around the hill, and wait for a poem to strike your mind. Try to render both of them novel and distinctive beyond the reach of my poetry. Confer long life on them by printing, and then let them circulate as rapidly as possible, so that people, on reading them, will say, "Mount I does not belong to Master Li anymore. It has been sold to this man."

Lu Ying's house on Shou-ning Lane was pulled down long ago. The *yü-lan* magnolias and the banana trees have also disappeared. Planners of "the new dynasty" have jammed storefronts and apartment buildings into her garden plot. But her daughters can still portion out the land, place the portals, and delineate its mood.

Chapter 7

FATHER

Chang Wu-ling, around 1935, in Soochow.

WU-LING NEVER HAD TO DO very much when his wife was alive. The
nurse-nannies looked after the children, tending to their activity and repose,
while keeping an eye on their minor transgressions. The tutors gave the children
a well-rounded education. His wife took care of everything else. He did not ask
many questions and did not seem concerned about how others ran their business.

Wu-ling spent most of his days reading. He was an indiscriminate reader
who devoured everything—poetry, essays, casual jottings, fiction, biography, his-

tory, the Confucian classics, plays, promptbooks, literary criticism, translated works, newspapers. He loved classical writings, but also took to vernacular literature. His house in Soochow was awash in books. "They were everywhere," Yun-ho said. "He had them arranged on shelves, stacked on tables and chairs, and piled on the floor."

Wu-ling had accounts in two large bookstores. He visited the stores at least once a week. The owners knew him so well that when they came upon items that they thought might interest him, they would simply have them delivered to his house. And every time Wu-Ling went to Shanghai, the wardrobe in his hotel room would be filled with the books he purchased from the local bookstores. Books of all kinds, even those printed in limited editions by small and often radical publishers, such as the Creation Society and the Violent Storm Society, would find their way into his home. One could say that Wu-ling was simply a collector of books, but friends who knew him well insisted that he read every book he owned. Wu-ling also subscribed to more than twenty different newspapers—the dailies and the weeklies, morning and afternoon papers, small local papers and papers with wide circulation. Each day he scanned all of them—*Shen-pao, Hsin-wen-pao, Ching-pao,* the *Times,* the *China Times,* the *Soochow Gazette,* the *Wu County Daily*—for local news and national news. This habit, a friend observed, often made for prolonged visits to the privy.

Like most educated Chinese at the time, Wu-ling was watchful and nervous about his country's future. In the first decade of China's fledgling republic, the ruling government had neither the strength nor the integrity to stop the warlords and the foreign powers from challenging its authority. Internal fragmentation continued into the 1920s as Japan became less discreet about her ambitions in China. For several weeks in the fall of 1924, Wu-ling and his family had to leave Soochow and seek shelter in Shanghai when two warring factions were fighting nearby for control of southeast China. Yet despite China's fragile state and a very bleak prospect, educated Chinese felt an excitement about what they could do. They had faith in the intellect, in the possibilities of intellectual inquiry, and in themselves. The 1919 betrayal by the West during the treaty negotiations at Versailles illustrates this paradox.

When Germany surrendered at the end of 1918, China, which had been an ally to France and Great Britain, rejoiced in the possibility of regaining those rights in Shantung it had lost to the Germans after the Boxer Uprising. But that hope was dashed when China's delegates learned that France, Great Britain, Italy, and the United States had sold out to the Japanese, who claimed that China's former premier, before he resigned in October 1918, had signed the German rights in Shantung over to them as payment for the secret loans they had made to him. The events in Versailles spurred mass protests in Peking and other major cities in China on May 4, 1919. For those who were young and sanguine, the demonstrations occasioned a great awakening. They were angry at those who betrayed China and disappointed in their own government, but they also felt ready to throw off the old and shabby and begin thinking about China's problems in a new light. Wu-ling was caught up in the spirit of the May Fourth movement.

Even before May Fourth, Wu-ling had been brooding about how best to use the wealth his grandfather had secured for the family through his successes on the battlefield. Like this ancestor, he wanted to do something—solve some immediate problem—for his country. But Chang Wu-ling was not Chang Shu-sheng. He did not envision his life or his achievements on a grand scale, and he was not a soldier. His grandfather, though himself a war hero, had carefully steered his own sons away from soldiery, and instead encouraged them to study for the examinations and to follow a career in civil service. By the time Wu-ling came along, the warrior instinct had all but disappeared from this branch of the Changs.

Another reason Wu-ling stayed away from the military might be that the profession had changed dramatically by the early twentieth century, especially for those in charge. The cost of training and maintaining an army had skyrocketed since the end of the Taiping Rebellion in the 1860s. Now everything was expensive: guns and artillery, modern weaponry from the West, wages and uniforms for the troops, and the transportation of men and equipment. But the price of losing a war was even greater. So the new breed of generals and heads of state emphasized expediency rather than principle, and often at the risk of long-term consequences. Some, like Premier Tuan Ch'i-jui, who was also a Hofei man, went so far as trying to mortgage China's autonomy to clear their own military debts. However weak and ineffectual the Ch'ing government was at the end of the nineteenth century, at least there was an imaginary center that officers could feel loyal to. In the second and third decades of the twentieth century, it was difficult to conjure up even this illusion.

Chang Wu-ling did not consider a military carreer, nor was he interested in an official's life. His father had been a bureaucrat, but when he died, Wu-ling was only eight, too young to have come under his influence. And since he was an only child, there was no older brother to guide him toward a public career. Finally, Wu-ling did not have the temperament and constitution of someone who would be successful in public service during a politically volatile time. His friends described him as a shy man, hard of hearing since childhood and nearsighted. He was born to comfort and was, in addition, favored with a good marriage and a peaceful domestic life.

When Wu-ling had first moved to Shanghai, he briefly considered investing some of his family fortune in a commercial venture, but that plan quickly fizzled. Then for the rest of his life he devoted himself to realizing just one dream: a school of his own that would give qualified young women a broad liberal education virtually free of charge. Wu-ling's school was different from the Academy for Practical Learning, which his grandfather had helped to found in Kwangtung in the 1880s. The Kwangtung academy was built with money Chang Shusheng had asked from the emperor, whereas Wu-ling's school was funded entirely from the assets Chang Shu-sheng had accumulated for his family.

Scholars in China have been creating privately endowed academies for at least a thousand years. They have done so out of concern about government interference and the quality of education in state-run schools. The founders of these academies hoped to create an environment where students could explore the bounds of knowledge and inquiry without having to worry about whether their reading was in line with government prescriptions or whether their education could help them pass the civil service examinations. The best schools—the White Deer Hollow Academy and the Echo Mountain Academy from the twelfth century, for instance—devised their own curricula and daily rituals, and they tried to present learning as something that had its own reason for being and its own good. On the whole, the schools reflected their founders' approach toward scholarship and cultivation. Most tried to hold on to their independence, which was not always possible since they could be closed down anytime the imperial court felt their teachings to be a threat to the state.

The earlier private schools were rather modest, usually centered on a great figure, a teacher of considerable standing within the scholarly community. Over time the concept got bigger, and so did the physical grounds. Ceremonial temples, lecture halls, dormitories, and kitchens became staples, and a salaried staff would be added to run the school from day to day. But to renovate existing facilities or to build from scratch required a lot of financial resources: ready cash plus endowed land that could generate a steady income. Fund-raising became crucial, and it was usually a communal project. Often the county magistrate would initiate it because, in theory, he was the moral guardian of his people and so was responsible for their education. Sometimes the local gentry would ask their magistrate to help them coordinate such an effort. And occasionally a group of educated gentry would try to organize the entire project themselves, from fundraising to construction and hiring, operating on the strength of their joint reputation and resources. (The West Hofei Academy was established this way, through the combined support of Wu-ling's grandfather, Chang Shu-sheng, and other commanders from the Huai Army. As the local history put it, "They were responsible for the construction of the school, and they also contributed income-producing land and urban real estate so that the students could have their basic stipends.")

In the 1600s and 1700s, the prosperity of the lower Yangtze and a renewed interest in rigorous scholarship spurred the growth of private academies in the region. This process came to a halt around the time of the Taiping Rebellion, but as soon as the war was over, the gentry started to rebuild their lecture halls and dormitories and, whenever possible, they tried to create even more schools. Because their country was in bad shape, these men had extra hurdles to overcome to get their projects off the ground, but they were stubborn. By 1900, the number of private academies in a province like Kiangsu (where Soochow was situated) had more than doubled from a century earlier.

From about 1910 through the 1930s, the situation changed. Even before the Ch'ing dynasty fell, the educated elite found that they no longer could count on the support of their magistrates or the local power brokers for their educational projects; and this was even more true during the early republican years. They had to rely on their own resourcefulness if they wanted to keep their schools private. Two prominent educators from this period, Yen Fu and Hu Shih, stressed how important it was for their schools to have independence. It meant that the administrators and faculty could determine the shape of the curriculum—the balance of the course offerings between, say, science and history, Western political theory and Confucian classics, and whether or not to teach Western literature and philosophy in the original languages. It also meant that the schools could have some flexibility in hiring. Writers without academic credentials could bring their skills to the schools; blacklisted scholars and radical intellectuals could find temporary shelter there. But the price of this kind of freedom was high both for the fund-raisers and for the students. One fund-raiser for China College—the school the third Chang sister, Chao-ho, attended—was so frustrated in his efforts that he committed suicide. And when private institutions were short on endowments, they were dependent on tuition and fees, which meant that only the well-to-do could afford to send their children there.

Between 1919 and 1921 Wu-ling consulted several educators in Soochow about his plans to establish a middle school for girls. (Two of the educators were actually running such schools themselves.) But in the end he conceived Le-i, as the school was named, essentially on his own. The idea was simple and very easy to implement: he, Chang Wu-ling, was to finance the school's construction, provide for its regular maintenance, and pay the teachers' salaries, mostly with his own money. This way, he did not have to raise funds among the local gentry and wealthy merchants (something he was probably not good at); he did not have to ask support from the government; and he did not have to charge his students a huge sum.

Wu-ling was not ambitious at first. He rented a house on Ch'i-ch'iao Lane, right off the street, Huo-lung-chieh, that cut through the center of the city, and he partitioned the space into classrooms and living quarters. School opened on September 10, 1921, just one month before his wife died. There was only one grade—first year, junior high—and one class. Twenty-three girls, ages from early to late teens, enrolled.

Wu-ling was unusually decisive in 1921. That year he also hired a professional actor to teach his daughters the skills of performing *k'un-ch'ü*, a highly refined southern-style opera. As Yun-ho remembered, this was how it happened:

> It was New Year's Eve. Preparing the New Year feast was a huge operation because there were at least forty people in our household. We were loud and rowdy that night, having such a good time. The kids and some of the servants were throwing dice and playing dominos and "driving the crow" at a corner, betting a few cents each round. My father, seeing what we were doing, was furious. He hated gambling, gambling of any kind, even just for fun and only once a year. So he made us a deal that night. He said, if we stayed away from games like dominos and "driving the crow," then we could have lessons in *k'un-ch'ü* opera, and he would have beautiful costumes made for us when we were ready to perform. Two days later, he found us a teacher and every week we learned *k'un-ch'ü* in his study.

Wu-ling's proposal was bribery. His daughters thought that it was arranged by the gods. Once their father made good his promise, *k'un-ch'ü* became inseparable from their lives, offering them pleasure and solace, and a means of self-expression. Through performing it, they also learned to be less afraid of public scrutiny and of hearing their own voices in a crowd. Their relationship with *k'un-ch'ü*, however, had begun long before that spring when they first took lessons in their father's study. They had been listening to operas while still in their nurse-nannies' arms, with their mother at their side in the old Shanghai theaters. Lu Ying loved all operas—*k'un-ch'ü*, Shanghai, and Peking operas. And when her daughters were growing up, they would create their own theater: the oldest, Yuan-ho, would write the script and assign roles to her two younger sisters, Yun-ho and Chao-ho, and to any visiting cousins. The first play they put on was based on *The Book of Family Names,* a primer they had been studying with their tutor. The book includes most Chinese surnames and is meant to help children build their vocabulary. Yuan-ho's "play" had only four lines:

"Chao, Ch'ien, Sun, and Li, please open the door."
"Chou, Wu, Chang, and Wang, please come right in."
"Feng, Chen, Ch'in, and Wei, help us entertain the guests."
"Chiang, Shen, Han, and Yang, pour tea for everyone."

After the family moved to Soochow, their father sometimes took them to the local native association to watch the Ch'üan-fu troupe perform *k'un-ch'ü*. Yuan-ho remembers a rickety stage, two posts in the front of the stage, two doors in the back (the left for actors to enter and the right for them to exit), a musty bro-cade curtain, and two rows of lights (one across the top and the other at the foot of the stage). The small theater was set up in the old style, complete with square tables and chairs, and tea was on the house. The audience would have in front of them their own thread-bound editions of the score. And as the actors sang, the audience would hum along.

In the early 1900s, the *k'un-ch'ü* theater was at a low point. Back then it was Peking opera that was packing the theaters. This younger derivative of the *k'un-ch'ü* had simpler phrasings; the music was also easier to listen to, and the move-ments and gestures were more obvious. On the whole, Peking opera had more mass appeal because it was not so abstruse. Moreover, the most talented and the most desirable actors at the time were all singing Peking operas onstage. As a result, patron support for *k'un-ch'ü* was flagging. The aging professional actors had no financial means to cultivate a younger generation to succeed them. The Ch'üan-fu was one of the few troupes still giving performances in Soochow, often in crumbling theaters and dank teahouses in front of a few loyal fans.

The first teacher Wu-ling hired for his daughters was an old actor from the Ch'üan-fu troupe. His name was Yü Ts'ai-yun. He specialized in playing the *t'ieh-tan*, or roles of working women—prostitutes, professional singers, and ser-vants—and of women who were rule breakers and mischief makers. Mr. Yü was probably a second-generation disciple of the troupe's founder, who had once been a bugle player in the Taiping army. After the government troops put down the rebellion, this bugle player formed an opera troupe. The name Ch'üan-fu was intended to commemorate the rebel leader Hung Hsiu-ch'üan.

It is a mystery how a bugle player could have become a *k'un-ch'ü* teacher, because the operas were very difficult to master. They were intended for a liter-ary audience, and often the dramatist would showcase his librettos by filling them with splendid lines and gorgeous poetry; even without the scores, many of the texts could stand on their own as great works of literature. The subtlety of the opera lies in the translation—from texts and scores to gestures and cadences. But most professionals could not read, never having had a chance for education because they had been entertaining since they were seven or eight. So they learned the operas by watching their teachers. The amateurs, on the other hand, were all educated. They would approach an opera always with an eye on the written words. Although few could match the stage presence and natural charm and fluency of the best professional actors, a learned amateur could adjust existing interpretations when he saw fit and restore nuances that had been lost. Such an amateur could even correct the mistakes professionals made, sometimes for several generations.

When Mr. Yü taught *k'un-ch'ü,* he worked with his students a scene at a time, instructing them on singing and showing them the nuances of each gesture and movement. A complex scene, such as "A Stroll in the Garden" from the late sixteenth-century drama *The Peony Pavilion,* took several months to learn. While Mr. Yü himself always played women from the lower class—"women of pleasure" and misbehaving women—as a teacher of gentry women, he instructed only those parts pertaining to them, such as daughters or wives of scholars, and highly refined courtesans who were no different in their sensibilities from the most respectable gentry. Throughout those years when Mr. Yü came regularly to Shou-ning Lane to give the Chang girls opera lessons, their father always stayed in the background. He never interfered with Mr. Yü's teaching, even though, being a learned opera fan, he could have had his own views about interpretation and aesthetics. This was how Wu-ling preferred things. It was his style as a parent and an educator. He would initiate an idea, get the right teachers for his children or the students in his school, and then leave everyone alone.

Wu-ling had given a lot of thought to his daughters' education, starting when they were little. He wanted it to be broad, to include both traditional and new learning. But since his wife had always insisted on respecting his mother's wish, not to send the girls out to a school, he knew that he had to try to implement his idea at home, replicating a modern-style school in the enclosed pavilion of his private garden. He employed three teachers to cover a wide range of subjects: history and literature, classical and vernacular writings, geography, mathematics, general science, physical education, and dance. His choice of teachers was interesting. Mr. Yü from Yang-chou was a scholar from the old school, a strict and forbidding figure; he taught the classics and the techniques of poetics. Mr. Wang Meng-luan, from Feng-yang, was a progressive young man; he taught history, geography, and the vernacular writings of contemporary critics. Wu T'ien-jan was a young woman from Soochow; she taught the girls arithmetic, general science, physical education, dancing, and a few simple English words.

While Wu-ling did not interfere with their instruction, he did help to organize the teaching materials. He would select essays and poems from a sixth-century collection called the *Anthology of Literature*, chapters from the *Mencius*, and biographies from the Han dynasty masterpiece *Records of the Grand Historian*. Then a Mr. Kan Ch'en-yü would hand-copy the selections in triplicate for Wu-ling's three daughters. No one remembers where Mr. Kan came from. He was what the Chinese would call a "permanent house guest," someone who eats and sleeps in the house, runs errands, and does odd jobs for the host. One can never get rid of such a person because he is either a distant relative or a friend of a friend. This Mr. Kan was a fine calligrapher; he wrote clearly and beautifully. His large characters against clean white paper were very easy on the eye. Mr. Kan also took wonderful photographs, but the children did not like him. "He drank like a fish," Chao-ho said. "And when our granduncles came to visit from Hofei or Shanghai, he would take them to the local brothels and get looped."

Wu-ling apparently tolerated Kan's occasional lapses, though as a rule he had strong views about bad habits and a dissolute life. The thought of anyone taking concubines or becoming addicted to drinking, gambling, or opium smoking depressed him. He did not permit it among his servants, and, without proselytizing, he also made his children aware of his stand. They intuited it from an early age. The only time they remember their father punishing a servant was when he flicked Yang San's forehead after he discovered that Yang San had been gambling outside. And occasionally he would make a sudden appearance at the fuel shed in the back garden, where the menservants liked to gather to play mah-jongg. Without comments or any obvious rage, Wu-ling would simply take a handful of the tiles from the table and leave. Days would pass, and there would be no news of the missing tiles. Some said that Wu-ling had tossed them onto the second-floor rooftop; others said he had thrown them into the garden pond. No one dared to ask, even though this meant that they had to pitch in and pay for the set they had rented.

Wu-ling held firm views but left most people alone, particularly relatives and friends who were of his age or older; he did not feel that it was his place to reform them. His own mother was addicted to opium for ten years. She first took it to relieve the pain in her legs. Then her intake became habitual. A block of opium, which the Chinese called *yün-t'u*, or "mud that smokes like cloud," was kept in her room. Every day, the concubine that her husband had acquired in Szechwan long before would prepare it for her, cutting a sliver from the block of "mud," heating it in a spoon over a small lamp, and pushing it into the bowl of the pipe with a twist. A row between the two women put a sudden end to her addiction. The old grandmother decided that she was not going to let her weakness for opium further her dependency on those around her. Her suffering from withdrawal in the days that followed must have been awful to witness. Wu-ling, his wife, and their oldest daughter prostrated themselves before her, begging her to end the struggle and give in to the demon. Wu-ling's behavior can be understood by way of what one might call Confucian logic. He regarded opium as wrong and hateful but still had to consider it as an option when it could alleviate his mother's pain. And he would never comment on her addiction, because it would not have occurred to him to judge her. This does not imply a lack of independent thinking; it is thinking in a different way—one that is inseparable from feelings.

It was a stroke of luck that Wu-ling did not grow up with his natural parents and his own brothers and sisters. Life would have been bleak if he had. He was carried off to the principal branch of his clan, to be the adopted son of Chang Hua-kuei and his wife and the heir of Chang Shu-sheng when he was only eighteen days old. It was a formal transaction. Hua-kuei wrote to his brother four months after the adoption: "[Our cousin] Po-chi had another son this autumn. This is his fourth.* Relatives of the clan drafted a contract for us, which says that I have formally adopted this child to be my heir."

Hua-kuei called his son Sheng-ching, with the alternative name Wu-ling. The two names each took a character, *sheng* and *wu,* from a line in the *Classic of Odes.* The poem in the *Odes* describes the founder of the Chou dynasty as *sheng-ch'i-tsu-wu,* or "having followed the vestiges of his ancestors." Hua-kuei wanted his adopted baby to be linked (*sheng*) to the accomplishments (*wu*) of his own father, Chang Shu-sheng. When his son was growing up, the boy was known formally as Wu-ling, but the family called him Hsiao-sheng, or "a little link." After Wu-ling became an adult, he chose a different name for himself, as men had often done in Chinese society when they felt that they had acquired a more distinct identity and wanted their names to reflect this. Wu-ling's new name, Chi-yu, means "waiting for the light to shine through the lattice"; it can also mean "hoping to enlighten others." But over the years, Wu-ling preferred its homophonic equivalent, which simply means "a good friend." He said that "a good friend" had considerably fewer strokes than "waiting for the light to shine through the lattice." It is in every way a lighter appellation, and it suggests the change in Wu-ling's disposition as he got older.

In the same letter, dated December 16, 1889, Wu-ling's new father also let his brother know his happiness in becoming a parent: "Only now at age forty

---

*According to the genealogy the Chang family compiled recently, Wu-ling was Po-chi's third son. It is possible that Chang Hua-kuei made a mistake in his letter.

have I experienced the joy of having a son!" The letter was sent from I-ch'ang in Hupei province to Hofei. Hua-kuei, his wife, and their four-month-old baby had been traveling from Peking to Pa county in Szechwan province and were stranded in I-ch'ang for a few days.

Once in Szechwan, Hua-kuei rarely returned home. He was an energetic and a competent man but he died too young to realize his full potential. He passed the top-level *chin-shih* examination in 1889, and spent nearly all of the last eight years of his life in Szechwan province, working first with the governor-general to give the salt administration near the Yunnan and Kweichow borders a thorough overhaul. Hua-kuei managed the task tactfully and efficiently; the local gazetteer said, "He brought order but did not disquiet the merchants who were affected by his actions." Peking very quickly recognized his talent as a troubleshooter and a skillful negotiator, and so moved him around a lot throughout his career. He was first circuit intendant of Szechwan's eastern districts; then he was sent to the southwestern and western districts before he was asked to return to his old position in the east, where he died in 1898. While in Szechwan, he handled mass demonstrations against missionaries, administered the collection of maritime customs at the treaty port in Chungking, and instituted a set of regulations for the *likin* stations. In 1896, when the chief Japanese custom official in Chungking violated the accord China and Japan had signed the year before, Hua-kuei made him retract. The local historians described Chang Hua-kuei as a man of integrity, someone who was fair and persuasive and who knew how to rectify abuses without incurring anger and indignation. So it seems fitting that he should have become Wu-ling's adoptive father.

There was nothing particularly wrong with Wu-ling's natural father, but the house he ran was in disarray because there were too many concubines and too many children. Since his principal wife died early, probably soon after Wu-ling was born, and he was not interested in managing his family, the family managed itself, which meant that the children of concubines had the most to lose. The fifth son, Ch'iao-ling, for instance, was so terrorized by his oldest half brother that he ran away from home several times.* Once, when he was only twelve, he got as far as his aunt's house in Wuhu, which was about eighty miles away. This aunt brought him back to Hofei; she told the family not to abuse this child anymore, and things got a little better. But before Ch'i-ling turned sixteen, he ran away one last time, to Chihli, where he enrolled in the Pao-ting Military Academy, the school Chiang Kai-shek had once attended. After grad-

---

*In the family genealogy, Ch'iao-ling was considered the fourth son because his older brother Wu-ling was adopted into another branch.

uation, like many of his classmates, he was recruited into Chiang's National Revolutionary Army and became one of the few commanders under Chiang to score repeated victories for him.

Ch'iao-ling's best moment came in 1930, when he was already a lieutenant general. That year, Chiang Kai-shek's tenuous hold on China, as head of the Nationalist government, was challenged by the combined forces of two warlords from the north, Yen Hsi-shan and Feng Yü-hsiang. Fighting broke out, and for a time it looked as if Chiang's defeat was inevitable. Then, in a brilliant play, Ch'iao-ling lured Yen Hsi-shan's top commander into a trap. By the year's end, the two warlords' coalition had collapsed. There were many reasons why the coalition failed, but Chiang himself considered Ch'iao-ling's action important enough to merit a reward of fifty thousand silver dollars. Later, when he learned that Ch'iao-ling had divided the award among his officers, Chiang sent thirty thousand more with the specific instruction that Ch'iao-ling was to use twenty thousand for private recreation and ten thousand to buy land.

With the twenty thousand, Ch'iao-ling learned to play; he acquired three concubines and became a patron of Peking opera. He also fought in the 1937 Sino-Japanese War, but he retired after the war was over because he refused to confront the Communists. He moved first to Hong Kong and then to Taiwan, lost all his money in bad investments, and became an amateur magician and the manager of a circus. When his elephants died of dehydration and his circus folded, his former officers from the army looked after him. Ch'ung-ho remembered her fourth uncle as a lively and zany man even in his old age. When Chiang Kai-shek turned eighty, Ch'iao-ling wanted to perform magic tricks to entertain his old commander. Chiang's son, a rather humorless man, thought Ch'iao-ling was mad and did not let him near the celebration.

Wu-ling's oldest brother, Yao-ling, was also a man of excess. Although he was Ch'iao-ling's tormentor when they were young, he shared with this brother a proclivity for reckless behavior and a love for romance. He once had an official position in the northwest province of Kansu, where there was a large concentration of Muslims. From the Muslim traders he bought Arabian horses and bred them for his own pleasure. In those years, he spent a fortune on horses, and when he was ready to come home, he found himself totally broke. He turned to Wu-ling first for help, knowing that he would not refuse him. Wu-ling gave him thousands of silver dollars to settle his debts.

Even though Yao-ling was a bounder, the children in the clan were drawn to him. He was tall and slender, with a handsome beard. He told wonderful stories, he wrote bold verses, and his calligraphy was imposing. In the children's eyes, he had style and panache. Once he told Ch'ung-ho about the performance he used to give on horseback. He called it "three lines." He would dress in a crimson rid-ing jacket, with a long blue sash tied around his waist and a lit cigar in his mouth, and behind him a servant would hold the horse's tail so that it was par-allel to the ground. When Yao-ling broke the horse into a gallop, the servant would let go of its tail. The blue sash, the cigar smoke, and the horse's tail would thereupon form three lines in the air. It was pure artifice, and hours of prepara-tion had gone into it just so that Yao-ling could have a fleeting image of himself looking spectacular.

There was, however, one nephew in the family, Ting-ho, who found Yao-ling's posturing absurd and objectionable. Ting-ho was the son of Yao-ling's second brother and until his death in 1936 was close to Wu-ling's children. He had joined the Communist Party in the late 1920s, and when, sometime in the 1930s, his subordinates shot and wounded Yao-ling, it was rumored that Ting-ho had given the order.*

Chang Ting-ho's hostility toward his uncle could not be explained simply by his politics. He and Wu-ling's son Tsung-ho and daughter Chao-ho were all liv-ing in Peking in 1932. Tsung-ho's description of Ting-ho in his diary of that year shows a reckless and often thoughtless young man who worked on secret assignments for the Communists but who also saw a lot of his relatives, spong-ing from them whenever he could—not out of malice, but because, like thou-sands of other young men and women in the cities, he was on his own and was out of money. Ting-ho also had friends everywhere: men in western suits, men just out of prison, scholars teaching in universities, and mysterious women from faraway places. He had connections wherever he went. He would suddenly show up when least expected, and disappear when one was just getting used to having him around. Those who knew Ting-ho were attracted to this side of him—his restless energy and impromptu actions, his extreme measures and exaggerated views—but they were also exasperated by his lack of consideration and his pushiness. That he had ordered his men to fire at his uncle was never proven, but he must have done something offensive and unforgivable, because after he was executed in October 1936, his parents refused to take his body back to his ances-tral home for burial. They also drove his widow and three young daughters out of their home in Hofei.

His children now say that Ting-ho died violently because he had a higher awareness, a noble motive. But in 1932 he did not seem to have a well-formed political view. Ting-ho liked having mysterious visitors and working on covert

---

*Wu-ling's third son is also called Ting-ho, but the *ting* in his name is a different word.

operations. He liked living dangerously. The republican police had caught him twice and let him go before they finally shot him. In many ways he was no different from his young uncle, who fought alongside Chiang Kai-shek, and his older uncle, whom he despised. They were all picaros, and they were all from the fifth branch of the Chang clan.

This was what Wu-ling was spared—having to live with inequity and excesses and having to grow up in a world that was dispirited and odd. His natural father never cut his queue even though he was not a loyalist to the former dynasty. Every morning a concubine would lovingly braid his hair. The old man also had a passion for collecting jade stones, which he liked to hang from his neck and waist. When he came to Soochow in 1930 to visit the son that he had given up for adoption forty years earlier, he was accompanied by his favorite concubine, a Miss Ch'en. On some mornings, father and son could be seen strolling together. They were a spectacle. The old man wearing a braid was an anachronism in a modern city like Soochow. Dangling in front of him was his collection of stones, big and small, round and jagged—they jingled as he walked. A few steps behind him was his son: slightly stooped and nearly bald, wearing gold-rimmed glasses and a long scholarly gown. The son frowned out of habit; his gaze was compassionate. He was not this man's heir. Anyone who saw them on the street in Soochow could tell you that.

Ch'ung-ho said this about her father: "He had no ideology and did not belong to any political party. He was consistent in that he would try to get anyone he knew out of the trouble he was in." Wu-ling lived by a set of principles—his children understood clearly what they were—but he did not let any of his principles mute his feelings. He was not a Buddhist, yet his belief in the power of compassion was as strong as that of Shih-hsiu, his aunt in Hofei. He did what he could for his relatives, his children's tutors, teachers at his school, friends, servants, and children of servants. He did not care if they had four concubines or none, if they were Nationalists or Communists, men with means or without, playboys or poor scholars. He tried to help them all. And it was not always money they needed. Sometimes it was getting out of a marriage betrothal or keeping a young girl in school; sometimes it was shielding a Communist Party member from the Nationalist police.

Wu-ling respected life and so encouraged everyone around him, including servants' children, to make something out of their lives. Because he said very little in public—and that, often, in a whisper—his optimism was not transparent, except to his children. Through him, his children have always known that life has a purpose and that one does not have to attain it by force. And like him, they regard humaneness as nobler than abstract principles, and they realize that it could never compete or be in conflict with the principles they uphold. Sanity, reason, purpose, and compassion were their inheritance from their father. These things do not necessarily add up to greatness, but as his oldest son, Tsung-ho, said in his diary at the age of seventeen, "It is already a fluke to be able to live steadily as an ordinary human being."

Wu-ling, however, was not without blame. His silence about Lu Ying after her death created much anxiety for his children. Two days before the tenth anniversary of Lu Ying's death, Tsung-ho wrote:

> I believe I have nearly forgotten my mother. I can't recall anything clearly about her or about the details of her death. All I do remember is that whenever I tried to approach her bed she would tell me to go away. "Big Dog, don't get near me," she would say. "I have a strong stench."* I also cannot forget her parting words. We had all been weeping. Mom turned to me and said, "Don't cry now. You have got lots of crying days ahead of you." Of course, a child without a mother cries when his mother is dying, but he will have plenty to cry about after she is gone. Dad has already returned from Shanghai. I don't know if he remembers what day is the day after tomorrow. Ten years ago this time, he was sitting by her bedside, gazing at her. How deep was his sorrow then! What is he thinking now? I don't understand. . . .

Tsung-ho's diary does not tell us what happened on the anniversary of his mother's death, whether his father made any gesture to show that he was aware of it. But the day after, Tsung-ho wrote: "Dad is still the best. He knew I was looking for reference books on the *Lyrics of Ch'u*. So this morning, even before I was up, he brought me the latest criticism on this work. It is called *A New Study of the* Lyrics of Ch'u."

Wu-ling never let his children know whether he missed their mother after she was gone or whether she was often in his thoughts. Yuan-ho remembers seeing him once sitting cross-legged on a low stool, watching her and her sisters play—there were tears in his eyes. It was the only time she had seen her father cry. Once Chao-ho showed her father a poem she had written not long after her mother died:

---

*"Big Dog" was Tsung-ho's milk-name. The Chinese call their children cats, dogs, pigs, or worse, in order to trick the gods into believing that there is no point in trying to snatch their children away because their children mean nothing to them. But the diminutives also express affection.

The moon shines through my window,
My heart is full of sorrow.
Misfortunes in my past bring uncertainty to my future.
I now know the loneliness of losing the pillar of my strength.
Hesitant, I pace back and forth.
Realizing there are many forking paths on this road of life,
I empty my cup and seek oblivion.

Wu-ling read it and had only one comment: "Your poem is in the style of [Ch'ü Yuan's] *sao*-lament." His restraint had its reasons. It helped to maintain stability and coherence. No one fell apart after Lu Ying died. It was also around the time of her death that he sent his daughters to their first school and threw himself into getting his own school off the ground. Wu-ling did not want his family to be consumed by grief, so when he read Chao-ho's lament, he responded to its style and not the emotion in it.

Still, his children sometimes could not understand his silence about their mother. He kept them guessing about his feelings toward her—whether he had forgotten her. But they knew securely that he cared about them. They were astonished by how much he picked up in their everyday conversations about what fascinated them. Then, they noticed, their father would nurture these interests so that they would not casually let them go. Once, when Yun-ho was only eleven, Wu-ling asked her who her favorite poet was. Yun-ho answered that it was Nara Singde, a seventeenth-century Manchu poet. Later she recalled:

My father was totally surprised. He was expecting me to say Li Po or Tu Fu. But my answer delighted him. Soon he produced two volumes of Nara Singde's lyric poems, "Drinking Water" and "Slanted Cap," for me to keep. He added, "Singde's nature and sensibilities were of the middle grade. It's a shame that he died at thirty-one. There have been few talents like him in history."

In three sentences, Wu-ling told his eleven-year-old daughter his assessment of Nara Singde in the context of Confucius' observation about human nature. Confucius put most people in the middle of three categories, between brilliant and dull, implying that nearly everyone needs to tend to his nature, in order to perfect its potential. Singde had promise, Wu-ling felt, perhaps more than others, but died too young to realize it fully. At the time, Yun-ho may not have comprehended all her father said, but eighty years later she still remembers his words.

Not all Wu-ling's efforts to fuel his children's interests succeeded. He loved etymology, his children said, the history of words, their ancient pronunciations, and the styles of writing them that were codified more than two thousand years ago. He covered the blackboards, the tiled floor, and even the lids on storage jars in his house with characters in a difficult "seal style." This caught the fancy of his fourth son, Yü-ho, who at the age of nine or ten decided to write down all the T'ang poems he had memorized in "seal style," simply by stretching the top and bottom of each character. When he showed his writing to his father, Wu-ling told him that one could not "invent" the "seal style," that each character had its exact form and strokes. He then took up a chalk and began to cover the table-top with the same characters written correctly, and when he ran out of tabletop, he got down on the floor and scribbled on the tiles. Yü-ho later wrote: "At the time, not only was I not impressed, but I had no idea what he was doing. I thought to myself, at least I could recognize my characters—yours are inscrutable." Wu-ling, seeing that he was not getting his point across, merely smiled, studied his own characters, not without appreciation, and left the room. The head of the literature department at Chinling Women's College in Nanking, who was a relative, once invited him to give a regular course in etymology. Wu-ling came home after only three days. Evidently his enthusiasm for words did not inspire students in the classroom either.

When his children got a little older, Wu-ling approached them like a friend, often dropping by their rooms to enjoy a joke, or to ask about their views on a book or a poem, or their thoughts on current events. Or he might ask how they felt about an idea on which he was brooding. Wu-ling's ideas were fanciful and wild, the sort little children had. Tsung-ho, as a young man, caught this side of his father with vivid transparency in his diary:

11/12/30: Seventh and Thirteenth Granduncle came to visit us. We played basketball. Dad appeared and said, "I want to join you!" He then got together a few teachers from his school and formed his own team. The final score was fourteen to zero. They didn't make a single basket. And Dad didn't catch any ball thrown in his direction.

12/14/30: Yesterday Dad came to see me at school. We chatted for a long time. He told me he wanted to build an ice rink and to improve the design of the bicycle—adding a wheel and making it into a tricycle.

12/17/30: Dad has erected a small indoor stage in the east wing of our house. It is constructed entirely out of stools and planks. A carpet is spread across the planks. He did this so that we can perform *k'un-ch'ü* opera at home.

12/24/30: In the evening, Dad came to see me, actually to show me Huang Ching-jen's poems, collected in the volume *Liang-tang Studio*. He also explained to me some passages from the Twelve Classics.*

3/1/31: Dad recited me a poem. I can remember only two lines: "Rustic inn, sprinkled fragrance, a dazzling spring. / Magnificent tower, immaculate clouds, a graceful moon."†

5/29/31: I got up a little after five, to study math. I heard someone coughing. It sounded like Dad, and it was him. He came to borrow Second Brother's copy of *Theater Monthly*. He chatted at length with him about this and that. He told me he planned to convert part of his school into a planetarium. He envisioned a glass dome filled with stars and planets. Dad also wanted to buy two trophies to give to the Soochow Sports Meet. He thought that the trophies could be first prizes for the discus and javelin throws. So I went with him to the trophy shop. All the way there, he was discussing poetry with me.

6/26/31: Around seven this morning, I thought I saw Dad, just his back. I rushed upstairs, and it was him. He had especially come to give me a silk gown so that I can wear it to the graduation. He was so proud of me that he wanted to show me off. What a father! He thought of everything.

10/10/31: Everyone asked Third Uncle to sing an aria from *Farewell My Concubine*. After hearing him, Dad composed an impromptu poem, "[Hsiang Yü] was hero and lover. He could shake the old firmament and seduce a great beauty. . . ."‡ At night, Dad came to my room to talk about national affairs and stayed until ten.

---

*This is an expanded version of the Confucian canon, which was most popular during the T'ang dynasty. It includes the *Odes*, the *Classic of Changes*, the *Classic of Documents*, three ritual texts, three commentaries of the *Spring and Autumn Chronicles*, the *Book of Filiality*, Confucius' *Analects*, and an ancient dictionary called *Erh-ya*.

†"Magnificent tower" (*ch'iung-lou*) refers to the palace on the moon.

‡The opera was based on the biography the Han historian Ssu-ma Ch'ien had written about the warrior Hsiang Yü. Hsiang Yü, knowing that he would be killed in battle the next day, "rose in the night and drank within the curtains of his tent." Ssu-ma Chi'en continued: "With him were the beautiful Lady Yü, who enjoyed his favor and followed wherever he

10/16/31: Last night Dad spoke enthusiastically about poetry. He also told us to do our best to dream in our sleep—to dream about the battlefield, and to dream about us winning the war. I slept all night and didn't have a single dream.

Wu-ling had reason to worry about his country. In September 1931, the Japanese army in Manchuria had begun a full-scale assault on the Chinese troops with the intent to bring northeast China within its sphere of influence. By the end of 1931, Japan had accomplished what she set out to do, with no armed intervention from the West, thus leaving the Chinese angry and humiliated. Wu-ling's wish on October 16 reflects China's desperation: it seemed that the Chinese could taste victory only by resorting to dreams. His other dreams—the planetarium and ice rink—also did not materialize. And he did not come up with a way to improve on the two-wheel bicycle. Wu-ling's children realized that their father was impractical and naïve, an extravagant and capricious dreamer, but they did not mind because he was their sustaining father—constant in his love for them and almost a child himself.

Wu-ling never quite knew how to be a father, but he was drawn to his children, all nine of them. He liked to spend time with them, listening to their chatter. He told them stories and shared his light verses with them. Wu-ling was not a great storyteller. His voice lacked range and volume; he was also not particularly animated and did not care to cultivate affectation. But he had a huge repertoire, mostly anecdotes with clever wordplay and a sharp bite. And seeing humor and hilarity in the ordinary was his grace note. In his view, any situation and any person could be funny, wittingly or not: a holy man's faux pas, a preposterous misreading, a spectacled myope like himself, or a lad riddled with pocks. Of the latter, he wrote, "[His face] is like a bare rump that had sat on a briar patch, the spikes removed but not the stubs." Most of all, Wu-ling liked the combination of ingenuity and wit. He told the story of a Hangchow prostitute in the eleventh century who, while chanting a poem written to the tune "Courtyard Full of Fragrance," mistakenly changed two characters in the first line. This forced her to give the entire poem an impromptu rewrite in a new rhyme scheme; the result was a charming echo of the original, but it also

---

went, and his famous steed Dapple, which he always rode. Hsiang Yü, filled with passion and sorrow, began to sing sadly, composing this song: 'My strength plucked up the hills, / My might shadowed the world; / But the times were against me, / And Dapple runs no more. / When Dapple runs no more, / What then can I do? / Ah Yü, my Yü / What will your fate be?" (Revised slightly from Burton Watson's translation of Ssu-ma Ch'ien's *Records of the Grand Historian, Han Dynasty I*, p. 45.)

reflected the prostitute's own diction and circumstances.* For Wu-ling, the point of the story was the poems themselves, the way the prostitute's mistake led to a slight change in tone through the turning of a phrase, or a reversal of two lines: "Soul-searing / This is the moment / The perfume bag is secretly untied, / The silk girdle gently torn apart" becomes "Soul, bruised / This is the moment / You gently tear apart the silk girdle, / Secretly untie the perfume bag." And even a reversal of two characters, say, from *huang-hun* (dusk) to *hun-huang* (a dull yellow), alters the mood: "The lights are up: it is already dusk" becomes "Flame from the lamp is already a dull yellow." Wu-ling would note all these nuances with delight.

Wu-ling's children also went to him when there was a personal crisis. His fourth son, Yü-ho, who once declined Wu-ling's instruction on the writing of "seal style" characters, years later told his high school teacher in political ideology that either he should be better prepared for class or not teach at all. For this he was expelled. The principal regarded his comments and the list of suggested readings that he signed and hand-delivered to his teacher as a deliberate attempt to humiliate a faculty member. When Yü-ho protested, a student dean explained that all instructors in political ideology were sent from the Nationalist (Kuomintang) Party—these were not educators, but all schools receiving government funds had to keep them on the faculty. Yü-ho finally asked his father what he thought. Wu-ling said that his son had not acted incorrectly and that the student dean also told the truth; since the situation could not be reversed, it was up to Yü-ho to decide what to do next. When summer came, Yü-ho took the entrance examination for another school.

Ch'ung-ho once made this comment about her parents: "Dad never knew who was bad or who did what, whereas Mom knew but would not make a fuss about it." Wu-ling probably knew a lot more than most people, including his children, realized. But being hard of hearing and amiable by nature, he did not come across as someone who was quick and perceptive. Still, he managed to be a loving father to all of his nine children and to keep the family together after his wife died. This was not easy once he remarried.

His second wife, Wei Chün-i, entered the Chang family a year after he lost Lu Ying. She was from a doctor's family in Chiang-yin. She had studied literature in Shanghai, and was hired as a teacher in Wu-ling's school. The marriage

---

*Ch'in-ts'ao was the prostitute, and Ch'in Kuan was the poet. Both were connected to the great poet Su Shih: one was Su's lover, and the other, his disciple. Someone must have used the poem to frame the three figures together in a story, but it is unlikely Ch'in-ts'ao was the author of this poem.

was arranged; her family initiated the idea. Her granduncle had known Wu-ling socially and had sold him the mulberry grove where he later built his school. He thought highly of Wu-ling's character, and Wu-ling's assets must have also been an attraction. Still, the decision was agonizing for Chün-i. She was twenty-three; he was thirty-three and a widower with nine young children. She could have said no to the proposal, but some unknown force tugged her the other way.

From the beginning, Chün-i was unhappy with her married life. The servants were hostile, she thought, and the children never needed her. The oldest, Yuan-ho, was only seven years younger than she, and more of a competitor than a stepdaughter. Chün-i felt that everyone resented her because she had taken Lu Ying's place.

From the children's point of view, their stepmother was difficult to love. She was smart and capable, a talented painter and writer, fiercely independent, but also edgy and ungenerous, moody and deeply jealous of their happiness. Often Chün-i would flee her Soochow home for her parents' house in Chiang-yin, especially when she was with child, because she did not trust the doctors in Soochow or the Hofei servants in the Chang family. Soon after she married, she had two babies in a row. Both died, despite the fact that they had Chiang-yin wet nurses and Chiang-yin doctors. Her third, a boy, became estranged from her when he was in his teens but remained close to his half brothers and half sisters.

Chün-i was a woman caught between two worlds. Her marriage put her in Lu Ying's world, but she did not have Lu Ying's grace or skills to make it work. One would have imagined her getting on well with Lu Ying's daughters. They were all ambitious and self-reliant; they all saw themselves as modern women. But Chün-i's nature and her circumstances did not allow this to happen. If she had been a young aunt or an older cousin, things might have been different. Ch'ung-ho said: "When a woman's husband dies, she remains a widow to keep the family together. The man nearly always remarries when his wife dies, and this brings trouble."

As Chün-i's husband, Wu-ling did his best to understand her. He often took her to Shanghai to be near the theaters, which she loved. Sometimes they attended classes together when a good scholar was giving a course or seminar on history or philosophy. And for three years, from 1932 to 1935, she was enrolled in the Shanghai Art Academy, studying Chinese painting. Wu-ling also made her the principal of his school, a position she held off and on for over half of Le-i's sixteen-year history. They shared many interests, and he did not talk about his first wife. His son Tsung-ho wrote in his diary:

2/28/31: It was after ten, at night. I was walking home. When I passed by Le-i's entrance, I noticed that the person sitting in front of the gate looked like Mother [Wei Chün-i].* She said she was waiting for our dad. Upstairs I saw that Dad was in Fourth Sister's room, telling her about how he and Mother had gotten into a fight. He asked us to go and persuade Mother to come home. Mother wouldn't. Finally he had to go himself. After much coaxing, he got her back. Then we all piled up in Dad's room, listening to his jokes. He told us the funny story of how our thirteenth granduncle and grandaunt fought. When we saw that Dad and Mother were talking and laughing, we knew things were all right, and so we all went back to our rooms upstairs.

Wu-ling's own family was able to contain Chün-i's anger and unhappiness; they knew when to keep away and how to clear the air. Children usually did, especially when the other parent showed them the way. The rest of the clan was not always so kind. When Chün-i and her husband moved back to West Hofei in 1937, on the eve of the Japanese occupation of Soochow, at first she quarreled with the Changs living in the ancestral home, but soon they left her seething on her own. They might curse her outside her door or behind her back, but they let her carry on alone. At the end, Wu-ling was the only audience she had for her harangues. Fortunately he knew how to find enjoyment despite her unhappiness. When he died the next year (from drinking well water the Japanese had poisoned, the family believed), Chün-i's eulogy was as much about herself as about him. It was a double mourning, heavy with blame and regret, and sadness for the human condition. "Fifteen autumns we got through together," she writes. "Suddenly one morning you let go of my hand and all the links were gone. / Even down in the underworld, you have your family joys, / Whereas I am left to wander here while my hair turns white."

> I have been in anguish for others, but myself never accepted pity.
> I have never found it natural to be entangled by feelings.
> Only now have I come to realize what such things mean.
> Already the gap between the living and the dead is over a thousand miles
>   wide.
> You built your school on Ch'i-ch'iao Lane and assembled the brightest talents.
> In groups and clusters, teachers and students worked together.

---

*Wu-ling's children called their own mother Da-da and their stepmother Ma-ma (mother).

Do you not remember the carefree elegance of that Chang Hsü willow,
*So like you, as the years went by, with your scholar's sleeves flowing?**

We were all wrong about how things would turn out:
Like swallows and sparrows, we thought we had to return to our original
*   home.*
Had we only known the utter disarray of our old nest,
We would have taken the risk and stayed in Soochow.

Soochow surpassed the immortals' isle,
Since from the immortals' isle, there can be no return.
Life is without its blessings; death is not so harsh.
Though I gave up my chances and effaced myself, disasters still come calling.

The bean stalks boil the beans, allow themselves to stew the other.†
It is rare that a nephew did not call his uncle a simpleton.
How your family envied your character and exceptional abilities!
And you carried your gifts to no avail. So there is the tragedy.

Families should have no "mine" or "yours," that is the natural way.
But your gentle sweetness sent your life awry.
When we at last perceive the extreme of differences,
We are like the spring silkworms tangled in the threads of our cocoons.

Chün-i's eulogy is a fierce indictment of Wu-ling's clan: "Had we only known the utter disarray of our old nest, / We would have . . . stayed in Soo-chow." And the "disarray" did not refer just to the dispirited life in West Hofei but also to the jealousy and hostility that, she felt, had become part of that world. The third-century poem she alluded to was about the tragedy of family relationships. Stalks and beans are from the same plant and so, by analogy, they are brothers. In the earlier poem, one is burning away, and the other is sweating and weeping. The one in the pot says to his brother, "We sprang from the same roots,

---

*Chang Hsü was from Wu, where Soochow is now situated. He lived during the fifth century and was noted for his elegance. The ruler of the Southern Ch'i dynasty used to point to the willow in front of the Ling-ho Temple, saying, "This willow is so lovely and charming, just like Chang Hsü when he was a young man."

†This idea comes from a well-known poem of the third century. The poem, "The Seven-Step Verse," was meant to reinforce stories about the poet Ts'ao Chih's strained relationship with his brother Ts'ao P'i, who was, at the time, the ruler of the Wei dynasty.

so why be in a hurry to cook me?" Chün-i accused Wu-ling's cousins and uncles of being grasping and petty, but she also blamed him for being weak and naïve: "You carried your gifts to no avail"; "your gentle sweetness sent your life awry."

In Chün-i's eulogy, even her accolade is set off by mockery. Her husband "assembled the brightest talents," and he had the "carefree," effeminate elegance of Chang Hsü and the willow. Chün-i's description of Wu-ling is a stark contrast to what she says about herself. She "gave up her chances," she writes, "effaced herself," and was unused to being "entangled by feelings." She was the nobler of the two but was not happy in her selflessness. Her "Eulogy" was followed by "Funeral Song," which contained this stanza:

> *Here and there, flowers in the cold, shaking off morning frost.*
> *My mind has been circling the long and narrow pond.*
> *I return, depressed, sit and face the imperfect mirror.*
> *With you gone, I am too weary even to sift through my dowry trunk.*
> *Weak as I am, how dare I claim to be a good wife?*
> *But you, we all know, were the prince of the romantics.*

Chün-i tells us that she had been revisiting the past, "circling the long and narrow pond," and that this depressed and wearied her. Looking back, she writes, she could not even "claim to be a good wife," whereas her husband, as everyone knew, was "the prince of the romantics." The expression for a "good wife" (*chung-kuei*) is found in the *Classic of Changes*. The commentary to the hexagram *chia-jen* maintains that "man and woman must keep to their proper places": the man's place is "outside the home"; the woman's place is "inside the home"—she "stays in" and "prepares food" for her family (*chung-kuei*) and "does not set off to pursue other matters." Chün-i said that she was not good at these things but did not seem terribly contrite. Her depression had a different reason. She was resentful at having married, perhaps, and at having had to accept her role as a married woman—unglamorous and thankless, she thought, while her husband glided through life with his "scholar's sleeves flowing."

Wu-ling's last poems, in a set of five, convey a different mood and different sentiments from his wife's, although they were also about Hofei. They echo a folk ballad written by the eighth-century poet-genius Tu Fu. Both men describe the joy of going home: one, anticipating it from his temporary refuge in Szechwan; the other, relishing it while there. Tu Fu writes: "When I heard that the troops had recovered the North, / My clothes were drenched in tears of joy. / I wanted so much to find my family and tell them the news. / Slowly I rolled up the scrolls of letters and poems, though I wanted to go wild with happiness. / To sing and get crocked in broad daylight." In Tu Fu's mind, he was already on his way home, "passing through Pa Gorge and Wu Gorge / Going downstream to Hsiang-yang and on to Loyang."*

Unlike Tu Fu, who had to seek shelter in the southwest when rebel forces occupied his city, Wu-ling chose to leave: "Away from my parents' home, / Neglecting the care of my ancestors' tombs." It was an impending war, years later, that forced him to return to Hofei, where it was safer to live. The homecoming brought him unexpected delights: "Hibiscus in autumn waters brighten the dawn. / Chrysanthemums in the western garden, reflected in an unkept pond. / Candied persimmons, honey-sweet, cool my mouth. / Steamed taros, soft and tender, fill my belly."

The last of the five poems was probably the last thing he wrote. Oddly, it was an endnote about himself, recounting his life and travels:

> As a baby I went up the Pa River with my father.
> I returned downstream, an orphan, clothed in white hemp.
> Growing up in Hofei, I lived with my uncles,
> Which meant I was never far from the ancestral hall.
> Then came twenty years in Soochow, 'til sated with perch and water shield,
> Nostalgic for the September scent of angelica and chrysanthemum in Hofei.
> Those lush cities of the South have become somber fortresses.
> To avoid the troubles there, I have come home.

Long before, when Chang Hua-kuei gave his adopted baby the double name of Sheng-ching and Wu-ling, he was hoping that his son would follow "the vestiges of his ancestors," meaning those of Chang Shu-sheng. Forty years later, Wu-ling described himself as someone "With only a bag of books and a writing brush but nothing to contribute." He said that he had been to places and loved life for itself—the taste of "perch and water shield" and "the September scent of angelica and chrysanthemum"—but when enemies came he dodged. In this sense he was not a link to Chang Shu-sheng. Yet at the same time, he shared with his grandfather a belief in the virtue of education. Both wanted to build schools and to restructure China's education based on Western models. They wanted to understand how Western learning, and learning as a whole, could fuel the spirit of a people and serve their practical needs. Wu-ling's romance with the world was with these things. He blundered at times and was a spendthrift, but this was his romance.

---

*The title of Tu Fu's poem is "Ch'u-chiang-hsing."

Chapter 8

THE SCHOOL

Between 1921 and 1937, Wu-ling spent over 250,000 silver dollars on his school for girls. There were less than three hundred graduates during Le-i Middle School's sixteen-year history. It was a most extravagant enterprise. The dean of students, in his foreword to the 1932 yearbook, asked whether it was wasteful to give so much to so few: Can one justify it, and how does one go about doing it? In his view, there was no easy way to assess the benefits of a Le-i education against its expenses. No judge or balance sheet could come to a fair conclusion. Yet he wanted the graduates to reflect on these questions and to be mindful of their experience at Le-i. He told them that the school had been precious for the benefactor—hundreds of thousands of dollars "came from him alone"—but also precious for itself. He wrote: "Know your school and understand her spirit. Think whether she is worth your remembrance. Did she lend you spiritual support?"

The benefactor, Chang Wu-ling, in his own foreword, refrained from offering any homilies. Instead, he told a story associated with the degree graduates of the eighth century:

During the T'ang dynasty, the new graduates of the highest, metropolitan degree, after their night of feasting and celebration, always signed their names jointly on the Wild Goose Pavilion in the capital. This was a much-told tale. Until the early Ch'ing, whenever there was a provincial or a metropolitan examination, graduates of the same year would record and publish their names together. They called each other "classmates" [*t'ung-nien*], and formed close bonds. But most scholars of the past studied alone in their own homes. They met only occasionally, usually when they were taking examinations together. However, once they had a chance to know each other, they cherished the friendship, and not just for themselves. Often their families for generations would remain close and would not lose touch with each other. And when they began to work in related fields or in the same profession, it would be less likely for such friends to have rifts or misunderstandings. All of you today have a greater advantage than past scholars who called each other "classmates." Ever since you came to this school, you have been in the same classes, sharing the same teachers. You learn in the same classrooms. You work and relax together; you refine each other and give each other encouragement. You know and understand each other intimately.

There were only nineteen graduates that year. Wu-ling had no grand dreams and no exaggerated words for them. He merely wished that they would hold on to the world they found in Le-i and the feelings they had cultivated as classmates. That was enough. Later, friends and family would explain that Wu-ling poured so much money into Le-i because he was committed to women's education. His own writings never made anything out of this. Like his first wife, he was a maker, a creator of worlds; he was a quiet man, not an advocate or an activist. The lyrics he wrote for the school song betray his deeper impulse: "Soochow is paradise, / civilized in early times / and suffused with glorious culture. / Long, long ago, T'ai-po and Yü-chung / brought their virtues here, / transforming local customs. / Our school, this hallowed ground, / rings with verse and music. / Scholars here are joyful and serene."

T'ai-po and Yü-chung were uncles of King Wen, the founder of the Chou state and the most glorious of all China's ancient kings. Long ago they had come to settle in Wu, the ancient home of Soochow. According to the Han historian Ssu-ma Ch'ien, after T'ai-po's youngest brother, Chi-li, married T'ai-jen,* a woman of the utmost refinement and decorum, and she bore him a son named Ch'ang, heavenly signs all point to Ch'ang as possessing the moral potentials of a sage king: "Knowing that their father wished to establish their younger brother, Chi-li, as his heir so that Chi-li's own son Ch'ang could eventually succeed him, T'ai-po and Yü-chung ran away to the land of the barbarians. They

---

*See chapter 1 for descriptions of T'ai-jen in the *Classic of Odes*.

tatooed their bodies and cut their hair short, in order to yield their right to rule to their younger brother." Confucius, in the *Analects,* called T'ai-po a man of "supreme virtue": "Three times he abdicated the right to rule over the empire. He also left behind nothing for which people could find praise." In Confucius' view, to yield and then to hide any trace of your accomplishment is the highest attainment of virtue. Yet even such a man could change the air, the customs, of a place merely by being there. T'ai-po civilized the land around Soochow long ago, and it was in Soochow that Wu-ling chose to place his own Le-i. He believed that from the strength of this "hallowed ground"—this plot he called "paradise" (*le-t'u*)—his students could find "compassion for others" (*i-jen*) and "contentment in themselves" (*chang-le*). This was his "optimism" (*le-kuan*) and his gloss on the meaning of *le* and *i*.

When the school first opened in the autumn of 1921, it was in a rented house on Ch'i-ch'iao Lane. The place was temporary, too small for any ambitious plans, and, some said, it was haunted because there had been a murder in the house a few years back. In early 1923, Wu-ling moved Le-i to an open space next to the Soochow Garden. Soon after, he also moved his family there, next to the school, on Chiu-ju Lane. Wu-ling wanted his children to grow up next to a school, to be near the Le-i students and to be able to play on the basketball court on holidays and during the summer break. By this time, he had married again. His wife wanted a new beginning, and since she also worked at the school, the move was a convenience for her.

The new campus covered three acres. In addition to fourteen buildings, each two stories high, and thirty-two rooms linked by verandas, it had a playing field, a thatched pavilion, and a profusion of winter plum trees. Originally the three acres included a mulberry grove and an old burial ground. The school was built on top of the abandoned graves. When it first opened, some mounds were still visible; occasionally an ancient skull would surface. The landscape changed over time. On one occasion, Wu-ling bought a garden just so that he could have its plum flowers moved to Le-i. The construction and landscaping cost over 20,000 silver dollars.*

Every year the school recruited students through the Shanghai and Soochow newspapers. It asked that all first-year, first-semester applicants submit their elementary school diplomas, and that transfer students submit transcripts from their previous schools. Admissions also required students to take examinations in Chinese, mathematics, the natural sciences, history, geography, politics, and

---

*In 1926, one silver dollar was equivalent to approximately fifty cents in U.S. currency.

English. Only the first-year, first-semester students were exempted from the English test. Students from outside Soochow assembled the day before the examination, and they stayed overnight at the school dormitory, taking their meals there. The charge for the examination was half a silver dollar. For the academic year 1932 to 1933, there were fifty spaces for the first-year students and thirty-five for transfers. (When the class of 1932 started Le-i in 1929, there were forty-four of them, but by the next year, the number had dropped to twenty-five; as the yearbook noted, "usually it was special circumstances that forced these students to leave.")

Le-i gave its students a broad, liberal education. Readings in vernacular and translated works were balanced with studies in poetics and traditional literature. The students also had physical education every day, and most of them participated in some form of intramural sports—track and field, soccer, or basketball. Le-i students were also one of the first groups of young women in Soochow to have their hair cut in a bob.

Le-i's tuition in 1932 was 20 silver dollars per semester; in addition, a room was 6 dollars, full board was 28, and there was a charge of 4 dollars for library, athletics, and miscellaneous fees. A full boarder paid a total of 116 silver dollars a year for her education—a bargain for private education in those days. The school reserved ten spots for scholarship students, four based on academic merit and six on financial need. The school's annual income from tuition was less than 3,500 dollars a year, while its expense for payroll alone was over 9,000 dollars. Wu-ling was the one who made up the difference. Before each academic year began, there was always a period when his own children were not sure if they would be returning to their schools; they all understood that Le-i's budget had priority over their tuitions.

The teachers in Le-i were adequately paid—about half a silver dollar an hour or around 40 dollars a month, which in the late 1920s was the average income of an urban middle school teacher.* The 1932 yearbook lists sixteen faculty members. Two of them were Communist Party members. In the 1920s, there had been many more. In fact, not only was the first meeting of the Soochow Communist Party branch held in Le-i Middle School in 1925, but the organizer, Hou Shao-ch'iu, was at the time the dean of the school.

When Wu-ling hired Mr. Hou away from his position as dean at another

---

*See Sidney Gamble, *How Chinese Families Live in Peiping* (New York and London: Funk and Wagnalls, 1933), p. 317; also quoted in Yeh, *The Alienated Academy*, pp. 195–96. The figures Wu-ling's son Huan-ho gave are not consistent with Wei Pu's in the 1932 yearbook. Since Wei Pu was the chief administrator of the school at the time, I have decided to use his.

girls' school, in Sung-chiang, a town just west of Shanghai, he probably did not know the details of Hou's Communist affiliations or anything about his political ambitions. Perhaps Wu-ling was naïve, or perhaps he was thinking only about finding a smart and able person to fill the position of dean. Mr. Hou had impressive credentials. In 1923 and 1924, he had helped two private schools in the Shanghai area to stay afloat without government subsidies. This alone would have satisfied many principals and school trustees who were looking for administrators at the time. In its first six years, Le-i had six different deans, which meant that Wu-ling could not afford to worry too much about a candidate's background beyond the relevant experience in education. Besides, people's political affiliations changed swiftly and dramatically during the 1920s and 1930s. Chou Fo-hai, who was head of the board of education in Kiangsu in the early 1930s and wrote the honorific inscription in Le-i's 1932 yearbook, was a good example. He was a delegate to the First Congress of the Chinese Communist Party in 1921; by the late 1920s he was a political theorist and a leading propaganda official for Chiang Kai-shek's Nationalist Party; then, in 1939, he joined Wang Ching-wei's collaborationist government and worked with the Japanese.

What Wu-ling did not realize at the time, however, was that Hou was a born radical, a firebrand—someone who was simply too hot to handle—and that his presence would have serious consequences for the school. The men Hou Shao-ch'iu admired most as a child were the nationalist heroes from the Sung dynasty, Yüeh Fei and Wen T'ien-hsiang. By the time Hou was in middle school, he was distributing, on his own, anti-imperialist propaganda on the street. And when he entered Nanyang Public College, his activism became more varied. He organized student strikes in Shanghai in the wake of the 1919 May Fourth demonstrations in Peking and was a chief coordinator of the Shanghai Student Union. He started his own journal and was often seen on the streets of Shanghai, delivering emotional speeches on the evils of the Japanese imperialists and the importance of having nationalist awareness. And for a while, he was so influenced by Bakunin's writings that he contemplated terrorist acts against Shanghai industrialists.

Hou Shao-ch'iu was also a famed radical on the campus of his school, Nanyang College (later called Communications University). Established in 1896 by the Ch'ing government at the suggestion of Li Hung-chang's protégé, Sheng Hsüan-huai, the college had goals that were clear from the start: it was to be a technical university designed to teach students science and engineering. While its curriculum concentrated on Western learning, the school's entire funding came from Peking, so its educational policies reflected those of the Ch'ing court, which at that time was stubbornly holding on to the position that

China was morally superior to the West. Consequently the students at Nanyang received a technical education along with a stiff dose of Confucian moral philosophy. The more perceptive and better-informed scholars and officials knew that this approach toward Western learning could not do much to solve China's problems. As Chang Shu-sheng wrote in his last memorial, Westerners had "attained wealth and power" because they had "a command of both the substance and function" of their learning: "China has abandoned the substance of Western learning, concentrating only on its function. So even if we move in great haste, we can never catch up."

Even after a revolution had dispensed with the Ch'ing court, Nanyang College remained cautious about any challenge to its conservative views of Chinese culture. The school maintained that it was still possible to implement the late ninteenth-century formula of letting "Chinese learning be the moral foundation of education and Western learning be its practical application." So as teachers of science and engineering were using more English in their classrooms, teachers of ethics were encouraging their students to write about the perils of aping someone else's steps and manners while forgetting one's own. When Hou Shao-ch'iu was a student at Nanyang, the president, T'ang Wei-chih, delivered weekly lectures on such subjects as the metaphysics of sincerity and how to guard one's inborn nature from corruption. The students were tested on the content of these lectures. Twice a month, T'ang also led the entire school in a formal ceremony to pay respect to Confucius' spirit tablet, and each year enforced a ritual celebration of Confucius' birthday. T'ang's crusade against the threat of moral debilitation and cultural contamination was not unlike the Purist movement of the 1880s, only lonelier, and by 1920 it also seemed more absurd. Sometime that year, Hou Shao-ch'iu and a group of classmates were expelled from Nanyang College for smashing Confucius' spirit tablet and suggesting through the student council that the school authorities abolish the celebration of Confucius' birthday. The school charged that Hou's "conduct had been extreme" and that "he did not set his heart on learning." Hou's Communist biographers claimed that he was in excellent academic standing at the time of his expulsion. Hou's own response is more telling. He said of the school authorities, "How could they change what I set my heart on?"

The project that was closest to Hou Shao-ch'iu's heart in 1919 and 1920 was the initiative he took to educate urban laborers and to raise their political awareness. In the summer immediately following the May Fourth demonstrations, he and three classmates established the first "free school" in Shanghai for workers and peasants, attracting nearly 50 adult students in the first year. By 1922, there were 113 students: 49 industrial workers, 12 handicraft workers, 16 shop clerks and apprentices, 24 school janitors, 5 peasants, 6 grammar school students, and 1 unemployed laborer. Working with their teachers in the evenings, between 7:30 and 9:00, in classrooms borrowed from a middle school, these students learned to read and write, and they were introduced to topics in history, science, and current events. The faculty compiled their own teaching materials, drawing articles from newpapers, magazines, and progressive journals. The students published a weekly journal, the contents of which reflect the influence of socialist thought. In a 1924 issue, a worker-trainee wrote, "The capitalists only knew to sponge the grease off other people, using it for their own enjoyment."

Around the time he was getting his "free school" off the ground, Hou Shao-ch'iu was also trying to save Ching-hsien, the girls' school in Sung-chiang, from total collapse. By 1923, Hou's activities were becoming more and more political. He joined Sun Yat-sen's Nationalist (Kuomintang) Party in May and the Chinese Communist Party in July. It was possible to do this in 1923 because leaders of both parties in that year decided to combine forces in an effort to reclaim China from the warlords and the foreign imperialists. As part of the stipulation of the "united front," members of one party could join the other and still retain their original membership.

Very soon after he became a Communist Party member, Hou Shao-ch'iu began to use the Ching-hsien Girls' School as a base for his secret meetings. At this school, members of the Communist Party developed strategies for expanding their influence in Kiangsu and Chekiang provinces. According to later Communist historians, Hou "personally cultivated a group of students and faculty for the Communist Youth League and encouraged the most outstanding ones to become Communist Party members." We know that in 1924 Hou accompanied Mao Tse-tung and the Communist Party secretary on an extended visit to Sung-chiang. Thus it is possible that Mao attended one of those meetings.

So when Hou accepted Wu-ling's offer to come to Le-i in 1925, it was probably not because he found the job particularly appealing. He had plenty to do in Sung-chiang and in Shanghai. He was dean of two schools, Ching-hsien and a large middle school attached to Shanghai University. He was fund-raising for Shanghai University and was steeped in the city's labor movement. There must have been some other business that took him to Soochow in 1925.

The Fourth Congress of the Chinese Communist Party convened in Shanghai during January of that year. The meetings produced a revised constitution, which made it easier for applicants to qualify for membership. Party members were also encouraged to go out on their own, to set up branch units, which they could then use to recruit new members. Before, they had concentrated on indoctrinating industrial laborers, who, they soon learned, were not necessarily interested in proletarian politics. So in 1925, the Communist leaders decided to absorb more categories of people—not just workers, peasants, and students, but all "class-conscious elements"—into their party. As soon as Hou Shao-ch'iu assumed his duties at Le-i in September 1925, he founded a Soochow branch of the Communist Party.

Hou brought three Communist Party members and five Youth League members with him to Soochow. The two women from the Youth League had been teachers at Ching-hsien Girls' School. They all joined the Le-i faculty at Hou's "invitation." The revised constitution from the Fourth Party Congress stated that in order to establish a branch unit, there had to be at least three party members. Hou had three, not counting himself, plus the five from the Youth League, who were on a trial run and on the verge of becoming full-fledged. This group held meetings at least once a week in the school. Wu-ling must have known about it, but he let them be.

The alliance between the Kuomintang and the Communists lasted until April 1927, when Chiang Kai-shek staged a violent purge of his party's left-wing elements in Shanghai with the muscles and guns of the criminal syndicate and with the help of the police in the foreign concessions. But even before the purge, some members of the Kuomintang—mainly the hostile right wing—found the presence of Communists in their party deeply unsettling. They distrusted their partners' motives and were jealous of their success in moving into leadership positions within the Kuomintang power structure. They accused the Communists of using a nationalist movement to prepare peasants and urban laborers for a socialist revolution. In Soochow, the local authorities pressured Wu-ling to dismiss Hou Shao-ch'iu in January 1926, only four months after Hou had assumed his responsibilities as dean. They said that Hou's covert operations were a menace to society. They also forced Wu-ling to shut down Le-i's senior high division and threatened further action if he did not comply. Wu-ling had no choice but to let Hou go.

After leaving Le-i, Hou Shao-ch'iu did not return to education. Instead he plunged headlong into the most dangerous political torrent. He worked with the Nationalist Party in Kiangsu province, trying to steer it onto a leftward track while feuding with those on the right. He died in a Nanking prison in 1927, as a result of Chiang Kai-shek's spring purge. The prison guards slit his throat and tossed his body into the Ch'in-huai River.

There is mounting evidence that early Communist activities were often associated with girls' schools. Representatives of the first plenary meeting of the Chinese Communist Party initially gathered in the classroom of a girls' school in Shanghai's French Concession. Hou Shao-ch'iu was affiliated with two girls' schools and used the schools as the base of his operation. Public schools and military academies had been revolutionary hotbeds since the beginning of the twentieth century, even before the last dynasty fell, and in the 1920s, the Communist Party specified "barracks and schools," along with "factories, railways, and mines" as ideal environments for recruiting members. But why girls' schools? Were the early Communists already thinking about grooming educated women for leadership roles in their revolution? Were there many teachers in girls' schools who happened to be party members? Did the girls' schools seem inconspicuous and so a relatively safe shelter for radicals? It certainly did not take the Soochow authorities long to become watchful of Le-i, and then to charge some of the Le-i teachers for carrying out subversive activities.

The accusations in this case were probably justified. Hou Shao-ch'iu's brief sojourn in Soochow was politically charged, and conspicuously so. He had arrived with a whole propaganda team and gone straight to work, proselytizing both in Kuomintang Party gatherings and among those who seemed most receptive to socialist ideas. Hou also invited well-known Communist Party members to Soochow to give public lectures in parks and auditoriums on such topics as the structure of customs collection in China and ways of combating imperialism. During the few months he was there, the number of left-wing Kuomintang increased from three to over twenty, and eleven joined the Communist Party. Out of these eleven, four were workers, five were teachers, and two were students. These developments were alarming for authorities, who had their own ideas about the possible consequences of a socialist revolution. So they accused Le-i of being "infiltrated with communism" and decided that Hou Shao-ch'iu and his team would simply have to leave town.

Just how much influence teachers like Hou Shao-ch'iu had on their students is hard to say. Hou was at Le-i for only a few months, and much of that time was spent on matters dearer to his heart. So he could not have affected the school's curriculum or its overall policies very much. For the students, however, it must have been exciting to have a new dean like Mr. Hou. He was young and idealistic—someone who had many plans for the future. Yuan-ho and Yun-ho, who were attending Le-i at the time, remembered him as a man of slight build, with gentle manners, but that was about it. In fact, the events following the May Thirtieth Incident, which was months before Mr. Hou arrived, made more of an impression on them.

May Thirtieth was the violent culmination of a series of strikes and protests the Shanghai workers staged against their foreign bosses. The crisis began on May 15, 1925, when a guard in a Japanese-owned textile mill shot and killed a striker. Protests and arrests followed. Then, on May 30, during a major demonstration against foreign imperialism in Shanghai's International Settlement, a British inspector ordered his constables to fire into the crowd, killing four of the demonstrators and wounding more than fifty, of whom eight later died of their wounds. The tragedy ignited a nationwide movement. Overnight, patriotism became a collective preoccupation. A general strike was called in Shanghai. Students, teachers, farmers, industrial workers, members of the Kuomintang and the Communist Party took to the streets in their own cities to show solidarity with the Shanghai workers. The Chinese Communist Party also created a Central Labor Union to help coordinate the general strike in Shanghai, and the members worked with labor leaders to launch strikes in Hong Kong and Canton. Activists such as Hou Shao-ch'iu gained a lot of credibility throughout this period and collected many recruits along the way, helping the party to revive itself from a long and paralyzing slump.

But what happened in Soochow was different, because the events organized there following May Thirtieth had nothing to do with the Communist activists, even though Communist historians later claimed otherwise. At Le-i, the administrators suspended classes for ten days so that the students could participate in rallies. The students also built a makeshift stage and put on performances to raise money for the Shanghai labor unions. According to the Shanghai newspaper *Shen-pao*, Soochow contributed more than six thousand silver dollars, and "Le-i gave more money than any other group."

Yuan-ho and Yun-ho describe the emotions of that spring as a mixture of rage and euphoria. It was exciting, they say, to march with teachers and workers on the streets and to solicit donations for the Shanghai strikers in the pouring rain. The high point was a series of three benefit performances the students gave before a Soochow audience. A few years earlier, such things would have been unimaginable for young women. But in 1925, students worked with teachers, deciding what to stage and how to do it. They adapted earlier dramas to produce their own short plays. Two professional actors were brought in from Shanghai to spruce up the show. But on the whole, those three days belonged to the students.

The scenes they put on were from classical sources: "Lady Wang Crossing the Border," "The Ruse of an Empty City," and "The Story of Hung-fu." Oddly, none of these had any patriotic themes. "Lady Wang Crossing the Border" was probably lifted out of the fourteenth-century Yuan drama *Autumn in the Palace of Han* and adjusted to the contemporary stage. It tells the story of Wang Chao-chün, a Han court lady who, for the purpose of political appeasement, was dispatched to a nomadic federation in the north to become the wife of its khan. The emperor who chose Chao-chün from among hundreds of women had seen only an unflattering likeness of her. When she came to his palace to bid farewell, he realized his mistake. And, as great stories go, he fell helplessly in love with her when it was no longer possible for him to have her. *The Ruse of an Empty City* is a Peking opera based on an episode from the classical novel *Romance of the Three Kingdoms*. At Le-i, in 1925, only the professional actors Wu-ling invited from Shanghai could have handled it. (The Chang sisters, who had some training by this time, were not yet ready to perform operas onstage.) This work, too, is about design—human, not heaven's as in the story of Lady Wang, and so without the tragic dimension. It tells how the strategist Chu-ke Liang tried to defend an empty city against thousands of enemy troops and won. Chu-ke was a genius at choreographing deception and also the consummate risk taker. In this scene he calmly sits through his game of bluff, strumming a lute. "The Story of Hung-fu," the third work, probably held more interest for the Le-i students who adapted it from a late Ming drama with the same title, written by a Soochow man also called Chang.* The central figure, Hung-fu, was from the sixth century. She worked as a maidservant in a minister's household, and despite her social disadvantages, she had uncommon intelligence and an uncommon sense of independence. One day a guest of the minister caught her eye. Realizing that he had exceptional talents, she followed him to his inn and offered to elope with him. The story is about their adventure and the great things they accomplished through their partnership. Again there was no obvious connection to the emotions that dominated those weeks that followed the May Thirtieth tragedy.

By the end of the 1920s, students were performing a different type of drama, plays written by contemporary writers and charged with nationalistic sentiments. Kuo Mo-jo's *Wild Cherry Blossoms* was a favorite. It was not a good play. Kuo had written it in the early 1920s, and later he destroyed all but two acts. He was twenty-eight or twenty-nine at the time, just beginning to get interested in socialist ideas and German expressionist style—not a favorable conjunction for creativity. His characters speak predictable cant, and his message about the evils of warlordism is crass.

Two years after he published *Wild Cherry Blossoms*, Kuo found Marxism. He wrote to a friend about his conversion and his latest views on literature. He characterized "the literature of yesterday" as "the unself-conscious and superior enjoyment of aristocrats" ("Lady Wang," "The Ruse," and even "Hung-fu" would all fit into this category), whereas "the literature of today is a literature embarking on a revolutionary path: the outcry of the oppressed, the yell of the desperate, the imprecation of the fighting will, the anticipational joy of revolution."

---

*The dramatist was Chang Feng-i (1527–1613). Six of his works are still extant.

The "literature of today" had immediacy and relevance, and sometimes it seemed indistinguishable from patriotic writings (this was how the Communists had profited from the nationalist movement). It was what many students at the time enjoyed reading and performing, and students at Le-i were no exception. It was also the sort of literature students themselves were producing. Everyone from Le-i's class of 1932 was asked to contribute a piece of her writing to the yearbook. There were essays, poems, short stories, and scenes from plays. Some of the pieces reflected an unease about social disparities; others were riddled with worries about China's future, which looked extremely bleak in 1932. (The Japanese had occupied northeast China in the autumn of 1931; a few months later they bombed and attacked Shanghai's Chapei district, where the Chinese poor lived.) The best essays in the collection were detailed and analytical: speculations regarding Japan's internal affairs, whether her more temperate statesmen could check the behavior of the militarists; the possible benefits and harm if China were to pursue better relationships with Russia and the West; and whether it was worthwhile to consider a peaceful solution with the Japanese and the warlords still in power. These writings show just how seriously the students had taken their political education and how alert they were about current events. They do not read like works of adolescents. Self-reference is rare.

The fiction from this yearbook is more difficult to evaluate. There are the obvious stories—tear-jerking scenes of mothers losing their babies, fathers selling their children, and grown men having no will to go on after Japan's savage assault on Shanghai in January. (The influence of writers such as Kuo Mo-jo and Ts'ao Yü is already evident.) Yet the subtlest of these stories is one called "Rich and Poor." The title might seem blunt, but the writing is deft, in a natural vernacular, and the characters are memorable.

> After it rained for nineteen days, the village heads called a meeting in Ken-fu's home. They liked gathering there. They liked walking into his clean and airy house. They liked being received by his gorgeous wife. A look at her would make anyone feel lighter. She greeted them with an entrancing smile and was as gracious as ever. Slices of steamed cake, neatly cut, were brought out.
>
> "No matter how depressed a man might be, the smile of a pretty woman is always lovely." Yin-shou, who was sitting on a long bench, thought this to himself and then took a long pull from his pipe.
>
> "Ken-fu is a lucky bastard with a wife like her. Who wouldn't squander all his money to have a pretty woman," another farmer was reflecting as he gave Ken-fu's wife another glance.

The author, T'ang Yüeh-hua, had won many prizes in writing. Her best friend described her as "taciturn," "someone who rarely speaks or laughs":

> Those who do not know her well think that she is arrogant and aloof, not realizing that this is her nature. Her thinking is always fresh and original; she does not follow other people's old ruts. Her passion is reading fiction. When she comes upon a brilliant passage, she will study it, mull over it, and feel after it. At those moments, she is always bright-eyed and enraptured though physically she might look exhausted.

T'ang Yüeh-hua's story was about those farmers who gathered in Ken-fu's house—about their desperate efforts to save their livelihood when rain had rotted their crops. But even in their gloom, they noticed Ken-fu's wife, her smile and her loveliness. The wife was not a major character, but she humanized the world the young author was trying to create. Not all the characters in T'ang Yüeh-hua's story are as strong or poignant. The landlord, the certain antagonist in this equation of good and bad, is the most unconvincing. Flat and contrived, he is the socialist archetype of all landlords, incapable of commiseration or of any human feeling.

One wonders what Wu-ling thought of his student's story, for he was also a landowner, one of the wealthiest in Hofei. And it was his tenants—through their payment in kind—who had been supporting the school that gave T'ang Yüeh-hua her education. This was the paradox of Le-i. Wu-ling lived with it; he even embraced it. He never tried to sort it out, with the result that teachers could congregate as they liked and students could write as they liked. Le-i was a paradise in this sense—not the ideal vision, the immaculate world, Wu-ling described in the school song. In this paradise, the virtues of T'ai-po and Yü-chung competed with forces that were deliberate and aggressive, and sometimes immensely seductive, and the scholars there were usually not serene.

The school closed in 1937. The Japanese were approaching, and the prospects were grim. Wu-ling and his wife moved to Hofei. When Ch'ung-ho and her sisters returned to Soochow after the war, everything seemed to have changed. While they were away, the Japanese converted Le-i into a hospital and then a prison. Rickshaw pullers had often come to the school to take prisoners to the execution ground. The windows of the classrooms had been moved higher, closer to the ceiling. There were marks on the walls. Prisoners had scrawled on them to bide their time.

Chapter 9

NURSE-NANNIES

Chao-ho's nurse-nanny, Chu Kan-kan,
with Ch'ung-ho in her Soochow home, around 1936.

AFTER WU-LING DIED, his children's tenderness for him became even greater. Other people, however, saw him in a different light. They pointed out that he had not made any practical use of his life: he squandered a huge fortune, and as a father he was indulgent, letting his children have too much say about their affairs. His children would respond that while this précis may be accurate, it does not describe their father. Without him, they say, their opportunities would not have been large and their views of life would not have been so generous. They would not apply conventional measures to approximate him. Their knowledge of him comes from their sentimental education, and it is private and incommensurable. After their mother died, they could share this secret knowledge only with their nurse-nannies.

Wu-ling had an amiable but unusual relationship with his children's nurse-nannies. He was gentle and courteous, whereas they were always a little skeptical of him. They respected his learning and his character but thought him sometimes not as sharp or quick as they were. And they were not convinced that when it came to contemporary things, his views and tastes were always smart or distinguished. The sassiest of the nurse-nannies was Wang Kan-kan, the woman in charge of Wu-ling's fourth son, Yü-ho. She came from a village in North Hofei. Her husband died soon after their son was born, while she was still a young woman. Yü-ho writes: "Wang Kan-kan had no culture, could not read a word, and was the most unclever among the nurse-nannies. Although she had lived in our Soochow house for many years, if she were to walk a hundred yards beyond our house, she would not be able to find her way back. She spoke calmly, but her choice of words was probably not suitable for respectable company."

Nurse-nannies told clean, "vegetarian" stories and fleshly, "nonvegetarian" stories. Even the girls in the family knew this. They, of course, had heard only the first kind. In front of them, their nurse-nannies all had restraint, to avoid over-stimulating the girls' imagination on certain matters. But according to Yü-ho, Wang Kan-kan was different from others in this. Her words were her own invention, not titillating or profane, but also not refined. She would say "to irrigate" when she meant "to drink," "to lie like a stiff corpse" when she meant "to sleep," "to pee like a cat" when she meant "to cry." Gossip for her was "chewed maggots," and "to have a stroll in town" was "to strut and swagger." Sometimes she would not distinguish snot from brains. "Look at you," she would tell Yü-ho when he had a cold. "Don't you know to wipe your brains when they are dangling from your nose!" And like all the nurse-nannies with their charges, she watched Yü-ho's every move, "from head to toe." He was not to make a sound when he was chewing his food, not to drop any rice on the dinner table, and not to whistle. "Your mouth looks like a chicken's ass when you whistle," she would scold him.

Wang Kan-kan took pride in the cotton shoes she made for Yü-ho—layers of soles sewn tightly together with fine stitches. But Yü-ho's feet were grotesquely shaped, and within a few days her smart shoes were as ghastly looking as his feet. The sight would send her into a rage. "I have never seen feet as ugly as these," she would declare. "If I had a pair like yours, in the middle of the night, because I wouldn't have time during the day, I would take a big cleaver and chop them off."

"Wang Kan-kan was quick and neat when it came to housework and fearless by nature," Yü-ho writes. "She alone dared to kill snakes thicker than the rope holding the bucket in the well." Sturdy though she might have seemed, she had lots of nagging illnesses—aches and pains, mainly. She thought that this was because she did not get a proper rest after childbirth, only three days of confinement before she was back in the field, working. To get rid of her ailments, Wang Kan-kan trusted folk remedies. When her back ached, she munched on dried geckos and centipedes sandwiched between two slivers of cake. When she had migraines, she ate pig brains. Pig brains were not as easy to get hold of as dried geckos and centipedes. She had to ask the cooks in the kitchen to buy them for her when they went shopping, and since pig brains were a delicacy, she usually saved up for weeks to pay for them. Finally, in order for the remedy to work, Wang Kan-kan had to pick an auspicious day, wait until everyone had gone to bed, take her bowl of pig brains in her hand, and circle the well three times to the right and three times to the left, all in silence. One night, while she was performing her rites, Wu-ling thought he had heard someone pacing by the well. This made him fear that a servant might be contemplating suicide. He got up, went to the courtyard, and saw Wang Kan-kan solemnly holding a bowl in her hand and doing her ritual steps around the well. "Lao Wang [Old Wang]," he asked, "what are you doing?" Wang Kan-kan was very reluctant to speak, knowing that this would break the spell and waste the efforts she had made. Wu-ling asked again. She finally answered: "What do you think I am doing? I am eating pig brains to get rid of my headache." Wu-ling probably did not catch the irritation in her voice and so teased her, saying, "If we eat pig brains when we have headaches, what do pigs eat when they have headaches?" Wang Kan-kan retorted: "How the hell do I know what pigs eat! Besides, how could pigs have headaches?"

On the whole, Wang Kan-kan was not impressed with educated men and women. It was her idea at first that her granddaughter, Liu Ts'ui-ying, should have a new name, a proper name, when she started school. When the granddaughter asked her teacher to give her one, the teacher decided on "P'ei-chu," "a match with pearls." But because *chu*, written with a different character, could also mean "pig," the sound of her granddaughter's new name made Wang Kan-kan furious. "She is already a cow [*liu* or *niu*, her granddaughter's surname]," she quipped. "Now her teacher wants her to marry [*p'ei*] a pig [*chu*]!"

Wang Kan-kan was also not taken with expressions that students and fashionable men and women at the time liked to use, many of which were reconstructed from classical terms or borrowed from the Japanese to reflect a modern way of life or to render ideas in new categories of knowledge, such as psychology, sociology, physics, chemistry, and the life sciences. Once she reproached Yü-ho for coming home so late: "So where have you been 'strutting and swaggering'?" Yü-ho responded, "I have been at school. Rehearsals. There is going to be a performance [*piao-yen*]. Do you know what is *piao-yen*?" "I am sure *I* don't know what you do at school," Wang Kan-kan snapped back. "So you 'mounted eyes' [*piao-yen*]. Did you 'paste nose' as well?" Yü-ho never quite knew whether his nurse-nanny was mocking his pretenses and the incrutable phrases he liked to use, or whether she was just a clodhopper.

Wang Kan-kan was not alone in her skepticism toward modern things. Other nurse-nannies also found most of them suspect. This was not always because these women were backward or obstinate; rather, they felt that modern things had no subtlety and could introduce new problems or breach propriety. They rarely voiced objections to Wu-ling's large collection of modern gadgets. The twenty or so cameras stayed most of the time in drawers because Wu-ling never learned to use them; the phonographs played *k'un-ch'ü* and Peking operas, which they loved; the movie projector showed Charlie Chaplin's silent shorts, which sent them into roaring laughter. But Wu-ling's fascination with Western art was a different matter. For a time he bought Western-style sculptures, either from Shanghai or from a fine arts school that was established in Soochow in the late 1920s, and he had them placed throughout the house. The open display of human nakedness was met with firm disapproval. "Scandalous, scandalous," the *kan-kan* would mutter to themselves as they walked past the sculptures. "And so ugly!"

The nurse-nannies also held their own views regarding literature. They preferred traditional dramas to modern plays, stories of men and women with refined sensibilities to stories of social inequity. They loved the traditional plays because they were well-told stories. They might not have understood all the poetry in an aria; still, they found the sounds more pleasing and beautiful and the emotions truer than those in modern plays, where characters spoke in a vernacular too strained to stir any human feelings. Contemporary writers may have been more sympathetic to peasants and servants, but these women were more attuned to dramatists who created from their genius rather than from the call of ideology.

The most literate of the nurse-nannies was "Big Sister Kuo." Her mother had worked for the Changs long ago in Hofei—in what capacity, no one quite remembers. After her own daughter was employed as a Chang nurse-nanny, this woman was a frequent visitor in Soochow, and the children called her "Granny Kuo." Granny Kuo was an opera enthusiast; sometimes she could get so caught up in a performance that she would stand up in a large theater and shout at an actor, "You sure are smart looking!" or "The beat is wrong!"

As a child, Big Sister Kuo had lived with her mother in the Chang house-hold. (This is probably why the children called her "Big Sister," not nurse-nanny.) Later she married an educated man with a licentiate degree. It is possible that he taught her to read. The Changs do not know what he did or how he made a living, but during the republican period, a low civil degree from the imperial era could have gotten him a teaching position as a private tutor somewhere. In any case, his degree could only have boosted his credentials and helped his status within the community.

After her husband died, Big Sister Kuo returned to the Changs as a servant. The sharp descent from wife of a licentiate to servant must have been a blow. Oddly, this did not seem to have affected Big Sister Kuo's rollicking disposi-tion. In the Chang household, she was entertainer and buffoon. The nurse-nannies adored her because she could sing and act, could manage tragic and comic parts, and was endlessly inventive. Her specialty was the *t'an-tz'u,* or lyrical narrative—a long ballade with one or two players acting out all the parts in a story. Big Sister Kuo always performed alone. Sequestered ladies and aged kings, gentle scholars and callous lovers—she could make them all come alive. She holds a libretto in one hand, a fan in the other: her massive, roundish body quivers with emotions as she sings. Nurse-nannies loved to gather in her room or on the veranda at the end of the day, to find refuge and empathy in her recital. Their favorite was "The Destiny of Rebirth," or *Tsai-sheng-yuan,* a bal-lade written by an eighteenth-century woman, Ch'en Tuan-sheng. It tells the story of Meng Li-chün, a woman forced by circumstances to leave her parents and live secretly as a man. With hard work and the right opportunities, she manages her new life with great success. She passes all three levels of examina-tions with the highest distinction and gets herself appointed prime minister while still young. As she flourishes in her career, people begin to suspect that she is not what she seems. Men think her womanly and are filled with desire when she is near. Even the emperor finds himself yearning to spend more time with his prime minister. Once, after an evening of drinking and poetry writing, he asks her to stay and share his bed.

Meng Li-chün drained three cups of wine in quick succession. She was so tipsy that she barely knew where she was. The emperor was so delighted at this sight that he began to pour out his feelings: "Prime minister, do you know what trouble I've gone through to protect you? Others in their memorials have been insinuating that you are a woman. If it were not for me, I fear that there would be no way to put an end to such rumors. I sent down an edict, demanding that this talk be stopped. Do you know about this? Now that I see your countenance, I don't blame people for being suspicious. You certainly are a great beauty. No man in the world could possibly possess looks and charm like yours. In these few hours, I have been happier than I have ever been in the women's palace. Be good to me as I have been to you. Stay, prime minister, stay. Let us spend our time here in abandoned delight. I will tell the attendants that I have asked you to stay and share a bed with me tonight. . . .

These words gave Meng Li-chün a start. Her expression changed. She was in shock. She heard the emperor's own pronouncement and his pathetic pleading. Suddenly she woke from her drunken gaiety—her face lost its flush. "Good God!" she said quietly to herself. . . .

The emperor continued, "Don't you remember that Emperor Han Kuang-wu used to share a bed with his advisor, Yen Tzu-ling? We, too, are ruler and minister and so have nothing to fear. We can spend the night, telling each other what is in our heart. If others want to talk, then let them. I can always have them interrogated and punished." When the emperor finished, he tugged at her sleeve. This made Meng Li-chün terribly alarmed. It was difficult to refuse the ruler, yet she had to find a way out. She thought that she could have a chance if she got ahead of him. "Your Majesty," she said, "when I accepted my office at nineteen, others had great doubts about me. I exercised restraint and was watchful of my conduct, but this still could not keep the slanders at bay. To be careless, and worse, to overstep the line would be asking for trouble. If we share a bed tonight, others, for sure, will say that I got my honors and my position through flattery and charm. It is best not to let others speculate about a ruler's relationship with his minister. I beg you to think through this again, and let the circumstances dictate your decision."

When she finished, Meng Li-chün prostrated herself before the ruler. The emperor turned pale, looking crestfallen. He stopped and gazed at her again, realizing that the prime minister's words and countenance did not seem womanly after all.

Drama like this shows off the performer's skills. An actor has to handle a whole cast of characters: father, mother, daughter, suitors, emperor, maidservants, daughter's best friend, adoptive mother and father. And Meng Li-chün's role adds to the challenge. In her scene with the emperor, for instance, she is constantly changing: now severe and proper, now flushed and seductive; now man, now woman. Her character is also stubbornly elusive. Even the author did not know what to do about her. Ch'en Tuan-sheng wrote sixteen chapters before she was twenty-one. She returned to it twelve years later, wrote one more chapter, but still left the story unfinished. To the end, Meng Li-chün resists letting the world know that she is a woman even though the emperor can prove that she is. (She was drugged in the palace and removed to a private room, where two female attendants took off her boots and socks and saw her small bound feet, "like golden lotus that remained underwater.") The emperor gives her three days to decide what to do about her life: she can continue to masquerade as a man and face the charge of "confusing yin with yang," which is punishable by death; or she can become his consort and find protection through him. In Ch'en Tuan-sheng's original drama, there is no resolution.* The heroine is last seen fretting in her room and coughing up pints of blood.

Meng Li-chün was infinitely fascinating because her actions did not always follow reason or the dictates of principle. She stood by her story at all costs, but not because she was reluctant to give up her career and take on a woman's traditional role of wife and mother. She was more original than that. Her independence was not something she planned or even sought; she realized it gradually as those that she could have and should have trusted—parents, friends, and her betrothed—turned out to be disappointing. Her story was tragic in this sense. One wonders if Big Sister Kuo caught all this. Those who had seen her perform said that she could hold her audience in sway, and her telling was never less than engrossing.

Because she was theatrical and large, Big Sister Kuo also made an exaggerated buffoon. She could invent a part and stage a show on the spot. Ch'ung-ho remembered her as a spirit medium: "Her body shook like the great firmament, her small, bound feet giving it only a precarious balance. She tells her audience that a dead widow has lodged in her, and then begins her lament." Most nurse-nannies regarded this as mirth; they all knew the sufferings of widows and were able to make sport of their condition.

Once, on a rare visit to Soochow, Ch'ung-ho's nurse-nanny, Chung-ma, found herself an unwitting participant in one of Big Sister Kuo's performances. Chung-ma was in Wang Kan-kan's room, surrounded by all the other nurse-nannies, when Big Sister Kuo curled her lip, pointing to Wang Kan-kan's round belly under the bedcovers. Chung-ma understood right away what she meant. She murmured to Big Sister Kuo, asking how Wang Kan-kan, after all these years, could have let down her guard. "You are so right," Big Sister Kuo agreed. Chung-ma took Wang Kan-kan's hand in hers, not knowing what to say, to

---

*Another woman writer, Liang Te-sheng, tidied up the story after Chen died. Quite predictably, everything ends happily in the extended version.

chide her or to comfort her. Suddenly Big Sister Kuo produced a small drum from underneath the bedding, and the crowd roared. Chung-ma, seeing that she had been tricked, chased Big Sister Kuo around the house, calling out, "Kuo, the Lunatic!"

Chu Kan-kan, Chao-ho's nurse-nanny, was the other "scholar" among the *kan-kan*. She was a late bloomer because she did not learn to read until her mistress, Lu Ying, launched her "literacy campaign." The ten to twenty characters she learned each day added up, so that by the time Lu Ying died, Chu Kan-kan could read simple stories and promptbooks.* By the time Chao-ho left for boarding school, Chu Kan-kan was reading classical novels and holding her own opinions about literature. Chu Kan-kan was stubborn and self-contained. She did not appeal to anyone for sympathy or ask lightly for favors, but she would pursue you down the corridor if she needed to know a word she had not seen before. Even more than Big Sister Kuo, who read better than she, Chu Kan-kan loved learning for itself and believed that her children and grandchildren should also get an education.

After Lu Ying died, Chu Kan-kan consulted Yun-ho and Chao-ho whenever she got stuck in her reading. At night she shared a bed with Chao-ho, who remembers:

> I slept at one end and Chu Kan-kan, the other. While I was sound asleep, she was often reading. When she didn't recognize a character, she would poke me with her feet until I responded. "What is this word?" she would ask. Usually I said something just so that she'd let me go back to sleep. And even when I was alert enough to realize that I didn't know the word either, I would still make up some sort of answer so that I didn't lose face.

One day, Chao-ho says, Chu Kan-kan quietly called to her and Yun-ho from the side room. "'Come, come,' she said," and then "she showed us the surprise— a big mandarin fish cooked in sweet-and-sour sauce—just for the two of us. Chu Kan-kan had bought the fish and asked the cook in the kitchen to prepare it as a treat for us, to thank us for helping her with her reading."

On those mornings that Lu Ying taught Chu Kan-kan to recognize characters from flash cards, she also showed her, stroke by stroke, the order of constructing each character. Whenever she found time, Chu Kan-kan practiced writing on paper with large square grids. She was not quick or particularly intel-

---

*These were the sort of promptbooks Big Sister Kuo used in her *t'an-tz'u* performance.

ligent, but she was determined to get herself educated. Eventually she was able to write letters. She also sent money home to Hofei, urging her son to use it for schooling. Years later, when Chao-ho decided to marry the novelist Shen Ts'ung-wen, her nurse-nanny disapproved of the match. She thought that Shen was not good enough for Chao-ho. He had some fame, but only through his modern vernacular writing; more important, he had barely finished grammar school, whereas Chao-ho had a college education.

Chao-ho was mindful of Chu Kan-kan's perception of her husband. So when she asked her nurse-nanny to come to Peking to help out at around the time her first child was born, she removed her husband's works from his study before Chu Kan-kan arrived. She did not want her to read his writings, knowing that her judgment would not be kind. Later Chu Kan-kan told her that she had leafed through Pa Chin and Lao She's works, which Chao-ho had left on the shelf. These were two prominent contemporary writers, but she found their stories "banal," "a far cry from classical novels and promptbooks."

Enlightenment came late for Chu Kan-kan, and she did what she did— learning the characters one at a time when her faculties were already slowing down—because it gave her pleasure. However, she did not embrace all aspects of social progress, and certainly not modern-style marriage, where men and women decided for themselves their marriage partners. She was not encouraged by Chao-ho's choice of a husband, because Shen Ts'ung-wen had no secure prospects and his family background and education were far inferior to Chao-ho's. Chu Kan-kan was not being a snob. Her concern for Chao-ho was entirely practical. The Changs did not know the Shens, who for several generations had been professional soldiers in West Hunan, where the landscape was unwholesome and barbaric. How would Chao-ho, reared in a cosmopolitan city and groomed to be a modern woman, fit into a family like the Shens? And how would she manage her life with Shen Ts'ung-wen if he had no money or property? What would she do if her circumstances declined? These were Chu Kan-kan's worries at the time, and they anticipated some of the problems in Chao-ho's marriage later on.

In fact, all the nurse-nannies disliked the ways of modern marriage. They found the premise shaky. They did not see how a marriage could last if it was founded on love and supported by the principle that one had the freedom to choose whom one loved. But if their young mistresses wanted to fall in love first before deciding on marriage, there was nothing they could do about it. Besides, the young mistresses' father strongly endorsed this. He never tried to arrange a single marriage for his children and dissuaded other families in Soochow from approaching him with such proposals. The nurse-nannies used to say: "The young ladies in our family are all free spirits [tzu-yu-te]. Even their husbands, they were free to catch themselves [tzu-chi yu-lai-te]." Ultimately the kan-kan never wished their young mistresses to fail in their marriages; they rooted for them as they had rooted for the heroines in the operas and ballades they loved, women like Hung-fu and Meng Li-chün.

In the 1920s, few from the servant class believed that it was possible for them or even for their children to have the freedoms that were taken for granted by families such as the Changs. One young woman, Chü-chih, the daughter of a servant woman in the family, tried and failed. Chü-chih had grown up with Wu-ling's daughters and studied with them when they were still being educated at home. Chü-chih's mother had arranged a marriage for her while she was a child, but when the time came for her to wed, the girl disappeared. The Chang sisters said that it was their tutor, Wang Meng-luan, who had persuaded Chü-chih to run away. She was never heard from again. Most people believed that she died soon after, of want.

At that time, it was women such as Chü-chih who were the victims of change. They had a chance for education and were encouraged to think and act for themselves. But when they tried to break free from their circumstances, they found that they could never be what their teachers had led them to believe about themselves; and that, unlike the young mistresses they had gone to school with, they could not expect anyone to lend them support. They could not even hope for the good fortune of a Hung-fu or even a Meng Li-chün—that was only for runaways in fiction. In the 1930s, things began to change. There was another young woman living with the Changs; her mother was a kitchen worker who wanted her to quit school and look after her younger brother. This time Wu-ling insisted on keeping her at Le-i. The woman went on to become a topflight athlete.

The girl the Chang sisters were closest to when they were living in Soochow was Kao Kan-kan's daughter, Chin Ta-chieh. Born just a few months earlier than Yuan-ho, she was in a way their older sister and childhood companion. She sat in the same classroom with them, played with them in the garden, and helped them to keep their baby sister alive for three days when their mother was dying.

Chin Ta-chieh's own mother was a remarkable woman. Born into the most desperate circumstances, Kao Kan-kan was indentured as a young girl to a family related to the Changs and was later pressured to become the concubine of the man who had bought her. To avoid this fate, she married another man, who turned out to be an opium addict. It was after her own children were born that she was hired to be Ch'ung-ho's wet nurse, but this did not work out: she had very little milk, and before her term was up, her husband forced her to come home. After her husband died, Kao Kan-kan returned to the Changs as a nurse-nanny to Lu Ying's third son. With the Changs, she found some peace and also appreciation for her talents—the memory and accounting skills that enabled her to help Lu Ying sort out her family obligations and keep track of household affairs.

Kao Kan-kan had a son as well as a daughter. The son was an opium addict, just like her husband. For years he panhandled and sold cigarette butts he found on the street to keep himself alive. Kao Kan-kan's daughter was her jewel. She called her "my little piece of gold" (*hsiao-chin-tzu*). The Chang sisters extended this endearment and called her their "Golden Older Sister" or "Older Sister Chin" (*chin-ta-chieh*). Knowing that "Chin" was not Chin Ta-chieh's real name, they eventually decided that they should find her a proper one. In the family school with their tutors, they had been reading the story of Ch'en She in Ssu-ma Ch'ien's history of the Ch'in and Han:

> When Ch'en She was working one day in the fields with the other hired men, suddenly he stopped his ploughing and went and stood on a hillock, wearing a look of profound discontent. After a long while, he announced, "If I become rich and famous, I will never forget you!"
>
> The other farmhands laughed and answered, "You are nothing but a hired laborer. How could you ever become rich and famous?" Ch'en She gave a great sigh. "Oh, well," he said, "how could you little sparrows understand the ambitions of a snow goose?"

Ch'en She did not have special talents. Neither had he acquired any skills in warfare. He did not possess the disposition of kings and nobles, and even heaven was not inclined to grant him any favors. But he was the first to rebel against the Ch'in dynasty, and his revolt spurred others to action, "like a great wind rising," "until the house of Ch'in at last crumbled." Ssu-ma Ch'ien wrote:

> Ch'en She, born in a humble hut with tiny windows and a wattle door, a day labourer in the fields and a garrison conscript, whose abilities could not match even the average, who had neither the worth of Confucius and Mo Tzu nor the wealth of T'ao Chu and I Tun, stepped from the ranks of the common soldiers, rose up from the paths of the fields, and led a band of several hundred poor, weary soldiers in revolt against the Ch'in. They cut down trees to make their weapons and raised their flags on garden poles, and the whole world gathered like a cloud, answered like an echo to

a sound, brought them provisions, and followed after them as shadows follow a form. In the end the leaders of the eastern mountains rose up together and destroyed the house of Ch'in.

The toppling of a dynasty, therefore, began with "the ambitions of a snow goose" (*ku-chih*). This idea inspired the three Chang girls to call their companion precisely that—Ku-chih. Older Sister Chin, however, did not live up to her new name and did not aspire to do so. She later married and had her own family. After her husband died, she returned to the Changs. She was first Chao-ho's servant and then Yun-ho's. The Chang sisters might not have considered her a servant. Still, she cleaned their houses, washed their bedsheets, and looked after their children. Chin Ta-chieh did not have to continue her mother's work, yet she chose to do so. Recently her grandson published an essay in China, explaining why his grandmother and great-grandmother considered the Changs their benefactors and guardians. The Changs say that it was the other way around, that without their Kao Kan-kan and their Chin Ta-chieh, they could not have gotten through some of the dark patches in their lives.

During the war, the Chang sisters' third brother, Ting-ho, had gone to Szechwan. When Kao Kan-kan heard that his marriage had collapsed and that Ting-ho was so consumed with grief that he could not even take care of his son, she made her way to the southwest from Hofei to be with them. Ting-ho says that it was Kao Kan-kan who brought him out of his depression and looked after his son, and that throughout the war he was too poor to pay her a salary and she never asked to be paid. Older Sister Chin was as generous as her mother. When the Chang sisters returned to Soochow in 1945, they were so short of money that they could not even afford to buy pots and pans. It was Older Sister Chin who brought over cooking utensils and cooking oil, bowls and dishes, pillows and padded bedding, and a washbasin.

The Chinese believe that reciprocity of feelings is the most powerful and most beautiful of human virtues and that coercion is its ruin. In a relationship between servants and their employer, this is more complicated. Kao Kan-kan and her daughter, however, insisted on keeping it simple. Moreover, their realization of this virtue was so deep-founded that children inherited it from their parents. Older Sister Chin's own daughter also worked for the Changs; in 1949, this woman followed Yuan-ho to Taiwan.

There is yet another mystery about these nurse-nannies. They loved the children put in their care as much as they loved their own. But these were "mothers" who expected nothing in return; these were women repaying the kindness of their master and mistress long after their benefactors were gone. The nurse-nanny who was most attached to her "child" and most demonstrative of her feelings was Yun-ho's Tou Kan-kan. When Yun-ho was a child, Tou Kan-kan always fanned her to sleep on hot summer nights, inside their grass-linen bed curtains, keeping her fan far above Yun-ho's head so that there would not be a draft. She would braid ribbon into the little girl's hair and then shape it into a plum blossom, a gardenia, or a bow. Yun-ho was her darling. And whenever Yun-ho was sent to the back room to reflect on her missteps, it was Tou Kan-kan who would carry on like a tragic queen, crying and complaining that the world had wronged her Yun-ho, that her mistress loved all her children except for Yun-ho. And while Yun-ho was usually triumphant when she emerged from her confinement, Tou Kan-kan would still be in a state. She would gather Yun-ho in her arms and quietly murmur her name.

Tou Kan-kan's husband was a peddler, selling odds and ends in towns near their Hofei home. One morning he left with his goods and never returned. Assuming that he had died somewhere on the road, Tou Kan-kan went to An-ch'ing with her young son and found employment in the magistrate's *yamen.** (This all happened before the dynasty fell.) One day the sons of the *yamen* officials took her little boy kite flying by the riverbank. They tied a kite string around his waist. The force of the wind carried him across the river to the other side, where the kite string snapped and the boy was hurled to the ground. Soon after this accident, Tou Kan-kan quit her job and came home to Hofei to work for the Changs, leaving her son with an aunt.

After Yun-ho left for boarding school, life was much quieter for Tou Kan-kan. This nurse-nanny stayed on for a few years before Wei Chün-i sent her home to the little market town of Che-chen, in Hofei county. During those years in Soochow with Yun-ho gone, whenever she missed her "Second Sister" (*erh-chieh*), she would take Yun-ho's clothes from a chest. She would stroke them and smell them. She would tell others: This is my Erh-chieh's scent.

By all accounts, Tou Kan-kan lived well after she retired. She was dead by the time Yun-ho went to Hofei in 1937. When Yun-ho traveled to Che-chen to visit her grave, the people there gathered around her. Her short-sleeved cheongsam was an object of curiosity—they wondered if it was, in fact, underwear. But they all seemed to have known Tou Kan-kan well and to have the highest estimation of her. She learned later that Tou Kan-kan had boasted to them about her "Erh-chieh."

All the nurse-nannies who worked for the Changs found it hard to let go of

---

*A *yamen* was where a magistrate had his office and residence.

their "children" when their terms were up. Yun-ho's fourth brother, Yü-ho, said that even his Wang Kan-kan broke down and cried when he left for Japan to pursue his studies. This surprised him at the time, because he did not know that she could form strong attachments. When her husband died, Wang Kan-kan had told Yü-ho, she climbed on top of his coffin, howled until she was tired and hungry, shoveled down a big bowl of rice, and wanted more. After her own son died, her daughter-in-law left her child with Wang Kan-kan and went to work in a Shanghai cotton mill. A few years later, this woman also died, of turberculosis. Yü-ho recalls: "Wang Kan-kan always said that fate had been cruel to her daughter-in-law, but there would be a smile on her face as she said this, unintentional and unself-conscious. Wang Kan-kan did not let these things affect her. 'It's nature's way. Nothing much one can do about it.' This was what she meant." But on the day her Yü-ho was leaving her, her sadness was so great that she simply could not be consoled. Yü-ho later wrote:

Kao Kan-kan, standing nearby, tried to comfort her: "The boy is going abroad to study. This is a good thing, a happy occasion. You shouldn't spoil it with your crying." My old mom—I call her my old mom—nodding her head, was still sobbing. She wiped her tears with her apron, but they welled up in her eyes again. At the time I was too callous and too thick to realize that this was farewell. I thought that she was making a fuss over nothing and so did not even pay attention to her.

During the war, she died in the Hofei countryside. Even after 1949, whenever I saw Kao Kan-kan, she would always tell me that my old mom should not have said what she said. Apparently, after I was gone, my old mom quit her job to go home. Just before she left, my father asked her, "When Yü-ho returns from Japan, are you coming to see him?" "I am not coming back," she said. "Not even when he marries?" my father went on. "Surely you are coming to his wedding." "I am not coming back! I will never come back," she persisted. Kao Kan-kan said, "She shouldn't have answered it this way. It was a bad augury."

Chapter 10

YUAN-HO

Yuan-ho onstage, in California, in the 1970s.

Y UAN-HO WAS HAPPIEST WHEN she was onstage. It is, therefore, not surprising that she married an actor. Her husband, Ku Ch'uan-chieh, was a *k'un-ch'ü* actor. For two years this man had the Shanghai audience enraptured. Then, at the height of his career, he gave it all up and moved on to something totally different. This happened in 1931, a long time before they actually met, yet throughout the years others would always regard Yuan-ho as an actor's wife—something she may have encouraged quite unintentionally.

Ch'ung-ho is frank about her oldest sister. She professes that they have little in common. Unless the topic is *k'un-ch'ü*, they have little to say to each other. They did not spend their childhood together. In that period, they saw each other at most once a year, when Ch'ung-ho came to visit her family in Soochow. Even then, she says, Yuan-ho was aloof. She was the oldest, slightly more mature than her siblings, with more gravity and self-awareness. The fact that their grandmother had always tried to keep Yuan-ho cloistered in her upstairs wing only further reinforced Yuan-ho's distance from the rest of her family. Still, growing up in the same household, Yuan-ho and her sisters Yun-ho and Chao-ho formed a trio when they were children. They studied with the same tutors and sometimes with the same teachers at school, shared similar opinions about servants and relatives, and attended the same important family occasions; they also played together and got into trouble together. In this regard, Ch'ung-ho was clearly at a disadvantage. She was not even home when their mother died and when their father brought back a new wife. And by the time she returned to Soochow in 1930, her oldest sister had already graduated from college and was teaching in Haimen, a town located on the north bank of the Yangtze River estuary, about fifty miles northeast of Soochow.

These two sisters would have been even farther apart had Ch'ung-ho not suddenly taken ill in Peking in 1935. Ch'ung-ho was a second-year student in college at the time. Her illness followed a bicycle accident, but the symptoms suggested an advanced case of tuberculosis. Yuan-ho left her job in Haimen so that she could go to Peking and bring her youngest sister home, and once they were back in Soochow, Yuan-ho decided to stay.

For the next two years, the two immersed themselves in learning *k'un-ch'ü* opera. Yuan-ho said that her sister was "spellbound," often coming home from a *k'un-ch'ü* gathering at a friend's house around two o'clock in the morning. *K'un-ch'ü* cured Ch'ung-ho of her mysterious illness; it also gave the two sisters some ground on which to build a relationship.

Yuan-ho's homecoming had other significance. Her absence had been long, nearly ten years. Everyone in the family knew why she stayed away. She and her stepmother did not get on, and so when there was a chance to be somewhere else, Yuan-ho took it, coming back only for short visits—a few days at a time. (Yuan-ho herself is reluctant to talk about those years when her stepmother first moved in—why they had been difficult for her.)

When Yuan-ho was a student at her father's school, one teacher gave her an unusual amount of attention. This woman, Ling Hai-hsia, came from a family very similar to Yuan-ho's. The Lings were not as wealthy as the Changs, but their home in Haimen was comfortable: plenty of living and idling space; plum flowers and pomegranates blooming in the garden, goldfish and turtles swimming in earthenware vats. Like Chang Wu-ling, Ling Hai-hsia's father was an educated man, and he wanted to send his daughter to school. Inexplicable reasons kept Hai-hsia mute until she was nine, and so when she began first grade, she was already sixteen. It took her only two years to finish grammar school; this was followed by six years in a normal school, another six in a Catholic university in Shanghai, and one year of professional school in Peking. Then civil war broke out in North China and it became too risky for her to remain in Peking to complete her degree in banking. So Ling Hai-hsia came home to look for work. This was 1925. She was already thirty-two.

Chang Wu-ling gave Ling Hai-hsia her first job. Ling thought Wu-ling's school "too relaxed," "lacking organization and direction," but she liked his children. "They were plucky and lovable," she later wrote, "especially Yuan-ho." She said that she got very close to Yuan-ho because Yuan-ho had a weak constitution and was "anemic." "So day and night I looked after her, making sure that she took her medicine."

Yuan-ho was probably not as sickly as Ling Hai-hsia would have liked to believe. Two photographs taken around this time show a delicate but healthy girl, comely and radiant, without any trace of illness. We know also that in 1925 and 1926 Yuan-ho was very active on the stage, that she designed sets and costumes and played leads in many school productions. Her grandmother had indulged her from the time she was born. For breakfast, Yuan-ho could pick through pastries and spring rolls, ham and minced meat, duck and chicken, sausages and salted gizzards. Even her congee, which was the breakfast staple, was fried with eggs. Rich food did not fatten her up, because she was a finicky eater, but she was never frail, not easily attenuated. Why, then, did Ling Hai-hsia remember Yuan-ho as a sickly adolescent? It is possible that she had to find some explanation for her single-hearted devotion to her young friend. At the time, some of her colleagues at Le-i thought that her behavior was unnatural, and they wanted Wei Chün-i to do something about it. Wei was the principal at the time and Yuan-ho's stepmother, and she was also inexperienced and very young. Ling later wrote that Wei had mishandled the situation and was duplicitous: she "listened to slanderous talk" and "could not distinguish between good and bad." For a while, Ling said, she was led to believe that the principal wanted her to stay; but by the next school year, her contract was not renewed.

Those who knew Ling Hai-hsia well thought her fierce and forceful, an opinionated and passionate woman, but also generous and maternal. Ling Hai-hsia never intended to marry and never gave in to the idea just because that was what most women did. Yet she wanted desperately to have a family of her own—a daughter or even a younger sister to look after for the rest of her life. Yuan-ho, at sixteen or seventeen, was the right person. At that age, she had already acquired grace and gravity, which were set off perfectly by her youthful energy. Even her sisters say that she was fetching. And as for Yuan-ho, she was ready to come under the influence of a smart and competent woman such as Ling Hai-hsia.

After Ling Hai-hsia left Le-i, her career took off. She had a lot of family help at first. Her father and older brother endowed a school in her name and made her the principal. She wrote: "My father founded the school with his life savings so that the poor students from our home district could get an education. My older brother, who had been so careful about his own expenses, also gave generously to the school. He did this out of love and respect for our parents." But within a year she was lured away. Ta-hsia University in Shanghai offered her a position, which she decided to accept. Yuan-ho was a first-year student there, and Ling Hai-hsia later recounted the joy of seeing her former student again: "My happiness was beyond words." Whether their reunion was chance or planned, no one knows. Yuan-ho herself had left for a boarding school in Nanking right after Ling Hai-hsia was forced out of Le-i. It is probable that the two wrote to each other or even saw each other before Yuan-ho got into Ta-hsia University.

The administrators at Ta-hsia recognized Ling Hai-hsia's talents right away. In fact, she did so well in the first year she was there that the board of education in her home county wanted her back, and they were ready to give her the position of principal of Haimen county's own middle school for girls. Ling Hai-hsia took the offer, but the job turned out to be taxing, much more complicated than she had anticipated. Haimen county school was a big institution; it received funding from the municipal government and was, as Ling later discovered, closely tied to local politics.

Yet even as she was facing these problems in her own career, Ling Hai-hsia was planning for Yuan-ho's future. As soon as Yuan-ho graduated from college, Ling had her employed as dean at her father's private school. Whether Yuan-ho wanted the job or not was probably not seriously discussed with her. By this time, Ling was also taking charge of other aspects of Yuan-ho's life. She appointed herself Yuan-ho's adoptive sister and declared her older brother to be Yuan-ho's adoptive brother. During winter and summer breaks, Yuan-ho stayed with Ling's family in Haimen. Young men who showed an interest in Yuan-ho could not enter the front door until Ling Hai-hsia had inspected them. Yuan-ho had many admirers—she was the school queen at her university—but, according to her sisters, few made it to the shortlist.

In a brief chronological biography based on Yuan-ho's own account, the four years she spent in Hai-hsia Middle School, from 1931 to 1935, were left blank. When asked about these years—what were students like and what were some of the problems she had to handle as the school dean—Yuan-ho usually has little to say. This is not because she cannot recall what happened. Rather, it seems Yuan-ho was not interested in her job. "It was, after all, Ling Hai-hsia's school," she explains.

Ch'ung-ho's illness in 1935 was of consequence to Yuan-ho. It gave her a chance to leave Haimen and go home to her own family. She could have returned to her school and her job after she had delivered Ch'ung-ho. Instead, she remained in Soochow and learned *k'un-ch'ü* from a Mr. Chou Ch'uan-ying. This, too, was of consequence. The next year, she fell in love with her future husband at a benefit concert in which both of them were performing.

Yuan-ho had gotten much better as an amateur actor in her year of study with Mr. Chou. Unlike her earlier teacher, Mr. Yü, who specialized in female roles, Mr. Chou always played male characters, particularly young scholars and officials (*hsiao-sheng* and *kuan-sheng*). He taught Yuan-ho to sing, walk, and gesture like a man in an opera. From that point on, Yuan-ho and Ch'ung-ho often paired up as man and woman, scholar and young lady in romantic scenes. But if an occasion called for someone to play the part of a young lady and Yuan-ho knew the part well, she could easily make that adjustment. "Playing a role is about becoming that role," Yuan-ho says. "If you have learned well all the nuances in singing and gesturing that give a character its distinction, then it doesn't matter whether you are a woman playing a man or a woman playing a woman because art is not about who you are. In fact, you should never bring any part of yourself—of your private feelings—to the stage." Her sister Ch'ung-ho is even more insistent on that last point. She contends that a performance without total self-abstinence cannot have integrity. And she herself, long ago, had decided that she would never allow herself to be enamored of an actor—professional or amateur. "Romantic attachment ruins the art," she says.

Yuan-ho did fall for an actor, though not on stage and long after the actor had quit his profession. Still, it was his performance of a scene from an opera that was the catalyst. When it happened, Yuan-ho was already twenty-nine. By her society's standards, she was late for marriage and even late for love. It is possible that during those four years in Haimen she realized that she did not want to follow Ling Hai-hsia's path or her plan—that it was not enough just to have students to guide, a school to administer, and Ling Hai-hsia as her companion. So when she came back to Soochow, she was ready for an adventure. Her own description of how it happened tells us a lot about what she was like in those years.

In 1935, when I was learning the *hsiao-sheng* [male scholar] role from Mr. Chou, a classmate of my brothers Tsung-ho and Yin-ho would sometimes drop by our house. If he showed up while I was having my lesson, I would stop right away. I knew who he was, Ku Ch'uan-chieh. A few years back, he was one of the hottest *hsiao-sheng* in Shanghai. He had since left his opera troupe and was now attending the same school as my brothers in Nanking. I would stop singing when he appeared because I was too embarrassed to continue. I didn't know him well then because he was my brothers' friend.

Then, in 1936, the Firemen's Association of K'un-shan sponsored a benefit concert. This was a big deal because K'un-shan was the place where *k'un-ch'ü* originated six hundred years ago. Professional actors and members of the opera clubs from Soochow all wanted to help out. My brothers and I also decided to go.

At the concert, Yuan-ho was onstage twice, performing the male-scholar role in two different scenes. That year Ku Ch'uan-chieh was also in K'un-shan for the same purpose. After he decided to leave the stage, Ku rarely sang in public. Occasionally, when he knew that his mates from the opera troupe were performing in Shanghai, he would show up and join them in a scene or two, out of nostalgia and out of affection for them. But as Yuan-ho's teacher Chou Ch'uan-ying observed in his memoir, Ku's performance no longer measured up to the grandeur and the subtlety it once had. Chou would know: he and Ku had started in the same troupe together when they were kids. Both sang *hsiao-sheng* roles, and at the height of their careers, the two were considered near equals.

Ku Ch'uan-chieh probably also realized that his stage presence and his technique were not what they used to be, and so he avoided occasions like the K'un-shan benefit concert. Why, then, did he go? Some said it was because of a young woman. He was pursuing her at the time, and she was going to be in K'un-shan. This woman was also from Soochow, the daughter of a silk factory owner. Her family forbade her to be near Ku Ch'uan-chieh; they even objected to her singing *k'un-ch'ü*. So she stole quietly away to K'un-shan when she learned that there was a chance for her to perform. Yuan-ho knew her. They were in the same opera club in Soochow, and this woman played the female lead opposite her male lead in the love scene from *The Red Pear.* Once Yuan-ho even encouraged her to run away with Ku, but "she didn't have the nerve."

In K'un-shan, Ku Ch'uan-chieh sang two of the most demanding roles in the male lead repertoire: Emperor Ming-huang in "Jolted Back to Reality" and the young official Wang Shih-p'eng in "A Mother's Reunion."* "Jolted Back to Reality" is scene 23 of *The Palace of Eternal Life*. Written in the early Ch'ing, the play uses a familiar story from the T'ang dynasty to comment on late Ming gaiety and insouciance—why these could be attenuating—while restating the late Ming's romance with the idea of love: that love transcends death and all things impermanent. At the beginning of "Jolted Back to Reality," the T'ang emperor Ming-huang is seen drinking with his favorite consort, Yang Yü-huan, or "Jade Bracelet," in the imperial garden under the moonlight. The emperor coaxes her to drink more. Jade Bracelet swoons from the effect. Delighting in what he sees, the emperor sings:

> *Holding my cup,*
> *I watch her closely,*
> *I am wordless.*
> *I see a blushing flower on each cheek.*
> *A drooping willow,*
> *A pliant sprig.*
> *Lazily swirling,*
> *She is my delicate oriole,*
> *My indolent swallow.*

The first half of the scene ends with the palace women escorting a languorous Lady Yang offstage to her chamber, the emperor's gaze still fixed on her. Suddenly the mood changes. Drums are heard in the distance: their sound "makes the whole world shudder." The prime minister enters. He announces: "General An-lu Shan has rebelled. His army is approaching the capital." The emperor is shocked. He quickens his steps; he speeds up the tempo of his recitative. He paces back and forth, stopping only to reflect on what discomfort this might bring to his Lady Yang.

The role of the young official, Wang Shih-p'eng, in "A Mother's Reunion" is just as difficult as that of Emperor Ming-huang. A son leaves his young bride and his mother to go to the capital to take the examination. He is placed first, gets an official position, and prepares to send for his family. Meanwhile, his wife and mother have learned from an unreliable source that he has a new bride. His wife's family forces her to remarry. She throws herself into the river

---

*The actor and opera critic Hsü Ling-yun thought that these two roles are artistically demanding. In his view, only one other role could be their rival, the young scholar from the drama *The Lute*. (See his *K'un-chü piao-yen i-te,* p. 104.)

and vanishes. The scene Ku Ch'uan-chieh performed begins with Shih-p'eng's mother arriving at the capital in search of her son. She finds him and, instead of feeling overjoyed, she is suffused with grief. Meanwhile, he is confused and anxious. He wonders where his wife is. Did she not get on with his mother? Is she all right? Is she ill? Is she dead? The actor and opera critic Hsü Ling-yun explains the difficulty of playing Shih-p'eng: "The character is bound by propriety to comfort his mother since she seems so distressed, but in his heart he is worried about his wife. He is vexed but cannot make this plain. He is unquiet but must appear calm. His patience with his mother must seem forced. This is the first thing the actor must grasp." Hsü continues: "And as Shih-p'eng's suspicion deepens, his manner becomes more and more unnatural. This is something the actor must also convey." Throughout this scene, the tension is sustained by the circularity of the conversation between Shih-p'eng and his mother and the circularity of their movement on stage. They are both unable to say what they mean: one is restrained by social decorum and the other by what she knows.

Ku Ch'uan-chieh sang "A Mother's Reunion" the first day of the concert, "Jolted Back to Reality" the second day. By the third day, he was exhausted and simply could not be persuaded to do another scene. Backstage, the Chang brothers, Tsung-ho and Yin-ho, cajoled him into giving them and Yuan-ho a private concert of "Written While Plastered." This is a short scene taken from the Ming drama *Variegated Brush*. Usually performed without the rest of the play, the scene is distinguished by its quick energy and pure lightness and is a vehicle for actors to show off their skills. The context is again the court of Emperor Ming-huang. This time, the emperor and Lady Yang play supporting roles to the poet Li Po, a man with great panache and wonderful peculiarities. The peonies are in full bloom in the imperial garden, gorgeous and lush like Lady Yang. The emperor, enchanted by the sight of these two beauties, sends for Li Po. He wants the poet to compose new lines, "fresh verses," to celebrate the occasion. But Li Po is in a wineshop, drinking with friends. Two eunuchs come to fetch him, and Li Po refuses to move. "I am gone, gone," he tells them, "so I can't go anywhere else." The eunuchs prop him up and deliver him to the emperor, who instructs the attendants to "find some elegant paper for Li Po to write on." He then orders his chief eunuch to take off Li Po's boots so that the poet can write more comfortably. He gestures to Lady Yang to hold up the inkstone for Li Po, "to give him encouragement"*

---

*In T'u Lung's original play, this scene is called "Taking Off the Boots and Holding Up the Inkstone."

"Written While Plastered" is about drunkenness—the different stages of drunkenness, and Li Po's drunkenness. Yuan-ho's teacher, Chou Ch'uan-ying, once remarked that only a good actor "is able to bring elegance to Li Po's dissolute state." Li Po must remain imperious in his addledness. "He only seems to have let everything go," and this distinguishes him from other drunks. Both Chou Ch'uan-ying and Ku Ch'uan-chieh had learned this role from Shen Yüeh-ch'üan, the consummate *k'un-ch'ü* actor of his generation. Ku Ch'uan-chieh's performance of Li Po that evening was "sublime, perfect in execution," Yuan-ho said, and she was enraptured.

Yuan-ho had seen Ku onstage many times when she was a university student in Shanghai. She and three female classmates from Ta-hsia were sort of a gang—they called themselves "the four warrior guardians of the Buddha's temple" (*ssu-ta-chin-kang*)—and nearly every Saturday and Sunday afternoon they would go to an opera at an entertainment center (*yu-le-ch'ang*). They would always see a matinee because at their university all students were expected to be back at their dormitory before dinner. Evenings were meant for studies. Also, matinee tickets were cheaper, half the price of evening shows. In 1926, for a tenth of a silver dollar, one could spend a whole afternoon in an entertainment center, seeing an opera (*k'un-ch'ü*, Peking, or a regional opera), a play, a musical, a magic show, a comic skit, a *t'an-t'zu* (ballade) performance, or a *mao-erh-hsi* opera sung entirely by a girl troupe.

From 1927 to 1930, when Yuan-ho was a student in Shanghai, Ku Ch'uan-chieh, was getting top billing on the theater program. Yuan-ho and her friends were fans, but they did not go to the theater just to see him. They loved operas and did not dote on particular actors. Once they wrote a joint letter to him—this was years before Yuan-ho met him in person—asking him to attempt the scene "Finding the Painting and Questioning the Painting" from *The Peony Pavilion*. The scene was rarely performed because the male principal sings solo from beginning to end, and most actors found the part too taxing. "Like-minded friend from the same literary circle," their letter began. "So serious, and so proper, isn't it?" Yuan-ho now says. "A few weeks later, he actually honored our request. We couldn't believe it! And it was a wonderful performance."

Ku Ch'uan-chieh was two years younger than Yuan-ho, so he was twenty at most when he received this letter. It is possible that he was charmed by the four young ladies' earnest appeal. He could also be doing his best to oblige his audience. The *k'un-ch'ü* troupes at the time were competing vigorously and nervously against other forms of entertainment for a share of the audience, and usually under the same roof, in the large entertainment centers that had become very popular in Shanghai in the 1920s and 1930s. This meant that while a *k'un-ch'ü* performance was going on, twenty or forty feet away a regional opera troupe or a jazz band might be onstage in the theater next door or just down the hall. "If you don't sing your heart out," Yuan-ho's teacher said, "your audience is going to get up and leave, and move to another part of the building."

K'un-ch'ü used to have its own theaters in Shanghai. The first one was built in 1851, in a bustling part of the city. It was called the Garden of Three Elegances. Unlike the entertainment centers of the 1920s and 1930s, this was a small and intimate space with a tended garden in front. In the 1860s and 1870s, there were many more such theaters, some considerably larger. Most of them were located in the foreign concessions, along Canton Road and Fukien Road. A theater monthly from this period described one: "In front of the stage, you will find five or six rows of square tables with five or six tables to each row, and five seats to each table." There were also box seats on the second level and chairs to the right and left sides of the main hall, with a small wooden table in front of each chair. Tea was free, but only customers sitting in the main hall and in the boxes were entitled to teacups with covers and to snacks: "On each table there are six small plates of nibbles—melon seeds, cheap fruits, and slivers of cakes. During intermission, a sweet soup is served—osmanthus flower and crushed walnut dumplings in spring and winter, mung bean or lily bulbs in summer and autumn. The food is usually not tasty, so customers rarely touch their snacks." An advertisement dated February 2, 1880, for a new and bigger Three Elegances Theater tells us the cost of going to the theater: "Three silver dollars for a table in the main hall. Separate seats are half a dollar each. A box is three and a half dollars; separate seats in the box are also half a dollar each. To hire a prostitute to watch the performance with you is seventy cents extra. Standing room is thirty cents in the back of the theater, and twenty cents at either side. The minimum charge is ten cents. For foreigners, it is a dollar."

Paying to see an opera was a radical concept in Chinese society. During the first two hundred years of opera's history, from about 1500 to 1700, gentry and merchant families either hired troupes to perform for small gatherings on holidays or special occasions, or they supported their own "family troupes" that would be on call all the time and perform any scene on demand. It did not matter if the owners were connoisseurs: "It was simply convenient to have a moderately good opera troupe around all the time to provide entertainment for your guests. On the whole they were for social purposes."

Depending on the pleasure of their employers, the troupes performed either in rented reception halls or on large luxury boats. In a reception hall, the stage was a piece of red woolen carpet at the center. Around the back and two sides of the stage were tables set up for a feast. Women and children could view the performance from behind a curtain. If the venue was a boat, the stage was in the bow and the kitchen was in the stern.

By the 1730s, another venue appeared. It probably began as a money-making scheme. Some clever entrepreneur in Soochow decided to open a dinner theater. He hired waiters, cooks, and opera troupes. Wealthy merchants simply rented a room from him, and he provided food, drinks, and entertainment. His idea caught on swiftly. By the 1780s there were more than twenty such restaurants in Soochow alone. But dinner theaters were mainly for socializing. The clients concentrated more on what they were eating and drinking and saying to each other than on the opera being sung onstage. A contemporary described what it was like:

> Inside, the cooks are roasting lamb and gutting carp to take care of the hosts and guests while the proprietor asks the actors to put on the latest opera. A balustrade surrounds the entire dining area. Outside, people could get a good view of the performance onstage. They could watch to their hearts' content all the operas the human world could create. Do they know how the story ends? Prosperity allows only a viewing like this. So you find your pleasure through the hullabaloo.

Those who were leaning against the balustrade, watching the opera, were usually servants and drivers waiting for their employers to finish feasting. They were the authentic audience, precursors to modern theatergoers. They would stand for hours because they were captivated. By the nineteenth century, the true enthusiasts bought a ticket at the gate, if they could afford it, and enjoyed an opera with or without a seat. Tea was still served, and snacks, but people hardly touched them because they were not there to eat and drink. By the early twentieth century, it was entirely possible for the master and mistress of the house to share their opera box with their servants. This was probably not a common sight, but Tou Kan-kan and Chu Kan-kan had often gone to the theater with their mistress.

It had taken the Chinese a long time to relax their rules about who could sit next to whom at a concert, but once *k'un-ch'ü* became commercialized, the change was inevitable. Yet even as certain social inequities began to disappear in that world, others remained stubbornly fixed. The actors' status was the slowest to change because it was hard for the Chinese to modify their views about entertainers. Up to the nineteenth century, actors were barred from taking the civil service examinations and so forbidden to have the chance, allowed to most men, to improve their social station. Even Confucius, a teacher of moral justness and human compassion, seems to have held strong opinions against entertainers. One early commentary says that at the height of his career as the judicial commisioner of the state of Lu, Confucius ordered the execution of a group of dancers and musicians, who had been entertaining at a peace-signing ceremony between the state of Lu and the state of Ch'i. "The dancers wore feathers and waved swords and shields as they danced," the account states. "The musicians played drums and shouted wild cries." Confucius considered their entertainment barbaric and offensive, a violation of the rites that were proper to such an occasion, and he told the officers of Ch'i, who had hired the troupe, to have the members put to death. This story has raised many questions about Confucius' judgment—whether he overreacted to a minor offense and whether he punished the wrong party. After all, it was probably the officers who instructed the troupe on what numbers to perform. And even if they were the wrong numbers, why should this have had any consequences on the signing of the peace treaty? In Confucius' view, it seems, the wild dance foretold a dark intent, perhaps a sinister design, and he could not simply sit back and let this intent come to fruition. To show the state of Ch'i what he knew and what he was capable of, he imposed a penalty severe enough to demonstrate his own strength but not so offensive as to jeopardize the peace between the two sides. Someone had to be punished, he decided; best that it be the musicians and dancers.

Yuan-ho's teacher Chou Ch'uan-ying once remarked, "People regard *k'un-ch'ü* opera as elegant but the professional performers as lowly." Tabloid history would like for us to believe that the Chinese regarded actors as lowly because of their sexual ambiguity. But this mean perception of actors had been around hundreds of years before some of them began to don women's clothes and transform themselves into women on stage. Actors were lowly because they were from desperately poor families. No parents would have sold their son to an opera troupe unless this was their last resort. There was a common expression: "As long as you still have three pecks of rice, you wouldn't send your son to an opera troupe." And once a child entered an opera school, his parents had to sign a contract stating that "from now on, Heaven would decide whether the child lives or dies" and the parents could no longer have any say about their child's life. Ku Ch'uan-chieh was from a Soochow family, the youngest of three boys and a girl. His father was a local schoolteacher. The situation at home was so hard that his parents had to send him and an older brother, when they were twelve and thirteen, to an opera training school.

Actors were also beneath others because they were skilled in the ways of giving pleasure—something nearly all the early philosophers, particularly the Confucians, found disquieting and vulgar. Confucians felt that the skills of actors were underhanded, easily winning but bearing no relationship to self-knowledge, and that they were unfair competition to attempts at moral persuasion. Most rulers preferred spending time with singers and dancers to listening to their ministers' counsel. And the morally astute would point out that it was not just rulers and the rich who were susceptible to entertainers' sway. One thirteenth-century scholar accused entertainers of luring ordinary people away from their work, of wasting their time and energy, and of encouraging proper women to have salacious thoughts. And a sixteenth-century Confucian, in his private "Family Instructions," tells his sons that interactions with actors may be hazardous because "what actors know is only how to juggle for power; what they talk about is only voice and veneer; what they pursue is only food and wine."

But *k'un-ch'ü* was an elegant art; it demanded much more from its performers than did other forms of entertainment. This was clear from the start of its flourishing. Scholars took an interest in it, as did musicians, poets, playwrights, men of taste, and men of imagination. They kept refining it and improving it, making corrections and adjustments, and writing new dramas that were compatible with *k'un-ch'ü* music; they also put pressure on the actors to do better, to add something new, and to claim some originality for themselves in a scene that had been performed hundreds of times before. It was expectations like these from critics, connoisseurs, and a generally alert and well-informed audience that helped to refine the aesthetics of *k'un-ch'ü*.

Even when *k'un-ch'ü* was in vogue, and actors were working under the most favorable circumstances, they could not better their social standing. Within the context of *k'un-ch'ü*, they could be seen as elegant, but outside of it, they remained lowly. During the sixteenth and seventeenth centuries, when *k'un-ch'ü* was in its glory, the opera troupes could name their price, and the stars among them could ask for horses and sedan chairs, brocade and ginseng broth in addition to their remuneration. Yet despite their vastly improved financial situations, they could not increase their social worth. Society's rules made certain of this. When the Ch'ing poet and critic Yuan Mei could not keep his hands off the young actors he patronized, the historian Chang Hsüeh-ch'eng publicly denounced him as a "shameless fool," someone who had "no regard for distinctions."

Social etiquette also worked to keep the worlds of actor and patron apart. An actor often spent many hours giving private lessons to families living in comfortable houses. Afterward, he went somewhere else to spend the night—a room he shared with other actors or a boat near the dock. And when things were going badly, he could rely only on his own family and friends. Most people who had studied with professional actors did not know what became of their teachers after their lessons had stopped. Ch'ung-ho said: "Professional actors could not even sit down and have a meal with you although they had been instructing you at *k'un-ch'ü* in your house. My family was an exception because my father didn't care for such rules." Her teacher, A-yung, often showed up for dinner wired from his snort of opium. Wide-eyed, he would talk for three hours about this and that—his life on the road, actors he knew—forgetting that he was there to give Ch'ung-ho her lesson. He would have a couple glasses of wine and some dried shrimp. By ten or eleven o'clock he would suddenly droop, his eyebrows would collapse, and his skin would grow darker and more wrinkled. Then he would slowly make his way to the door and disappear into the dark.

Rules became more exacting when professionals and amateurs appeared on the same stage. Actors had been singing with guest artists since the beginning of *k'un-ch'ü* performance. By the nineteenth century, a new phenomenon appeared. The popularity of *k'un-ch'ü* had declined. Professional actors could hardly find work themselves, much less guest spots for enthusiasts, and so amateurs formed their own *k'un-ch'ü* clubs. Sometimes several clubs would rent a theater together and stage a joint program. (The theater owners could hardly refuse the opportunity, since the clubs provided their own costumes and headdresses, hired their own extras, and then paid for the use of the space.) Members of a club would work with a professional actor for weeks to prepare themselves for a public performance. To draw a large crowd, the apprentices could advertise that the master would appear with them. But this was the amateurs' show: they made the arrangements and paid the expenses, and they wanted to play the leads. Moreover, most gentry considered it improper for a professional actor to have equal weight with them in any situation, even a fictive one. So the teacher could have only walk-on parts.

This practice continued into the twentieth century. In 1936, Ch'ung-ho was associated with a large opera club in Nanking that boasted many celebrities: top officials from the Republican government, wealthy industrialists, writers, composers, university professors, and an older brother of the last emperor. That year the club hosted a *k'un-ch'ü* troupe from the north, and the local celebrities and the actors gave several performances together. At the time, Ch'ung-ho worked with Han Shih-ch'ang, an experienced actor who specialized in female leads.

A few days before the performance, Ch'ung-ho learned that her plan to have Mr. Han play the maidservant opposite her Li-niang had met with firm disapproval. The man who objected most strongly was Ch'u Min-i, a senior member of the club. Ch'u was also a prominent figure in the republican period, known for his work in medical education, public health, and the arts. (He had received

a medical degree in France and had traveled extensively in Japan and Europe.)
He was a sophisticated man, yet he could not allow a professional and an amateur to undertake roles of equal importance onstage. He called it a breach of
propriety. Ch'ung-ho had just turned twenty-three in the spring of that year, so
she was a mere youngster, but she would not yield. Insisting that the rule was
unreasonable and wrong, she withdrew from the program. This could have
ended in a deadlock, which, her brother Tsung-ho pointed out, might have been
awkward for the actors. They appreciated Ch'ung-ho's show of loyalty but also
needed to be on good terms with the amateur clubs in order to survive.

All of this explains why Yuan-ho's marriage to Ku Ch'uan-chieh came as
such a shock. Shanghai's society page described it as a case of "a gentry woman
marrying beneath herself." Yuan-ho believed that her father would have given
full consent to her plan to marry Ku. (She wrote to him about it, but her letter
arrived a few days after he died.) She also believed that her father would not
have worried about who Ku's parents were, how he ended up as an actor, or what
others might say of the class disparity between the two families. Ch'ung-ho had
another point of view. She believed that if you loved *k'un-ch'ü* well enough you
could never be involved with a *k'un-ch'ü* actor. Did Yuan-ho fall in love with Ku
Ch'uan-chieh's art? Or did she fall in love with him because he sang "Written
While Plastered" backstage? Was he more intoxicating up close?

A critic said this about Ku Ch'uan-chieh when Ku was only eighteen: "Seeing one of his performances would make you ruminate for the next ten days." Ku
had grace and presence, and he was a superb ruler onstage. His best roles were
the big kings, those who made grand their weakness and fallibility, men such as
Emperor Ming-huang and Emperor Ch'ung-chen, the last Ming ruler, who
hanged himself from a tree in his garden on the last day of his dynasty. Ku had
a tendency to frown, and this became his distinguishing trait onstage—it made
him an even more convincing tragic hero. His colleague Chou Ch'uan-ying
remembered that once Ku Ch'uan-chieh was so consumed by the role of
Emperor Ch'ung-chen that after he uttered the last line, "this most wrenching
regret that a dynasty's three hundred years should finish in a day," he rushed
backstage and coughed up a mouthful of blood. After that episode, he stopped
playing the role.

Chou Ch'uan-ying always thought that Ku had the genius of an actor. The
two had grown up together—both came to the Ch'uan-hsi opera school when
they were kids. The school had opened in 1921, and it was the only one in Soochow that specialized in *k'un-ch'ü*. Chou Ch'uan-ying said: "Most people
wouldn't want to go to a *k'un-ch'ü* school. If they had to learn opera, they would
probably go to a Peking opera school. We ended up in a *k'un-ch'ü* school because

we were poor and because we heard that the school was good and we were also from Soochow. Soochow has always been best in *k'un-ch'ü*." Families in Soochow must have known about Ch'uan-hsi by word of mouth. Five boys from Chou and Ku's neighborhoods started in the school at the same time.

Ch'uan-hsi was located in a desolate part of town, where families stored occupied coffins not yet ready for burial. In China it was common to see coffins on a temple ground or a vacant lot, either exposed or under a temporary cover; until they found a suitable gravesite and an auspicious date, families would wait for months, sometimes years, to bury the dead. Their attempt to do the right thing for the deceased often had a disagreeable, if not spooky, effect on the living. The actors who attended this *k'un-ch'ü* school could recall, years later, the dread of being so close to the dead when they were children. Chou Ch'uan-ying said:

> Our school bought half of "Five-*mu* Plot," which was the name of this place. The coffins on our side were moved next door. In front of the school was an execution ground. On one side was the funeral home, which was always dark and eerie. We were all so young at the time, the oldest being no more than fourteen or fifteen. The younger ones among us would be too scared to go to the privy at night unless we had an older brother or a group of friends guarding us. I remember there was a boy with the nickname "Little Eggplant." He was literally frightened to death.

The founder of this school, Mu Ou-ch'u, was both a practical man and a dreamer. He learned enough English to get into the Chinese Maritime Customs Service and then earned enough credits through a correspondence school to get himself enrolled in an American university. His education in Western things was thorough—science, language, mathematics, agriculture, economics, and politics—the kind of education that Chang Shu-sheng had wished for all Chinese. In 1922, with a bachelor of science degree in agriculture from the University of Illinois and a graduate degree in textile industry from Texas A & M, Mu was already the owner of three cotton mills and a bank in Shanghai. The year before, he and a group of opera specialists and enthusiasts had met in Hangchow to discuss the future of *k'un-ch'ü*. The old Ch'üan-fu actors were probably not going to be around in another ten years, they said. What would happen to *k'un-ch'ü* then? Who would keep this art alive? And what could they—bankers and industrialists—do to help? At this gathering, Mu Ou-ch'u decided to make a huge contribution—fifty thousand silver dollars, according to some sources—to start a *k'un-ch'ü* school for boys. He was also willing to cover all the expenses.

Mu Ou-ch'u had many ideas for his school. He wanted it to be a modern-style school, where physical punishment was forbidden and students learned to read and write in addition to receiving opera training. The school provided room and board. Every child was well fed. The instructors were the old actors from the Ch'üan-fu troupe, and among the staff were Yü Ts'ai-yun, Yuan-ho's first teacher, and Shen Yüeh-ch'üan, the most venerated *k'un-ch'ü* actor of his time. Mu Ou-ch'u called his school *ch'uan-hsi*—"to pass on what one has practiced." The name evoked an idea, found in the *Analects*, that later became central to the Confucian discussion of knowledge and its transmission. The *Analects* says that Confucius' disciple Tseng Ts'an asked himself every day, "Have I passed on to others [*ch'uan*] anything I have not tried out [*hsi*] myself?" Every actor trained at Mr. Mu's school had the word *ch'uan* in his stage name. The word identifies them as the *ch'uan* generation of actors.

From the beginning, Ku Ch'uan-chieh's teachers noticed that he had unusual gifts: an expansive and shimmering voice, and movements that were light and lithe. They took care to cultivate them but never singled him out. All the boys were treated equally—this was also the style of the Ch'uan-hsi school. Later, when they began to perform in the theaters in Shanghai, it became apparent very quickly that the audiences were coming to see Ku Ch'uan-chieh and a handful of others. Even so, their patron, Mr. Mu, saw to it that these actors did not always get top billing, that they sometimes took walk-on parts and played supporting roles. Chou Ch'uan-ying explained it in this way: "We were all classmates and brothers, sat at the same table and ate from the same pot. We were all professionals on the stage, trying to earn a little spending money on the side." There were slight differences in their pay, but "they were always appropriate."

In 1927, Mu Ou-ch'u's textile business faced serious financial troubles, and he had to withdraw his support. Two other industrialists, Yen Hui-yü and T'ao Hsi-ch'üan, took over the school. They changed the name of the opera troupe and many of its rules, creating a "star system" and huge discrepancies in salary and amenities. Those actors whom Mr. T'ao and Mr. Yen liked to plug got special treatment: "They stayed with T'ao and Yen, had meals with them and lived separately from their colleagues." T'ao and Yen did not allow their favorites to play supporting roles. The "stars" decided which scenes they wanted to be in. "They would arrive in rickshaws with their patrons at their side just before they went onstage. And they would leave the same way, usually as soon as they finished singing." These actors also received private gifts, "silk in the summer, fur in the winter." Chou Ch'uan-ying thought that their new patrons did a lot of harm to the troupe, spoiling the love and loyalty the actors had for one another, and spoiling their work and their morale.

In 1931, Yen Hui-yü and his partner decided to terminate their contract with the Grand World Entertainment Center, where their actors had been performing, and to cut their ties with the Ch'uan-hsi troupe altogether. Yen was willing to send his favorite actors to college if they wanted to go. Out of the three he plucked, only Ku Ch'uan-chieh took the offer.

Yen Hui-yü's relationship with Ku Ch'uan-chieh was not what one would expect between a patron and an artist. Yen thought Ku smart and capable, and so encouraged him to do something else. He probably did not believe that there was much hope in an actor's life. Other members in the troupe noted that Mr. Yen liked *k'un-ch'ü* well enough but his heart was not really in it. In fact, they were not at all surprised when Yen suddenly withdrew his support in the middle of a season. The cultural historian Lu O-t'ing believed that what happened to Ch'uan-hsi was inevitable—Yen Hui-yü could not be completely responsible. He wrote:

> Mu Ou-ch'u and others tried to prolong the lifespan of *k'un-ch'ü*. What they did was admirable, but they did not give much thought to the more stubborn problems, much less their solutions. Once you have put together what you believe is a modern-style opera troupe, where do you go from there? You must think about reform, how to make the organization better and how to modernize the art of performance. Also you must consider what sort of audience you want to attract and what sort of impression you want your audience to have about your troupe. [At the early stage of Ch'uan-hsi's history,] all these questions were either pushed aside, or they got lost in the wishful thinking one indulges in when one has had a few successful perfomances.

When Mr. Yen and Mr. T'ao cut off their funding, the actors decided to go it alone, negotiating their own contracts and handling their own publicity and accounts. The Ch'uan-hsi troupe lasted another six years. The first few years, the actors worked all the time and wherever they could find work—small theaters, entertainment centers, department stores, private homes, riverboats, in towns and villages, up and down the Yangtze—sometimes crowding several performances into an afternoon and evening. The most each person could make in a day was around a silver dollar—a living wage if there was work all the time, which was not the case.

Then, on August 13, 1937, Japanese planes bombed Shanghai, destroying several department stores and the Grand World Entertainment Center, where the troupe had been performing. Soon the troupe disbanded, because in the middle of a war no one wanted to hear *k'un-ch'ü,* and the actors all had to make their own way. Some became waiters; others, factory workers or day laborers. The actor who had played the chief eunuch to Ku's Li Po in "Written While Plastered" ended up as a fortune-teller. A few, like Chou Ch'uan-ying, joined other types of opera troupes, and whenever they could, they also gave private lessons in people's homes. The most desperate ones slipped into a dark corner and died. The male lead who succeeded Ku Ch'uan-chieh after 1931 ended up this way, and was buried in a common grave in Shanghai. A drummer for the troupe committed suicide—he quietly laid himself down on a railroad track one night.

Did Ku Ch'uan-chieh know in 1931 that his life might come to this if he stayed with his *k'un-ch'ü* troupe? Even his wife cannot say what he was think-ing at the time. She knew that when he left the theater he still loved opera and still enjoyed performing it. Ku had a few good years in Shanghai, but he prob-ably realized that this would not last. The *k'un-ch'ü* theater had a brief revival in the late 1920s, but that was because the three patrons, Mu, Yen, and T'ao, pumped a lot of money into it. Their support would have had to stop sometime. Ku also thought that an actor's life was "complicated," so near the edge that it was easy to give in to temptation. Many of his fellow actors were taking opium to keep going. Twice, his partner onstage collapsed in his arms from having had too much to drink.

Ku Ch'uan-chieh was probably also self-conscious about being an actor. An actor could not even sit at the same dinner table with many of the men and women who came to the theater to see him every night. Just before he and Yuan-ho got engaged, his patron, Yen Hui-yü, asked Yuan-ho why she wanted to marry Ku Ch'uan-chieh. Yuan-ho answered that it was because he had "high aspirations." But what sort of aspirations? Those of Ch'en She from the Han— the "aspirations of a snow goose"? Aspirations of leaving a life that was beneath others and aiming for something high and proper?

In the end, Ku Ch'uan-chieh paid dearly for his aspirations. He had to give up the genius others recognized in him. His sister-in-law Yun-ho used to say, "Every scrap of him was suffused with theater. His own character might be flawed, but could he perform!" And to step up, Ku had to go back to middle school when he was already twenty-two years old.

Yen Hui-yü probably told Ku that education would be his passage to inde-pendence and respectability. Yen himself had only a primary school education and one year in a technical school, yet before he turned thirty, he had been the vice president of a Shanghai bank, had managed a cotton mill, and had founded his own tobacco company and coal mining company and begun to lay the groundwork of an ambitious agricultural project. He believed that his protégé could have the same entrepreneurial success as he, with his drive and intelligence, but he wanted Ku first to get the education he never had. Throughout his life, Yen supported many young people through school, sending them to universities or abroad with the money he'd earned. He did not know most of them—many were scholarship students. Ku Ch'uan-chieh, however, was his private pick.

Yen's expectations must have been a persistent pressure on Ku Ch'uan-chieh. For someone who had been an actor in an opera troupe, starting over was not easy. Ku learned to read and write in opera school and had an early introduction to aesthetics through performing *k'un-ch'ü*, but it was a limited education—there was no mathematics or science, no practical knowledge. There were not even readings in the classics or vernacular literature. By the time the school had become a professional troupe, the actors worked every day, two shows a day, matinee and evening, plus performances in private homes. Whatever time these actors had, they used to learn new scenes, to add to their repertoire.

Ku Ch'uan-chieh must have done all right in middle school. It took him two tries to pass the entrance examination to one school, but he got into Chinling University in Nanking, and he prevailed. Yen Hui-yü urged him to study agriculture, and he did. After graduating from college, Ku taught for a while in an agricultural school in Shanghai. This was also his patron's wish. Yen probably had more ambitious plans for him, perhaps to have him manage one of his farms in Chen-chiang. Yen also wanted Ku to marry his oldest daughter.

Ku's life could have been very different had he married his patron's daughter. In 1936, Miss Yen was only eighteen. Her father was grooming her to become a sericulturist someday, and she was devoted to him. Marrying her would have made Ku Ch'uan-chieh an heir to Yen's farming business and given him good connections to the Shanghai banks and a new identity, as the son-in-law of Yen Hui-yü. Either Ku did not accept the offer or decided not to wait for it to be made formally. Miss Yen was eleven years younger than he. She had spent most of her life in agricultural schools, learning how to raise silkworms and run a farm. She was practical and diligent, but it is unlikely that she had much polish or poise. At her age, Yuan-ho was acting in plays and choreographing her own dances. Miss Yen had a sensible education, whereas Yuan-ho had a charmed life.

Both women's fathers had considerable means. But Yuan-ho's father, Wu-ling, was living off old money; his life was one of ease and elegance, with the least amount of anxiety because he never did very much. Yen Hui-yü, on the other hand, was industrious and competitive; he thrived on taking risks and not having enough time to do all he wanted to do. His mother used to say, "It seems like he has eight pots of soup on the stove with only seven lids. So he never gets a break, always rotating the covers to keep the soup bubbling." Wu-ling founded one school; Yen supported three, plus a hospital and projects in famine relief. Yen practiced calligraphy, but it was not so much for enjoyment as to teach himself perseverance. He enjoyed *k'un-ch'ü* but could do without it.

Miss Yen probably would have made a more suitable match for Ku Ch'uan-chieh. They both shared her father's views about how best to spend one's life and how best to use one's resources. But at the end Ku wanted Yuan-ho. He and Yuan-ho had little in common except for their elegant art, yet once they were together, her fate became inexorably linked to his.

Yuan-ho remains loyal to Ku Ch'uan-chieh even now, thirty-five years after his death. She does not murmur anything critical about him—we don't even know if he had any irritating habits—and she does not tell any of their secrets. Yuan-ho is guarded. It is difficult to notice this in conversation because she is so exuberant, so sunny, and she always seems so composed. She sticks to her script when talking about her husband and cannot be rattled. Most scenes in her account of Ku Ch'uan-chieh have an operatic setting: her meeting with him in K'un-shan, seeing each other again in Shanghai, her wedding, and their social life in Shanghai during the war. She also talks about his particularities: that when he was performing in Shanghai, he liked to go to the public bath after midnight when no one else was there; that just before he went onstage, no matter how loud the noise level around him, he could be completely alone, stretching his arms and legs and muttering to himself; that privately he enjoyed singing female leads. Yuan-ho also remembered that after they married, when he came home from work and was in a good mood, he would do an acrobatic leap and fall gracefully into bed.

We do not know what Ku Ch'uan-chieh thought of Yuan-ho's singing. Since they both performed male leads, he must have had an opinion of her voice and her training. Did they talk about the aesthetics of *k'un-ch'ü*? Did they disagree? Did she defer to him? He taught her the female lead in a scene from *The Peony Pavilion*. How did he teach her? The seventeenth-century critic Li Yü pointed out that teaching a woman to sing either the male or the female role required subtle skills: one should "emphasize naturalness." "Don't let her imitate the style of a male actor," he wrote. The teacher, Li Yü continued, should understand a woman's natural gifts and instruct her accordingly. Was Ku Ch'uan-chieh a sensitive, empathetic teacher? Yuan-ho's response to such a question is usually sparing and imprecise. And if asked a more direct one, whether her husband ever regretted leaving his earlier career, she will say no, without elaboration.

It is hard to guess what Ku thought about his life, but he must have been a disappointment to himself. He failed at everything he tried after he left school. His desire to do better never got him anywhere; it just made him seem more anxious, his intentions more transparent. Other people also did not let him part with his past. His eagerness to please only reinforced their opinion of him as someone who knew he was inferior. Yuan-ho was aware of this and seems to have decided a long time ago to side with him. Each time he failed in business, she was willing to let him try again. So Ku Ch'uan-chieh was a stock speculator, a tobacco buyer, a scout for reclaimed land; he also sold traditional medicine and was a retailer of wool and woolen products. Yuan-ho's family was loyal to her. Her siblings simply accepted Ku as their brother-in-law. The fact that their father had approved Ku and Yuan-ho's courtship was also important. Yet, in spite of this, Yuan-ho was made weak by her marriage to Ku Ch'uan-chieh.

Unlike her sisters, Yuan-ho makes no claim to great passions. She is not for or against anything; she has no strong views regarding human characters and no strong love for anyone besides her husband and her son. She does not rant or exaggerate the good. She copes well under any circumstance, and even in situations where most people would become frayed, she is an elegant presence.

During the war, Yuan-ho was the only one among her siblings to remain in Japanese-occupied China. She and Yun-ho were together in Hankow in 1938. The Japanese had already marshaled their troops in Shanghai. From Hankow, like many other refugees from China's coastal cities, Yun-ho—who was already a mother by then—and her children headed for Szechwan, where the National-ist government had relocated. Yuan-ho could have gone with them but chose not to. Instead, she returned to Shanghai to be with her adoptive sister, Ling Hai-hsia, and with Ku Ch'uan-chieh. By the next year, Yuan-ho and Ch'uan-chieh were married. They celebrated at a Western-style restaurant. Ku's former classmates from the k'un-ch'ü school sang for them at the banquet. Even though Ling Hai-hsia did not take to Ku Ch'uan-chieh, her family gave Yuan-ho a thousand silver dollars so that she could pay for the wedding and have some-thing left over to start a new life.

Yuan-ho has said that life was "all right" under the Japanese. She was still receiving a regular income from the family estate manager in Hofei, an arrange-ment her fourth brother had made for all his brothers and sisters just before he left for the southwest. She and Ch'uan-chieh had their home in the French Concession, which was a relatively peaceful place to be before the war in the Pacific broke out. At that time the Japanese could not move into any of the for-eign settlements because the Western powers, in principle, were maintaining a neutral position in the Sino-Japanese conflict. Wealthy businessmen and poor refugees, plus journalists, writers, spies, and anyone who was likely to get into trouble with the Japanese police, all fled to the foreign settlements in 1938. The Chinese living there spoke of their condition in those years, from 1938 to 1941, as one of being on a "solitary island"—a trope that suggests not only isolation but also privilege and protection.

The "island" life was also strange and deeply ambivalent. There was a brief period of prosperity in 1938 and 1939. The industries that were relocated here from nearby cities and the "Chinese areas" of Shanghai could still purchase raw materials through the international market and sell finished products to Southeast Asia and the United States. At the same time, plenty of refugees were willing to work for low wages. By 1940 the boom was over. The Japanese imposed a tighter blockade around the "island," thus slowing its commercial traffic with the outside world. The price of staples shot up, and this, in turn, encouraged speculation and profiteering. Most people with some cash at hand could not resist the chance to make easy money. Ling Hai-hsia wrote in her memoir that a friend invested smartly and became a wealthy woman within a few months. Ku Ch'uan-chieh either was a stockbroker or played the market himself in those years, but he made no fortune.

Things became more complicated for the Chinese toward the end of 1939, when Wang Ching-wei, a national hero from the Republican revolution and one of Sun Yat-sen's most trusted lieutenants, decided to throw in his fortune with the Japanese. Those in Wang's coterie had also been ardent loyalists and powerful partisans within the Nationalist government. These men had been fighting the Manchus and the foreign imperialists since they were kids. Thus it confounded all common sense when Wang announced that the government he was putting together would be working with the Japanese to drive out the Westerners in China and to build "a new order in East Asia." If Wang and his advisors had not been zealous nationalists for so long, it would have been much easier for the Chinese to dismiss their sophistry. These men were not scoundrels. They had seen a lot of the world and thought a lot about China; they had proven their courage and worked on big problems. After the war was over, when Wang Ching-wei's men were put on trial (Wang himself had died in 1944), they claimed that they were reluctant collaborators, victims of Wang's relentless pressure and glib persuasion. When their defense failed, they faced life imprisonment or the firing squad with quiet dignity. Even their end added to their enigma.

Ku Ch'uan-chieh's patron, Yen Hui-yü, was a close friend of one of them. This man, Chou Fo-hai, before 1937 had been the minister of education of Kiangsu province and Chiang Kai-shek's minister of propaganda. He was second in command in Wang Ching-wei's pro-Japanese government. In 1924 and

1925, when Chou was the minister of education in Kiangsu, he and Yen saw each other nearly every day. Yen was also a godparent to Chou's oldest son. During the war, their relationship changed. Yen did not let Chou near his house. Chou, now minister of finance and minister of police, offered his old friend a fat position as general director of the central reserve bank. Yen refused. Chou then had Yen's house watched. Yen left for British Hong Kong in 1940. The Pacific war brought the Japanese to Hong Kong the next year, and Yen returned to Shanghai.

By the time Yen came back in 1941, the "solitary island" had also ceased to exist. The Japanese seized all the foreign-owned businesses. They tagged all the Westerners, except Germans, Italians, and Vichy French, with red armbands, and then gradually dispatched them to internment camps just outside Shanghai. Now the whole city was under Japanese control. Chinese industrialists and businessmen who had moved their operations to the foreign concessions in 1938 were forced into "cooperative partnership" with the Japanese either through a Japanese firm or through one of the puppet government's economic agencies. Yen Hui-yü had two factories in the French Concession, a cotton mill and a cigarette company called Ta-tung. In 1942, his cotton mill came under pressure to take on a Japanese partner, but when some members at a board meeting intimated that they were ready to accept such an arrangement, Yen got up and left, saying that he would never go along with it. After this incident he essentially gave up his interests in the company. The situation at Ta-tung Cigarette Company was somewhat different. He had founded the company in 1922. After its headquarters were destroyed at the start of the war, Yen relocated to the foreign concessions and built a new factory, which managed to stay in operation until 1943; but he relinquished most of his responsibilities after he returned from Hong Kong. In the last years of the war, Yen collected paintings and calligraphy, and opened a small antique store.

Ku Ch'uan-chieh, meanwhile, became a vice president in Ta-tung Cigarette Company after his own retailing business in Chinese medicine had folded. Yuan-ho remembers that when they were living in Shanghai her husband would go to Yen's house every day to pay his respects. Ku Ch'uan-chieh regarded Yen as his "teacher." Yen never taught in a school but he had many students who had either apprenticed with him through his businesses or had once been actors in his k'un-ch'ü troupe. Ku knew him in both worlds and so was especially close to him. In 1941, he and Yuan-ho moved next door to Yen, who let them use a villa an old friend had put under his care. "It was a quaint and comfortable place," Yuan-ho remembers. She and Ch'uan-chieh lived there until the end of the war.

Most people who had known him said that Yen Hui-yü was not a temperate man. During the war, he would eject from his house anyone who had ties with Wang Ching-wei's government, including old friends and favored students. It seems that Yen never had doubts about Ku Ch'uan-chieh and never lost his affection for him. Yet in those years, Ku and Yuan-ho often went to the house of Ch'u Min-i to sing *k'un-ch'ü*. Ch'u was a patron of the arts, and, in the early 1930s, a top official in the executive branch of the Nationalist government. (He was also the man who had accused Ch'ung-ho of being indecorous because she invited a professional actor to perform a principal part with her on the stage.) During the war, he worked with Wang Ching-wei, as his secretary of foreign affairs. A self-assured man and a known philanderer, Ch'u was the toast of society—of whatever society there was in Shanghai at the time—and was frequently photographed with Japanese visitors in Nanking and with his Japanese hosts in Tokyo. Given his own interest in *k'un-ch'ü*, Yen Hui-yü must have known about these gatherings at Ch'u Min-i's house, but he never went there and did not forbid Ku Ch'uan-chieh to go. Yen probably distinguished between those who did business with the collaborators and those who socialized with them after work. Ch'u was executed after the war.

Theaters were scarce during the war. Many were destroyed, and others had a hard time staying in business. After 1941, the Japanese, now in complete control of Shanghai, forced all of them to close down, together with foreign-published newpapers and major publishing houses. They viewed all cultural activities with suspicion. In the meantime, amateur *k'un-ch'ü* clubs continued to meet once or twice a week in small groups and then once a month in a more formal gathering with performances in the afternoon, followed by dinner and more singing. Professional actors were begging for work then. Twenty or thirty dollars a month could hire an actor to give weekly group lessons. Club members who took turn hosting the monthly gatherings all had to have some means: the house had to be large enough to hold forty or fifty guests, and the host had to be well-off enough to feed just as many. According to Yuan-ho, most of them were doctors, lawyers, bankers, and businessmen, along with their wives and sometimes their daughters, and the most lavish of such gatherings were at Ch'u Min-i's house.

This house had a theater with about a hundred seats, where Ch'u's friends could watch a private show. The singers, all amateurs, would ready themselves in full gear—costumes, headresses, and makeup—as they would if they were performing in a commercial theater. Because the event took place in a collaborator's house, one would like to imagine secrets being exchanged, deals cut, and confidences betrayed while the music was playing. This probably did not happen. They were there to sing *k'un-ch'ü*, Yuan-ho said, and the audience was there to listen: "It was no different from the past."

A city under occupation had it own rules and its own views about expediency. It tried to keep some sort of dignity, and life continued. People living under occupation could not easily be divided into the good and the bad, the constant and the duplicitous, the patriot and the collaborator. A man such as Yen Hui-yü could withdraw from the world and live by his principles because he could afford to. In his absence, others kept his factories running, and the businesses were still his. He had other advantages as well. While Yen may have offended an old friend like Chou Fo-hai, who was now working with the Japanese, and Chou may have retaliated and ordered the secret police to put a little pressure on him, that was as far as he would go. Because they were once friends, decorum had to be observed. So during the war, a collaborator like Chou may have ended up being Yen's most powerful protector.

Most people living under occupation, however, could not afford to have moral clarity. So what did they do? A shadowy publication from this period—a literary magazine, backed by the puppet government—offers some clues. The magazine, *Ku-chin*—"Past and Present"—ran fifty-seven issues, from March 1942 to October 1944, with about twelve essays per issue. Most of these essays are "occasional writings"; they imitate the style and tone of the seventeenth-century writers but without the freshness and genius one finds in the works of Chang Tai and Li Yü. Nevertheless, they reflect how the educated elite bided their time: what absorbed them and distracted them; what they remembered about life before the war; how they'd compare past and present, China and the West. The topics also included strange things people had heard and seen, rereadings of the classics and popular novels, and reflections on social practices and human relationships. The magazine emphasized that these writings were a miscellany: "that nothing is excluded, from the vast universe to the smallest birds and insects, from the most trifling of gossip to erudite studies of novels and dramas." Oddly, the Japanese do not figure in this medly, and politics is barely audible. These were awkward subjects for everyone, including Wang Ching-wei and his supportors, who contributed regularly to the magazine.

One author wrote on the virtues of lychee and red bayberries, what poets and scholars said about each. Another remembered "home cooking in Peking on hot summer days": five ways of preparing cold noodles and seven ways of cooking eggplants (braised with chopped pork or dried shrimp, sauteed with slivers of lamb or chives, layered with pork and then steamed, stuffed with pork and then fried, or roasted and then dressed with sesame butter and soy). Food was a popular subject. So were love and divorce, men and women: whether a woman should divorce and how a man should propose; men who were giants, men who were castrated, and men who were "afraid of their old ladies"; women with mustaches, women with considerable notoriety, women who died for love, and women who prostituted for a living. The magazine also revisits powerful men of the previous century, eccentrics from fifteen hundred years before, poets who had no restraint except for the discipline of their art, and opera performers and opera critics.

Some people believe that occasional writings are a veritable record, that both the light and jocular and the heavy and staid conceal a deeper truth about how people really feel about their government and who they think is worthy and who is not. "They catch the details of a generation," one critic contends, "and so must come close to the actual." These readers treat all miscellanies as social commentaries, so even an essay on Yang-chou pastries must be masking a complaint against the shortage of food. Yet an essay such as "Peking Home Cooking" cannot but convey the delight the author takes in thinking about the taste of eggplants when prepared this way or that. He wrote the piece during the worst period of the war, and it appears that he was still unwilling to give up his inclination for pleasure. The same could be said about those who were merely exercising exegesis or adding bits to the history of minutiae, and those who went to their weekly k'un-ch'ü practice and the monthly performance. There was still some panache left in occupied Shanghai.

Along with war and its effects, insouciance also set in. Yuan-ho did not work in those days. Her school in Haimen had been destroyed in a fire, and finding another teaching position would have been difficult because schools were few. Many disappeared and others merged to save space and cost. But Yuan-ho did not even look for work. She had a baby the year after she married—a girl with "beautiful hands and feet." The baby's father called her "Chüeh," which means "a pair of jade." Eighteen months later, Yuan-ho was pregnant again, but soon had a miscarriage. Her adoptive sister, Ling Hai-hsia, came to see her right away and left with the baby and the wet nurse. She said she wanted to help look after the baby while Yuan-ho was still recovering. Ling Hai-hsia never returned Chüeh to her parents. She even changed the baby's name from Ku Chüeh to Ling Hung, which meant that this child now belonged to the Ling family and Ling Hai-hsia. Ku Ch'uan-chieh was furious. Yuan-ho was upset only because of her daughter's new name. Otherwise, she later recalled, "I didn't care one way or another." Her mother-in-law told them to leave Ling Hai-hsia alone: "Let her have her way. Let her change your daughter's name. Someday your daughter is going to marry and have a different family anyway. What's in a name!" Ku Ch'uan-chieh was not assuaged by his mother's philosophizing. He insisted that Ling Hai-hsia had snatched their daughter from them.

This was not the first time Ling had snatched someone's daughter. Ku

Chüeh says that between her mother, Yuan-ho, and herself there was another girl. This girl lived with Ling until she was thirteen, at which point her own parents demanded that she come home. Ling was heartbroken when she finally let her go.

Yuan-ho never put her foot down regarding the fate of her daughter. She could have done so when she was leaving for Taiwan in 1949 with her family or when they first arrived on the island. She and her husband wrote to Ling Hai-hsai at one point, asking her to send their daughter across the strait. Then it was still possible to travel between Taiwan and the mainland. When Ling Hai-hsia stalled, Yuan-ho did not pursue it further. She also had another child, a son, the year after her daughter was taken from her. Her husband called him "Kuei," his "lump of dirt." Ku's "lump of dirt" was the object of Yuan-ho's affection. It is unclear whether this was because she had only this child to love or whether she preferred him from the start: "Once Ku Chüeh—she was called Ling Hung then—came to visit. Her brother pushed her, and Ling Hung said, 'I want to go home.' So you see, Ling Hai-hsia's home was *her* home. We all thought it was funny."

When the war was over, there was a brief euphoria. Yuan-ho saw her brothers and sisters again, and for a few weeks they camped out in her house and talked around the clock, filling in the six years they had missed. Then they all went their separate ways. Uncertainty returned in the next few years: this time the Chinese were fighting among themselves, the Nationalists against the Communists.

In early 1949, Yen Hui-yü was considering buying a stretch of reclaimed land and turning it into a dairy farm, a mulberry grove, and a *t'ung* tree plantation. He sent Ku Ch'uan-chieh to Haimen to look into its real estate. Ku stayed with Chi Fang, a relative of Ling Hai-hsia's family and a powerful military and political figure in that area. At the start of the war, Chi had organized his own peasant guerrillas, quite independent of the Nationalists and the Communists, and waged an effective resistance against the Japanese. When the Communists' New Fourth Army moved into this part of Kiangsu in 1940, he joined forces with them and placed himself under the Communist commander. Chi Fang was never a Communist Party member; he had his own political party, which people referred to as the "Third Party." But over the years, he worked with Communist activists, their party leaders, and their field commanders. From him, Ku Ch'uan-chieh learned about the discipline within the Communist army, and the rules and reasoning in that world. When he came home, he told Yuan-ho that they would have to move to Taiwan, and that if she was not going with him he intended to go alone.

Even now, Yuan-ho does not fully understand why her husband was so determined to leave. He said repeatedly that there were no moderates among the Communists. Does this mean that his worries about what the Communists might do to a person like him were so overwhelming that he was willing to risk a long and uncertain separation from his wife, the son he adored, and his mother? At the time Yuan-ho had no one to turn to. Yun-ho and Chao-ho were in Peking, which was already in the hands of the Communists. Ch'ung-ho was in America with her husband. And Yuan-ho was not seeing much of Ling Hai-hsia after Ling "abducted" her daughter. Finally a friend interceded. He told Ku Ch'uan-chieh that if he was going to Taiwan he had to take his whole family with him.

Ku had only a few days to organize the trip. The garrison commander of Shanghai, a friend, found tickets for them on a steamer. An ounce of gold a head. Ku bought six and left Shanghai with his wife, their son, his mother, their son's nurse-nanny, and Kao Kan-kan's granddaughter, who had been their household help for several years. Their daughter was still living with Ling Hai-hsia in Soochow, where the fighting made the roads impassable, but even if Ku Chüeh could have traveled to Shanghai to join her parents, Ling Hai-hsia would not have let her go.

Yuan-ho's steamer left Shanghai on May 18. Ten days later, the city fell to the Communists. Yuan-ho did not see her daughter until thirty-one years later, by which time both Ku Ch'uan-chieh and Ling Hai-hsia were dead. In fact, the two people closest to Yuan-ho died in the same year.

Ling Hai-hsia gave up her profession after her schools in Haimen closed. The war also muted her ambitions. For many years she simply lived on the money her brother sent her. After 1949, her brother also decided to retire. He had been an enterprising man, had made a lot of money as a banker and given a lot away to his family, friends, and home community. Communism was disagreeable to him, and he was too stubborn to concede and too tired to fight back. So he simply stopped working. When his resources ran out, his sister became desperate. She tried growing jasmine flowers at first. In Soochow one could only cultivate them in the suburb, several miles from the town center, and Ling Hai-hsia had to travel that distance nearly every day in the spring and early summer to tend her plants. Then, when the weather was mean and hot, the buds were ready to harvest. To catch the buds while they were still pale and tight and right for tea, Ling Hai-hsia would work day and night under the most wretched conditions.

After a few years she gave it up. For the next twelve years, she raised laboratory mice for a living, hundreds of them. "I don't know what happened to me after the Japanese were through with us," she wrote just before she died. "I lost my fighting spirit. I lost my resolve." She continued: "I have bid farewell to my parents, but they can still visit me in my dreams. What pains me and infuriates me is that I can never bring back the career I have worked so hard to build."

Yuan-ho's regrets were linked to her husband's. After they moved to Taiwan, Ku Ch'uan-chieh tried to get things going on his own. His patron, Yen Hui-yü, stayed on the mainland, and like Ling Hai-hsia's brother, he chose to do nothing. The Communist government collectivized his farms. None of his plans could go forward. So he donated his considerable art collection to the Chen-chiang and Nanking Museum and went back to his reclusion. Meanwhile, Ku was having his own troubles in Taiwan. He could not get anything off the ground and accumulated a lot of debts. Opera specialists approached him, hoping that he would help them to revive k'un-ch'ü in Taiwan, but he let their interest lapse and continued to brood about his next project. A mushroom farm, he thought, or a beer with his own label.

Ku Ch'uan-chieh did not give another performance on the stage. Yuan-ho says that he simply could not be persuaded. In their modest house in Taichung, he would occasionally sing the part of a tragic hero, with only Yuan-ho listening. Early in 1966, Ku fell ill with hepatitis, and it did not seem that he would recover. By April, he was gone.

After her husband died, Yuan-ho began to perform in the amateur theater again. Once she played Emperor Ming-huang from *The Palace of Eternal Life,* in a scene in which the emperor is forced to have his concubine, Jade Bracelet, commit suicide. The scene ends with Jade Bracelet's burial—her body, wrapped in silk, is placed in a shallow grave. Years later, Yuan-ho mused at the irony of her situation that night: "The jade I buried was not Jade Bracelet but Ku Ch'uan-chieh." *Chieh* means "jade," and Ku Ch'uan-chieh was jade because of his talent and what he was to her. It was appropriate that Yuan-ho buried him onstage.

Chapter 11

YUN-HO

Yun-ho (*left*), with Yuan-ho, when she was a college student in Shanghai.

WHEN SHE WAS A CHILD, Yun-ho did not like love scenes in an opera, or scenes with sensitive young men. They put her to sleep. She preferred extreme characters, men who were violently brave and fiercely upright. The warrior Lord Kuan was her favorite.

In the Chinese imagination, everything about Lord Kuan was godlike—his appearance, his character, and his accomplishments. A protracted civil war at the end of the Han dynasty gave him a chance to be great; the storytellers filled in the rest. One account from the sixteenth century described him as "nine feet tall, with a long two-foot beard, and a face [red as] jujube. His lips are like painted rouge, with cinnabar phoenix eyes, and reclining silkworm brows."

Yun-ho, at the age of five or six, was not afraid of Lord Kuan's red face and long beard. They might have seemed strange and exaggerated, but it was a countenance so stern and forceful that it permitted no injustice or duplicity. One poet wrote: "His manly spirits had power like wind or thunder; / His glowing purpose shone like sun or moon." It was this aspect of Lord Kuan that impressed Yun-ho. She also liked the mood of a drama with him in it, which was always religious and dignified because he was a god. The scene she loved best opens with the night after Lord Kuan was beheaded in the town of Mai. The vapor from Lord Kuan's soul "remained undissolved, floating attenuated until it came to rest on Jade Springs Hill in Tangyang county, Ching-men-chou." Yun-ho remembers the smell and sight of burning incense permeating the stage—Lord Kuan's "undissolved soul." "It was mysterious and full of foreboding," she says.

The novel that inspired the opera continues:

On the hill lived an old monk whose Buddhist name was P'u-ching, or "Universal Purity." He was the abbot of Cheng-kuo Temple at the Ssu River pass. In his jaunts through the realm, he had come to the mountain, and, attracted by its charmed scenery, had built himself a thatched shelter there. In this hermitage he would seat himself for meditation each day, searching for the truth of life. Besides himself was a single novice; they lived on the food they begged.

The night Lord Kuan died, the moon glowed pale and a breeze blew cool and fresh. Some time after the third watch, as the monk was sitting in meditation, a voice called out, "Return my head." P'u-ching scrutinized the air. A man was riding the steed Red Hare and brandishing the sword Green Dragon. Two men were in his train, a general of fair complexion and a swarthy man with curling whiskers. Together the three alighted from a cloud onto the summit of Jade Springs Hill. P'u-ching realized that it was Lord Kuan and struck the door with a deer-tail whisk for protection against the spirit.

Lord Kuan appeals to the abbot: "I have met with calamity and am now dead. Please teach me how to find redemption. Show me a way out of this wandering in darkness." The abbot says to him: "Yesterday's wrong is today's right, so there is no point arguing about right and wrong. Yet one thing is always true: every consequence has a cause. Now you cry out for your head, having been cut down by Lu Meng. But what about Yan Liang, Wen Ch'ou, Ts'ao Ts'ao's six pass guards, and all those you have killed? From whom shall they seek their heads?" Suddenly Lord Kuan understood, not only about himself and his circumstances, but also the inevitability of Buddha's law—they were all clear. "He bowed his head in submission and departed. From time to time, he manifested himself as a divine sage on Jade Springs Hill, to give protection to the people there. To repay his kindness, the local dwellers built a temple on the summit and made offerings to him each season."

Yun-ho believes that she was born with Lord Kuan's extreme temperament but not his ability for self-scrutiny and self-effacement. When she talked back to her tutors as a child, or slapped her younger sister for resisting her bullying, she never felt the slightest remorse, she says. Why should she, if she could get her way, as she nearly always did with her nurse-nanny as her tireless defender? Tou Kan-kan was as unreasonable as she and just as vocal. They were an irrepressible team, Yun-ho thought.

Yun-ho attributes her nature to the circumstances of her birth. It was her fighting spirit that allowed her to live at all, so, she figured, why not thrive on it? When her tutor, the amiable Miss Wan, first tried to teach her to read, she put up a struggle. Miss Wan was only ten years older than she, so still a young girl in Yun-ho's eyes, and of the ten characters this teacher introduced to her, she already recognized eight. Yun-ho's behavior in the classroom at the age of six even made her nurse-nanny anxious. Tou Kan-kan would sit next to her and act as the mediator: "The character is *ch'ai* [hairpin]," she would repeat after the teacher, hoping that Yun-ho would be more willing to yield to Miss Wan's instruction if she, her nurse-nanny, had done it first. It would take several bouts of tantrum before Yun-ho gave in to the idea of learning from someone who was too young and tender to have authority.

Five years later, the situation was reversed. Her sister Ch'ung-ho had come home to Soochow for a few weeks to be with her family. Their mother assigned Yun-ho to be Ch'ung-ho's "little teacher." "I was four years older," Yun-ho explains, "and my two other sisters, Yuan-ho and Chao-ho, each already had a younger brother as their student." This was in 1920, the year the Chang family had gone full-force to teach their nurse-nannies to read. Yun-ho writes:

Mom also bought us blue cotton cloth, asking each of us to sew a book bag for the student we were responsible for and to give the student a formal name, a name appropriate for school. We older sisters were terribly excited about this, and we all pandered to our students because we wanted so much to be liked. I believe I was the most eager, yet my student was the most difficult to handle.

Although Ch'ung-ho was only seven, back in Hofei she had two older scholars to teach her to read classical texts. Her knowledge of classical

Chinese was not in any way less than that of her three older sisters. But we knew who Hu Shih was, and she didn't. And we had more exposure to modern Chinese literature than she did. All this gave me more confidence. On the matter of her name, after much thought, I decided to call her Wang Chüeh-wu, therefore changing not only her given name but her surname as well. I was so pleased with my ingenuity that I carefully embroidered the three characters, *wang, chüeh,* and *wu,* on her blue book bag with pink thread.

My little fourth sister was not impressed. One day, she suddenly asked me, "Why did you change my name to Chüeh-wu?" I explained, "After experiencing enlightenment [*chüeh-wu*], a person is awakened, which means that everything is clear to her, and she understands everything." She pressed on, "Tell me, then, what do I understand?" I hemmed and hawed, and, trying to give her a response that sounded serious and correct, I said, "Now that we live in a new world, we are all beginning to understand the importance of reason. We also understand that we need science and democracy to save China." She shook her head and wouldn't let me go. "Let's say that the name you gave me makes sense even though it doesn't. I have another question for you, you who claim to understand reason so well. Why did you change my surname? My name is Chang, not Wang. *Wang* means 'king.' Kings are no different from bandits, thus the saying, 'If you succeed, then you are a king. If you fail, then you are a bandit.' Are you suggesting that bandits are enlightened? What an absurd name you have chosen for me! I don't care for it." My little sister was relentless. She curled her lip and dealt me the final blow: "*You* consider yourself a teacher, but you don't even know how to choose a proper name for your student. Ha!" Her mockery made me furious, but I could not hit her or scold her. So I said, "Give me back your school bag! I won't be your teacher anymore." Holding a pair of scissors, I then proceeded to take out the characters on her bag, one by one. It was a tearful trial. The word *wang* was easy to get rid of. *Wu* was more complicated but still manageable. *Chüeh* was a different story—it had twenty-one strokes!

Ch'ung-ho was a rare guest in her own family's home, a novelty. Her presence was so desired that even a natural bully like Yun-ho was willing to take her verbal blow and quietly undo her own blunder. The three older sisters insist that Ch'ung-ho's infrequent appearance was not the only reason she was so popular. They claim that they were in awe of their little sister. Even though she spoke a provincial dialect and was not dressed as smartly as they were, in their hearts they knew that she was cleverer and more capable. "At her young age, Ch'ung-ho had already begun studying the techniques of calligraphy, copying in free-hand the works of the former masters," Yun-ho said. "The few characters she wrote for us had caught something of the original, the spirit, maybe, or the intent."

So it was out of respect for Ch'ung-ho that Yun-ho refrained from making a show of her displeasure. In her behavior toward her other younger sister, she observed no limits. Yun-ho could be nasty even when Chao-ho was most vulnerable. If Yun-ho had just finished potted chicken and smoked ham for breakfast (her nurse-nanny liked to indulge her), and knew that Chao-ho had only rice congee and pickled cowpeas in her bowl, she would insist on taking a look, to see what was there.

Even now, at ninety-one, Yun-ho is the provocateur. She and Chao-ho are liveliest when they jest. When they were children, however, one would strike and the other would run or take her hurt silently. Their mother was aware of this situation. If she gave Yun-ho a scolding, Yun-ho would pace back and forth in the corridor, ranting and complaining that she had been wronged. She would cause so much unease in the household that in the end even her mother gave up reproving her. Lu Ying used to say, "This Erh-mao-tzu,* it's impossible to discipline her. Lao Tou [Tou Kan-kan] is always protecting her. There is nothing I can do."

Yun-ho loved her father, but she believed her mother to be perfect. Lu Ying was open-eyed and openhanded, easy of manner yet regal and roc-like. Yet even such a parent could not manage her. It was not until much later that Yun-ho learned to put her unruly spirit to good use. The change began with her mother's death. The shock of Lu Ying's absence reined her in. Life also became heavier because her older sister, Yuan-ho, would soon leave for boarding school, giving her the responsibilities of the oldest child.

But Yun-ho's change was not simply the result of circumstances. There was much about her that had been concealed when she was younger and her willfulness was indulged. It was hard, then, to see that she loved strongly and that changes affected her strongly. Of all the sisters, she is most attached to the past; her memories of that past are also keenest. So even when her energy ran rampant, she picked up many things along the way: menacing portents, despairing glances, the shape of yearning, the sight of the good, the sounds of death and blight, the joys of childhood recreation. It would take her a few more years to

---

*Erh-mao-tzu means "Second Kitten." Lu Ying and her husband called their children by their diminutives. Daughters were kittens (mao-tzu). Sons were puppies (kou-tzu).

sort out what they all meant, and to apportion their degrees of importance, but all her life she was interested in these moments and concerned with the consequences they might have on human life. Yun-ho regarded herself as a quester and a blunderer, someone easily fired up by the presence of injustice. She was not impartial and did not always play a fair game, as she readily admitted. In this way she was kindred to Lord Kuan.

Lord Kuan possessed a hero's sense of justice, which was decidedly inferior to that of a philosopher or a monastic man. The abbot of Cheng-kuo Temple pointed out the difference between the two, the night Lord Kuan descended on Jade Springs Hill to ask for his head back. The old warrior thought that since he had never failed to risk his life, fighting for a righteous cause, it was only fair that his body be made whole again after he died. The monk replied that if Lord Kuan was appealing for cosmic justice, what about all those men he slew on his quest: "From whom shall they seek their heads?" This is a problem with heroes. They are insensitive when on the job and mere scrappers in Heaven's eyes. They can be insular despite their magnanimity. So even after people have benefited from the hero's service, not all are grateful.

Born a "petulant little thing," Yun-ho was endowed with the hero's sensibility. But she was also "scrawny," physically unfit for heroic feats. Girls in Chinese society were usually compared to flowers—lily, lotus, morning glory. Friends of the Chang family thought that Yun-ho looked like a slip of chive, which did not amuse her. When she was older, they were more tactful. They likened her to Lin Tai-yü, a principal character in the eighteenth-century novel *Story of the Stone*. This was even more insulting, as Lin Tai-yü was a bad-tempered and consumptive youth. In the aftermath of the New Culture movement, the ideal beauty was someone healthy and strong, a woman fed on milk and optimism.

Yun-ho compensated for her physical deficiencies with sheer audacity. Early training in *k'un-ch'ü* prepared her to be unafraid: "I was not afraid of performing in front of hundreds of people and of making mistakes in front of hundreds of people." When she was in middle school, Yun-ho was also good at public speaking, and even better at confronting the opposition in public. Her first major opponent was her stepmother. In Yun-ho's memory, the new parent was so jealous of their mother that she was determined to wipe every trace of her and everything their mother had cherished from their lives. A child's eyes "should never forget the countenace of his deceased parents, nor his ears their voices," one early ritual text says, "and his heart should always remember their small pleasures and deepest yearnings." Yun-ho, even at a very young age, realized this. She also realized that just as the dead relied on the living to hold them back from eternity and the void, we, the living, could not exist without them—"we for whom grief is so often the source of our growth."* So when her stepmother tried to repress her grief, she rebelled.

Yun-ho was sensitive to repression. When her stepmother first moved in, the relationship between them was so explosive that at times she had to retreat to a grandaunt's house to defuse. Finally it was this elderly woman who helped turn Yun-ho around. She said to her: "Why destroy yourself? Why let yourself become so upset that you have a breakdown? What would that accomplish?"

Although Yun-ho was compared to Tai-yü in *Story of the Stone,* and she learned the role of Li-niang from *The Peony Pavilion* as a child, her life was not like theirs. Emotions consumed Tai-yü and Li-niang, and they died young. They were examples of unbridled passions—an antidote, perhaps, to forced reason and an inhuman order, but only as a last solution because these women had nowhere else to go.

When Yun-ho and her sisters were younger, their lives, like those of Tai-yü and Li-niang, were also enclosed and guarded. A gatekeeper kept an eye on them whenever they played in the garden. They slipped out a few times to buy snacks from the vendors. Once, while they were still living in Shanghai, after Yun-ho and Chao-ho had gotten out, Yuan-ho shut the gate behind them and locked it. "We screamed, begging our sister to open it for us," Yun-ho recalled. "The girls living down the lane swore at us from their upstairs window in Shanghai dialect, which we didn't understand. The louder they shouted, the harder we banged on the gate. Finally Yuan-ho appeared, and the three of us returned their insult, calling them *hsiao-wu-tzu,* and then quickly shut the gate tight." *Hsiao-wu-tzu* was the worst slight they could come up with; it meant "little girl servants" in Shanghai dialect. The gatekeeper dutifully reported this to their mother, and they were all punished. Lu Ying and Wu-ling absolutely forbade their children to call people names, but what their daughters did that day was worse: "To call the girls outside 'little servants' implied that we were young ladies. Our parents considered this very bad." Yun-ho remembered being shut up in the back room. It was miserable but not as terrifying as being out in the street with the gate shut behind you and strangers, albeit girls of your own age, mocking you in a foreign tongue. Later she thought her sequestered life in

---

*Rilke, "First Duino Elegy," Mitchell's translation, p. 155. Rilke, of course, believes that the dead do not need us to hold them back. In the elegy, he says: "In the end, those who were carried off early no longer need us: / They are weaned from earth's sorrows and joys, as gently as children / outgrow the soft breasts of their mothers." In another poem, he writes: "I have my dead, and I have let them go, / and was amazed to see them so contented, / so soon at home in being dead, so cheerful, / so unlike their reputation." ("Requiem for a Friend," Mitchell's translation, p. 73.)

Soochow was paradise, but it lasted only as long as her mother was alive. After Lu Ying died, everything had to change. Her father's school helped her to make the transition.

At Le-i, Yun-ho was fascinated by concepts in geometry and mathematical reasoning. She also put to use "her quick eye and deft hand," her tireless energy and knack for argument. The school also introduced her to philosophy and biology, intramural sports and contemporary politics, subjects that distracted her from her unhappiness. This was the advantage a twentieth-century gentry girl had over her predecessors, especially if she was fortunate to have a parent as liberal and sympathetic as Chang Wu-ling. Her favorite teacher was her geometry teacher, a Mr. Chou:

> Mr. Chou had two children. Both had died some time ago. Every Sunday he would ask me over for lunch. I was not well-behaved. I ate very little— could hardly finish even half a bowl of rice. Instead of concentrating on my meal, I would talk and talk. Once my teacher suddenly put down his chopsticks and said to me, "Little girl, if you don't eat your food, you are going to vanish." I still remember his words, spoken in Chiang-yin dialect. The dish I loved best at his house was lake shrimps. In the summer, I often saw Mr. Chou walking along May Thirtieth Avenue. I didn't like the burning sun, so I would trail in his shadow. His robe cast a long one, completely enfolding me in it.

Yun-ho could be impetuous even with Mr. Chou. Once she tore up her geometry test in front of him because she did not receive a perfect score. Mr. Chou responded with calm and reason, something she remembers well, even after seventy-five years. It was men and women like Mr. Chou and her parents that impressed Yun-ho most. They possessed the strength of yielding and a natural gift for finding what will suffice, something Yun-ho herself was not born with and had to learn with arduous effort.

Whatever Yun-ho lacked, she tried to make up for with virtues she had in abundance, and the results were often remarkable. When their stepmother refused to let Yuan-ho return to Ta-hsia University a second year because the tuition there was too high, Yun-ho stood at the gate of Le-i, where the stepmother was school principal, telling all the students to boycott classes. Yun-ho contended that if their school principal was unwilling to support her own stepdaughter through school, then it was pointless for Le-i students to attend classes. Her solitary crusade caused the Changs so much embarrassment that the clan elders decided to raise enough money from land rent to see Yuan-ho through graduation. Probably it was because of this incident that Wu-ling's children all managed to finish their college education without the threat of another financial crisis.

Yun-ho and her sisters Yuan-ho and Chao-ho all attended private colleges in Shanghai, and before that, boarding schools in Nanking. Private institutions charged much more than public ones, sometimes twice as much, anywhere from 350 to 450 silver dollars a year. Many of these institutions were created impulsively, often as the result of a split between the administrators and a group of faculty and students at a school. The disagreement might have been about how to restructure the curriculum or whether their school should take a political stand, especially after a major national incident. In the case of missionary universities, the disputes usually reflected the tension between China and the West in the larger world. Yuan-ho and Yun-ho's alma maters, Ta-hsia and Kuang-hua, were founded this way in the 1920s. Chao-ho's school, China College, was ten years older. A group of overseas Chinese students, returning to Shanghai from Japan, started this school in protest against Japanese treatment of the Chinese students in Japan. The wealthy gentry helped such schools at first with permanent endowments and private contributions, but when their funding slowed, private colleges depended more and more on student tuition and fees as the main source of income.

In the 1920s and 1930s, only the wealthy could afford to send their children to private colleges. Chang Wu-ling had three daughters in such places. The family probably felt some financial pinch, but not enough to alter the way Wu-ling lived his life. He did not cut back his support of Le-i; his household staff did not shrink substantially; and he continued to visit Shanghai just for its operas and books, often staying in hotels for weeks at a time. If Wu-ling could afford his daughters' private education, why was his wife reluctant to go along? It is possible that Wei Chün-i was skeptical about the merits of such an education in Shanghai. Many children of the well-to-do went to private colleges just to obtain a credential—in other words, to procure respectability. It was not difficult to get in and not too strenuous to get by since most of these schools were desperate for students and eager to keep them there. For recreation in Shanghai, one could go to the theater, the dance hall, a night club, or an entertainment center, not to mention the seedier places for the more adventurous. Yun-ho remembered how some of the Kuang-hua students passed their time:

> They partied every Saturday night. Often the male and female students would pair up and spend a night in a hotel. Most of them had attended missionary schools before coming to Kuang-hua, St. Mary and McTyeire,

for instance. They were used to wealth and comfort and speaking English. The women wore loud-color dresses and spiky heels. Every day, they looked like they were going to a banquet or a wedding. So how could they be interested in their schoolwork?

Yun-ho scoffed at these women and also at the jocks. She despised their snobbery and their posturing. She was one of the few students who had graduated from a Chinese middle school outside of Shanghai. Nevertheless, the women students elected her their representative to the student council.

Yun-ho had transferred to Kuang-hua from China College in her second year. She had begun China College at the same time as her younger sister Chao-ho. She probably moved to Kuang-hua so they could give each other room. But even as a freshman at China College, Yun-ho plunged into student politics and was known among her classmates for her firm views and irrepressible voice. She spared no chauvinists or bombasters, and was equally contemptuous of the vapid and spineless, men or women. She was able to contain her tantrums by this time because she was older, but Yun-ho did not modify her behavior significantly. Anger did not make her ill anymore, and she had sharpened her debating skills. These were about the only improvements she had made.

In her first year of college, she wrote an essay called "When Flowers Shed Their Petals." The title was assigned, not her choice. The subject was all too familiar; whatever one tried to say would sound like this: The autumnal wind scatters the flower petals and brings about a melancholy in the air. Yun-ho did not write about melancholy: "I said that the best time of the year is when flowers lose their petals. The sky is clear, and the air is crisp. It is a maturing season, a time for harvest, and also the best time for young people to plunge into their studies. Spring and autumn lament is the business of a dejected woman in her boudoir. I grew up in an enlightened age and always considered myself a woman of the May Fourth generation. So why should I have sorrow and regrets?" The next year, after she had transferred to Kuang-hua, Yun-ho won a speechmaking contest. She employed the same upbeat rhetoric, urging her classmates to "arrest the present" and make good of it. Now Yun-ho says her words were high-handed and absurd. She heartened others to take the difficult path in life when she herself was just as much a slacker as they were.

It was around this time that Yun-ho fell in love. She had always felt uneasy about women who were so intent on falling in love while they were in college that they were either too quick to settle down, or else too casual in their relationships with men. She had known Chou Yu-kuang, her future husband, since she was sixteen: she and Yu-kuang's sister were classmates at Le-i and saw each other's family often. Then Yun-ho went off to boarding school in Nanking, and Yu-kuang, who was five years older, was attending college in Shanghai. It was not until Yun-ho herself was in college that Yu-kuang renewed their friendship. He was cautious at first and discreet. This was his manner, which suited Yun-ho well. Yun-ho probably knew early on that this was the man she was going to marry. He was patient and gentlemanly—someone she could respect and strong enough to check her excesses. They could have married earlier, but she chose not to.

Yun-ho's college education was interrupted twice. A fire in the women's dormitory at Kuang-hua suspended classes for a while, and the bombing of Shanghai by the Japanese in January 1932 forced her to transfer to a college in Hangchow for a semester. It took Yun-ho four and a half years to get her degree in history. She insisted on finishing because, she said, she did not want to disappoint her parents. Her father believed that a woman should have economic independence, which only a proper education and a proper profession could allow. Her mother's influence was more distant and more difficult to assign.

Yun-ho and her sisters remember a song their mother used to sing about a woman called Yang Pa-chieh, who met the emperor by chance on his travels to the south. The emperor asked her to be his wife, and she said she would consider it if he met her ten conditions. Her list began with objects: pearl-sewn shirts and robes embroidered with gold and silver threads; bolts of silk, "stretching from Nanking to Peking"; and a golden bowl. Then her demands became more outrageous and finally unattainable: "a pair of stars from the night sky," "celestial cranes to take part in the wedding rites," and "a phoenix to receive the imperial bride." The hubris so offended the emperor that he declared Yang Pa-chieh unmarriageable. "Tens of thousands of strings of cash could not win her heart," he says.*

Yun-ho did not think that Yang Pa-chieh was "unmarriageable": "She'd marry when she wanted to and to the man she wanted to marry." The idea is old, Yun-ho insists, ennobled in the "feudal tradition" and expressed as female virtue in fiction. "We four sisters were all influenced by operas, which the Chinese now characterize as 'feudal' and 'reactionary.' And because our judgment and our principles are rooted in that feudal world, we dare even to spit on the emperor."

Just before their wedding, Yu-kuang wrote to Yun-ho, telling her his misgivings. He was afraid that "he could not provide her happiness because he was so poor." Yun-ho responded with a ten-page letter, which boiled down to one thought: "Happiness is what we create ourselves." Yun-ho was the first among her siblings to marry. Her father gave her two thousand silver dollars as dowry. It was

---

*The Yang Pa-chieh in this song is not Yang Chia-chiang, the famous woman warrior from the southern Sung dynasty, who was called by the same nickname.

a fluke that Yun-ho got anything at all. A relative working in the local bank unexpectedly found twenty thousand dollars sitting in one of Wu-ling's accounts. Wu-ling had either forgotten about this account or kept no record of it.

The nurse-nannies in the family sent nativity information about the new couple to a fortune-teller, who predicted that Yun-ho and Yu-kuang would die before they reached thirty-five. The wedding went ahead anyway. More than two hundred guests were invited. The bridegroom was in tuxedo and black tie, the bride in a white gown. Ch'ung-ho sang an aria from "A Fine Occasion." After the ceremony, Yu-kuang asked Yun-ho whether her sister understood what she was singing. The song was about lovemaking: "Oblivious of her tumbling hair and pins awry, she slants her head / While he, oblivious of the cold on unclad limbs, stirs up the bedclothes in a storm."

In the winter of 1932, just months before Yun-ho married Chou Yu-kuang, a high school classmate came to see her in Shanghai. This woman, Tai Chieh, told Yun-ho that she was ill. She said, her belly was full of parasites. It did not take long for Yun-ho to figure out that Tai Chieh was with child; in fact, she was already six months pregnant. Tai Chieh wanted an abortion. Yun-ho advised her against it, saying that it would kill her along with the baby.

An unmarried woman with child in 1930s China would have been completely alone. Her family would not want her back, and she probably would not seek refuge with them anyway. Her transgression would be thought to reflect on her upbringing, and so she would do everything possible to avoid implicating her parents. If she went home, her parents would have to discipline her severely. Relatives and neighbors would not allow them to be lenient even if they wanted to. Therefore, such a woman would hide somewhere for as long as she could. Her prospects were dark.

Yun-ho offered Tai Chieh a place to stay until the baby was born. She hoped that this would buy them some time to think what to do next. That winter, Tai Chieh lived with Yun-ho's family on Chiu-ju Lane, next to the Le-i campus. But once Yun-ho married and moved to a place of her own, she put her friend in a small space behind the bedroom she shared with her husband. This nearly ruined her marriage. "Who has ever heard of such a thing?" she says. "A pregnant, unmarried woman hiding in the newlyweds' back room. We were setting ourselves up for mockery. The old lady next door just couldn't keep her mouth shut. She said to my mother-in-law, 'What is the matter with your new daughter-in-law? She takes in an unwedded woman with a bastard child in her belly. Is she as loose as that woman?'"

Yun-ho's mother-in-law was not happy. Yu-kuang was her only son, and his wife had managed to embarrass all of them even before the couple settled down to their new life. Yu-kuang also had a rough time. He found both women difficult to handle, and himself in a moral predicament. To drive Tai Chieh out of their house in her condition was wrong, but to let her stay and be the source of his mother's anxiety was also wrong. And then there was the problem of his sisters.

Sometime before, Yu-kuang's father had evicted his wife, four daughters, and Yu-kuang from their home because they made it inconvenient for him to live with his concubine in the way he preferred. For years, the six of them struggled to survive. His sisters were capable women. They looked after their mother and put Yu-kuang through college. Now, his sense of obligation brought him under their influence. On the matter of Tai Chieh, they sided with their mother and put pressure on Yun-ho. Chao-ho later observed: "What they didn't understand was that my second sister could never be forced to do anything she didn't want to do. In fact, the more pressure you put on her the harder she resists and the more likely that she will do something completely inconceivable."

After Tai Chieh's baby girl was born, Yun-ho tried "something completely inconceivable"—and reckless:

On July 20 [1933], Tai Chieh and I took her daughter and a wicker suitcase, packed with baby clothes, and rode the train to Hangchow, where the baby's father's family had been living. After we arrived, we checked into a hotel, using false names. The next morning, we fed the baby and placed a note under a pillow. The note was addressed to the baby's grandmother. We then changed our clothes from cheongsam to Western-style dresses, left the hotel, and got on a train bound for Shanghai.

On July 22, the people of Hangchow read in their local papers that two mysterious women had stepped into a hotel, abandoned a baby in their room, and vanished. The baby's grandmother refused to acknowledge that the child was her family's and so placed her in an orphange. For the first few years, a family friend who was studying in Hangchow would go to the orphanage and look the child up, but when the war came, those who knew about her lost touch, and she disappeared.

Yun-ho's act of chivalry exacted a price from her marriage and her relationship with her husband's family. Chao-ho and Ch'ung-ho have both said this, though neither implied that Yun-ho should not have done it. These two sisters knew Tai Chieh well. She had spent a lot of time in their parents' house, often standing in front of a bookshelf in the library, reading through the dynastic histories in their father's collection. Tai Chieh was smart and unusual: a fierce intellect and a tireless romantic. She came from a prominent family in Szechwan, with two good scholars as brothers. When she was fifteen, she ran away with the young man she was in love with at the time. On their flight to the southeast, they encountered sinister people and stayed in shady establishments. Once they found a corpse under their bed. When they reached Nanking, her young man died. She buried him and enrolled in a boarding school. It was in this school that she met Yun-ho and Chao-ho. Just who supported her through school is a mystery. Her parents could not have sent her the money; a normal relationship with your daughter was not possible after she had slipped away with a man and spent many nights with him on the road. Her brothers could have been giving her money secretly. The siblings saw a lot of each other during the war and may have been in contact all along.

After high school, Tai Chieh studied biology in Chung-shan University in Canton. On a field trip to Hainan Island, she fell for a classmate and conceived their baby under a waterfall. It was this baby she and Yun-ho left in Hangchow. Tai Chieh was impulsive and she fell in love easily, but she was not at all like the women Yun-ho belittled. She did not wear high heels and fashionable clothes, and in her own eyes, she did not sleep with men casually. She was a slightly bizarre romantic heroine. Her life did not end when her lover died. She did not wallow in self-pity when a second lover abandoned her, pregnant with his child. She did not even have the looks one would expect from a romantic heroine. Short and stocky and quite "unlovely" was how people described her. When her life was bleakest, she said that she could not even sell sex because she lacked physical allure. During the war, she became a top researcher in Szechwan's silk industry. Later, she married one of her junior colleagues—"a handsome and agreeable man"—and had three children with him.

Yun-ho had her first child exactly a year after she was married. She used to tell people that her son, Hsiao-p'ing, was born on her wedding day—a blunder it took her some time to recognize. Her daughter, Hsiao-ho, arrived the next year. Three more pregnancies followed. One ended in abortion; one baby was too small to survive; the next baby probably caught an infection during childbirth—he lived only twenty days.

Chao-ho says that Yun-ho had not lived a peaceful day since she was twelve. First, their mother died; then a stepmother moved in; then, after Yun-ho married, she had to share her family life with a mother-in-law and four sisters-in-law. Yun-ho sees things differently. Tension in personal relationships, she believes, can never bring about the sort of hell created by wars and a tyrant's ideological demands. The first stage of her hell, she says, began in August 1937, on the eve of the Japanese occupation of China. From that month until the end of the war, she made at least "ten major moves and twenty small moves." She started her journey with twenty pieces of luggage and seven people—two children, two nan-nies, her husband, her mother-in-law, and herself—and came home with five pieces of luggage and four people. She had lost a daughter and a nanny to illness; the second nanny had decided to settle down with a man in Szechwan.

The first stretch of her flight took her back to her birthplace in Hofei. Her stay was brief. When the Japanese planes came, Yun-ho moved her children and mother-in-law to Hofei's west suburb, to her ancestral home at the base of Chou-kung Mountain. A hundred years before, at the time of the Taiping and Nien conflicts, her great-grandfather and his brothers had turned an old family dugout into a military stronghold. They used the surrounding streams as a nat-ural buffer, and then encircled the living quarters with earthen walls. Apertures were set within the walls for firing. In 1937, the fortification stood much the way it always had and so still gave the appearance that it was safer than the world outside. The Japanese bombardiers could have flattened it in a matter of minutes, but it was not likely that they would waste their ammunition and fuel on the Anhwei countryside.

Just as Yun-ho and her children were settling into a new rhythm in West Hofei, Yu-kuang sent a telegram from Shanghai, asking them to leave for Wuhan and from there to continue to Szechwan, where he would join them. He had decided to make his way to Chungking with colleagues at the bank where he was employed. A friend of the Changs sent a truck to pick up Yu-kuang's family. Yun-ho said good-bye to her father, who had also moved back to Hofei. This was the last time she saw him.

From Wuhan, Yun-ho went upstream on a boat to Chungking. Fifty years earlier, her grandfather had made the same journey with her father, the eight-month-old Wu-ling, to take up his duties as circuit intendant of the Pa region in Szechwan. Yun-ho's boat also carried Tseng Kuo-fan's granddaughter. In the 1860s, Tseng Kuo-fan and Yun-ho's great-grandfather Chang Shu-sheng had been commanders of the imperial army; together they had helped to defeat the Taiping rebels. Now their descendants were refugees.

The boat reached Chungking after ten days. It was nearing the end of 1937, a year Yun-ho calls the longest and the most taxing in her life. This, however, was only the beginning of her peregrinations. When Chang Wu-ling put "legs" on his daughters' names, he probably did not realize that they would be on the road all the time.* From Chungking, Yun-ho and her family took a smaller boat.

---

*The first characters in the names Yuan-ho, Yun-ho, Chao-ho, and Ch'ung-ho all share the same radical, *jen*. *Jen* means a human being. In certain contexts, it also can mean "a person walking," and it looks like two legs.

They traveled thirty miles north on a Yangtze tributary to Ho-ch'uan. Her friend Tai Chieh was working there and was willing to look after Yun-ho's children and mother-in-law while Yun-ho went on to Ch'eng-tu to take up a teaching position in Kuang-hua Middle School. Ch'eng-tu was a long distance away, two days and a night by truck to Chungking. No railway connected the two cities then, and the roads were too dangerous for most buses to pass down. The arrangement was impractical, but Yun-ho felt that she had to work and put her skills to use.

By the next spring, her husband had arrived in Szechwan and was employed in Chungking. Yun-ho moved her son and mother-in-law to the Chungking countryside while she and her daughter lived in the city with him. Air raids were common, and Yu-kuang was often away on business. So Yun-ho was left to solve "every conceivable problem" alone: "When there was no water or food, I walked every corner of the city to find it, sometimes in total darkness." She came to know the meaning of "deadly stillness" and the smell of charred air; she saw brains and guts smeared across the road and coffins piled up taller than a man. But she was lucky, she thought: "When they bombed the area around Seven Star Mound, I was living in the neighborhood of the Temple of Supreme Pureness. When they were destroying the houses around the Temple of Supreme Pureness, I had just moved to Jujube Valley."

Yun-ho's luck ran out in May 1941. They were living in Chungking's suburb, and Chou Yu-kuang was again away. Their daughter, Hsiao-ho, one day complained of a tummyache. Her temperature shot up, and there was no doctor in sight. After three days, Yun-ho found a way to have her transported to a hospital in Chungking, but it was too late. Hsiao-ho's inflamed appendix had ulcerated, and infection had spread. It took Hsiao-ho two months to die. Watching her die was excruciating, the darkest period of Yun-ho's life. Even now she cannot talk about it.

During those two months, Ch'ung-ho and their fifth brother, Huan-ho, spent a lot of time with Yun-ho, doing everything they could in a hopeless and agonizing situation. In the last few days of Hsiao-ho's life, even Yun-ho's spirits were quashed. She could no longer carry her daughter or comfort her. To Hsiao-ho's plea for relief, she could only say, "Why don't you die?" Ch'ung-ho remembers the day Hsiao-ho died:

> It was a sweltering July day. It was so hot and humid that I felt my sister and I needed to get away for a while from the dying girl. I suggested finding something cold to drink. We asked our brother Huan-ho to guard Hsiao-ho. By the time we returned, maybe hours later, I don't recall, I saw

a small, unpainted coffin sitting by the door. I knew that Hsiao-ho was dead. I told my sister that we should spend the night somewhere else, at a friend's house. I am not sure if she saw the coffin that afternoon. The next day, we went home to bury Hsiao-ho. Our brother had stored the coffin in an air raid shelter overnight. At the simple ceremony, my sister did not cry.

A year and half later, after Yun-ho had moved back to Ch'eng-tu with her family, her son was struck by a stray bullet. The bullet entered through his waist and punctured his organs in six places. For a while, the doctors did not know if he could pull through. Yun-ho's husband was again on the road when this happened, and when he received the news in Chungking, he rushed to Ch'ung-ho's house and banged on her door. A housemate answered it. Ch'ung-ho recalls that when she heard her brother-in-law's voice from upstairs she was sure that something awful had happened to her sister: "My knees went weak. I don't remember how I made it downstairs."

Chou Yu-kuang had come to see Ch'ung-ho because he knew that only Ch'ung-ho could help him find a seat on a bus bound for Ch'eng-tu the next morning. Ch'ung-ho managed this through a friend, a *k'un-ch'ü* enthusiast, who was head of a hydroelectric company. Two weeks later, Yu-kuang sent Ch'ung-ho this letter:

After we parted at the Chungking bus station, I carried this heavy heart throughout my rain-filled journey, all the way home. When I got here, it was already six o'clock in the evening on the twenty-ninth. I stood at the entrance and didn't go in. Through a small opening on the door, I asked our manservant, how was Hsiao-p'ing. He said, "He is still in the hospital." From the tone of his voice, I could hear the news. I knew Hsiao-p'ing was all right. Only then did I feel a relief. Otherwise, I don't think I would have dared to enter the house. Upstairs, only my mother was home. She was sewing a pair of shoes. Immediately I started toward the hospital. On the way there I saw Yun-ho. She did not seem upset. In fact, she was all excited. . . .

In the first three days, Hsiao-p'ing remained unconscious. Only by the fourth day, his condition began to stabilize. It is like watching the breakers dashing against the seawall in Ch'ien-t'ang from Pa Fortress. A peaceful sea could give rise to waves hundreds of feet tall. By the time I got back, the tide had receded; everything was calm. I could only see the traces of the storm left on the beach.

I remember that when [your brother] Ting-ho was going through his divorce, he was so upset that he didn't want to live. I used the argument that "life has many facets" to try to get him out of his funk. He was stubborn at the time, but he sees my point now. I know that Yun-ho had put all her hope in Hsiao-p'ing. If something awful happened to him, she would be so much more bereft than her brother had been. The only solace I could offer her would be what I'd told Ting-ho, that "life has many facets." But this time, I needed to argue with myself and to convince myself first. On the bus home, the bumpy ride made me tired and numb, and even calmed me down. Still, I knew, if things were bad, nothing could pep me up again, not even the many interests I have in life. What's more, I could no longer believe in my own optimism. I have studied in missionary schools since I was a child, but was not baptized until after Hsiao-ho had died. I had never prayed until now. I said a silent prayer for Hsiao-p'ing. I believe that slowly I am losing my faith in human strength and have vaguely become dependent on divine power.

Our cousin, I-ho, said to me, "If things do not look good for Hsiao-p'ing, I think it will be difficult for Yun-ho to keep on living. The blow will kill your mom, too. Probably only you could stay alive, but just barely. Wouldn't this finish your whole family?" She was right, you know. When I came home and asked the servant how Hsiao-p'ing was doing, if he had given me a different answer, the world would have taken a different color and a different light altogether. It is impossible to fathom life's sudden dislocations. . . .

The letter also says that Ting-ho, who had been so dispirited because of his divorce, had just had a premiere of his new musical compositions, which was a success; that Ting-ho brought the chorus to Yu-kuang's house to give Hsiao-p'ing a private performance of the concert he had missed; that Yun-ho bought her son a pair of white rabbits to keep him company; that the lunar New Year was approaching. The world was mended.

The same letter mentions that Chao-ho and her husband had wired more than ten thousand dollars. "We are going to use it for now, but must return it when we are able to. They, too, are pressed for money. Unlike the time when Hsiao-ho was ill—there was nowhere to turn—these days we can still find ways to borrow money. This is why Hsiao-p'ing is luckier than his sister."

Yu-kuang believed that had Hsiao-p'ing not been in Ch'eng-tu at the time of the accident and had there not been a good hospital nearby and doctors who operated on him right away, he, like Hsiao-ho, would have died, and his death would have killed his grandmother and his mother. Timeliness was what saved all of them. Yun-ho had another point of view. Yu-kuang was not in Ch'eng-tu when the bullet hit their son. She and the landlady rushed Hsiao-p'ing to the air force hospital, and for three days and three nights she could not sleep. It was not until the fourth day, when Hsiao-p'ing was out of danger, that Yu-kuang came home. "Women are left to deal with most of the crises," she said of her married life. It was not a begrudging remark, just a statement of fact.

Yun-ho also relied on the kindness of her brothers, sisters, and friends to get her through a bad time. In her diary she keeps a log of what they have done for her so that, if it is money they sent, she knows how much to return, and if it is something incalculable, she won't forget it. In 1964, for instance, when she was spending seven hundred yuan* a month from a monthly family income of 241 yuan to buy Western medicine for her aged mother-in-law, her sister Chao-ho as well as old friends—childhood friends—sent large sums, money they themselves could not afford, to help out with the medical expenses. And when, during the Cultural Revolution, Chou Yu-kuang's salary shrank to thirty-eight yuan a month (part of the penalty for being a "bad element"), Chao-ho lent her sister three thousand yuan over the years so that Yun-ho's family would not starve. Yun-ho writes: "[Chao-ho and Shen T'sung-wen] were having a rough time themselves, but they always did their best to find money for us. All my life, I hated borrowing money. But when I came to the end of my road, I could only beg. Maybe this is also a necessary part of the human experience."

Yun-ho came to what seemed like the end of her road several times between 1966 and 1972. Each time, she managed her escape through a rhetorical sleight of hand. Often, she says, her operatic experience came to her aid. On August 13, 1968, during the most violent and most volatile period of the Cultural Revolution, two radical extremists, flanked by neighborhood busybodies, stormed into her two-room apartment. They identified themselves as special agents from the external affairs division of Peking University, investigating a certain Chang Chih-lian. Yun-ho thought to herself: Chang Chih-lian? He was once the principal of Kuang-hua Middle School. I taught there. He is ten years younger than me. Is he in trouble? The two, she recalls, "fired a series of questions at me about this Chang Chih-lian, to which I could only answer, 'I don't know.' After I'd repeated this a few times, they were fed up with me. The young man to my left pointed to the teacup I was just about to reach for and snapped, 'Move that aside! Don't you drink that tea!'" So, "like a good girl," Yun-ho took her teacup to the next room and "hurried back."

---

*A yuan is a Chinese dollar, about forty cents in U.S. currency in 1964. It is difficult, however, to assess its purchasing power in China at the time.

Earlier, Yun-ho's goddaughter had poured her the cup of tea. They did not offer any to their visitors. Yun-ho knew that the young men would not want it because "to drink tea made in a bourgeois household would blur social distinctions." Her account continues:

Just as I was about to sit down, there was another loud bark: "You are not allowed to sit!" I was not quite in my seat yet, so I got up, holding on to the side of the table. Once I was on my feet, I realized that the chair behind me was pressing against my legs, so I rested my weight on the table in front. This sight displeased them. The same youth shouted, "Don't lean against the table! Move back two steps!" I followed his order and pushed the chair back. Now my legs were leaning on the chair. Probably, they were thinking, we told you not to lean on the table, and so you are leaning on the chair. The young man gave one more command, "Step forward one pace!" I obeyed his instruction once more. "With no village ahead and no inn behind," I had nothing for support. This, I believe, satisfied them.

I steadied myself and thought: I am nearly sixty. These two boys are directing me in an opera. I wonder what lines they want me to sing. They seem so stern and so strict about what they want to be done, and here I am, a nice, cooperative actor, following their directions exactly.

I raised my head. Outside the window, the children were watching. I see only their sweet faces and big, astonished eyes. The huge gourd leaves dangling from the trellis are no longer in view.

I waited for more orders and more shouting, and the young man to my left obliged. He must be tired, I thought. But youths are never tired, especially on occasions like this.

The young man sitting across from me said, "Think carefully. What sort of political collusion has Chang Chih-lian been involved in? Why cover up for him?"

I rather appreciated this young man's gentle manners. I said, "We were colleagues for not quite two years. He was the principal. I was a teacher. We saw each other a few times during meetings. That was about it. We rarely talked."

It was the person "with gentle manners" who decided to let Yun-ho have five minutes to think things over. This gave Yun-ho a brief reprieve: "Everyone in the room seemed to relax a little. Even the children, hanging from the trellis or gathered around the window, were a little quieter." Yun-ho had a chance to study the young man across from her. He was "a handsome lad," she thought. "Fair complexion, delicate skin, and bright eyes, probably only in first year of college. I am sure he is very sweet and amiable when he is courting a girl." Yun-ho told herself not to be angry: "As long as I could find something amusing about these kids, then I could be quite agreeable."

> I had my arms crossed in front of my chest. I thought about resting my chin on my right hand. It would have helped me to reflect, but then it might have given the wrong impression. So I kept my hands where they were.
>
> At that moment, the young man to my left made a coughing sound. I suddenly felt alarmed. This is not fun, I thought. A public struggle is face-to-face. It's nasty and malicious. One might get physically hurt. Or worse, it might be deeply wounding. One might even die from it. Maybe the time has come for me. Maybe it's now.

Just as Yun-ho became aware of the danger she was in, the tough young man got up and stretched his arms, which gave her a start. He was merely taking a deep breath. She noticed his appearance: he had dusky coloring and was coarse. Yun-ho decided that this was Chang Fei and the other was Chao Tzu-lung. Like Lord Kuan, Chang Fei and Chao Tzu-lung were big heroes from the Three Kingdoms period. They fought on the same side and never swerved from their purpose, but they were two different kinds of soldier. Chang Fei was brave and boorish: "eight-foot tall with a panther's head and round eyes, pointed chin and tiger's whiskers, a thunderous voice and force like a galloping steed." He had the manners of a man from the wilderness even though he had "farmed a little, sold wine, and slaughtered pigs." Chao Tzu-lung was as valiant as Chang Fei on the battlefield, but a gentleman warrior, restrained and dignified—the one readers preferred.

From Chang Fei and Chao Tzu-lung, her thoughts drifted to the theater and the roles she enjoyed playing as she got older. In the 1950s, when she was a member of an opera club in Peking, she played the clown several times. She felt that every opera needed a clown. A clown added merriment and charm—just like now, she mused. She needed to think of something funny to ease the pressure. But in this scene, if it was a scene, she was not sure who was the clown, "them or me," or who was spoofing whom. Yun-ho was relieved that "these two have no idea what is going on in my head right now. If they do, they will, no doubt, give me a belting."

By this time, Yun-ho's five minutes were up. The young man she thought of as Chao Tzu-lung because of his softer countenance "looked at his watch and said, 'Why don't you give us an answer? Surely you have remembered something by now. Did you ever ask anyone what this man was up to?'"

Suddenly I was jolted back to Chang Chih-lian, to the question of whether he was a counterrevolutionary. So I put my thoughts about clowns aside temporarily. If they were to give me five more minutes, I could write an essay on clowns.

"You ask me to give you an answer, but I don't have an answer," I said. I didn't dare to speak too quietly. I didn't want to shout either. So I adjusted my voice to what I thought was the right level, and I spoke slowly. "He was the school principal, and I was a teacher. I have never been to his house, and he has never been to mine. I have never asked any-one about his past. I wasn't interested in anyone's curriculum vitae. So I don't know what he did."

The fierce one, the "Chang Fei" to my left, was furious with me. He said in a loud voice, "You don't know! What sort of nonsense is this!"

Yun-ho thought his last sentence had a "strong, dramatic effect." "He con-tinued: 'You are not going to be honest with us? You cover up for him, just as Lin and Chang covered up for you. You are all scoundrels!' I felt that this was a rather nice summary of things." By this time, everyone else in the room was try-ing to convince Yun-ho to go along with her inquisitors.

They were all talking at the same time, saying the same thing, "They will be lenient if you are frank, but unmerciful if you resist." They wanted me to give these investigators from "external affairs" an answer. Otherwise, they repeated, I would be sorry.

But what was there for me to say? At this point I lost all my reserve. I told them, "If I say I don't know, then I don't know. I can't make up rumors and invent lies. I can't pick someone out of a crowd and smear his name. I can't betray my people and my country."

Yun-ho found these words herself. She was singing her own lines, not the script her young directors had been trying to force on her. And it seems to have worked. No one—not the representatives from "external affairs" nor the neigh-borhood cadres—could say that it was wrong for her not to want to "betray her people and her country." The young man who still had a trace of civility got up and said to her: "All right, why don't you give us a written response? We will come back and pick it up in three days." It was his way of letting everyone off the hook.

This was not the first time Yun-ho had faced down a pack of wolves. In 1946, she walked into the house of a Shanghai crime boss and made a series of demands for a friend she had known since middle school. The friend, a woman by the name of Hsü Shu-yin, had married a law student in the early 1930s and had a daughter with him. Sometime before the war was over, Hsü's husband had forced her out. By the time Yun-ho saw her again in Soochow after the war, Hsü Shu-yin was a wretched woman, scared and without means. Her husband was a legal counsel for a Shanghai criminal syndicate, and so could have afforded to look after her financially. Yun-ho confronted him right away, asking him to give his wife and child a house to live in, money to buy clothes, and basic monthly support. Nothing came of it, and her friend was too weak to pursue it further. Yun-ho, however, insisted on taking her grievances to Hsü Shu-yin's husband's employer in Shanghai, to a person he called his "teacher," a Mr. Chan. She and her friend made an appointment to see him:

> I told Hsü Shu-yin, if we couldn't get anywhere with these men, then she would have to perform—she would have to pretend to be so desperate that she'd rather jump from a second-floor window and die than be rebuffed. I also told her not to go too far, not to do anything silly, that she should only feign an attempted suicide. She, of course, was terrified. I assured her that all she had to do was to play her part, should the negotiations fail. That I was going to take care of the rest.
>
> As soon as we arrived at Chan's house, I knew that we would have to put up a show. The two men stalled, and our talks were not going anywhere, at which point my friend ran toward the second-floor window and her daughter fainted on the floor. The men were not expecting this. The drama unfolded so quickly that they didn't have time to think it through. However, neither wanted the publicity that this act of desperation could have generated should things go wrong. After some scrambling, they were ready to meet our conditions. They asked me to be present at the formal signing of the agreement. I went and behaved rather smugly. All along they probably thought that I had some powerful backer. But it was all bravado.

Yun-ho's private war had point and clarity. Her adversaries were genuine scoundrels. Their professions were scandalous. Yet twenty years later, two self-righteous punks called *her* a scoundrel because she would not tell lies that could destroy people. During the five-minute reprieve they gave her to think things over, it had crossed Yun-ho's mind that the world had gone mad—that even she could not tell whether she was good or bad: "Every person thinks of herself as good and her opponent as bad. But to say that you are good does not make it so, and for your opponent to say that you are bad also does not make it so."

Yun-ho could not have shared these ideas with her detractors. Unable to see that she was directing these questions at herself, they would have misappropriated her argument. Yun-ho noticed that since the Communist victory, the world had become more complicated and, at the same time, simpler. Past distinctions were turned on their heads and present distinctions were declared absolute. No one among the political bullies wanted subtlety, not in thinking or creating, not in the act of finding moral rightness.

Yun-ho was an early victim in this new world. For about two years during the war, she had received rent from her family's property in Hofei. In the Communist China created in 1949, this made her a landlord, and therefore a negative element in a moral construct based on class struggle. The labels "counterrevolutionary" and "tiger," fastened to her since 1952, cost her her job on the editorial board of the People's Education Press.

Before becoming an editor, Yun-ho had been teaching history in a Shanghai senior high. She realized at the time that she "did not have much goods to deliver." So as she was teaching, she was also learning, trying to absorb as much as possible from whatever books she could get her hands on. She also joined a workshop, where history instructors met regularly to discuss how to revise the materials they had been using in class. Some of her colleagues at the workshop encouraged her to write down her ideas, which she was happy to do. "I love being praised," Yun-ho later said: "I got so excited that I wrote twenty thousand words on the subject." She sent her long dissertation to an educational journal but heard nothing in return. Her unpublished manuscript must have traveled to Peking because, not long after, some of her views appeared in a long editorial in the *People's Daily*. The senior editors at the People's Education Press read the editorial. They had been trying to formulate guidelines for revising and rewriting history textbooks for the new government, and they liked Yun-ho's suggestions about including more sources in the history of technology and science and bringing literature and philosophy to the teaching of history. They also liked her call for making the teaching of history livelier and more relevant and giving more weight to the study of non-Han Chinese. They hired her as an editor and asked her to help them compile a general history for high school students. Yun-ho was excited about her job and about "starting a new professional life." But all this came to a swift end when she was labeled a counterrevolutionary.

After being "ostracized so early in the game, in the first wave of political move-ments," Yun-ho decided to retire and become a "stay-at-home tiger."

Almost as soon as she left her position, the Communist History Commis-sion assumed total intellectual control of school textbooks. Yun-ho does not know how she would have fared, had she stayed: "If I followed their rules and prescriptions, writing a history they wanted me to write, how could I say that my work had any integrity? Also, wouldn't I be corrupting the youth?"

After she lost her job, Yun-ho was in a funk at first, angry and disappointed. She did not want to be in Peking and be reminded of her hurt. So she went home to Soochow. Her fifth brother had moved back to their old family house on Chiu-ju Lane after the war, and she stayed with him. The two revisited childhood haunts, and Yun-ho began to see friends from her *k'un-ch'ü* club again. By the time she returned to Shanghai a few months later, she had freed herself from her "terrible state." Every Saturday, she studied *k'un-ch'ü* with Chang Ch'uan-fang, her brother-in-law's old classmate from the Ch'uan-hsi troupe. Together they compiled a manual on movements and gesturing—in other words, a director's handbook for the actors. Such manuals, rare in the *k'un-ch'ü* tradition, are extremely useful, since operatic scenes are usually staged with-out a director. Professional actors and amateurs often collaborate on such projects: one draws from his years of experience onstage and the knowledge handed down to him by his teachers; the other offers her reading of texts—her understanding of the dramatist's art and intent.

In 1953, Yun-ho and Chang Ch'uan-fang worked on six scenes from six sep-arate operas. She later said:

> My relationship with *k'un-ch'ü* had changed over the years. What had once been an interest gradually evolved into a profession. The unhappi-ness from the year before did not destroy me. My love for *k'un-ch'ü* saved me and restored me. Who would have guessed that a loss might turn out to be a blessing? Over the years, I realized more and more that the whole affair was a fortunate turn for me. If I had not been dismissed earlier, if I was still working during the Cultural Revolution, I would have certainly been dead. Either I would have taken my own life, or they would have racked me to death.

From 1956 to 1964, Yun-ho was head of liaison at the Beijing K'un-ch'ü Research Institute, an organization supported by the Cultural Ministry. In the late 1950s, she even helped to write contemporary dramas, churning out lines such as "Upstairs we have silk and brocade, / downstairs, garlic and onion," which were meant to extol the virtues of the people's communes. She says that these works were inconsequential, produced under pressure from the Cultural Ministry. The center was shut down in 1964, and when it reopened in 1979, Yun-ho returned as a chief officer.

If one asks Yun-ho what she has done since 1952, she will insist that she has been a "housewife" and an "ordinary person." She lived on her husband's income. (Chou Yu-kuang had become a linguist. He was fluent in English and a man of "many interests," so was able, on short notice, to make a huge career change, making himself indispensable to a new government eager to launch a language reform.) The Chinese government never paid Yun-ho for writing correspondence and arranging concerts at the *k'un-ch'ü* center. She volunteered her time and worked as hard as anyone. Up to fifteen years ago, every wage earner in China under Communist rule was, in theory, a government employee. Yun-ho's decision not to become one was probably a calculated move. She knew that she would not survive Communist politics and tactics. She was too blunt and too loud, too easily provoked by what she regards as injustice and too stubborn to compromise her principles. So while she preferred to teach history or edit textbooks, she chose to become a housewife.

In the past, when the world was faced with uncertainty, men with either extraordinary potential or a tendency to get themselves into trouble would pretend to be ordinary and clumsy to avoid being singled out. Very few succeeded. Being ordinary is hard work, the philosophers say. Who, after all, would not want to display his talents and to have them appreciated? Even the most cultivated—say, a mythic figure such as Lieh Tzu—could not stop others from treating him as special. Lieh Tzu observed that he ate at ten inns "and at five they served me first." Thus he feared, despite his attempt to be ordinary, "something still oozed from [his] body and became an aura" that might get him into trouble. Yun-ho called herself a housewife. It took her a long time to accept this appellation. But in the end, she was pleased with her cover.

In 1969, her husband was sent to a small community in Ninghsia, near the Inner Mongolia border, to reform himself through physical labor. The place, according to him, was like a concentration camp, bleak and isolated. The nearest town was twenty miles away. Chou Yu-kuang stayed for two years and four months. Yun-ho could have accompanied him there but decided not to. She told her husband to go and have his hardship. She says, "I was too frail and too tired to endure it with him." Yun-ho remained in Peking and looked after their granddaughter.

For years, Chou Yu-kuang had been suffering from glaucoma. Without his eyedrops he could have gone blind, and the small clinic in his labor camp did not stock such medicine. Only Yun-ho could get it to him from Peking, and this was not easy to manage because during the early years of the Cultural Revolution everything needed official approval from one's work unit, even a prescription for eyedrops. In 1969, most of Chou Yu-kuang's colleagues were in Ninghsia reeducating themselves. Two men guarded the office in Peking: a young teacher and a fifteen-year-old Red Guard. The morning Yun-ho went there to get the approval for her husband's eyedrops, only the Red Guard was there. His name was Wu K'ai-ming. Yun-ho still remembers the conversation.

> YUN-HO: Comrade Wu K'ai-ming, my husband needs the medicine for his glaucoma. Could you write a permission for his prescription?
> WU: Tell him to get it from his clinic.
> YUN-HO: His clinic does not have it.
> WU: Tell him to get it from the hospital.
> YUN-HO: The hospital is twenty miles away. Besides, they don't have it either.
> WU: Then tell him not to use it!
> YUN-HO: If he is blind, then he can't do any physical labor, and he won't be reformed.

Yun-ho said that she could not argue with this "little Red punk," much less scoff at him for being so thick. If she had, he would have beaten her. So she simply refused to leave until someone had yielded to her importunity. Toward the end of the day, the young teacher showed up. He scribbled a few words, which allowed Yun-ho to pick up a prescription for her husband. "So every month, I mailed him his two bottles of eyedrops in a small wooden box. Sometimes I added a few bars of chocolate with the medicine."

It helped that Yun-ho was a housewife when her husband was stranded in Ninghsia without resources. The political commissars could not fix blame on her even for small transgressions because hardly any records had accumulated in her dossier. They could have rummaged through her personal papers and found some incriminating evidence there, but she was way ahead of them. At the beginning of the Cultural Revolution, sometime in 1967, Yun-ho had torn up nearly every personal paper in her possession—letters, diplomas, diaries, and the essays and poems she had written. Her son disposed of the photographs. It took them a week: "My fingers were hurting. Every part of me was aching. I destroyed every precious thing I had."

Fifteen years before, when Yun-ho was initially labeled a "tiger" and a bad element in the first round of political movements, the commissars had dispatched their lieutenants to her home, and these men took the letters her husband had written to her over the years for "further study." To Yun-ho, their conduct was "deeply humiliating." "What sort of self-respect are we left with," she said, "when they could display in public the little bit of privacy a man and a woman should have in a marriage?" For days she could not eat or sleep. Finally she went to the commissars and confronted them: "I told them, 'If you think I have ideological problems, then find a way to deal with me. Otherwise, please return my husband's letters.'" After a few days, the letters all came back in a package. In 1967, Yun-ho destroyed them herself so that she would not have to suffer the humiliation again. This way, she managed to keep her "little bit of privacy."

After 1949, Yun-ho only had one sister, Chao-ho, with her in China. Yuan-ho had left with her husband for Taiwan at the end of the civil war. Ch'ung-ho, after marrying a Westerner, had moved to America. Yun-ho remained close to Chao-ho and her husband, Shen Ts'ung-wen. In 1988, the day before Shen Ts'ung-wen died, Yun-ho wrote an essay about him, about all of them, and about what had happened to their world in the last fifty years:

> My third sister and I were married in the same year, she to Shen Ts'ung-wen and I to Chou Yu-kuang. We had our sons in the same year. Mine is called Chou Hsiao-p'ing, and hers, Shen Lung-chu. After the Marco Polo Bridge Incident [in July 1937], our families went their separate ways. The Shens settled in Ch'eng-kung, Yunnan. The Chous drifted around in Szechwan, from Ch'eng-tu to Chungking, from the Su River to the Min River. Altogether we moved over thirty times. After the Japanese surrendered, the ten brothers and sisters of the Changs gathered in Shanghai in 1946.* We had a photo taken in a studio of our ten-family reunion. After this, we each pursued our own path, and never would we all be together again.
>
> By 1956, there were three families living in Peking, my third sister's, my third brother Ting-ho's, and my own family. We could say that life was still joyful. Ten years passed, and suddenly there was the Cultural Revolution. Now we could not even keep our separate families together. Two more years went by. Of the three families, only four persons were left in

---

*Lu Ying had nine children, and Wei Chün-i had one. The Chang sisters always regarded their half brother as a sibling.

Peking: Shen Ts'ung-wen from the Shens; Ting-ho's son, Chang I-lian, from the Changs; plus my granddaughter and me. I-lian was twelve and was living alone. My granddaughter was nine. My third sister was sent to Hsien-ning in Hupei. She was busy carrying manure and planting crops. My third brother was looking after sheep somewhere. As for the five in my family, my son and daughter-in-law had gone to Ch'ien-chiang, also in Hupei, to transplant seedlings and grow vegetables. The grandfather, Chou Yu-kuang, was dispatched to P'ing-lo in Ninghsia. He gleaned wheat fields, wove screens, and looked for coal dust. There were also the endless self-criticism sessions. Most of them took place on an open field. Once a flock of wild geese flew by and together dumped their droppings on the meeting below. This was convenient for birds but not for humans. Luckily my Yu-kuang wore a big straw hat that day. Whenever he remembered the wild geese in Ninghsia, he always said that this was the funniest experience in his life. It seems that wild geese are more orderly than men. So goes the saying, "Men are not as good as birds and beasts."

Life returned to some order and sanity by the 1980s. Over the years Yun-ho has found various resources to calm her nerves. The Heart Sutra is one such remedy. The words are about the cessation of anxiety—the end of vexations. One arrives at this through the realization that all things are empty. "Form, sensation, perception, predisposition, and consciousness; eye, ear, nose, tongue, body, intent" are all transient and so empty. Thus one should not become attached to them. "With this obstacle removed, you are no longer scared," the text says, "and your miseries are miles away." Yun-ho recites these words to find refuge from her worries.

But Yun-ho is not a believer and does not think that she could give up her attachments, so when her spirits are low, she sometimes sings the raunchy aria from "A Fine Occasion," written five centuries ago. In this scene, a young mistress and her true love are stoking up their fire in bed, while her maidservant is outside her door, imagining the goings-on:

> Young mistress, young mistress,
> So full with your ripeness.
> Young master, young master,
> Awash with your talents.
> Oh, what a blending of talents and beauty!
> What a grand to-do!
> How I long for them to be a perfect match.

. . . .

So gently one pushes the other away.
So startled the other to be there at all.
How the young mistress flushes in shyness.
How the young master pounds with desire.

These words also offer her solace.

At ninety-one, Yun-ho still loves recounting stories of her heroes. She could have ended up like them—head severed and limbs torn—but instead she kept her body whole. People say that she knew how to nourish life and keep alive. She follows no special diet, and does not rely on spiritual strength. In fact, there is no mystery about her. Yun-ho clings to her earthly attachments, never pretending to have inner composure, and she delights in recreation.

In the 1980s, Yun-ho was able to see her sisters Yuan-ho and Ch'ung-ho, who, by then, were both living in the United States. She came to California on one visit and spent several weeks with Yuan-ho in Oakland. By this time, she was keeping a diary again, after having stopped for nearly twenty years to avoid trouble. On August 2, 1984, she wrote:

Yesterday was a whole day of opera. We started putting on makeup at eight o'clock in the morning. My oldest sister worked on me first and then herself. She still takes her time, as in the past, fixing the fringe on my forehead, strand by strand, and then arranging the hairdress. It was already five after one when we finished. We had a bite to eat and then began going through the movements and gestures of "A Stroll in the Garden," and snapping shots of each other to keep a record.

[Our first *k'un-ch'ü* teacher] Yü T'sai-yun's movements and gestures were considered the standard during his time. Even Mei Lan-fang and Han Shih-ch'ang had to consult him when they were rehearsing this scene. It was sixty years ago when we sisters first performed "A Stroll in the Garden" together. We couldn't have been more than thirteen and fifteen then.

Four in the afternoon: my sister adds a streak of black on my right cheek and paints my upper lip a little fuller. She takes photos of me as the clown in "The Misplaced Kite." The light outside is not good enough. The conditions are not ideal.

Chapter 12

CHAO-HO

Chao-ho with her husband, Shen Ts'ung-wen,
in Peking in 1934, the year after they were married.

IN JUNE 1931, Chao-ho's future husband, Shen Ts'ung-wen, wrote to her from Peking:

> X X,* I beg you, please let me do what I wish. Whenever I try to say
> something to you, treat me like a fool but not someone you despise. Allow

---

*During their courtship, Shen Ts'ung-wen would sometimes address Chao-ho as X X in his letters to her.

me to be abject and say these words. It shouldn't be hard for you. Every time I say I love you, don't get embarrassed, and don't insist on saying "You don't love me" simply to resist my falling in love with you. Your strategy is like a child's. It just won't work. Some people say to Heaven day and night, "I praise you, O Lord!" Others tell their ruler, "I praise you, Powerful One!" Have you ever heard either Heaven or the emperor, or, for that matter, the moon, beautiful flowers, or exquisite art, telling its admirer, "But I don't want to praise you"? Anyone worthy of praise, anyone with enormous sway, is king or queen of the universe. When she runs everything and rules everyone, it all seems so natural, not a bit forced. A good person—a virtuous person—also has the power to bend, to give rise to a shift of mood or a change of nature while herself remaining aloof, high on a throne, not having to give a single declaration. Anyone who uses her virtue and her beauty to seize possession of another person's soul has illimitable authority to decide this person's fate, and she never has to utter a thing. The sun, clouds, flowers—there are endless examples. Other than the oriole, who cannot be silent because people admire her song, almost everything else with such powers is silent. X X, you are not an oriole. . . . X X, you are not an emperor. . . . X X, you are my orb. . . .

X X, I think of you as like the moon. And, yes, I am thankful for my fortune. Yet I feel smothered by anxiety and am often in despair. (I can't say that writing to you right now gives me happiness.)

Shen Ts'ung-wen was not exaggerating his unhappiness. The year before, not long after he had met Chao-ho, he blurted out his feelings to her one day, all at once, and she told him that she was concentrating on her studies and did not need a boyfriend. She was a second-year student at China College, and he was her teacher.

In the late 1920s, Shen Ts'ung-wen had created quite a stir in the literary world, winning praises with his prose. He was raised in a small town in West Hunan called Feng-huang. He had been enrolled in school since he was four, but he spent most of his childhood playing by the Yuan River and watching the goings-on in the streets and temple grounds of Feng-huang: rope makers and basket weavers working side by side and next to men shadowboxing; an umbrella store "with its door flung wide open" so that one could see a row of apprentices assembling their wares; an old man "with big glasses" concentrating on needle grinding; butchers and barbers, starch makers and dye makers; bean curd shops and shops that rented sedan chairs for weddings, funerals, and miscellaneous occasions. At the age of fifteen, he entered a military school to become a soldier, because "it was a way out, the only way out" for a young man born in West Hunan. Then a serious illness, coinciding with the death of a friend, became a turning point in his life. He did not want to die before he "had seen many places and known many things," so he decided to leave Hunan and come to Peking to study. He wrote: "If I can't study, then I will become a policeman. If I can't become a policeman, then I'll give up and not make any more plans." This was in 1922. By the late 1920s, Shen Ts'ung-wen was a well-known writer, someone who dazzled Chinese readers with stories that were created from his recollections of West Hunan. The eminent historian and cultural reformer Hu Shih, who was the president of China College in Wusung at the time, hired him as a professor of Chinese literature, knowing that Shen did not even have a high school diploma. "With a talent like Mr. Shen," Hu Shih remarked, "one should make exceptions."

In spite of what others thought of him, Shen Ts'ung-wen did not have a high estimation of himself. He never presumed that his success would or should have any sway over a woman whose affection he could only hope to win. So when Chao-ho rejected his love, he was not angry. Her rebuff simply broke him. He told Chao-ho's best friend: "Because I love her, I have destroyed my life in the last half year. I can't do a thing. I want to go far away, which will let her pursue her studies peacefully and spare me my miseries. I have also considered getting myself killed in a war, to free myself from these entanglements. But this is a childish thought. It won't get me very far."

When Shen approached Hu Shih for a leave of absence, Hu asked him to reconsider. He even offered to help, to talk to her family if they were the obstacle. Shen begged Hu not to intervene. Instead, he asked Chao-ho's friend, Miss Wang, to find out from her whether it would ever be possible for Chao-ho to love him or to need his love. Miss Wang told him that Chao-ho was more rational than she was emotional: "She can never be persuaded by a friend's argument or give up her views because of a friend." Miss Wang also warned Shen that her friend had an irrepressible nature: "Just when you are most pleased with yourself, thinking that you have convinced her, she will say, 'I won't.' She still has not slipped out of her childlike temperament. If you press her on a point, then she will say no, even when she wants to go along with you. She does not care what consequence her response might cause."

On the evening of July 4, 1930, Chao-ho copied into her diary the conversation Miss Wang had with Shen, which was related to her in a letter. She added her thoughts at the end:

I have been living in this world for nearly twenty years. I am not without feelings, not a piece of wood or rock. In the last ten years, my mother's

death and having to part with the teachers I loved in school moved me to
tears. Violent oppressions and wide inequity between rich and poor have
incensed me and stirred me to compassion. Also moonlit nights, stars at
dawn, windy mornings, and rain at dusk—all weathers affect me. I feel
sorrow, desolation, frustration, all sorts of emotions in my heart. But it is
no more than feeling them. All this has not inspired me to write a compelling poem or pointed me to attempt some astonishing feat. I am an
ordinary girl. I don't understand what love is, the sentimental love that
poets and novelists glorify in their works. I have been looking for it in my
own world, and sometimes I could feel its presence in a flash, with my
parents, my sisters, my friends, but only in a flash. Love appears and dis-
appears like lightning, and when it's over, we return to the wind and rain,
to the darkened sky, to this frail and frightful world. I have always sus-
pected that love may not exist. But *they* have tried to prove me wrong,
especially Yun-ho. So I am confused again.

Four days later, Chao-ho went to see Hu Shih. Lots of students and young
scholars, writers and cosmopolites, had gone to see Hu Shih because he was a
man who knew a wider world and had absorbed huge amounts of learning of
many kinds. Some of his young visitors also believed that this man could advise
them in matters of love. It was widely known at the time that when Hu was a
student at Columbia University in New York, he had fallen in love with an
American woman. Even though he never left his wife (their marriage had been
arranged when he was twelve), Hu remained sympathetic to those who were
made miserable by love, and to lovers who made other people miserable because
of their love for each other.

Chao-ho did not show up at Hu Shih's home to seek his wisdom on this matter or any other matter. She was there to explain herself. She had learned from her
friend that Shen Ts'ung-wen had let Hu Shih know about his feelings for her. She
was not sure what he'd said, but since she found Shen tortuous and incoherent
on the subject of love, she wanted to tell Hu herself where she stood. When she
arrived, she could hear through the garden gate that a lively crowd was already in
the living room. Chao-ho decided not to go in because she realized that she
would probably recognize "half the people there." Hu asked her to come back two
hours later when they could talk alone. That night Chao-ho wrote in her diary:

Thereupon, I mentioned Mr. Shen. [Mr. Hu] also told me what he'd
learned from Mr. Shen about us. He praised Shen, calling him a genius
and the most promising Chinese novelist right now. He went on and on

about him until I made my point that I don't love Mr. Shen. Then, he stopped. I believe he really wanted to help me with my problem. He asked me whether Mr. Shen and I could become friends. I said that in principle I didn't see why we couldn't but Mr. Shen was not like other people. I told him that even if we were just friends, the misunderstandings would persist, which would then be followed by quarrels and lots of them. At this point, Mr. Hu leaped to his friend's defense again. He said, "Since the world has this genius, everyone else should help him and let him have a chance to develop his potential." He added, "He certainly worships Miss Chang to an extreme." In fact, he repeated this several times in our conversation. I said to him, "Too many people feel this way about me. If I have to deal with them one by one, then I won't have time for my studies." That kept him quiet for a while.

Hu Shih was to explain in a letter to Shen Ts'ung-wen two days later why he was "quiet." But before she closed her diary, Chao-ho had more thoughts about this man who was probably the most prominent public intellectual of his time and the most admired, and also a man whose work she had studied since she was a girl of nine or ten:

> Just as I was about to go, [Mr. Hu] said, "I am glad that you two have told me about this. I always feel that such things are sacred, so don't worry, I won't carelessly let it out." "It's sacred," so "don't worry," "I won't carelessly let it out." What was he saying? When I left, I didn't feel as if I had just talked to a famous scholar!

It is difficult to imagine another person of Chao-ho's age who could have responded to Hu Shih in this way. Hu Shih was not a genius—he probably realized this when he called Shen Ts'ung-wen one—but most people, especially the young, looked up to him. They respected his views and his character, and the fact that he could handle problems in the Chinese exegetical tradition and issues in Western analytical philosophy with equal aplomb. Chao-ho, however, had her doubts, about his understanding of her and of human nature. She found his comments about her recent troubles banal and so saw no reason to come under his influence just because of his considerable reputation.

Shortly after he learned about this meeting, Shen Ts'ung-wen wrote to Chao-ho. In his letter, he acknowledges his stubbornness and pays tribute to hers; he then congratulates them both for not yielding an inch. "I respect your stubbornness," he begins. "From now on I am going to try not to put any more pressure on you. If each person can live in his stubbornness—'I love you and you don't love me'—then it is indeed a very good thing. When I realized this, I was not terribly crushed because it is what it has to be." Thus, with sadness and irony, he praises the virtue of stubbornness: "I wish that your prejudice is followed by happiness—your stubbornness is your happiness."

Shen Ts'ung-wen's insight into Chao-ho's character was proof of his genius. No one else, not her best friend, her sister Yun-ho, or Hu Shih, understood this about her. And Chao-ho herself merely lived in her stubbornness—she was not self-analytical. Her diary tells us that around this time Yun-ho took her to task on a point she had made a few years earlier. Yun-ho believed that it was possible to have unconditional love, whereas Chao-ho insisted that all love is for an end, even when the person does not intend his love to be expedient. They argued all night on this question.

Hu Shih, having formed an opinion of Chao-ho when they met, put his thoughts into a letter to Shen Ts'ung-wen and forwarded a copy to Chao-ho. It was an honest gesture. He wrote:

> Miss Chang was here two days ago. What she said on the whole agrees with what you already knew. I tried not to put any pressure on her.
>
> These are my observations. This woman does not understand you and, even less, your love for her. You have misplaced your affection. I said this to you the other day—love is not the only thing in life. (Those who say otherwise are mad.) We all have to withstand the test of success, and even more, that of failure. Don't let a little girl boast that she has once broken the heart of Shen Ts'ung-wen. . . .
>
> That day, when I suggested that she should write to you, she said, "If I do the same to everyone, then when will I have time to study?" I was quite concerned when I heard this.
>
> This person is too young and too inexperienced. Therefore, she treats everyone who expressed love to her as "them." And she takes pleasure in turning "them" away. You are just one "among many."

After Chao-ho read Hu Shih's letter, she wrote a rebuttal. It was intended only for herself, so she put it in her diary.

> Mr. Hu only knows that love is precious, and he feels that as long as the love is sincere, then one should accept it. This is a very simplistic view of things. If the beloved loves the person who loves her, then there is no problem. But what if this is not the case? What if the beloved doesn't care

for the person who offers his love? If she accepts it purely because his love is sincere, then this will provide the leaven for greater trouble and suffering. Mr. Hu did not see this. (Perhaps his interests are different.) He considers Shen a genius. So there is no doubt in his mind that a woman who scorns the earnest love of genius must be too young and too inexperienced. If his advice could convince Shen to give up pursuing an ignorant and stubborn woman and thereby ease some of his pain and some of my troubles, then I would be terribly grateful. It would not matter if he did this on purpose or not.

That night, Chao-ho thought about writing a letter to comfort Shen because "after all, he has a good heart." Yet she was afraid to mislead him. She writes:

This is a weakness we women have. We are full of compassion yet reticent about showing it. One shouldn't blame us. We are meek and a little scared because our thought and action are repressed from being rigorously scrutinized. If we are incautious just once, then we are marked for life, unable to wash away the blemish left on us.

The diary entry under July 14, 1930, is long, and it is almost as if two women had a hand in it. One exudes a childlike arrogance, unfazed by the opinions of famous men. The other is so tightly guarded and so fearful about making a misstep in her conduct that she seems years older than her age. This aspect of Chao-ho has always troubled her sister Yun-ho. We do not have the full account of their conversation about love two nights earlier. (Chao-ho wrote in her diary that Chu Kan-kan "had repeatedly urged us to go to bed," and so she did not have time to jot down everything after Yun-ho left her room.) Probably some of their argument was about Chao-ho's excessive vigilance. Yun-ho was a different kind of woman. She, too, was watchful of her conduct, but she had had her adventures. She believed in the possibility of love, so she was more willing to let it happen. Yun-ho also did not think that making a mistake, even in romantic love, could mar a woman's character for life. She had more faith in a woman's strength and resourcefulness and in the kindness of others should there be a mishap. Chao-ho was timid because she was cynical. She disliked repression and thought women had to endure more of it than men, but she would not take risks to change things.

Yun-ho felt that her sister had not always been like this. Years later she said:

Since childhood, Chao-ho liked to dress in men's clothes. So she volunteered to play the role of [the woman-warrior] Hua Mu-lan. . . . Later, in the school play *The Three Knights-Errant,* our oldest sister was Hung Fu while she [Chao-ho] played [Hung Fu's lover] Li Ch'ing.* When she sat in the "dragon chair," her feet couldn't even touch the ground. She looked so small and shy in that chair, swinging her legs back and forth. It was very funny. Still, these were not her favorite parts. What she loved best was comical skits. She would paint her face in a mess and act in plays she invented herself, with titles like "The Multipurpose Scholar" or "The Visitor from Outer Space." She was lively in school and often made a spectacle of herself. She would be missing from her room in the middle of the night, and we would find her dancing under the moonlight all by herself. When she saw candies, sitting on the windowsill, covered with ants, she insisted that ants had noses. Comments like this made the girls in the dorm laugh so hard that they couldn't go back to sleep. This never had any effect on Chao-ho. She would be snoring away, as if she had nothing to do with it. What she was like then and what she is like now are completely different.

Yun-ho insisted that "life's hardship" changed Chao-ho. But was she so different earlier on? Her diary from 1930 already showed her as taciturn and shut in, which seemed a contradiction to her other self—the pugnacious and plucky girl Shen Ts'ung-wen fell madly in love with. According to Yun-ho and Chao-ho herself, there were many other men, besides Shen Ts'ung-wen, writing love letters to her at the time. Chao-ho rarely responded to these letters and would not send them back. She put them all in her collection, assigning each a code and a number. Among these letters, was one from a former teacher in her middle school. This man waited until she was in college to write to her and to ask her whether she would at all consider marrying him, because another girl had expressed an interest in him and he wanted to know from Chao-ho first if there was any chance of the two of them being together, before responding to the other girl. Chao-ho was stunned. She liked the teacher but had never expected him to approach her with a question like this. She wrote back, saying, "Your letter made no sense." Her answer was blunt and curt so that there was no misunderstanding.

When Shen Ts'ung-wen first fell in love with Chao-ho, he found words like these—spoken without feeling—both heartbreaking and entrancing. He wanted Chao-ho to know about feelings she had never known before. At the same time,

---

Three Knights-Errant was a modern play Kuo Mo-jo adapted from the Ming drama *The Story of Hung-fu.* (See chapter 8, p. 108.)

he wanted her to be spared if she was living in perfect happiness. In his letter of
June 1931, he wrote:

> I am able to see the moon countless times in a year, and it is the same
> moon wherever I go. This selfless moon not only illuminates every corner,
> but it has been glowing since I was a child. But you, who are my private
> moon, are not always in sight. Human conditions have been clouding my
> view. Days, not nights, have taken away some of my youth. They cannnot
> dull the radiance you have impressed on me, but they are slowly forcing
> me to change. "A woman in a poem can never age. Not so the poet who is
> creating her—he is already older." Whenever I think of this, I am filled
> with sadness. Our lives are fragile. We are not any more able to endure a
> storm than flowers. Thus looking at human life with nature's eyes, I would
> never regard lightly the randomly entwining tendrils of human relations.
> With any one person, it can happen only once. All my life I have seen only
> one perfect moon. . . . I have crossed many bridges. I have glanced at many
> clouds. I have tasted many kinds of wine. But I have loved only one
> woman, who is always at the perfect age. . . .
>
> X X, . . . I regard you as my goddess. I respect you. But for convenience
> I must explain some things about which even true goddesses might get a
> bit confused. . . .Many strange things happen in this world. . . . For
> instance, whenever I think of the person I love, my blood flows faster than
> usual and I become feverish. And when I hear someone mention this per-
> son's name, I am both excited and alarmed. What is the reason? Books
> like to speak of such things, but none can give a clear explanation. Some
> call it an illness. . . .
>
> You have never been struck with this illness, so you don't know how
> serious it can be. Some people, I believe, will never catch it. In the same
> way, some will never catch the measles or typhoid, so they will never
> believe that typhoid can cause a person to go mad. X X, I think you are
> unable to contract this illness, so you don't understand the people who
> have it. It's a blessing. Because this illness is the nemesis of a childlike
> heart, I hope you will always remain a child and will never have to under-
> stand these things.

Shen Ts'ung-wen, of course, did not mean what he said. He often did not.
For example, the same day on which he wrote Chao-ho that he respected her
stubbornness and was going to try not to badger her anymore, he sent her
another letter, which reads, "If it is your misfortune that I love you, then your

misfortune will last as long as I am alive." In the letter, dated June 1931, after he tells Chao-ho that he wants her to stay always "a child," he immediately adds: "But nature won't allow it." He goes on: "Just as nature turns apples from green to yellow, at the right time, it will turn you into a mature woman. So when you feel that you are no longer a child and want to be an adult, tell me. I want to know where you are, what you are doing, and what you are thinking."

Shen Ts'ung-wen was incorrigible, and he was wrong about nature. Nature did not turn his wife into a mature woman, he did. He brought his awareness of this fact to a short story he wrote three years after they married. The story, "Housewife," uses a he-says-she-says type of narration, which curiously echoes the way Chao-ho organized her diary. A 1930 entry from her diary would often begin with his letter to her, which would be followed by her interior dialogue with him, and sometimes she would include a third person—say, her best friend or someone like Hu Shih—to comment on both. The woman in "Housewife" is called Bibi:*

Today is the fifth day of the eighth month in the lunar calendar. Three years ago, on the same day, she married a man whose life was completely different from hers and whose temperament seemed quite odd. To start their new life together, the two of them hired a car and went shopping all around the city from the east side to the west, from Heavenly Bridge to the North Gate. Together they chose all the essential items for their new home—from the bedding in their room to the pots and pans in the kitchen. They managed to move everything into their house amid laughter and squabbling, friendly discussions and small complaints.

Everyone—her older sister from Shanghai, her mother's relatives from even farther south, the two younger sisters in school, and the few friends—seemed like wind-up dolls. [For days] they had been running around in circles, getting things ready: gauze shades for the windows, red lanterns, red envelopes for the servants' gift money, and gold-speckled stationery for writing thank-you notes. Finally the joyful occasion arrived. Just as she and her older sister were cutting out tiny characters of *hsi* [happiness] to put on cakes and pastries, the dressmaker arrived with a new set of clothes. "Whose is this?" "The young lady's." She took it and ran to the small dressing room behind the wedding chamber. As she was changing in front of the mirror, she thought to herself: Everything is coincidental,

---

*To be consistent with the romanization system I am using, this should be Pipi. Her name, however, is pronounced Bibi.

this moment or that. It's not easy to arrange a rendezvous, but once you have a chance to meet, it would be useless to try to run away. Only a year ago, I had this romantic notion, to dress myself like a man, in gray student uniform, and make my way to Peking to study there. Who could have guessed that here I am, getting ready to become a bride, and perfectly willing to be a little housewife for some man.

So why did Chao-ho marry Shen Ts'ung-wen? She "didn't like him" when he first told her that he was in love with her. She "didn't even like his stories" then, and she thought it strange and unseemly that he should have nosebleeds so often. Even now she remembers his behavior in those years as "exasperating" and "the source of her irritation." Their long marriage and her loyalty to him throughout his illness and after he died did not soften those memories. She says she married him "because he wrote good letters." His story "Housewife" elaborates this remark. It is from his point of view, so he is gentler on himself.

After she graduated from high school and began her first year at a private university, those who knew her all thought her "beautiful." She was a bit surprised and couldn't quite believe it. How could I be beautiful? she would muse. It must be a mistake. They are just ignorant. She also carefully avoided flatterers. And then she met him. He thought her gentle and sweet, intelligent yet artless. By the time they could say more than a few words to each other, he told her that he thought he was in love with her. This was very similar to what she had heard from other men, yet maybe the way he said it was a little different. At first, she thought that this was going to be "the usual," so, as usual, she let the whole thing lapse. Then as things became more complicated, she felt she had to distance herself from him even more and to give the impression that she was not at all gentle and sweet. It went on like this for two years. In the meantime, classmates continued to pay their addresses, adding some diversion to her student life. And as she was quietly enjoying the attention, it gradually became a habit for her to wait for his letters to arrive. The letters were full of humility and admiration, mixed with a helpless sadness. She would read each from beginning to end, give a long and gentle sigh, and put a number on it before storing it away in a little box.

It was not only Chao-ho but also her sisters who were surprised by how men looked at her and considered her after she turned nineteen. At home, no one really took notice of her appearance or her demeanor. Her complexion was dark.

She cropped her hair short, like a boy's. She was also plump and healthy, bull-headed and not very graceful. To her siblings, Chao-ho was not the "black phoenix" or "black peony" her admirers liked to call her behind her back. Their oldest sister, Yuan-ho, was the beauty of the family and the mysterious one.

Chao-ho's early memories of herself do not differ much from what her sisters remember about her. She enjoyed strolling with her father in the evening, "reciting the classics" with her sisters, writing "just two pages of large characters a day" and "one page of small characters," and chewing the coarse rice the old gatekeeper fed her from his bowl. But no one indulged her or wept on her account. There were no precious stories to tell. Her mother loved her because she was the youngest of her daughters living at home, but she did not have much time for her. She would put Chao-ho in her room in the morning when she was busy with her chores, leaving a string of candied crab apples in the washbasin as a treat. Her father was hard-of-hearing, and so gave Yun-ho, who was the loud-est, the most attention. Her *kan-kan* was a woman of much sense and little ten-derness. She believed in self-reliance and forbearance.

When the family was still living in Shanghai, their tutor, Miss Wan, would arrive early in the morning and take her breakfast in the classroom, often with the children, before starting their lessons. Yun-ho's nurse-nanny, Tou Kan-kan, was in charge of breakfast, which usually included congee and side dishes of assorted pickles, fermented bean curd, salted peanuts, and sliced cucumbers. Chao-ho had a huge appetite. At meals, she was usually the first to sit down and the last to leave; whenever she was allowed, she would have an extra bowl of rice with the leftover sauce on a dish. So in the morning, when Tou Kan-kan was laying the table, Chao-ho was already in her seat, waiting for her breakfast:

> Then one day Tou Kan-kan said to me, "Shoo, off you go! It's only you who are so impatient. Your teacher isn't even here yet, and you are already anxious to start." When Chu Kan-kan learned about this, she was so enraged that she said to me, "We don't want their breakfast. I'll get pick-led cowpeas for you." Then she fished two long segments of cowpeas out of a pickle jar and put them on top of a huge bowl of congee. From that day on, this was my breakfast. Whenever two segments of cowpeas was not enough, I would open the jar myself and take one more.

Chu Kan-kan taught Chao-ho not to be covetous and not to look plaintive or feel sorry for herself when she could not have what she wanted. She also liked her charge to be physically sturdy, and to be tough without being contentious. Her ways suited Chao-ho, which meant that Chao-ho had a rougher childhood than her siblings. She would not cry when her tutor, the fierce Mr. Yü, caned her with a wooden ruler, and she did not let out a peep when Yun-ho played the tyrant. She suffered more because she did not let others know. Yun-ho now says, "Why didn't you scream like me? No one dared to touch me, not even Mr. Yü." Chao-ho had her reasons. She did not mind working things out herself and preferred to keep her own counsel, which was what her friend Miss Wang told Shen Ts'ung-wen years later.

Even when making mischief, Chao-ho liked to attempt it alone and quietly. At home, she was called "the little destroyer." She pulverized a clay doll with her little stool; she tore a cloth doll into shreds with her bare hands. Finally her parents gave her a rubber doll, thinking that it would be indestructible. Chao-ho studied it for a while, then fetched a pair of scissors from Chu Kan-kan's sewing box and cut the doll's head off nice and clean. Chao-ho could also slip her body between and around the banister rails. The nurse-nannies were startled at first, seeing her attempt something so risky; soon they were cheering her on for another performance. "No one ever fussed over me," she explains, "except for my mom; but she died so early." And whenever Chao-ho felt dejected, smarting from her tutor's punishment or her sister's bullying, Chu Kan-kan would say to her: "Forget it! It's no big deal. Go and have your congee and pickled cowpeas, and you will be all right."

All this added up to a curious personality. Chao-ho is obstinate and a brooder. She can seem inflexible, but is also generous and forgiving. As a young woman, she wanted passionately to do well in school and to have a career. She saw herself as inconsequential, someone of no importance to anyone in her family, yet she did not feel shortchanged and did not hold a grudge. She was not born with poise. *K'un-ch'ü* lessons could have improved her deportment, but an accident in the family made it impossible for her to continue after the first year:

Our grandfather's concubine stepped on a pair of scissors, which pierced one of her bound feet. The gash just wouldn't heal, so she went to Shanghai to have it treated. She wanted me to go with her to keep her company. First the doctors amputated her toes and then her foot. Finally she died of gangrene. The summer I stayed in Shanghai with her, my sisters, Yuan-ho and Yun-ho, learned "A Stroll in the Garden" and "Awakening from the Dream." Afterward, I could never catch up with them.

Chao-ho still joined her sisters onstage in school plays. Serious parts made her nervous, and she could be at ease only when she was in a farce. A few times, she nearly turned a solemn scene into a farce. Once she knocked down a cardboard tree and another time Yuan-ho's headdress. Chao-ho probably would have liked to remain a child, the child that she was in Soochow, but her marriage with Shen Ts'ung-wen made it impossible.

For over three years, Shen wrote to her because he knew she would accept his letters, first from the other side of town, then from Peking, and after that, from Tsingtao, "the city by the sea." When he had nearly run out of words, she moved to that city, and they married. This segment of their life also appeared in "Housewife":

> [He told her that] he had known many women. Only she had the power and the skill to tame him, to make him whole. She thought his explanation interesting but not very honest. Nevertheless, it was beautiful, close to being flattery yet different from ordinary flattery. She could not quite understand the delirious effect and the profound meaning a person could have for another. So powerful was this that one only wants to be trusted and be acknowledged by the beloved. She had wanted the two of them to know each other better and to be closer. She was waiting for "the surprise" to fade before making any plans. Still, she became engaged to him, and then married him.

When Chao-ho agreed to marry Shen Ts'ung-wen, Shen wrote to her family, asking for permission. He says in his letter, "Let a man of country stock have a taste of your sweet wine!" Wu-ling and his wife did not need any persuasion, and Yun-ho, who could not wait to let Shen know the good news, hopped onto a rickshaw and headed toward the telegraph office: "On the way there, I thought to myself, How shall I wire this message? I realized that at the end of the telegram I would have to put my name. But doesn't my name, *yun,* mean 'consent'?" So Yun-ho sent a one-word telegram, YUN, which pleased her. When she told Chao-ho about it later, Chao-ho did not say anything. She was worried that Shen Ts'ung-wen might not understand her sister's message because it was too clever. So she quietly dispatched one herself: "Let the man of country stock have his cup of sweet wine. Chao."

Chao-ho was neither happy nor unhappy in her marriage. She *was* often disappointed. But, unlike the character Bibi, she was not "disenchanted" because "she could not tame" her husband, and she was not "tired of a housewife's life." She worried even less about the feeling of "surprise" gradually "being eaten up by the details of everyday life." This was her husband's problem, and he made it hers when he re-created her in his story. Chao-ho's concerns were about practical things: his spending habits, and how she could get them through the month with so little money. It was her life with him that turned her into a housewife, and this happened swiftly.

> We had nothing to start with. It was expected that when I married, I would get a proper dowry. When Yun-ho married a few months before me, our oldest sister confronted our stepmother and managed to secure two thousand yuan for Yun-ho. When it was my turn, Shen Ts'ung-wen wrote to our father and stepmother, saying that we didn't need any money—even though we didn't have any, we still didn't need any. Of course, my parents were relieved. Not long after we were married—we were living with our friend Yang Chen-sheng at the time—one day, Shen Ts'ung-wen sent out a pair of trousers to be washed. The laundryman found a pawnshop receipt in one of the pockets and told Mr. Yang about it. As it turned out, Shen Ts'ung-wen pawned a jade ring my aunt had given me. Mr. Yang later remarked: "When a man marries, he should give his bride a ring. Shen Ts'ung-wen not only did not give his bride a ring, he took hers and pawned it because he needed the money."

It was also around this time that Shen Ts'ung-wen's "Little Ninth Sister" left her Catholic missionary school in Peking and moved in with them. "Little Ninth" was the baby of the Shen family, an enchantress and a troublemaker from the time she was a little girl. She was their mother's favorite and had learned to manipulate her brothers' affections at will when they were growing up in West Hunan. As she got older, no one could have any control over her. Her mother brought her to Peking in the 1920s when she learned she had consumption, and entrusted her to Ts'ung-wen. Until Little Ninth married, which was more than fifteen years later, she was her brother's joy and appendage. They made merry together, just like when they were children, carousing and eating from restaurant to restaurant, and often buying meals on credit. Chao-ho recalls:

> Little Ninth was bubbling over with new ideas about spending money. So Shen Ts'ung-wen's monthly salary would be gone in a week, leaving me to worry about how to pay the cook and the nursemaid. When I was a child, Chu Kan-kan fed me big bowls of rice, and I was plump. My plump days were over when I married Shen Ts'ung-wen. I have been skin and bones ever since.

When Chao-ho married Shen Ts'ung-wen, Little Ninth also became her appendage: "She always carried an English book, which she never read, under her arm. She didn't bother with studying or going to classes when she was enrolled in a school. Whenever she was around, she plunged her brother's life into chaos and made mine miserable."

Bringing Little Ninth into their home was not the only thing Shen Ts'ung-wen did that made Chao-ho's life difficult. He was obsessive about collecting, not expensive paintings and calligraphy, not bronzes and jades, but "trifles" and "bric-a-brac," things "other people didn't want." In his story "Housewife," he tried to explain his compulsion to buy and hold on to the hundreds of small jars and bowls, vases and lacquer boxes. The character who is Bibi's husband says: "Everyone needs a hobby. But once you have one, it's easy to let it become an obsession." Privately, the collector admits feeling "loggy"; his spirits have become "a little lazy," "a little abandoned." The trinkets are "like sandbags weighing down on his keener impulses." Yet he also believes that his compulsion has "a deeper meaning," that "he is pursuing some forgotten things in his memory."

For Shen Ts'ung-wen the author, it had always been the quest for obscure objects, for those ghostlier impressions from the past, that made him most happy and most miserable. He loved the chase. Collecting offered some solace and a possible way to the past, but for more than twenty years he was unclear regarding what he was meant to do about it. There was also his writing, a nobler pursuit, maybe, and nearly all-consuming. His fiction and autobiographical writings from the early 1930s attest to his labor and the demon he had within.

His letters to Chao-ho during a visit to his family in West Hunan in 1934, just four months after their wedding, also give evidence of his hunt. (In these letters, he calls her San-san, or "Three-three." She is the third daughter in her family.* He calls himself Erh-ke, or "Second Brother." He is the second son in his family.) The first letter was sent from T'ao-yuan, or "Peach Blossom Springs."†

T'ao-yuan, January 12, 1934, en route to Yuan River

San-san,

I have arrived in T'ao-yuan. The journey by train was comfortable. My friend Tseng escorted me here. We stayed with a family that sold wine yeast.

---

*San-san is also the main character in a short story of the same title he wrote in 1931.

†The fifth-century poet T'ao Ch'ien, in the preface, or prose account, to his poem "Peach Blossom Springs," tells the story that around 221 B.C., a group of men and women, fleeing from tyranny, had settled in T'ao-yuan (Peach Blossom Springs). Because of this work, T'ao-yuan or T'ao-hua-yuan suggests an otherworldly existence in the Chinese imagination.

We also went to look for a boat. I chose a new boat, and the owner agreed to fifteen dollars for the ride. We board tonight. Right now I am still at my temporary shelter, trying to catch up with friends and speaking country phrases. . . .

On the way here, I saw this notice, which was very charming. It reads: The person who posted this notice is Chung Han-fu. I live by Pai-yang River in Wen-ch'ang-ke, under a big pine tree in a house on the right-hand side. Recently I have lost one virtuous daughter-in-law, aged thirteen, by the name of Chin Ts'ui. She has a squat face, a broad mouth, and a protruding tooth. Her destination, unknown. Anyone who can find her and bring her back shall be awarded two silver dollars. With this big tree as my witness, I will never go back on my word. I am yours sincerely.

San-san, I have copied it all down, without changing a word, to share it with you. With a bit more reading and a bit more work, this person could be a great writer.

January 13, 1934, on the boat
Our boat is going upstream through the rapids. I am sitting under my covers and leaning against the side of the boat as I write this long letter to you with my fountain pen. . . .

Around this time of year, there are still green trees and green mountains along the banks. The water is transparent. Two men are pulling the small boat, which glides upstream in the clear pool. One boatman is smiling, his mouth closed. I asked him, "What is your name?" "Liu." "How many years have you been rowing boats?" "I am fifty-three this year. I have been doing this since I was sixteen." San-san, you can calculate it for me. This man is amazing. Four hundred miles of waterway, he knows every rise and dip, every change of course. He knows how many rapids and pools this river has. And if it were me writing about him, I would also say that he knows how many rocks there are in the water!

January 16, six-fifty in the afternoon
Our boat came to a stop. We moored at Duck Nest Village. . . . The hanging terraces are astonishing. Stacked high along the banks, they are a miraculous sight. The mountains are deep green. The roof tiles on the terraces are white. The wooden boats in the river pool—about twenty of them—are pale yellow. Sheep are bleating. Women are calling, "Erh-lao" and "Hsiao-niu-tzu," their voices piercing through the air. One could also hear the sounds of firecrackers and gongs in the distance. . . .

It's too bad the weather is cold, so cold that I can't go ashore. I like the multistoried houses suspended in the sky. The timber here is cheap. When the water rises, it spreads a far distance, so these houses are all over thirty chang *away from the shore.* It is an enchanting sight from the river. I could hear the singing of simple tunes and ballads. Where these sounds came from—and the lights—are places where the boatmen are getting their pleasure. The young masters and boat owners are also there drinking. The women must be wearing gilded rings. What a moving scene! Just mentioning this makes me sad because I know something about their joy and sorrow. And watching them dispatching each day as the day before, I feel an inexplicable rush of sadness. . . .*

The dogs are barking again. In the dark, someone is saying, "Come again. After the New Year, come again." I am sure a woman is seeing a client off—a woman from the hanging terrace is seeing her sailor to the riverbank.

The wind is fierce. My hands and feet are thoroughly cold, but my heart is warm, and I don't understand why. As long as I am near you, then I don't feel so bad. It seems as if I am still the same person from more than ten years ago— alone, without possessions, getting a ride on a boat carrying military uniforms, traveling upstream and without a clue about the life ahead. Then I was only hoping for a clerical job that paid four dollars a month, and even that was too much to wish for. I wanted to read but didn't have a book. I wanted to go ashore but didn't have any money. . . . The nights were long. The sailors loved to play dice and tiles. They let me watch as they squatted on the deck, pursuing their games by oil lamp. That was me! Me, San-san. Fifteen to twenty should be the most beautiful years in a person's life, and this was how I spent it. Can you imagine what that was like? But here I am, back at my river, on this little boat, reliving my past! This is something I didn't expect. Even more astonishing is that on this little boat, I am right now thinking of a gentle and beautiful face far away, and *this dark-faced woman is at the same time thinking of me from where she is. So much to muse, about fate. . . .*

It is already eight-thirty. You can hear people talking everywhere. This river is a lively place. I can also hear the banging of drums in the distance. It's possible that people are making good on their promises. The wind is vigorous. It's cold in the boat. But if a person loves someone, he is warm inside. It wouldn't matter if his body freezes. The wind is hard. I fear that there will be

---

*Thirty *chang* is about 100 meters.

snow tomorrow. The sheep is still calling. I thought it strange, so tried to listen to it more closely. It seems there is another sheep calling from the other shore. They are answering each other. I also heard singing—the voice of a young woman, piercingly beautiful. I've tried to understand the ballad she was singing but couldn't. I know many ballads. Just thinking about the joys and aches of people like her brings me sorrow. Because of her song, I recall the time I was in Chin-chou, staying in an inn. I heard a woman, a storyteller, singing her story to the beat of her drum. She sang for half a night, for an audience of mule drivers, to help them pass the time. I was alone in bed, listening to the sound of her singing, which was mixed with other people's laughter and chatter. This is also your Erh-ke! You must have been in Chi-nan at the time, studying. Every morning, you had to get up and do your morning exercise. Life's fate makes us feel at a loss. Love me because only you can make me happy.

> *Erh-ke*
> *the sixteenth, eight-fifty in the evening*

The next letter describes the last stretch of his river journey. The boat owner had to hire a tracker to help them get through a succession of rapids. He was an old man: "His whiskers had turned white, teeth all fallen, but as strong as a Roman youth." Shen Ts'ung-wen was struck by his likeness to Tolstoy: "bushy brows, big nose, long beard." He continues:

But this man looked a bit more refined because he grew up by the water. He also seemed cleaner than Tolstoy. Just now, he perched on a rock. Watching him counting his money, realizing how old he was and how hard he worked, and listening to him haggling with the owner about a hundred yuan, I asked myself, Why does this man want to live? Does he ever think why he wants to live?

The next day, Shen Ts'ung-wen is still brooding about these questions. He tells Chao-ho:

I've been standing at the back of the boat, gazing at the water. Suddenly everything is clear to me. I feel I've gained a lot of wisdom from the river. San-san, it's true, I've gained wisdom, not just knowledge. . . . It seems that there are no dregs in me, no opacity. The river, the sunset, the tracker, the boatmen, I love them all and so warmly. Remember the history we have read. What do books tell us except that in the past, childish men, idiotic men, hacked and killed one another? A river is the veritable history. The rocks and sand, the rotting trees and plants, the broken bits of wooden planks in the ever-flowing, perduring water—they stir me up when for so long these feelings about the pains and joys of another people, another time, have become muted. Earlier I mentioned these people who lived their lives as if unconcerned about its consequences. I was wrong about them. They don't need our pity. In fact, we should love them and respect them.

Shen Ts'ung-wen loved the river: life on and around the river, lives bound to the river, the river as a metaphor for life, and the paradox of that metaphor—the constancy of the inconstant. He says to Chao-ho, "It seems as if I am still the same person from ten years ago." Yet he knew he had changed. His aspirations and expectations were different now. Also, he now had a dark and beautiful face to concentrate on; he had gained her and a world. But he did not simply rejoice in the new. Life's possibilities and the "coincidences" that helped him to create a life baffled him and made him feel uneasy. They sharpened the distinctions between him and his wife because without the possibility of the unexpected, they could not have been together. He tells her that while he was listening to the storyteller singing her heart out to a handful of mule drivers, she was in her Chi-nan boarding school. He imagined her getting ready for the morning; he dreamed of the calisthenics and the order of that life. In 1934, Shen Ts'ung-wen was still smitten with his young bride. He believed that love could blur or even override the disparities. So when he is most uncertain, he says to her: "Love me because only you can make me happy."

Much of Shen Ts'ung-wen's happiness was imagined, but it was not a lie. He tells his wife in his letter, even before he arrives home: "Once I reach land, the relatives I'll see along the way will be asking about you first, I'm sure. I want so much to tell them, when they ask, that in fact you are in my pocket." The last letter from this batch was sent from Hu-hsi, still two and half days on foot away from Feng-huang. He writes:

> Tomorrow will be the twentieth. Time passed swiftly yet slowly. Along the
> way, yesterday and today, I saw many white pagodas and many women
> pounding their wash on the rocks by the river. Also cave houses in cliffs and
> stone rollers propped up in the air. I have already reached "Pai-tzu's" stream
> and "Ts'ui-ts'ui's" hometown.* The sun was glorious at midday. Since then,

*Pai-tzu is the main character from a 1928 short story with the same title. Ts'ui-ts'ui is the female character in his novel *Frontier City*.

the light has softened, so my yearning for you has also changed its shape—it is
gentler now. My heart calls out to you all the time. I have been saving tens of
thousands of words, endless phrases, and mounds of smiles and kisses for you. I
know that when I get home and see everyone, because I miss you so much, I
will say foolish things, which no one will understand. Therefore, when
someone asks me, "How were you in Peking?" I will tell him, "My San-san,
her face is dark, so life is fine in Peking." If I don't answer this way, it will be
something very close to it. In any case, I will give them lots of chances to tease
me. Mom is getting old. When she sees that I have such a sweet and gentle
wife and knows how close we are, she will be extra joyful. When I was in
Ch'en-chou [Yuan-ling], [my brother] Yun-liu told me, "Mom is still saying,
'Do you have any idea how Ts'ung-wen learned to pick a wife? It won't do if
he finds someone just like him, and worse if he finds someone unlike him.' But
this is perfect. There is actually someone who is neither like him nor unlike
him." You cannot imagine how happy the family is about us being so good to
each other. They love you even though they haven't met you.

The stars and the new moon are exquisite tonight. There is nothing like
gazing at the sky from a boat. I didn't care how cold I was. My eyes were fixed
on the stars for a long time. If tonight or tomorrow night you also look for the
same big star in the sky, then its glimmer will draw us together, I know.
Because each night, this star will be just like your eyes when they are so
swallowed up by my gaze that they cannot glance sideways. San-san, from
your end, this star will have become my eyes.

Your Erh-ke
nine at night, on the nineteenth

This was how Shen Ts'ung-wen resolved the distance between himself and
his wife. He carries her in his pocket; he makes the stars and his family his allies.
He composes a self that is a companion for him.

We have only one letter from her to him while he was away in Hunan in
1934. There is romance in it, but her words are quieter:

Dear Erh-ke,
You are gone for only two days, yet it seems like a long time. After you left,
the wind started blowing. It is a bullying wind, a mad wind with a boorish
roar. Right now is ten o'clock at night. I can hear the tree branches making
strange sounds. I imagine that you are just getting off the train, or getting
ready for your river journey; or you are quietly walking the three miles to the
river, trying to keep up with the porter who is carrying your bags. Is the wind

*in Ch'ang-sha as brutal as ours, turning my Erh-ke's body into a block of ice?
Because of this wind, I am worried, and my heart is ice cold even though I am
sitting in a cozy room. I don't see how you can endure it. When I say I am
worried, I am not at all untruthful.*

*Because I miss you so much, during the day I concentrate on reading your
manuscript. Then comes the night. The demonic wind keeps on howling, and I
can't do a thing. Sometimes I think about what it will be like ten days from
now. By then you will have been home. I imagine how happy your family will
be, which in turn gives me solace. But that's ten days from now. The ten days
in between are hard to get through. Come to think of it, it's probably better to
wire a message to you. The road between here and your family home is long,
and the passage is difficult. It would take at least ten to fifteen days for a letter
to arrive. And by the time you receive this letter, my situation will be different
from now. . . . . Perhaps you and your brothers are sunning yourselves under the
eaves. Perhaps you are chatting with your mother in a room. (Most likely you
are chatting with your mother.) In the room a charcoal fire is burning. A pot
of dark and red dates is bubbling on the stove, giving off a warm sweetness.
You and your mother talk of this and that. Sometimes you stretch out your
hand to feel if her clothes are too thin. Suddenly your younger brother comes in
with my letter. Surely this will make you happy. You open it and read what's
in the letter. It's all this talk of being worried and cold, which is not in tune
with your feelings. Am I not right? I want so much to write like this: "Erh-ke,
I am ecstatic. Little Ninth and I jumped up and down, celebrating for half a
day. We guess that you must be home by now. So tonight we each had three
bowls of rice." These words, I am sure, would please you more. But I will write
this ten days from now. When you receive this letter, think that while you are
reading it, we are all happy for you here.*

San-san
night of the ninth

Even in high romance, Chao-ho tried to hold back. It was a way of reining
in her reveries lest she be dishonest or inaccurate. If she had let herself go, pursuing what she had started to say, "Little Ninth and I jumped up and down, celebrating for half a day," her husband would have been more pleased. Not
because this was "in tune" with his happiness but because the scene she had
begun to compose could have been delicious had she followed it up. Shen
Ts'ung-wen would not want her to lie about whether she was happy or not. Yet
he would probably feel a little sad if she gave up an idea when the idea had
somewhere to go. His regret about her was that her spirits were too earthbound.

At the same time, he admired this in her because his own existence was nearly all aerial. In the story "Housewife," Bibi's husband describes her as like the grapevines, "so firmly planted in the ground" and "living so close to what is real and practical." He realizes that living things cannot sustain themselves in the sky, and so decides to emulate her, "to live closer to earth."

In real life, Shen Ts'ung-wen could never emulate his wife. Marriage made them more resistant to each other's influence. Things got worse by 1937. They had two sons now, many friends in common, a shared interest in books, and little else besides. Neither Chao-ho nor the boys went with him when in August of that year, a month after the Marco Polo Bridge Incident that led to full-scale war with Japan, Shen and several friends left Peking. It took this group nearly a year to reach K'un-ming, a major city in the southwest province of Yunnan. Scores of writers, scholars, scientists, and teachers from the north were making their way to this place after the Japanese moved into their cities and created an atmosphere in which it was impossible for them to work.

When he boarded the train in Peking, Shen Ts'ung-wen had no idea where he might end up or what the next stage of his life was going to be like. Since his marriage he had done a lot of writing, but mostly essays. In 1936, he had published *Notes on a Trip to Hunan*, a work based on the letters he had written to Chao-ho two years before, and he was very pleased with this book. His output in fiction had been thin. He was spending more time editing and compiling stories he had finished earlier. He had also joined the editorial staff of a literary supplement to a major newspaper in Tientsin. He had become more practical now that he was a father.

Probably one reason for his decision to leave Peking was that he would be traveling with Yang Chen-sheng. Yang was his closest friend, someone Shen had come to depend on when he was in a funk or short of money. In early August 1937, Yang, a novelist and a professor at Peking University, was deeply involved in talks of combining China's three most prestigious academic institutions—Peking University, Tsinghua, and Nankai—into one, and having this "union university" relocated in Ch'ang-sha, a city nine hundred miles southwest of Peking, in Shen's home province, Hunan. He probably persuaded Shen to leave with him, knowing that he could always find his friend a teaching position in the new university if Shen could not make a living as a writer. Chao-ho and the two children did not join Shen until the fall of the following year.

In the interim, Chao-ho wrote Shen many letters; his letters to her were far fewer. She was twenty-seven at the time but already feeling "old and tired." Her tone in these letters was grating. Her worries were mainly about him, but not about his being cold or hungry on the long journey or any of the concerns she expressed in her 1934 letter. Instead she imagined how much of a burden her husband was to other people. When she learned that he and his traveling companions would be staying with his brother in Yuan-ling for some time, Chao-ho wrote:

> I think that it makes sense for your group to stay with your family in Yuan-ling. It will take some burden from Mr. Yang. But I wonder if you have considered these two things: (1) Your older sister told us several times in her letters that there had been many guests at the Yuan-ling house. And just now, Little Ninth was talking about going home. So don't be vague about your plans. Since you are bringing a huge group, don't you think you should warn your brothers first? Don't give them too much inconvenience. This way you can avoid not knowing where to put everybody once you get there. (2) You have completely exhausted your financial resources. Even though the Yangs have been taking care of all your daily expenses, the truth is that you haven't got a cent, and now you are the host. Does this mean that you are going to put all the responsibilities on your brothers? Maybe you think I worry too much. Maybe you have thought through this yourself. But from what I know about you, you usually don't plan ahead, and you attend to this but not that. You also tend to make promises you can't keep, so nothing gets done and people get angry at you. I can think of lots of examples. So of course I'm worried. . . .
>
> And speaking about what we are going to live on in the future, I agree with your long-range plans. But what about our more immediate concerns? Yes, for the time being we are all right. But what about next year? I hope you will think of something soon. I know that Ling Yen-ch'ih had told you that you didn't have to worry about being hungry for a year.* And I am sure that if I ask my Hofei family for help, they will not refuse. But can we be at peace with that? My hope is not to seek anyone's help, not even my father's, if we can possibly manage it ourselves. You should understand my predicament. If my own mother were alive, do you think

---

*Ling Yen-ch'ih was the brother of Yuan-ho's best friend, Ling Hai-hsia. A successful Shanghai banker, he had become a sort of guardian angel to the Chang family. Ling helped Yun-ho and her family move to Wuhan during the war and put up the money for Yuan-ho's wedding expenses. He was also a collector and a man of refined taste. He and Ch'ung-ho shared a love for calligraphy.

we would even have to ask? You know how I feel. When you write to Hofei, no matter whether it's to our oldest sister or our brother Tsung-ho, please, don't mention a word about asking Dad for help. Until we really have no choice, I will write myself. I don't want these words to come from you. It's not appropriate. You should know this.

Chao-ho never asked for money from home. Her oldest sister sent money to Shen Ts'ung-wen a few times. His letters did not explain whether this came from Yuan-ho's private account, her father, or the Ling family. Chao-ho told Shen Ts'ung-wen in an earlier letter: "You understand the temperament of 'that mother' of mine. Why should we give her an excuse to vent her anger on our Dad? If we could get by, why go begging for help?" Chao-ho is the most austere of the Chang sisters. She denies herself extravagant things and an easy life because she believes that simplicity is good and self-reliance is a thoughtful gesture—it takes the weight off someone else. She says to her husband:

You have always blamed me for being so hard on myself. You say that in trying to save a little, I lose a lot. Now you realize that I've been right all along. No one at home knows how to be frugal. So I have to keep an eye on everything. If I don't save, who will? The way things are now, even if we were to save and save, it's already too late. If you can provide for yourself on your side, without borrowing money, it will be best. If it's absolutely necessary to borrow, be sparing. Mr. Yang doesn't have much money. Plus he has many expenses. (I know this from his letters to his sister.) So don't ask him for more, no matter what. . . .

I don't like to "slap my face to give myself a puffed-up look." To pretend that you are a gentleman when you are not is so unnatural. We must live as our situation permits. I much prefer "drawing the water and pounding the rice myself."* I never consider physical exertion a hardship. Most important is that we are flexible enough to adapt to our circumstances. After the war, I won't allow us to have extravagant wishes and to be wasteful. I want us to do our best to be thrifty and to make some contribution to the new China. We should get rid of our old habits and try earnestly to improve our character. I don't care for outward appearances. So I won't let you force me to wear high heels and to have my hair permed. I will do the washing up myself, and I won't let you stop me

---

*Traditionally this is considered "women's work." The phrase has come to mean managing a household.

from doing it just because you don't want me to have a pair of rough hands. I don't care if our food is coarse or fine, our clothes are tasteful or not. We are lucky to stay alive.

It is hard to imagine that Chao-ho herself needed to reform her habits. Long ago her nurse-nanny had convinced her that pickled cowpeas tasted as good as potted chicken, and were nobler because they were rightfully hers—she did not have to beg or grab them from anyone. Chu Kan-kan also taught Chao-ho the virtue of thrift. In one of her letters to her husband, Chao-ho mentions that Chu Kan-kan had thought it "a waste" that Shen Ts'ung-wen was sending his mail express to Peking. Chao-ho concurred, saying that in fact regular mail was often faster than express. Her letter does not acknowledge his probable intent in this superfluous act—that his heart was impatient, that perhaps he, too, realized the impracticality but still went ahead and did it.

And could he have forced her to "wear high heels" and to have her "hair permed"? Could Shen Ts'ung-wen have forced Chang Chao-ho to do anything she did not want to do? His only power over her was to imagine her extravagantly—to make her his dark angel and muse. Chao-ho tried to resist it, but at times even she found this kind of excess intoxicating. Shen guessed at this, and it did not take him long to realize that rather than wanting him there with her, she much preferred to have him hundreds of miles away, writing to her. During his trip to West Hunan in 1934, he had teased her about this, saying that she should have been "a bit more ruthless" and "squeezed a few more years of letters" out of him before agreeing to marry him. By 1937, the thought made him despair. He was on the road again, this time not knowing when he would come back. His wife stayed behind in enemy-occupied territory with their two young children. She could have joined him, but was reluctant, despite his pleas. "It seems that you don't understand yourself," he writes.

You are doing your best accommodating to your situation, in order to avoid making any commitments to me. You know you are prevaricating. It seems, also, you are not interested in our having a life together. While other people are yearning to be with their families in the chaos of war, you are letting go so many opportunities that would allow us to be together. Frankly, when you say that you love me or you love my character, it is more accurate to say that you love me writing letters to you. You are happy to have me far, far away. You would rather that I stay anxious and angry and depressed than spend a quiet life with you. You feel that a quiet life means that I have been neglecting you. What you don't understand is that such a life will give me some rest—it will allow me to concentrate on producing something enduring.

Shen was probably right about Chao-ho. She was evasive in her letters to him, dodging his questions about why she was staying in Peking even when it was clear that the Japanese had dug in and both sides were preparing for a protracted war. She complained a lot in these letters, not about the cook, the maid, money being tight, or food getting scarce. The children tired her, but they were her joy. It seems that she saved all her disapprobation for her husband. He wrote to her that if indeed she felt "life was simpler and happier" when they were apart, then they should have "a long-term plan." He added: "If in Peking there is someone who cares for you and you for him, and if you are remaining in Peking for this reason, then I won't feel jealous or angry," because "even a healthy person can catch malaria or typhoid, let alone finding yourself in love or being loved."

In two long letters, he urged Chao-ho not to miss her chance should such a thing happen. He said: "I will never stop anyone from loving you or you from loving anyone else. As long as you have gotten your happiness, I won't be in your way. I love you, but I shouldn't, because of this, hold you back." And about himself, he claimed that he had foreseen this to be his fate:

I am someone who was born with a tragic character. When I am compassionate, I am extremely compassionate. When I am naïve, I am extremely naïve. When I am muddled, I am hopelessly muddled. It's difficult to explain my character, but I can offer several reasons: (1) I inherited some germ of madness from my ancestors. (2) I spent too much of my childhood daydreaming. (3) The books I read are too eclectic, and I have gone through too many colossal changes in my life. (4) I lost too much blood through nosebleeds. This, combined with using my head too much, gives me endless cycles of depression.

Chao-ho's response to Shen Ts'ung-wen's heartrending letters was short and brisk: "Your words were full of rubbish. What is this talk about giving me freedom? I don't ever want to hear it again. You are not me, so what is in your head is yours, and you feel this way because you are depressed. If you write like this again, I simply won't answer." She did not want to fall in love with someone else or to have someone else fall in love with her. What she wanted was her husband's yearning for her all his life. This was her only vanity.

She also cared a lot about his writing, whether he was doing his best or whether he was writing at all. "I don't think that writing reviews and critical essays suit you," she tells him.

> Your observations are subtle but fragmented. You see other people's short-comings but not your own. You talk a lot but do less. So even a layman like me feels that many things you say in your critical pieces are inappropriate. In the past, you still listened to my suggestions and made slight revisions. But in the last year or two, you won't even show me your shorter essays. If you think that I am not someone you could have a rapport with, then I have nothing to say. Still, I feel that your strength does not lie in this type of writing. You have been letting go your creative energy, the charge that allowed you to write those beautiful stories. You have broken it up, so now you are just churning out fragments of miscellanies that are of no consequence to anyone. I think it's a pity. It's heartbreaking to watch someone taking a piece of material that was meant to be a seamless, celestial robe and tearing it to shreds. I know I am being blunt. I hope you won't take offense.

Just as Chao-ho regarded superfluous things as extravagant and artifice as evidence of moral decay, she felt that clever "miscellanies" could ruin a writer's divine gift. She referred to the miscellanies as "outward things and trifles" and did not want her husband to waste his energy on them. She says to him: "Your original countenance is clean and pure and simple. Any kind of covering would not be right. You are originally good. It's a shame that you have been spoiled* by so many different kinds of fancy, unsuitable tricks."

From reading these letters, it's hard to believe that Chao-ho was eight years younger than her husband and that he was once her teacher. It is also hard to believe that she was the one who grew up in a household overflowing with servants, tutors, and extravagant things; that he was a man of "country stock" and she was his "cup of sweet wine." What Chao-ho gained from her family's shelter and the steady march of a good and well-rounded education was an unwavering sense of how things should be and what constituted integrity. This confidence she shared with all her sisters. So even with her husband, she would risk offending him and tell him how he should best use his talent. She wanted him to keep his countenance immaculate because no covering would be suitable.

Shen Ts'ung-wen's most "beautiful stories" were those of West Hunan. But

---

*She uses the English word *spoil.*

even when he was writing about the people and places he knew well, using no "tricks," he was an artificer. Chao-ho takes notice of this fact and makes no comment. She simply reads and hopes for more.

*April 13, four o'clock in the morning, Yuan-ling**

Third Sister,

It's not yet dawn. I can make out dimly the outlines of trees on the mountain and a patch of fog. I don't know which family has been having a funeral. They have been banging drums and gongs the whole night. It was a dull and weary sound. Everyone must have been tired. They all have been tottering in the candlelight: the monks, the watchman, the children of the deceased, and the guests who came for the wake. They rely on the sounds of drums and chanting to keep them braced. Cocks are also crowing in the distance. I reckon that the rice pudding and the lotus broth are waiting for us in the pot. The drums from a thousand years ago probably sounded just like this, with nothing changed.

The cries of cuckoos are everywhere. They are anxious and mournful—lucid and mournful. These birds are strange. They always wait until dark to call their mates. Their call is loud, so they must be far away from their mates, and there must be fewer of them. We also have cuckoos in the north, but they don't sound the same. There is nothing remarkable about their color or their shape. They look spotty. And when they are ready to fly, they seem always in a hurry and distracted, as if fleeing from something—their form far from graceful. It is only their cries that are impressive: clear and distant, sad and baleful.

We are hoping to be on the river around five-thirty. This means that we have to call for someone to open the city gate, to call for the ferry, to call for . . . This is what it takes to travel in the hinterland. "The sound of a cock, a moon hanging over a thatched hut. / Footprints of men, frost on a wooden bridge"— this couplet describes precisely what it is like setting off early in the morning. The scene on the river just before the boat gets going is most beautiful. The bamboo sparrow and the myna are probably dreaming. They hear in their dreams the sound of drums and bugles inside the city walls. Maybe they are having another dream. They dream they are being chased by a huge bird or being caught by a ferocious dog. Or they dream that they have become friends with the oriole. All the birds are in pairs except for the oriole. The oriole sings about his aloneness. The woodpecker is also alone, but his aloneness explains

---

*Shen wrote this letter just before he and his friends left his brother's house in April 1938 to get on the road again, heading toward Yunnan.

his circumstances: he finds his own food, and he is independent. This bird is different from the oriole, who is simply self-absorbed.

Everyone is up, waiting to get on the road. We will have to walk down a mountain path and go past a street, called Yu-chia-hsiang, that is lined with brothels. Maybe the dogs will bark when we pass. Maybe the girls, who spent their night alone, think that other people's clients are leaving. . . . Once out of the city gate, we will come upon the river, the eternal river! If we have to wait for a while before our boat leaves, we can see the young women who spent the night with their clients coming back: their clients getting ready for the next stretch of journey, the young women on their way home. On many occasions, during my river wanderings, I have seen a woman like these, standing quietly on a boat. What was she thinking? Who treated her well? Who betrayed her? Who deceived her, who cheated her? Ah, life. Every woman is like the sea, deep and wide, without borders or coasts. I hear that there are over five hundred decent women, proper women, doing this type of business here. If only they could write, how many stories they could tell!

The cock is crowing eagerly now. The porters have arrived. In another twenty minutes, I will be by the riverbank. Hsiao-hu must be waking up at this moment. The light in your little room is already lit. Hsiao-lung, just turning over in his bed, is calling for his nanny.* On this piece of paper, there should be the cries of cuckoo, the sounds of bugles and drums, the crowing of roosters, and the murmurs of Older Brother and Sister-in-Law downstairs, making arrangements for our bags. Also there should be another sound, my little babe.

Kiss the children for me.

Fourth Brother†
five-ten in the morning

Chao-ho waited until late August of 1938 to make up her mind. By that time the two major inland routes, through Wuhan and Ch'ang-sha, had become impassable as fighting around these areas escalated by the summer of 1938. The safest option left was to take a steamer—probably British operated—to Hong Kong from Tientsin, then to continue the journey by sea to Vietnam, and to take a train from there to K'un-ming. Even after her husband had gotten all the

---

*Hsiao-hu is their younger son and Hsiao-lung their older son. They are also called Hu-hu and Lung-lung.

†Even though Shen is the second son, hence Second Brother, in his family, he is also the fourth child. So sometimes he refers to himself as "Fourth Brother."

documents ready for her to pick up in Hong Kong so that she could reenter unoccupied China by train through Vietnam, Chao-ho was still shilly-shallying. This time he was fed up. He wrote to her, saying: "I wish I could talk about the weather, or things of human interest, . . . but I won't" and "So are you planning to come or not? Do you still want me or not? Of course, I suspect there is some other reason why you are not on the road when you should be."

What was it that forced Chao-ho to act, especially when it had become much more difficult—and expensive—for her and her children to travel to the southwest? Did she want to put a stop to her husband's suspicions? Mail from the southwest now had to be routed through Hong Kong. Was Chao-ho worried that soon she would no longer be able to receive letters from Shen Ts'ung-wen? Or was she finally persuaded by his argument that being in the same place, bringing up the children together, was better than facing life alone?

Years later, Shen Ts'ung-wen would observe that Chao-ho was slow to act; that she would rather "accommodate" herself to her situation, no matter how undesirable, than brave change. Having a home and two children reinforced her inertia. She told Shen that it was cumbersome to be on the road because their children were so young, and that she also could not bear to part with their books and letters. Yet her sister Yun-ho had made the journey to Szechwan the year before with two small children, an elderly mother-in-law, two nursemaids, and fourteen trunks. When Chao-ho finally wrote to her husband on August 25 to tell him that she was ready to set off, even she must have realized that if she brooded any longer, she would be letting the Japanese decide her fate. So she said yes to him, and then delayed her trip for another month, waiting for the sea to calm down.

Chao-ho and the couple's two sons, Lung-chu or Lung-lung (Dragon's Pearl) and Hu-ch'u or Hu-hu (Tiger Cub), did not reach K'un-ming until November. Shen Ts'ung-wen was shocked to see how much their children had grown. Lung-lung had been two and a half and Hu-hu only two months old when Shen left Peking in the summer of 1937. From K'un-ming, Shen sent a full report to his brother in Hunan: "Hsiao-lung [Lung-lung] has a lot of energy. He doesn't need anyone's attention but makes a lot of noise. No one can quite manage him. He is a completely wild kid" and "Hsiao-hu [Hu-hu] is untamed and strong. He is loud when he speaks and takes big strides when he walks. He shouts, 'More,' even while he is eating. He adds a lot of life to the family." The younger son writes, years later: "My brother and I couldn't care if there was a national crisis or if our family had a steady income, our bodies just kept growing, and our stomachs were always hungry." Their father used to say, "In the air, we have flying machines. At home, we have digesting machines."

When the Japanese planes began to bomb K'un-ming in the spring of 1939, Chao-ho decided to move to the countryside with the children, to a small town called Ch'eng-kung. She chose this place because there was a school for refugee children not too far away where she could get a teaching position. It was her sister Ch'ung-ho who had first learned about this school. Ch'ung-ho knew that Chao-ho had not been happy in K'un-ming, so she urged her sister to apply. A year earlier, when Chao-ho was still in Peking, Shen Ts'ung-wen, in his letters, had also encouraged her to take up some work she might enjoy. He suggested translation because Chao-ho had read English in college and had done well in it. He said: "It does not matter what you translate. Sometimes I know you better than you know yourself. At school you were so conscientious in your studies, and you have such a subtle mind. The two kids can spend only your physical energy but not your imagination or your intellect." Chao-ho, however, did not take her husband's suggestion kindly. She snapped back: "You said I should start translating books. How could you be talking about translating books in this day and age? It sounds like you have been talking in your sleep. I don't have the time or energy to do it. Furthermore, who is going to read it? Who still reads that sort of thing these days?"

Chao-ho responded differently to her sister's advice. She moved her family to Ch'eng-kung and every day walked seven miles to her school and back, passing by the wheat fields and stretches of yellow rape and banksia flowers. She loved teaching and was truly pleased about her independence. Her children both knew how to look after themselves. Lung-lung walked to school every morning. "And when he hears the air-raid warning, three gunshots in the distance," Shen Ts'ung-wen wrote, "he runs a mile home, darting across the footpaths like a monkey. No adults can keep up with him." Hu-hu "becomes the master of the house when his mother leaves for school. He sits on a low stool and eats his meal."

Shen Ts'ung-wen was now employed by the Southwest Consolidated University (Lian-ta) in K'un-ming. This was the "union university" that brought together Peking, Tsinghua, and Nankai Universities in the fall of 1937. The school had a temporary stay in Ch'ang-sha before it was moved farther west to K'un-ming in the spring of 1938. There, Shen taught modern Chinese literature. On weekends, he would make the long commute home: "He jostles his way into a small train, clutching his cloth bundle; rocks from side to side for an hour to the wails of the steam whistle; and then gets on an elegant little Yunnan horse and rides ten miles home."

The house Shen Ts'ung-wen rented for his family in Ch'eng-kung had been built by a local landlord long before. It took twelve years to finish: "The old man went to the mountain himself and selected every rafter and pillar from the trees that grew there." The groom Shen Ts'ung-wen had hired to look after his horse on his first visit to Ch'eng-kung told him to take a close look at details of this house:

> You can see that no two cabbages, gourds, toads, or rabbits carved on the window lattice are the same. This is the work of a single carpenter. He shaped everything with his hatchet. Also the front gate and bolt, the iron bar that tightens and locks the door, the stone drums with carved designs that hold the pillars up, and the big wooden bed that couldn't squeeze past the front door—which of them is not the work of our county's best craftsman? In the past, when the old master of the house was still alive, anyone who had seen the house would stick up his thumb and say, "Old timer, your house is the very, very best in Ch'eng-kung." The old man would smile and reply, "Who says!"

According to the groom, the former master of the house had an odd temperament. Even when the house was completed, he left most of the rooms empty. He then hired four carpenters to prepare a coffin for him. It took them a year. By the time they finished "his house in the ground," the old man died.

When Shen Ts'ung-wen saw this place, an elderly woman was in charge. She was married to the old man's second brother, and people called her "Grandma Number Two" (*erh-nai-nai*). It appeared that after the old landowner died, his brother moved the whole clan into this house, but he took a concubine, who did not get along with his wife. Eventually he and his concubine returned to his original house, letting his wife manage the new house. Over the years, the younger generation of the family all went away. The family had also lost a lot of its former splendor. Then, in 1923, "the bandits took a fancy to their house. They moved in for a few days and left with two loads of jewelry and silverware, and more than ten loads of silver coins and blocks of Yunnan's best opium." This was the story the groom told Shen Ts'ung-wen when they rode back to town.

Of their life in this house, Shen's younger son writes:

> My brother and I not only had insatiable appetites but also inexhaustible spirit and energy. Our mom racked her brains, commanding all her skills to satisfy us. Therefore, we were all familiar with the nursery rhymes Chu Kan-kan used to sing to her in her local Hofei dialect. We even learned a few Soochow ditties her classmates taught her at school. English songs were her attempt to introduce us to "advanced education." My tongue was clumsy, so I could only listen. Mom also knew a few arias from Peking

opera. Not wanting the neighbors to hear her, she would sing these softly. . . . *K'un-ch'ü* was another story. We couldn't make head or tail of it. But whenever Mom was with Aunt Ch'ung-ho and Uncle Tsung-ho, they loved to sing this kind of music together—so elegant and refined that my brother and I could only spoof it to entertain ourselves. . . . If Dad was home, and Mom was running out of tricks, he was glad to take over to give her some relief. It was effortless for him.

Shen Ts'ung-wen laid a drawing board on top of two wooden crates—cans of Shell oil used to come in these crates—and this became "the family's cultural center." Hu-hu writes: "Mom corrected papers on it. My brother practiced calligraphy on it. And when Dad was home, we would often find him bending over the wooden board, scribbling away." This was also where the family gathered when they relaxed. "An oil lamp, with a flicker no bigger than a pea, hung on the wall." Sometimes on these occasions, Shen Ts'ung-wen would break into a song, "the only one he knew": "Yellow River, Yellow River, you arise from the K'un-lun Mountains. / Rolling past the Mongol Plains, / you cut through the Great Wall! / One, two, one, / One, two, one!" He had learned this song when he was a young soldier in West Hunan. When the family teased him about it, "he would never be upset": "'No good?' he would say. 'Well, then, let me tell you a story.'" Shen Ts'ung-wen told tiger stories and wild boar stories, and stories of how hunters caught pythons in the wild. He described the arrogance and majesty of these beasts, and could imitate their sounds and "the sounds of ten different birds chattering at the same time, himself like the sparrow, intoxicated with his own happiness."

According to his sons, Shen Ts'ung-wen could never exhaust his source: "When he finished one, he would start another." "That was nothing," he would say to Lung-lung and Hu-hu. "Wait until you hear this." And he would continue, with stories of hard-driving widows. One in a fit of anger sank a chestful of gold and jewels. Another—a soy seller—went after a bounder with a wooden bat. To keep his young audience—his two "digesting machines"—interested, he would include "some delicious props." He told them this story:

When your mom was in college, she wouldn't pay a heed to me. Whenever she saw me, she would run. One day she went to a bookstore. Under her left arm were two books, like this, and in her right hand, she was holding a box of cakes. The back of her hair was cropped short, like a boy's. Her fringe came down to here, which nearly covered her eyes, and she would toss it up and down—wow, she looked smart. So she walks into the bookstore. Suddenly she sees Mr. Hsiao, standing behind the counter. Mr. Hsiao in his black-framed glasses looked just like me. So she thought she was looking at Shen Ts'ung-wen. She dropped her box of cakes, dashed for the door, and ran for dear life.

His young son remembered being worried about the box of cakes Chao-ho had left behind: "'And then what happened?' 'She disappeared and that was the end of the story.'" The father smiled. "I still could not let go of the cake, so I pressed him again, 'But then what happened?'"

Shen Ts'ung-wen also played a complicated game with his two sons, based on a traditional drama, *Beat the Drum and Curse Ts'ao Ts'ao*.* The drum (*ku*) was the "thickest part" of his sons' backsides (*ku*).

[Dad] could play a sequence of the most complicated rhythms, his head swaying and his mouth uttering some vague and abstract denunciation of the enemy. Maybe his hands were so lost in the rhythm that he could not stop cursing. My brother often could not wait any longer. He would edge closer and say, "Dad, it's my turn, it's my turn."

Shen Ts'ung-wen had many reasons to feel rotten. He was teaching in China's best university at that time, but he knew that some of the faculty at the Consolidated University strongly objected to his being there. He was first an instructor at the inferior teacher's college, and then held a joint appointment in the college of arts—a job probably procured for him by his friend Yang Chen-sheng, who was an administrator and a professor at the college of arts. Like Hu Shih, Yang had always maintained that Shen's achievements as a writer qualified him for an academic position. Not everyone in the school shared this view. China's long tradition of using the civil service degree to validate a person's intellectual worth could have been responsible for some of their skepticism. But Shen's detractors were subtler. They held him to a higher standard—their own measure of scholarship. One such person was Liu Wen-tien, noted both for his annotations of *Huai-nan-tzu,* an abstruse Han text on political theory and cosmology, *and* for his expositions of the Ch'ing novel *Story of the Stone*. Liu had

---

*This opera is from the *hsi-p'i* tradition, a type of music that uses a lot of drums, gongs, and clappers. The story is from the history of the Three Kingdoms. Ts'ao Ts'ao, the prime minister of the Wei kingdom, asks a smart and talented man, called Mi Heng, to play the drum for his guests. By using Mi Heng as an entertainer, Ts'ao Ts'ao is hoping to humiliate him. Knowing that this is Ts'ao Ts'ao's intent, Mi Heng strikes back. As he drums, he chants a long diatribe against the host. (See *Hsi-tien,* vol. 1, pp. 254–66.)

said, "Chen Yin-k'e is a real professor.* He is worth four hundred dollars a month. I am worth forty dollars. Chu Tzu-ch'ing is worth four dollars.† But I wouldn't give forty cents for Shen Ts'ung-wen."

Shen Ts'ung-wen was also feeling pressure from Chao-ho. In one letter, she tells him that his use of the particle *ch'i* is "often wrong." She then writes out a sentence from a recent letter he sent her, points out his mistake, and gives a sample sentence in which the particle is used correctly. She adds: "I was afraid that you might make the same mistake when you write to other people. So don't make fun of me and call me a linguist." Chao-ho liked to edit her husband's work. She admitted that he was nervous about her reading his manuscripts because she "could not keep from tampering with them." He would say to her, "You have gotten rid of my style. After you are through with them, these writings are no longer mine—they are no longer Shen Ts'ung-wen's."

His essays from the K'un-ming years reveal that he felt yet another type of pressure from his wife. Whether this was imagined or not, it was a darker force and more serious, and he felt it most acutely when she was silent and agreeable and when she smiled. He writes:

> This smile should have suggested to most people understanding and tolerance, affection, and sympathy. But for me, at this moment, it has become a force that tries to ostracize me. It sends me to a place where I feel totally isolated and helpless. I know that before me stands a woman with a simple and kind heart, that nothing—no impossibilities of mine and no personal setbacks of hers—could have taken away that smile which represents her truest self. That her life is sound and complete is apparent, not only in her disposition and her sense of responsibility, but also in the fact that she is always full of energy and takes a lively interest in everything. Years might have added some limitations, but they are of no consequence to her. Troubles connected with having a home and children have only deepened her gentle, maternal nature. When I am reminded of her singularly good points, I feel rather resentful.

The passage is from a piece entitled "Green Nightmare," the first of three "nightmare" stories he wrote about the two of them in the Yunnan countryside.

---

*A linguist and a historian of China's medieval period, Chen was, perhaps, the most respected scholar at the university.

†Chu Tzu-ch'ing, a great stylist of the vernacular essay, was also a professor of Chinese literature at the university.

Throughout these stories, or "autobiographical reflections," he calls her "the housewife." The children are "Lung-lung" and "Hu-hu" whenever they appear, and other people call him "Mr. Shen." Only the Chao-ho character is referred to without a name. Perhaps he wanted his readers to realize that this was the continued chronicle of "Housewife" from seven years ago. In the Yunnan countryside, the housewife has become his conscience and his competition, only now her competition has made him feel "resentful." Against her illimitable goodness, he can only say, "I used my brains, so I am tired." In the story, he tells her that he "needs music to rinse his mind, to let it rest for a while," and "to rein in his imagination." He goes so far as to say "music is more important to me than you and the kids." She does not flinch when she hears this—he is rarely declarative—and she can never be jealous because she is "sound" and analytical. In his head he composes her response to him. She points out to him that he is tired because he uses his imagination to scare himself and to defeat himself. And, of course, she is right. He says: "I am like an anomalous star caught by the spatial equation of some young mathematician. I admit total defeat to the housewife."

The interior war continues in "Black Nightmare." In this story, Hu-hu's eyes have caught his father's notice:

> They are big eyes, wide-open, gazing into the distance. The going-ons along the river and the glory of stars in the night sky have influenced me all my life. I know that they will have the same effect on him. I couldn't help but feel slightly worried about his beautiful pair of eyes. So I told him the Buddhist story, the story of Prince Gotanara:*
>
> *That prince had the most beautiful pair of eyes. Then he became blind, and then his sight was restored. His eyes were just like yours, dark and luminous, and he could see everything. In daylight, he could stare at the sun without blinking. At night, under a lamp, just like this one, he could see the tiniest mosquito on the ceiling. This was because he was noble and just, and believed in virtue. The prince's father wandered throughout his kingdom, carrying a gold and purple alms bowl in his hand. The young and beautiful girls, when they heard what had happened to their prince, became so moved that they wept. The father collected more than half a bowl of their clear, immaculate tears and brought it home to his son. Once bathed with their tears, his eyes were radiant, just like before.*
>
> The housewife smiles but says nothing. Her bright gaze seems to sug-

---

*I have not yet found the story of this Indian prince and so could only approximate his name from the Chinese transliteration.

gest a gentle gloss of her own: "In the old story, after the prince was made blind by an evil man, he had to wash his eyes with the tears of beautiful women. But now people can only be saved when they are beheld by virtue and justice."

Shen Ts'ung-wen continues:

> Since I imagined her saying this to Hu-hu, I simply had to add something myself: "My little boy, a person can also be saved by someone's beautiful and gentle gaze. For instance . . ."
> The child's heart was completely won over by the story. His eyes were wide open. Looking at his mother softly, he said to her, "Mom, your eyes are also very bright, brighter than mine!"

Shen Ts'ung-wen believed that the gaze of a woman could do as much good as virtue and justice. Chao-ho could never go along with this. The difference between them lies in their beliefs. Her family and her childhood in Soochow had helped to shape hers. The source of his belief is more difficult to locate: his impressionable soul, maybe, his extreme passions and innocence, his early peregrinations, the landscape of West Hunan and its violence. He would never give up his belief, but he always seemed rattled and defensive under her gaze—the same gaze that filled their sons with love and warmth.

Long after her husband died, Chao-ho would discount his imaginings of her, of her calm and her confidence. She said that she did not earn his full respect until she started teaching during the war. She felt that every woman should work and have her independence: "Otherwise her husband would never consider her his equal." In Shen Ts'ung-wen's eyes, his wife had virtue and the will to live. These things alone made her supreme. Her concerns about a job and her independence had no significance in his estimation of her. "Housewife" was queen and goddess in his world, and he was always slightly afraid next to her.

In Chao-ho's version of the two of them, she could be as rattled as he, and he was not as diminutive as he'd thought. In fact, she felt that her life in Yunnan sometimes was as unsettled as his. Apart from the war, she says, Shen Ts'ung-wen was most responsible for the disquiet. For a while Chao-ho believed that her husband was in love with someone else, a woman he had tutored in Peking in the 1930s and who ended up in K'un-ming during the war. Chao-ho was not alone in her suspicion. Many people who knew Shen assumed this because he was often seen with this woman in K'un-ming. Around this time he also wrote a short story called "Gazing at the Rainbow," which some regarded as proof of his infidelity. It is more likely that the woman in this story was a montage of characters the author had known, reconstructed as the narrator's interior paramour. Still, he did not let Chao-ho read "Gazing at the Rainbow," and copies of it nearly disappeared.

Chao-ho continued to share with her husband the burden of his younger sister, Little Ninth, who made her way to K'un-ming in 1938, around the same time as Chao-ho. During the war Little Ninth carried on with her life as in the past. She loved gallivanting in the city, eating in restaurants and going to the cinema. After a while, she wore her brother out completely. Chao-ho said, "Friends in K'un-ming told me that even when Shen Ts'ung-wen was pale from exhaustion and his endless nosebleeds, he still worked around the clock to try to support his sister's lifestyle." Shen finally sent Little Ninth to Ch'eng-kung. It was safer for her to be in the countryside with his family, and less expensive. Chao-ho took her in even though their relationship had deteriorated since Chao-ho had become a mother. "Little Ninth was jealous of Lung-lung immediately after he was born," Ch'ung-ho remembered, "because her brother had another object of affection."

Little Ninth stayed a troublemaker even after she moved to Ch'eng-kung, always trying to steal back to K'un-ming. When Chao-ho and Shen Ts'ung-wen refused to give her train fare, she walked. And often she would pilfer from the pantry, giving whatever Chao-ho had prepared for the family to the beggars living in the caves. Little Ninth preferred to spend her time with beggars if she could not be in the city spending her brother's money. She was either dressed in finery or covered with lice. No one could quite understand her or her behavior.

Sometime in the early 1940s, Shen Ts'ung-wen decided to send Little Ninth to Yuan-ling, where his oldest brother and his wife had their home. These two had more authority and were willing to treat her with greater severity. They, too, failed. Little Ninth would disappear for days at a time. Finally her guardians locked her up in an upstairs room. Once she broke a leg when attempting to escape from her second-floor window, but this incident did not deter her from trying again. When she succeeded, she did not surface again until many months later. By then she had married a bricklayer and was carrying his child. Her oldest brother said to her: "Take your things and get out. Go and live your life. I don't recognize you as my sister anymore." Little Ninth "did all right" initially with her bricklayer. They had three children together. But during the famine years in the late 1950s, she died of starvation.

After the war ended in 1945, Chao-ho and her children stayed in the southwest for nearly another year. After the Americans pulled out, she was able to buy the butter and canned fruits they left behind. "I baked cakes in coffee tins," she recalls, "and the children were ecstatic. Life wasn't easy, but I loved it, especially when I could make the children happy."

Shen Ts'ung-wen returned to Peking first, half a year ahead of his family. Peking University hired him as a professor of Chinese literature, and this entitled him to faculty housing in a large yard on Chung-lao Lane, with twenty-some other families. Shen began building his collection again, "not only lacquer boxes and old books, but blue-and-white porcelain, and large amounts of antique papers from the Sung and Ming." He did a lot of buying before his wife came home.

Chao-ho and her two boys slowly made their journey back to Peking, first by rail from K'un-ming to Shanghai, and then by boat from Shanghai to Tientsin through Tsingtao. The last part of the trip from Tientsin was again on a train. "The train was filthy, crowded, and slow," her younger son recalls. "A grayish-yellow hue dominated the landscape. Only the large and small military pillboxes stationed along the way made an impression on me." Chao-ho sewed little pockets on her children's undergarments and placed in each two silver dollars and a slip of paper with their father's address in Peking. She had heard that Communist troops were cutting railroad lines and capturing trains, and so she was preparing her children in case they got separated in the confusion.

No crisis visited them on their journey. Soon the family was together again and settled to a new rhythm in the city. Their son writes:

> Although we were reunited, we no longer sat around a table, laughing and chatting to our hearts' content, like the way we were on Dragon Lane [in Ch'eng-kung]. Dad was very busy. He did not have time to play with us. I didn't mind. I was older, and Dad was a little different. . . .
>
> After a while, I realized that he would study an old tree, a peony petal, or stare at a pottery, an old building, and quietly murmur to himself, "Now, that's beautiful." It was just like him in Yunnan, lying on a slope behind our rented house, watching the clouds. Only now he sighed more. He loved beautiful things but would always worry about their loss, their destruction.

Hu-hu often went with his father to antique stores and antique stalls, looking around. Shen Ts'ung-wen preferred browsing to making a purchase, and when he bought something, he did not mind if the bowl or jar had a crack or a chip. His son said: "I had no interest in these things but would never give up a chance to be with him. We would walk the streets of Peking, from the south side to the north, covering several shops on a trip. There was a lot to say to each other." On these outings, Shen Ts'ung-wen told his son about his life with a young writer in Peking in the 1920s, pointing out to him the apartment he once shared with her and her lover, Hu Yeh-p'ing. Hu was executed in 1931 as a Communist agitator, and the friend, Ting Ling, "had gone to the other side, meaning the Eighth Army, the Communist side." Shen wrote three books about the couple and never wavered in his affection for them. His son said:

> My dad would never deny his association with someone who had been a friend, and he would never conceal his affection for a friend even after the world had ostracized and trampled on him. His friends could have beliefs completely different from his and they could have chosen paths different from his. But there must be some good in them, in their lives or in their characters, which Dad saw and admired. So he would never forget them.

During the first two years after their return, their home in Peking was often full of guests. Many young people came to ask advice about writing. Shen Ts'ung-wen did not worry if they were university students or not—he treated them all equally. But even as he persisted in this way of regarding his friends, the world around him was changing, and people he knew well were formulating positions and taking sides. In the summer of 1948, he had a brief reprieve from the political storm in Peking when he was offered the use of the northeast corner of the imperial summer palace. Peking's mayor had originally planned to use this "garden within the garden" as his summer home, but the civil war put such plans on hold, so the rooms in the corner building stood empty. Yang Chen-sheng, who knew the mayor, got permission to move into these rooms that summer, and he took along several friends and their families—among them Shen Ts'ung-wen and Chang Chao-ho. Chao-ho could not stay very long; her sister-in-law took ill and needed care, so she returned to Peking. In this short span of no more than two weeks, with one in the city and other in the suburb, twenty-five miles away, Shen Ts'ung-wen wrote Chao-ho several letters. He says in the first:

> At this moment, as I am writing to you, I feel that I am composing a love letter to you again. It's that sort of happiness—full of affection and small things I have been saving up to tell you. Maybe it's hard for you to understand, but I have to be alone in order to digest you completely, and to let you become a belief and a part of my character and strength. When we are together, your commands keep me dazed and addled. Recently there

seem to be a tad more of them than before. A truly holy mother is taciturn.* I know that your orders are a form of love, but it seems that you are
giving me more than my share. So my mind has become duller and more
stupefied.

In this letter, Shen Ts'ung-wen seems more assured about his marriage and
less afraid of his wife's judgment. He knows how to handle her now. He humors
her, calls her "the holy mother" and "my little mom," and even tries remon-
strance, but always gently and playfully. He also loves her more strongly now. He
writes:

Once I am apart from you, you seem to be moving nearer to me. It is a
slow getting closer, so what I perceive must be the pure beauty of your
character, mixed with impressions and memory. . . .

My little mom, life itself is a kind of miracle, and you are the miracle
within it. I am so pleased that in my lifetime, I possess so many lovely por-
traits. What I find even more moving is those eight years in the Yunnan
countryside. You accepted life's circumstances with such courage and
strength. How can there be a novel or a movie more compelling than this?
Every scene is dazzling and gorgeous, yet the background is plain. My little mom, recently I feel even more blessed than before because I can see,
on your face, truly joyful smiles. Your empathy for me is also complete.
This must be a new beginning for us. Let's pursue it, and let's rearrange
our life. We must try to apply this love to our work. I want to write
another chapter of "Housewife" to celebrate our new beginning. . . .

Don't worry about my "weariness." I will try to resolve it with humor.
Why don't you and Lung-lung go to Hsi-tan and do some shopping? Buy
beef. We can afford to put beef on the table. I want to use this time of
being apart from you to become youthful again. I want to write to you
every day. . . .

The tone of this letter suggests a Shen Ts'ung-wen fourteen years earlier,
when he was writing to his bride of three months with the fresh eagerness of
a smitten youth. His words are still lyrical, but they mean more now because
he and Chao-ho have lived through a war together and raised two children,
and he has come to accept her smile as a smile, not something else. He calls

---

*The term *sheng-mu* can mean a holy mother, a sage mother, an emperor's natural mother, a
goddess, or the Madonna.

her "a kind of miracle"; he says she creates a "dazzling" scene against a "plain" background.

By the end of the war, Chao-ho had come back to him as his muse. Shen Ts'ung-wen was impatient to start again, to write as he used to in the early thirties. He could feel the rush. In the next letter, he tells her about a conversation he had with their younger son that day:

Young Hu-hu said, "Dad, some people claim that you are the Chinese Tolstoy. One reader in ten in this world knows Tolstoy's name but not yours. I think you are not as good as he."

I said, "You are right. I am not as good. This is because I married and had a good wife. Then the two of you arrived, one after the other. Then there was the war. In these ten years or so, I didn't do much, just trying to get by. My accomplishments are shabby. I can't be compared to Tolstoy."

"So you have to try harder."

"Right. I must. In fact, I've been telling this to your mom. I want to have a good writing spurt. I want to write ten, twenty books."

"What? You can write that many, just like that?" (Hu-hu was being polite. If it were you, you would say I was boasting.)

"As long as I want to write, it shouldn't be hard to write that many. But to write well is difficult."

Shen Ts'ung-wen did not finish even one of those "ten, twenty books." And he did not attempt another chapter of "Housewife." He had the desire to write, but forces beyond his control took it away from him.

By the autumn of 1948, the Nationalists had lost Manchuria and most of the northern provinces. By December, the Communists had surrounded Peking, and for two months the city was under siege. The pressure was, on the whole, psychological. Chao-ho's sons recall that the artillery fire often missed its targets, hitting residential areas instead of arsenals. But children like them were euphoric, as children often are about any disruption of routine. They helped with digging ditches and storing food and fuel: "We were so excited about the final confrontation in Peking."

Most people were unsure about what a Communist revolution might bring. The auguries were not good, yet they were reluctant to put themselves on the road again even when they had a chance to leave. "What could Chinese do to the Chinese?" they would reason to themselves, and hunker down. On December 7, Shen Ts'ung-wen wrote to a contributor to a literary supplement, the *I-shih-pao*, of which he was an editor:

Mr. Chi-liu, We can't publish your piece because our journal has closed. Everything must change. . . . Yet when a person approaches middle age, his temperament is set. Or maybe this person is, by nature, inward inclined and short on social skills. So for years when he writes, he always begins with thinking and contemplation. But now suddenly, he has to begin with a [political] belief. I think that it would be difficult for him to make this drastic change. So after a while, even if he is not forced to put down his pen, he will have to. Some people from our generation will end up like this. It is different for those who are at the peak of their youth. They are pliable and adaptable, and their characters and views have not yet taken definite shapes. They can learn to write from this new point of view. They can write for human progress and service. It is much easier for them to bring about a fairer and more reasonable society.

Shen Ts'ung-wen was already anticipating the rest of his life even before the Communists marched into Peking. Still, he could not have known how the end would unfold for him and for many like him. Already in March 1948 he had some inkling as to how he might fare in the new society, should the Communist revolution succeed, and what the new commissars might want from him. In the first issue of a Communist journal published that month, he was castigated in two separate essays. One called him "a panderer to the landlord class" and "a slavish dependent on the wealthy." Another called his works "peach pink" or "soft porn." The second of his critics was the veteran revolutionary writer Kuo Mo-jo, whose plays Chao-ho and her sisters had performed when they were students in Le-i.

These words must have stung Shen Ts'ung-wen, but as his letters to Chao-ho that summer attest, they could not have sent him into depression. His love for his wife and children and his desire to write were still much more powerful than criticisms that were empty of aesthetic content. In November, he was still strong enough to defend his position in a literary forum that literature should come from the person creating it, from "thinking and contemplation" and not from any outside beliefs. But something happened in December. First there was the siege. Shen must have known that by the end of it, he would have to terminate his literary career. In his December 7 letter, he says that even if he is "not forced to put down [his] pen, [he] will have to." Then the students on the campus of Peking University began to denounce him in wall posters. This must have been a bigger blow than the earlier disparagements because Shen had taught some of these students and had grown fond of them.

By January 1949, Shen Ts'ung-wen was clearly ill. His younger son writes:

The sound of artillery fire was subsiding with each passing day. Finally there was silence.

The repeated explosions in Dad's head were just beginning. Gradually he sank into a hopeless and isolated state. "It's time to settle scores," he would say. He felt he was being watched, and he talked in a low voice, insisting that there was someone next door listening. He thought that a lot of people were having a hand in his life; that they were methodically tightening a big net around him, forcing him to destroy himself.

His son says that no one could help his father unravel the tangle he was in because it was all in his head: "For a long time, he would sit and mutter to himself, 'Life is frail. The life of a gentle person is frail.'" His family was "slow at" understanding what was haunting him, and this in itself worried him. "But tens of millions of people all over the country were in a mortal struggle," his son explained. "A writer who belonged to neither side was ill. So why should anyone care?" Still, friends came by, bringing comforting words and food "that was difficult to come by in a city under siege." Chao-ho was patient and constant. She would greet everyone and try to smile, but she was "clearly tired."

Five days before the commander of the Nationalist troops in Peking handed over the city to the Communists, friends who were teaching at Tsinghua University invited Shen to come and stay with them for a while. The campus was about twelve miles northwest of the city, in the suburbs. It was quieter. During his two-month convalescence, Chao-ho probably never went to see him. They still wrote to each other. His letters were close to being "ravings of a madman." He writes to her: "How do I thank you? I am so tired. I need rest. It's only because of you, I am struggling to survive." She to him: "Because of your illness, I've been so anxious and nervous. If you can come home full of life, it would be a total relief to me." She also tells him to rest his mind, to chat with his friends, and to play with their children. "There is absolutely no need to do any writing. Even letters, the less the better."

On one occasion, Shen writes his letter as a paragraph-by-paragraph gloss to her letter from the day before:

Is it nice staying on the Tsinghua campus? Yu-t'ang, Meng Chia, and Kuang-t'ien, I believe, must have all arrived. Try to listen to their conversations. Otherwise you will be daydreaming again.

[My head is useless. How could I be daydreaming?] . . .

Only your own willpower can help you to recover. No one else could do it for you. It shouldn't be too hard. Just give it a try.

[What is my willpower? Everything I have written is improper. That's what other people say. Now I don't even know what I've written.] . . .

The weather is pleasant. I am sure it is nice where you are. The mood in the city is a bit heavy.* I didn't let the kids go out.

[Let me have a not-so-painful rest. Let me not ever wake up again. No one understands what I say. Not one friend is willing or dares to acknowledge that I am not mad.]

You should get a haircut and take a shower. Get Jui-chih to help you.

[What's the point?]

If you have a letter for me, Jui-chih or someone else can bring it into town. I hope so much to know how you are feeling and what you've been thinking. I do hope that you are optimistic.

[My little mom, why should I be pessimistic? I have finished everything. I can rest now. But if I force myself to be agreeable and submissive so that I can have some temporary peace, what good will this kind of optimism do? Let other people be optimistic. *I* am not pessimistic.]

The cotton underwear is yours. When Chong-ho† returns to school in two or three days, you can give your laundry to him, and he can bring it back for me.

[What difference does it make if my clothes are washed or not? Do you suppose that I will be better if I am cleaner? I should get a divorce. Otherwise this will drag her and the kids down.

My little mom, no need for you to write to me anymore. It doesn't matter if I exist or not. All is the same because I know life is no more than this. Everything has lost its connection to me. People around me are trying to serve me and to entertain me. It's like a ritual sacrifice, only I am still alive.]

Chao-ho's letter was returned to her the next day with her husband's comments. It must have been painful for her to read them through. Some things in it were not kind, and he talked about a divorce. She wrote him another letter the same day. It was an emotional letter, but not about what he had written the day before. She mainly wanted to tell him how moved she was by what their friends had done for them. She said that they had galvanized her, making her feel even more determined to see herself and her husband through this crisis. But she added:

---

*This was January 31, 1949, the day the Communist troops moved into the city.

†This is Chao-ho's cousin from the fifth branch. To avoid confusion with her sister Ch'ung-ho's name, I have romanized his as Chong-ho.

Wang Sun mentioned another person—the one you have considered your friend, but who does not feel the same way about you—and things that were truly upsetting. When he said you were too honest and naïve, I couldn't hold back my tears. This was the first time I cried in front of a guest. Later I felt quite embarrassed about the whole thing. After Wang Sun left, I wept and wept and felt much better.

The "other person" was probably Ting Ling (Ding Ling), the writer friend who, with her lover Hu Yeh-p'ing, in 1924 and 1925 shared their lodging with Shen Ts'ung-wen in Peking. In those days, the three were inseparable. They read and wrote in the same space, pooled what little resources they had, and helped each other to get their bits and pieces published. After the Nationalists executed Hu in 1931, Ting Ling threw herself into left-wing activities. She joined the Communist Party, wrote revolutionary stories, edited communist publications, and helped the party to indoctrinate young recruits. She was kidnapped by the Kuomintang in 1933, lived under house arrest for three years, escaped to the Communist area in 1936, and made her way to Yenan during the war. In 1949, Ting Ling was riding high in the victors' camp—one of few writers who could claim to have lived through the Yenan experience and to have sat down and discussed land reform with the peasants. She had just published a novel on the contradictions of peasants and landlords and was given her own literary magazine to run. And now she stood with other Communist writers in their judgment of Shen Ts'ung-wen—this despite the fact that in the 1930s, it was Shen who had seen her through her loneliest and most desperate period, right after Hu was killed, and it was Shen who had persisted in writing about her, after she disappeared in 1933, so that others would not forget her.

When Shen Ts'ung-wen read Chao-ho's sad lament on the frailties of human relationships, it was his turn to comfort her. He writes: "Let's not say any more about those who do not consider us friends. We should know that these are the rules of the city dwellers. Because we don't understand them, we end up like this." In this letter, we find a postscript: "My little mom, all your love and all the good you have done for me—nothing could save me from harm. This is fate. I will be sacrificed."

Not long after he came home, Shen Ts'ung-wen tried to take his own life. He drank kerosene and cut his wrists and throat. Chao-ho's cousin, who happened to be visiting, found him half-conscious and in shock: "He kept repeating 'I'm from Hunan. I'm from Feng-huang.'"

Shortly before his attempted suicide, Shen had tried to see Ting Ling. It had been thirteen years since they'd last seen each other. His whole family was excited about their impending reunion, despite their misgivings about her. They believed that these two had once shared a secret life, an interior life, that no one else could be privy to, and because of their understanding of each other, now only Ting Ling could "turn him around." Shen Ts'ung-wen took Hu-hu along on this visit. His son later wrote: "I had no idea that her place was so near. Dad held my hand tightly and was so quiet all the way there. I understood that he was full of anticipation." Ting Ling offered him nothing: "It was like being received by a senior officer. . . . The room was big and warm. The mood was cold and indifferent."

Before her husband tried suicide, Chao-ho had taken steps to keep life from descending into melodrama. She knew that society's rules as well as human relationships had changed. At times she felt as hurt as Shen Ts'ung-wen when friends became estranged. Yet Chao-ho believed that she could adapt and be of some use to the new society. So when a local cadre suggested that she "catch up with the times" and "get herself reeducated in the revolutionary tradition," she agreed. She applied to North China University, a school established for such a purpose, and was admitted a few weeks later.

There was much speculation about why Chao-ho took this step at a time when her husband was so ill and when the communists themselves could not say for sure that they had won the war. Was this purely a practical move for her, to give her family a footing, in case the socialist vision was going to be China's future? Was she thinking about work? Chao-ho was always worried about not being able to put her education to use and not having a proper career. Did she feel that the new society could give her better opportunities if she underwent indoctrination? Or was Chao-ho drawn to the socialist vision? Her education at school, both in Le-i and in Nanking, was highly politicized. Then, every national crisis was an occasion for raising awareness, and even physical education was brought into the discussion of nation building. Chao-ho was a good student and an athelete in college. While her sisters were steeped in the arts, she was training for the all-round category in her school's annual sports day. In her diary from 1930, she said that "violent oppression and wide inequity between the rich and poor" incensed her, but she was not ready at that point "to attempt some astonishing feat." Did she feel that she was ready in 1949?

Chao-ho's teenage boys supported her decision: "To think that Mom might be a cadre in a Lenin suit—how smart!" Lung-lung and Hu-hu preferred their mother's way. Where would they be and what would they do if they had accepted their father's reasoning? His depression had dragged the whole family down. They loved him, but it was unbearable to be in his presence, to hear him sigh, to see him so dejected and so scared. Hu-hu wrote:

Dad was stricken at the worst possible time and with an illness that was most inappropriate. His illness had become the family's collective anxiety. It weighed so much on us that we couldn't hold our heads up. Our mom, my brother, and I wanted so much to understand how it got started and how it declined to this point. So this was what we talked about when we were together. We would rack our brains and still could not get anywhere.

Chao-ho postponed her plans to be at North China University until her husband had come home from the hospital after his bungled suicide, and was showing signs of coping with his depression. Their sons were living at home and could keep an eye on him. Shen Ts'ung-wen's recovery was slow. Music became his companion, and Puccini and Verdi, his healers. He told Chao-ho that "truths in books and well-intended words did not sink into his head," that "repression and exclusion" could not persuade him, that even self-analysis could not reform him. But he could "totally surrender" himself to "beautiful music." "This is because its instruction lies in the process, not in the mechanics of right and wrong." Shen Ts'ung-wen would sit by the radio. Sometimes the music made him weep. He would scribble poems and tear them up as soon as he finished. He would guard the radio long after the station had signed off.

Peking University canceled his classes when the fall term began, and by the winter of 1949, Shen was assigned a new position: he was to label the artifacts in Peking's Historical Museum. His younger son remembers the "dark and dank storehouse" where his father worked. "The place was not allowed to have a charcoal fire. [In the winter] the filthy rags used for cleaning the artifacts would freeze into lumps. . . . Sometimes, to keep the dust out, Dad tied a handkerchief across his face, letting only his eyes show. I thought he looked like Jesse James, but without the swash—he was too civil, too weak."

Shen's work at the museum required little thinking, and that was the way he wanted it. It also allowed him to handle objects to which he had been drawn emotionally since he was a young soldier in the army, working as the cataloguer of a Hunan military commander's private collection. But most important, the job gave him something to do, and it was useful and safe work, work that could not have attracted anyone's notice. So eventually people forgot about Shen Ts'ung-wen, and that too was what he wanted. Early Chinese literature on the art of reclusion points out just how difficult it is not to come out of one's lair when summoned. Harder still is it to live in anonymity after one has known fame. The fifth-century writer K'ung Chih-kuei called those who "retired on impulse, with hearts still contaminated" "imposters." Of one such man, he said: "When the belled messengers entered the valley / And the crane summons reached his hill, / His body leapt and his soul scattered / His resolve faltered and his spirit wavered. / Then / Beside the mat his eyebrows jumped, / On the floor his sleeves danced. / He burned his Castalian garments and tore his lotus clothes / He raised a worldly face and carried on in a vulgar manner."

In a letter written years after his recovery from depression, Shen Ts'ung-wen told Chao-ho that he had been reading *Notes on a Trip to Hunan* and thought the author (who was himself) was a fine writer:

> But I have heard that he keeps his identity hidden. What can one do to get him to use his pen again? This is a real conundrum. Alas! This is just the way we feel about Ts'ao Tzu-chien. We wonder why "he did not write more poetry." What we don't understand are his intellectual and social conditions, and his private circumstances. From his biographies, we can see that lots of his contemporaries were ready to bow to every wind. These were the people that battered him until he was beyond recognition. So at the end, he drifted from place to place with a band of old retainers until he expired. And [the other writer] Ts'ao Hsüeh-ch'in simply died of destitution. They were only around forty when they passed away. The author of *Notes on a Trip to Hunan* is fortunate after all. He is half a century old, still vigorous and strong. At home he has a precious treasure—she is dark bronze and black jade, known far and wide (especially here)!* Perhaps a person needs to endure extreme straits in order to write well. Without it he can never make a name for himself. Or perhaps there are other reasons why this is so.

In this letter, Shen Ts'ung-wen refers to himself in the third person as the author of *Notes* and places himself in the literary tradition of Ts'ao Tzu-chien and Ts'ao Hsüeh-ch'in, two of the most arresting writers of their times, one a poet from the third century and the other a novelist from the eighteenth century. Both Ts'aos were isolated and repressed. They died young and in straitened circumstances, but the author of *Notes* was "luckier," his trump being his wife— his "dark bronze and black jade"—and the fact that he was better able to keep his name concealed. If people did not know him anymore, it was not because he had not suffered for his writing or he no longer had what it took to be a good writer: There were "other reasons" why this was so. The "wind," or political climate, made writing a perilous pursuit, and there was also the problem with "art."

---

*"Here" means Hunan. Shen was writing from Ch'ang-sha.

Shen could not see why his contemporaries would refer to certain activities as art and certain things as beautiful: "I don't understand art anymore," he tells Chao-ho in the same letter. "And what I do understand, I don't know what we are supposed to call it."

It is possible that Shen Ts'ung-wen intended these words as a criticism of his wife even though he acknowledged her as his "precious treasure." She had been encouraging him to write again, and so he asked her rhetorically whether she thought anything could rouse him to pick up his pen once more. During his long retreat from the literary world, Chao-ho had become an editor of *People's Literature*—in other words, an arbiter of literary worth in the socialist dominion. She and her husband debated art and literature passionately in their letters, when Shen was on the road for reeducation or work. Several of these letters, dated between 1951 and 1957, have survived. Shen had extended stays in Szechwan and Shanghai during this time, and he also visited his wife's home in Soochow and his own home in West Hunan. He wrote frequently, as did she, whenever she could, sometimes sending him works by his contemporaries. He tells her in a letter posted from Shanghai on October 29, 1956:

> *Third Sister,*
>
> *Thank you for sending the essays. I have read them and didn't find any interesting. They are all crass simplifications. Plus there are many mistakes, some close to being pure nonsense. And whenever the subject is literature, the writing is even more shallow, "like a dragonfly skimming the water surface," completely wide of the mark. . . . I feel that many of the editors [working on books and essays] are also not being responsible. When you find over thirty mistakes and misprints in an essay, is this supposed to be funny, or a way to educate the reader?*

Shen sent a piece of his own—an essay based on the artifacts he had been studying—to a pictorial, although he knew that "it did not fit their requirements":

What these magazines wanted was simply captions copied from the catalogues of the Imperial Museum. . . . Anything intelligent, they wouldn't get, so regard it as unnecessary. What a waste of my time! In a way I do understand why the writings have been so flat and without any energy. It's because no one dares to say the wrong thing. So the banal writing continues. But maybe smart editors should do better. At least they should correct the obvious mistakes.

We do not have Chao-ho's reply. But from a letter to him written nearly a year later, we learn something about her view, an editor's view:

> It's best that you read more fiction by contemporary writers. That way you will have some idea of the creative energy and the standard in current literature. Some rightist authors say that there hasn't been any good writing since the liberation, that everything is formularized and generalized. Although I haven't read that much, I have come across some good manuscripts in my work. I can say that they hold up quite well against the standard.

Three days later, Chao-ho amended these words slightly. She conceded that good writing was, after all, hard to come by, and that this was a problem for editors who had to find something to publish. She said that most writers were "being mobilized for political campaigns" and so couldn't do any writing. And when they did write, their works either lacked "appeal and meaning" or, "if they had aesthetic values," were riddled with "serious political problems."

When Shen Ts'ung-wen received this letter, he was at a retreat in Tsingtao, with a group of writers and artists affiliated with the Cultural Ministry. His description of them explains why his wife was having problems soliciting manuscripts and selecting from her slim pile anything worth publishing:

> Most people here seem not to have any interest in books, and so they can't really be interested in writing. The weather is so pleasant, yet four would sit around a table and play mah-jongg all day with such intensity and glee. Some take turns with those around while others are just glued to their seats. This really puzzles me. Perhaps some people, by habit, don't think much about life's purpose.

These people in Tsingtao were different from the boatmen and trackers along the Yuan River and the women living in "hanging terraces," who "dispatch each day as the day before." Shen Ts'ung-wen had no love for these new acquaintances and no desire to write about them. They did not stir him. This was yet another reason why he abandoned his art. His subjects had vanished.

For years his wife mistook his inactivity in creative writing for "a loss of confidence." She thought that his critics had scared him into silence: "Therefore, you are so indecisive. To write or not to write? Of course, writing is hard. . . . The important thing is to try to overcome the difficulties, to actually start the creative process and then go from there. If you don't write at all and just proclaim

a lot of empty theories, then you won't leave behind anything significant."
Chao-ho also accused her husband of "not having a comprehensive view of
things." By this she meant that he had not factored in the goals of the state and
was wanting in political awareness:

> You still cannot let go of your personal attachments and your sentiments;
> this, as a result, has stopped you from seeing so many things worth getting
> excited about. You are not inspired, so you are reluctant about helping us
> put into words the passion and enthusiasm we have for our present society.

Chao-ho also could not understand why, years earlier, when they had very
little and were always pressed for money, her husband would write day and night
even while he was suffering from his endless nosebleeds. "Now," she says, "the
Party cares so much about writing and gives writers so much encouragement
and support. When you finally can write, you don't write."

Shen Ts'ung-wen did not stop writing altogether. In the 1950s and 1960s, he
produced books on ancient lacquerware, silk embroideries, T'ang and Sung
dynasty mirrors, and Ming dynasty brocades. He also published articles on
architecture, decorative art, and folk art, and finished a multivolume history of
Chinese costumes. And when he was at the right place, found the right subjects,
and did not feel constrained by requirements, he still wrote the way he used to.
But after 1949 he had only one person to write to, and that was Chao-ho. They
had chosen different paths and worked in different ways, but she remained the
person to whom he could tell everything, whether or not she understood it or
felt empathetic.

On a trip to Hunan, he described to her again what it was like to be home in
Feng-huang:

> The streets are being built all the way to the old city walls. There are still
> a lot of run-down areas in this town. The place is too old. Yet, as a whole,
> it has the feel of a painting, a painting from the Northern Sung.
>
> Today, starting from the house I grew up in, I walked the whole town.
> It was just like years ago when I was an urchin. It's very odd. There are
> only about ten people who still know me. Several were from my old
> neighborhood. I hear that they were either hauling goods or growing veg-
> etables. Even if I see them, I wouldn't know what to say to them. In my
> memory, the place is so familiar. Yet when I am actually here, I feel I don't
> know it so well anymore.
>
> I think my impression of this place now is that it is "strange." Strange,

because lots of things seem changed and yet not changed at all. Many kids were walking on stilts, trying to knock each other down. It was what I liked to play as a child. Stands that sell sour radishes are everywhere, just like before. Lots of old women are still guarding the stands. They sit, with their arms huddling their chests, and they chat to each other so affectionately. Yes, they are poor but seem satisfied.

Seven days later he writes from Ch'ang-sha:

In Feng-huang, I spent some time with my parents and grandparents by their grave mounds. Our sister-in-law carried a bamboo basket with some cured meat and oranges in it. Two cadres also came along. There was a light drizzle, and everyone wore a rain cape. The whole thing seemed like a page from a Turgenev novel. From the top of the mound, one could see the trucks and cars go by on the new highway. . . .

Around here there is a place called the Stone Lotus Pavilion. Besides the beautiful scenery around it, it also had a sculpture of [the bodhisattva] Kuan-yin in white, with a smile that made her look real. The main part of the building had been torn down. A new hospital stands in its place. The people here could not bear to see their Kuan-yin destroyed, so they moved her to a cowshed, which belonged to a local co-op. If someday someone decides to expand the cowshed, it would be unlikely that they could hold on to their Kuan-yin. Several teachers wanted to take me to see their Kuan-yin. So I went. The whole thing looked just like the Nativity with Jesus and the Madonna. . . .

The inns along the way, all multilevel, feel as if they could collapse anytime. The floor creaks and wobbles when you walk on it. Thin boards divide each floor into small rooms, but you can hear everything going on next door. The beddings weigh over ten kilos. . . . In the morning, someone rings a bell, to get the guests off the bed and on the road. The good thing is that these inns still follow the old custom of providing you with hot water to wash your face and feet. On the streets, there are gangs of dogs, and ducks and kids. . . .

The best is still all the goings-on along the river. On the way back, passing by Hu-hsi, there were more than ten boats and rafts floating on the water. The river and the mountains were like a picture—so gorgeous! When I arrived at Ch'eng-te, I went to visit relatives on Ma-yang Street. Several Ma-yang old ladies were guarding a cigarette and wine stand in front of a dog meat restaurant. Hanging across the roof beams were forty-three dog legs and on the counter were six or seven jugs of wine. It's a shame that we can't see Wu Sung or any of those characters like him coming to the shop to feast. . . . Our bus passed by the Peach Blossom Springs, and we stopped briefly. The Shui-hsi Co-op has a shop with three or five tables, and sitting at the tables were several young girls—all looking pert and pleased with themselves. At the stand in front of the shop, a middle-aged man in a cadre suit was buying cigarettes. The only thing there that had the feel of something old was a jug of wine. But even this came from Ch'eng-te! Peach Blossom Springs is no longer an otherworldly place.

Shen Ts'ung-wen's losses were private. During the Cultural Revolution, nearly all the writers from pre-Communist China were marched around the city and humiliated in public. He was spared. He was sent to the May Seventh Cadre School in Hupei's countryside for three years but he did not have to do hard labor. Chao-ho was at the same camp. She left for the school earlier, so stayed there longer. For nearly all the time she was in Hupei, Chao-ho was in charge of guarding the outhouse, to discourage others from stealing the night soil. It was light work compared to carrying the night soil to the vegetable patches, which she had been assigned to do when she first arrived. In 1972, she and her husband came back to Peking together.

Because of their parents' class background, Lung-lung and Hu-hu were not allowed to go to college. Lung-lung first worked in a factory and then raised flowers in a nursery. Hu-hu never lived the sadness his father thought he would. For a while, he was blind—he might say, blind to his father's suffering—but his sight was restored, not by the tears of young girls, but by the love of his father. He first learned a mechanic's trade, but has been editing Shen Ts'ung-wen's works with Chao-ho's help ever since his father's death in 1988.

After they returned to Peking, Chao-ho and Shen Ts'ung-wen lived separately for a while. During that time, he took his meals in her home and then returned to his one-room dwelling half a mile away. We do not know if he wrote her letters then.

Their physical separations, sometimes by choice, do not quite have the tragic ring that they might in a marriage. A meal together, or a letter, sometimes brought them closer than sharing the same space ever could have. Chang Chao-ho and Shen Ts'ung-wen lived stubbornly in their separate worlds. They might each use the same words to describe what they wanted yet what they wanted would turn out to be different things.

Chao-ho understood her life's purpose as a task, a big task, something to conquer, to overcome—making things better, maybe, or rectifying a wrong. Even

in her eighties, she remembered her awareness as a child of how she was compared with her siblings. She was not quite gentry stock, not delicate and refined
like her sisters. Even the nurse-nannies seemed to feel this way. And it was not
her parents' or even her siblings' doing that she felt slightly repressed. It was
something she put upon herself. It was how she imagined others regarded her,
and being stubborn, she would not let others know her feelings and she would
not complain. When she was a young woman, she was still not clear about her
purpose, but she was not in a hurry to figure it out. Her family was a warm place
to be, she had good schools to go to, and she did not like to take risks. Then she
got married, and her life became inseparable from her husband's. Chao-ho rarely
had ease as a housewife. Still, she loved her children and looked after her family. She was also compassionate to her friends and developed a huge tolerance for
those who were unlike her. Yet her anxiety was not quelled until the communist
revolution allowed her a chance to look for a purpose outside of her immediate
circumstances. Because the society's rules had changed, she could now let go,
somewhat, of what had once been a woman's principal responsibilities.

For Shen Ts'ung-wen, life was meaningful only when it was a contemplative
life. He thought of himself as "a man of country stock," yet he could never live like
one; he could not be like the tracker who never asked "why he wanted to live."
Shen's stories and essays are products of his reflection. And when he no longer
could write for himself, in the way he thought meaningful, he stopped. In 1961,
Mao Tse-tung and Chou En-lai personally urged him to try again, and for three
months he labored over the story of Chao-ho's cousin Chang Ting-ho.* Ting-ho
was the early Communist Party member who had been close to Chao-ho when
Chao-ho was living in Peking in 1932. The Nationalists shot him in 1936, and
so the Communists considered him a martyr. Shen Ts'ung-wen never finished
writing Ting-ho's story, and he destroyed what he had begun. Such behavior must
have frustrated Chao-ho.

In 1995, seven years after Shen Ts'ung-wen died, Chao-ho published their
letters. In a postscript, she wrote:

Sixty years have passed. In front of me, on this table, are so many words.
I have read them and revised them, and now I don't know if they all happened in a dream or they belonged to someone else's story. The experiences seem so absurd and odd, yet so ordinary. . . . Ts'ung-wen and I
together in this life—were we happy or unhappy? I have no answer. I

---

*This Chang Ting-ho also appeared in chapter 7, p. 85.

didn't completely understand him. Later I began to grasp what he was about, but not until now did I truly understand his character and the pressures put upon him. . . .

But all is too late. Why didn't I try harder when he was alive? Why didn't I try to help him in every way I could? Instead we had so many conflicts we could not resolve. It's too late for regrets!

Chapter 13

CH'UNG-HO

Ch'ung-ho during the Sino-Japanese War,
in a small Buddhist chapel that had been converted into an apartment.

EVEN WHEN CH'UNG-HO was a child of seven or eight, her sisters knew her to be different from them. They had the advantages of young cosmopolites: regular visits to the theater, early impressions of a modern city, and an awareness of those distinctions particular to being modern. Their knowledge also had more breadth, certainly more categories, and their vocabulary showed greater currency; they could also discuss science and politics. Yet they considered their little sister more learned and more assured than they were. Even the poems Ch'ung-ho wrote were fresh and original, while their phrases and sentiments were appropriated whole from poems they had memorized. They were children, but they could intuit aesthetic distinctions, and they accepted Ch'ung-ho as superior.

Ch'ung-ho's sisters attributed her special character to her education—to the attention her tutors gave her each day and the effort she made to comply with her tutors' expectations. But the fact that Ch'ung-ho spent her childhood apart from her siblings and nearly alone, with few companions to play with and then only on special occasions, must have been consequential to the way she worked and thought and the manner of her repose. Ch'ung-ho's early life was a contemplative one, without the pressure of competition or the need for argument or analysis. She learned to recite poetry from memory before the age of three. Primers to the Four Books were added to her curriculum in turn. Before she was ten, neither her tutors nor her grandmother Shih-hsiu explained what the words meant. "I merely gathered the phrases and sentences at that age," she says. "In time their meaning became self-evident." Around age seven or eight, Ch'ung-ho also began to write parallel couplets, which graduated into poems. Her tutors would read her poems and make a few corrections, without comment or explanation. This was the first stage of her learning. The hours were long, and she had few distractions. All this gave her the habits of a scholar and time for reverie. Later, she wrote about these years:

Outside my window is a little yard. It has a banana tree and a small garden. Only lilies are left. They grow in a neat row. . . . Facing my desk is the wall of a separate building. At the top is an opening. It is the third-floor window, the only one on this side, which seems a little odd on a tall wall. The lattice design on the window is intricate. For many years, no one bothered to change the paper pasted over the lattice. . . . It's dark inside. I have never gone up to the third floor of that building. . . .

No one lived even on the second floor, just piles of leather cases and wooden crates stored up there. Sometimes when servants went to fetch things from the second floor, I could slip unnoticed into the general hurly-burly. But the third floor was completely off-limits to me. Even grown-ups rarely got up there, and when they did go, they would do it in groups of three or four, to bring down lanterns, bronzes, porcelain, tables, and chairs, all sorts of utensils and furniture for the New Year festivities. I could never join them on these trips. They said that an old fox spirit lived up there, so I shouldn't get near it.

Fox spirits have been around in the Chang family for a long time. Ch'ung-ho's mother had seen one in a mirror during a brief visit to Hofei. Her grandmother burned three sticks of incense a night at the fox altar in her Buddhist chapel, and this seems to have satisfied them. "They did not cause any trouble," Ch'ung-ho wrote. "And if they played a prank, they did it without malice." What worried Ch'ung-ho as a child was not fox spirits but a crack on the belly of the tall wall that faced her study. The crack gave the wall a sorrowful look. "The unsayable sadness of so many people seemed to have gathered there. The mouth was deep and dark—it was a melancholy mouth."

In those days, Ch'ung-ho's closest friend, the little blind nun Ch'ang-sheng, told her many of her dreams: "They were strange and novel. She said that she often saw her mother in her dreams, sitting on a lotus adorned with jewels." The two girls also bartered, sight for sound. Ch'ang-sheng chanted sutras for Ch'ung-ho; in return, Ch'ung-ho would take her to the top of the city walls, "to look at the scenery." "I'd say: The sun is just above the pagoda and a boat is gliding by on the river below; on the boat is a child; he is barefoot and is chewing a piece of watermelon rind." All this gave Ch'ang-sheng enormous joy. Ch'ang-sheng would also ask Ch'ung-ho to tell her the colors of things: clouds, sky, Ch'ung-ho's clothes: "As long as she had her answer, she was satisfied." Once Ch'ung-ho asked her friend whether she had ever seen any of these colors, to which Ch'ang-sheng answered, no, never. Then why bother to know? This was her reply:

> I have never seen colors, but I can distinguish between them and not make a mistake. Whenever you mention red, I do not associate it with purple. Sometimes I might get anxious. For example, you say that the color of your jacket is purple. If you lied to me, I wouldn't be able to tell from touching it. Also, take my hand-chime. The handle is red sandalwood. The chime is yellow brass. If someone were to paint them in other colors, I wouldn't know either. Even though colors do not have much to do with me, I still want to know. Learning two more colors means more to me than learning two scrolls of sutras.

After this, whenever her friend asked about colors, Ch'ung-ho would tell her all she knew about them, using every palpable device. Later Ch'ung-ho wrote, "If now I am able to describe to you the beauty of a color, it was all because of the training I had then."

Ch'ang-sheng's favorite object was a round fan Ch'ung-ho had given her. On the fan, she was told, there was a painting of a remote mountain, a patch of clouds, a stream, an old pine; under the tree was a boy; next to the boy was an old man; the old man was a visitor and he was talking to the boy. Above the painting, someone had inscribed a poem: "Beneath the pine, I ask the boy, where is your teacher? / Gone to pick medicine, he says. / I know he is in this mountain, / but not where because the clouds are thick." Ch'ang-sheng liked to quiz people when she showed them this fan. She would ask, How many persons are there in this scene? When they said two, she would say three: "One is hidden in the clouds." This was the other thing Ch'ung-ho liked about Ch'ang-sheng: her keen sense of the reality of nature—that it was and was not—*and* her pursuit of the unseen as purely an act of her mind. Ch'ung-ho thought that her friend, in total darkness, had mastered a high form of playing.

Under this kind of influence, and the influence of her grandmother, who was nearly a nun herself, Ch'ung-ho was barely aware of the goings-on in the outside world. So when planes suddenly appeared in the Hofei sky in 1927, she thought that they were large kites snapped off from their strings. "But they kept coming back, like hawks, encircling the sky three or four times." She was studying Confucius' *Analects* with her tutor, Mr. Chu, that day.

> My teacher's face turned pale. I ran to the window to look. He seemed alarmed, and then, as if commanding me, he said: "Go and take cover! That was an airplane. Yesterday I heard the news at Wang Hsing-yun's teahouse, that these are airplanes. They are dangerous because they might drop bombs. Do you hear? They don't seem to go away." Sure enough, soon after Mr. Chu finished, we heard explosions in several places far and near.

The planes had been sent by the Shantung warlord Chang Tsung-ch'ang. The year before, Chang Tsung-ch'ang had watched with great unease the Nationalist Army's aggressive drive against regional power brokers such as himself. But in the spring of 1927, there was a lull. Chiang Kai-shek, the commander of the Nationalist Army, had shifted his attention to another matter, which, he thought, had greater urgency: he was planning to spring a surprise assault on the Communists and union sympathizers in Shanghai. Up to this point they had been allies in his campaign to eradicate the warlords and unify China. Shortly after Chiang carried out his purge, Chang Tsung-ch'ang moved his troops into Anhwei and laid siege to Hofei. The siege lasted two months, during which time the people of Hofei witnessed a bizarre show of force. Besides his regular forces, Chang employed White Russian mercenaries and warplanes for the task. Either he was mad or he was hoping to stun the residents into submission. Ch'ung-ho wrote:

> Huo-san, a hired hand in our house, told me just now that the hawk dropped several strange eggs from the air. Some fell on the mud paddies

without much of a stir. But those on hard ground made big craters. One killed a woman by Five Mile River, a pregnant woman near childbirth. The baby was blown out of her, and her legs were nowhere to be found.

The woman was the mother of one of Ch'ung-ho's friends, a servant's son, a boy who loved building kites and flying them in the open air.

When Ch'ung-ho was a child, the only boys she was allowed to play with were servants' sons. She recalled another boy, "Big Precious," who was the son of Chang-ma, a woman Ch'ung-ho's grandmother had hired to give her nurse-nanny Chung-ma some relief from menial work. Occasionally this little boy would come from the countryside to visit his mother, staying overnight in her room. Big Precious was a little younger than Ch'ung-ho, and maybe because of this, he was her most boisterous companion. He had a "ga-ga" sort of laugh, and he roughhoused with Ch'ung-ho as if she were a boy. Then one day Big Precious turned into a young man. He was only about fourteen, but he looked more like a man than a boy. It was the New Year. He came to pay his respects to his mother and to Ch'ung-ho's grandmother, and when he saw Ch'ung-ho, he kowtowed, which made her furious and hurt. Ch'ung-ho thought that they "shouldn't have grown up." It finished their friendship.

With male cousins, there was never friendship to begin with, she said. She would see them when they came to visit. They were cordial to each other but would hardly exchange words. Servants' children were different. She could have adventures with them and raise a rumpus, and it would be acceptable. Yet once they turned fourteen or fifteen, there was a sharp demarcation: a gentry lady was a gentry lady; a servant's child was a servant's child.

Ch'ung-ho had another childhood companion in a distant relative. The girl's father was a cousin of Ch'ung-ho's grandmother, which meant that Ch'ung-ho's friend was her senior in rank, even though the two were only a year apart in age. This was not uncommon in large Chinese families. The girl went to the local public school and came to visit when Ch'ung-ho had her day off from her tutor, which was every ten days.

The girl's parents had met when her father was working in Shantung. He was a married man at the time. Her mother was a graduate of a teacher-training school; she and her classmates were probably one of the first groups of women from their province to have received a Western-style education. When she married, she did not know about her husband's other wife back home. By the time he took her to Hofei, they were a family of four. When the woman learned about her husband's past, she went mad, and he moved back to live with his other family in the countryside. The woman's mother, who had moved to Hofei with her, looked after her mad daughter and her two granddaughters for years. She took in washing and did some sewing, which brought a little income, but, on the whole, the family relied on the kindness of others. Ch'ung-ho's grandmother owned a lot of property in Hofei, and she gave them a place to live. It was a modest house, constructed of bamboo, only a block away from Shih-hsiu's own residence. When it was time to collect rent, Shih-hsiu's manager would skip this family, as he was instructed to do for families that were desperately poor.

Ch'ung-ho says that the condition of her friend's mother was especially tragic. After this woman became ill, she would proposition any man she met and would have sex with anyone who was willing. Often she would just turn up at people's houses. Whenever the woman's mother sensed such a moment was coming, she would beg friends and neighbors to help her tie her daughter up. Even under such awkward circumstances, Ch'ung-ho's friend managed to grow up as normal as one could have hoped. She went to local schools and was expected to get a high school education and to have a profession afterwards. This probably would not have been possible if the girl had not been descended from gentry.

Ch'ung-ho had only these few friends in Hofei. When she moved to Soochow to be with her own family, her relations with the outside world did not change much. She could move about more easily now and get to know more people, but she still preferred being alone. She spent one year at Le-i and was not particularly taken with the school that was her father's pride and lifetime investment. Her history and literature teachers could not offer her anything she did not know already. She dreaded biology class, and especially dissection. (In her grandmother's residence, the kitchens were set far back from the living quarters.) Yet what she disliked most were commemoration days—for instance, Sun Yat-sen's birthday, the anniversary of his death, and the day of the founding of the republic. On such occasions, students were gathered in the auditorium to stand in front of Sun Yat-sen's portrait and observe a few minutes of silence. This was followed by a recitation of Sun Yat-sen's will and many speeches after that. Ch'ung-ho recalls, "The flag waving, red and white in turn, plus the long speeches made my head swim."

Ch'ung-ho also did not care for her political education class. Based on Sun Yat-sen's Three Principles of the People, this was a staple in every middle school's curriculum during the republican period. She did like geography, mostly drawing maps, but did not know north from south. She took part in extracurricular activities, but only under pressure. "In this way I was different from my sisters," she noted. "They loved to get on a stage and perform for an audience. I was used to being left alone to do my own things."

Ch'ung-ho never liked performing, though she was good at it. After each performance, she felt as if she had just come through a long illness. And the off-stage politics, of who should sing which part and of what scenes to perform, exhausted her, as did the more complicated questions of propriety. For instance, once in Soochow, she sang the female lead opposite her sister Yuan-ho in "Awakening from the Dream." Soon after, a well-known actor, probably the best male lead in the *k'un-ch'ü* theater at the time, invited her to play the same role opposite him in Shanghai. Ch'ung-ho was willing to play any role but this one, because she did not want to give the audience an opportunity to compare her sister's performance with his. She thought that it would not be fair. It took long negotiations for her to have her way, and much of the joy of the occasion was gone by the time these questions were settled.

Her sisters Yuan-ho and Yun-ho gravitated toward big fanfares and a chance to showcase their skills, but Ch'ung-ho preferred singing with friends at home or at a club gathering. "I love the music and being with those who love the music as much as me," she says. While the older girls' earliest training in opera was with a professional actor, who had been preparing them for the stage from the start, Ch'ung-ho came to *k'un-ch'ü* by way of books. She says:

My adoptive grandparents in Hofei had their private library upstairs, in a large storage area. The grandfather I'd never met didn't care for books that would have prepared him for the examinations. Instead, he liked to read sutras and fiction—books most scholars considered "unrespectable." These books could not be kept in the main library, which had the Thirteen Classics, the twenty-four dynastic histories, and the most comprehensive collectanea of commentaries written during the Ch'ing on the classics—all big books.*

When I was growing up, I was free to explore the private library upstairs. My grandmother never stopped me from reading whatever plays or novels I found up there even though most of them contained love stories with a sufficient amount of salacious scenes and dialogues. I remember my first long fiction was [the Ch'ing drama] *Peach Blossom Fan*. This was followed by *The Peony Pavilion* and classical novels. I enjoyed reading these works but didn't know that the dramas could be sung, not until I came home to Soochow, and my father began to take me to the *k'un-ch'ü* theater. It was there that I realized I'd read many of the librettos before.

---

*The collection of commentaries is the *Huang-ch'ing ching-chieh* in 1,400 *chüan* (chapters).

Usually I could place a scene in long drama right away and I'd recognize the phrases in an aria. This feeling of familiarity, of having known it in the past, was my way into *k'un-ch'ü.*

The same could be said of Ch'ung-ho's studies at the university. If the subject was the *Classic of Odes,* or the *Tso Commentary,* or any of the classics or early histories, she could recite from memory most of the passages her teacher referred to in his lecture. This, she thought, made learning easier. In her early education, Ch'ung-ho also had the advantage of studying with tutors of different interests and teaching styles. Mr. Tsou, the degree-holder, loved poetry; he encouraged Ch'ung-ho to write poems and taught her techniques of composition. Also because he was a degree-holder, his pedagogy was of the kind used to prepare a student for the civil service examinations. Mr. Chu, the tutor with whom Ch'ung-ho learned most and studied longest, preferred histories and the writings of philosophers. In the past, tutors almost never introduced, in a classroom, works of philosophers outside the Confucian tradition. These texts did not appear on the government examinations, and they were considered "unorthodox." Mr. Chu did not follow these guidelines. He chose his own materials and got Ch'ung-ho interested in abstruse subjects she probably would not have attempted on her own. His approach was also analytical. Lectures on homonyms and syntax were added to the curriculum as his student got older. Ch'ung-ho says that his instructions were extremely helpful later on, when she took the entrance examination to Peking University in the summer of 1934.

She had gone to Peking the year before, in September, for her sister Chao-ho's wedding, and for no particular reason she decided to stay. Family and friends urged her to take the college entrance examination the following summer, and she thought she might. Chao-ho offered her a place to stay, she began auditing classes at Peking University, and a few months later she moved into her own apartment.

Ch'ung-ho did not spend much time studying for the entrance exam. Of the four areas covered—Chinese literature, Chinese history, mathematics, and English—her tutors in Hofei had been preparing her for the first two since she was six. She had taken English classes at her father's school and then for another year at a Shanghai middle school, and she found the language manageable. Mathematics was different. She was unable to learn it in the classroom, so scores of people tried to help—her brothers and their friends, her sisters and their teachers, college graduates and even those with advanced degrees from the West. None succeeded. Mathematics simply vexed her. She hadn't been introduced to it until she was sixteen, and then suddenly she was faced with proofs and algebraic equations. She could not see the point of it all and did not know where to begin. She was also stubborn. During the few months she was preparing for the exam, she barely thought about mathematics, much less pursued remedial measures. Thousands of students all over China had come to Peking that year to compete for just a few hundred places among the country's five best universities. On the day of the examination, her family presented her with a compass and square. "I didn't use them," she says, "because I couldn't even understand the problems."

Her mark in mathematics—an indisputable zero—caused a lot of trouble for the examination committee because she also scored a perfect hundred in Chinese literature. The senior scholars on the board wanted to have such a student at Peking University, but there was an examination rule that a candidate with a zero score in any of the four subjects could not be admitted. The examination committee put pressure on the teaching assistant who had graded Ch'ung-ho's paper, asking him to reread her answers and see if he could allow her just a few points. This man reconsidered her paper and came back with another zero. Finally the committee had to act on their own to let Ch'ung-ho in. (A few years later, Ch'ung-ho and her grader would meet in person and become friends. They would banter about the rights and wrongs of that business in the summer of 1934, each congratulating himself or herself on his or her triumph.)

Of her perfect score in literature, Ch'ung-ho said there was nothing to it. She did not have to compose poems or gloss classical passages—just answer some questions on grammar and punctuate a few pages of texts, something that came easily to her. The examinees were also asked to write an essay in vernacular on "My Life in Middle School." Since Ch'ung-ho had not had any life in middle school, certainly not anything that made an impression during her brief and erratic stay in two schools, she decided to make the whole thing up. The graders liked it enough to mark it perfect.

Ch'ung-ho's admittance to Peking University was so unusual that the local papers picked the story up for their columns on college news. The student's name, however, was given as "Chang Hsüan," the pseudonym Ch'ung-ho used when she signed up for the exam. She did not want to be associated with her brother-in-law Shen Ts'ung-wen through her sister Chao-ho. Shen was a well-known author then, and Ch'ung-ho feared that her relation to him might bias the examiners, many of whom knew him either personally or through his works. Ch'ung-ho was also protecting herself and her family, just in case she did badly. Her brother Tsung-ho had a friend who had been a school principal in Ning-hsia, and this man produced a high school certificate for Chang Hsüan.

There was only one other woman student besides Ch'ung-ho in the department of Chinese literature, but many more were admitted to the science departments and the schools of law and education. Hu Shih, who once played a part in Shen Ts'ung-wen's courtship of Chao-ho, was chair of the literature department. Although he did not learn about Ch'ung-ho's relation to Chao-ho until Ch'ung-ho had left the school, on several occasions he showed approval of her scholarship and urged her not to quit when it appeared that she might. Peking University was not giving Ch'ung-ho the superlative education one might have expected, even though she had sterling teachers: Hu Shih and Ch'ien Mu on intellectual history, Fung Yu-lan on philosophy, Wen I-tuo on early literature, and Liu Wen-tien on Six Dynasties and T'ang and Sung poetry. Ch'ung-ho felt that she was partly to blame for not making the best of her years there. But students on the whole were restless. Many were drawn to radical politics. "There were many goings-on I didn't know about," she recalls, "political meetings and Communist study groups."

Ch'ung-ho herself preferred to spend her time learning opera. At nearby Tsinghua University, a professional *k'un-ch'ü* teacher held informal classes once a week. Any college student or teacher could enroll. Ch'ung-ho and her brother Tsung-ho, who was a student at Tsinghua, went regularly. Of all her siblings, Ch'ung-ho says, she was closest to this brother. They were only a year apart, and they loved *k'un-ch'ü* the same way, singing in small ensembles and mostly for their own enjoyment. When Ch'ung-ho left Peking suddenly in early 1936 because of illness, Tsung-ho stayed on to finish his degree, but as soon as he graduated that summer, he wrote to her in Soochow, asking her to join him and a friend in Tsingtao for a holiday. He wrote in his memoir:

> I believe it was only the second day after we got here that Fourth Sister arrived by boat from Shanghai. We met her at the dock. Later she took a room next to ours, so adding a lot of gaiety to our small band of vacationers.
>
> While she was in Shanghai, this "opera nut" learned that Shen Ch'uan-chih, one of our *k'un-ch'ü* instructors from Soochow, was in town, giving private lessons in opera clubs. She even managed to find out where he was staying and his phone number. Right after we placed a call, Shen rushed over here, telling us all about the opera scene in Ts'ingtao.

In Tsingtao, the more notable amateurs in the *k'un-ch'ü* world were government officials and their families. As soon as they heard about Ch'ung-ho and Tsung-ho from their instructor, they sent out an invitation, asking them to attend their club gathering that evening. The host dispatched a car to pick them up. "Fourth Sister was all decked out, looking pretty." The two learned later that they did not make a favorable impression.

This was especially true for Fourth Sister. She had put on lipstick. And before we arrived, Shen Ch'uan-chih told our host that we'd just come from Shanghai, which led everyone there to believe that we were professional actors. And then after Fourth Sister finished singing, while others were still clapping, she got up, cupped one hand in another, and returned their compliment. This made things worse. Now they were sure that we were professional actors. They must have thought to themselves: Who ever heard of a woman gesturing like that unless she sang *k'un-ch'ü* for a living? In Soochow, however, this was the standard practice—it applied to everyone.

The misunderstanding did not persist. And once the club members learned that the visitors from Soochow, like them, had only an amateur's interest in *k'un-ch'ü*, their relationship with them relaxed. Ch'ung-ho and her brother ended up staying for more than a month.

In the world of amateur musicians and actors, all were equals, so a merchant and a college president could be playing music together in the same room, and an elderly scholar could defer to a young woman on matters of aesthetics and art. Even young children who showed musical talent could join their parents in club gatherings. During the war, among Ch'ung-ho's friends in the southwest there was a peerless *pipa* player from Shanghai, an enterprising man called Mr. Li. Every few weeks, he would load his truck in Lashio, probably with goods that had come from Rangoon, travel more than seven hundred miles along the Burma Road, and arrive at K'un-ming three days later. He would take his goods to the local distributors, reap his profit, go to the little town of Ch'eng-kung, where Ch'ung-ho was living with her sister Chao-ho and Chao-ho's children, throw a party for his musician friends there, make music for several days, and return to Burma with his empty truck. Along with the usual composers, music critics, and scholars of music history, a general manager from the Russia-China Airline would join them whenever he had business in K'un-ming. "It was a fine ensemble," Ch'ung-ho says, "because we all were at the same level."

On weekends, a different group—a constituency from the Consolidated University in K'un-ming—would show up. This included the president of the university, junior and senior faculty members, and teaching assistants. Most of them were not musicians. They came to seek refuge, to get away from the politics in the city, which was uncomfortable for them because these academics relied on their government for work and so could not take a firm stand on many issues, not even on some of the policies affecting their school. In Ch'eng-kung, they could talk freely, about any subject.

There were several prominent figures from the world of literature and art living in this small town, but visitors liked to be in the house where Ch'ung-ho and Chao-ho had their apartments. When Chao-ho's husband, Shen Ts'ung-wen, first saw this place, he decided to rent the three rooms near the front garden for his family, the two rooms across from them for a friend who was a painter, and, directly above the painter's apartment, six small rooms for Ch'ung-ho and whoever else needed a place to stay. Of the six rooms upstairs, one was a Buddhist chapel with a half room adjacent to it. Ch'ung-ho moved into this suite. It was quiet, being in the back and upstairs, but soon it became a gathering place. The lute player and the zither player liked to be where the flute player was, and those who loved listening to music followed them. The poetry and calligraphy group also gravitated toward Ch'ung-ho's room. They liked its atmosphere; they also liked her inksticks, inkstones, and writing brushes. Ch'ung-ho says of herself: "Even when I was poor, I was particular about my things. I didn't fancy gold or silver but wanted my inkstones and brushes to be the best." A wooden plank placed on four kerosene containers—a near replica of the family table in her sister's home—served as their writing desk. Just behind it was the altar: the Buddha and the bodhisattva Kuan-yin, flanked by Confucius and a small image of Jesus. (The original owner of the house took a practical view of divine protection: he thought that more was always better than less.) Her apartment was not as peaceful as before, but Ch'ung-ho did not mind.

To help her with cooking and cleaning, Ch'ung-ho hired a seventeen-year-old girl, already married, from the minority Miao tribe. The girl's in-laws were desperately poor and abusive, and her husband was a cripple. It was his family's idea that she go out and look for a job, and her own good fortune that she ended up in Grandma Number Two's house, working for Ch'ung-ho. The Miao girl and Ch'ung-ho got on well. Ch'ung-ho liked the fact that she would sit down and share a meal with her, without being the least self-conscious. "She didn't have a servile demeanor and did not see herself as inferior, which was different, say, from Kao Kan-kan," she recalls.

Kao Kan-kan was like family to us, yet she always thought of herself as a servant, so that she could never allow herself to sit with us at the dinner table. On her sixtieth birthday—this was in Chungking during the war— we begged her to join us, but she wouldn't, saying that she simply could not bring herself to do it. So she prepared a big meal for us and then retreated to the kitchen. But this was her birthday!

Kao Kan-kan also insisted on eating spoiled food, so as not to waste it, and meat covered with a layer of white slime, which she'd bought cheap from the butcher. The Miao girl ate whatever Ch'ung-ho ate, and when Ch'ung-ho sent her to the market to buy food, she came home with vegetables she had plucked from someone's field, saying that nature grew them so they belonged to everyone, not just the farmer. Ch'ung-ho also taught her and another woman to read.

The Miao girl was slower than Chao-ho's servant, Mrs. Li, who was a young widow. It would take her hours to learn a few characters, but once she learned them, she wouldn't forget. Mrs. Li was quicker, smarter. She could handle ten, fifteen characters in less than half an hour. But as soon as something upset her, her little boy, for instance, or if she was reminded of her sorrowful life, being so young and already a widow, then everything she had just learned would suddenly vanish. So she would have to start all over again.

When she was living in Grandma Number Two's house, the Miao girl was essentially a free person. So Ch'ung-ho and the two young ladies living upstairs figured that it should be possible for her to leave her married life and start all over again. The three began to plan her getaway. They thought that it would be best for the girl to be in a large city like K'un-ming. It would be easier to lie low in a city, and her husband's family, being country folk, would also be reluctant to go there to look for her. The distance from Ch'eng-kung to the railway station was long but still manageable on foot. One could hire a pony, as Shen Ts'ung-wen had often done, but this would involve bringing extra people into the plot and attracting unwanted attention—risks they could not afford. On the day the Miao girl left Ch'eng-kung, no one except the principals knew, not even Chao-ho. The girl quietly took to the road. Ch'ung-ho's housemates met her along the way, and the three walked to the station. Not long after, Ch'ung-ho heard that the Miao girl had married a driver and was living somewhere in K'un-ming.

Ch'ung-ho herself had lived in K'un-ming for about a year before she moved to Ch'eng-kung. She had come to this part of the southwest because of a job Shen Ts'ung-wen helped her get. Before he joined the faculty of Consolidated University, Shen was part of a three-member textbook selection committee, and when the Ministry of Education put him in charge of fiction, he recommended his sister-in-law for the position of general editor of poetry. The ministry made Ch'ung-ho an offer, and she accepted it. It would be difficult to weigh Ch'ung-ho's credentials by any conventional standards. She had attended Peking University but never completed her degree: her illness in 1936, which doctors at first thought was TB, forced her to take a leave of absence from college. After her recovery, she had worked for a while as the editor of features at the *Central News,* a daily paper in Nanking. Then the war arrived. During the brief period between her return to Soochow and the war, word about her learning must have gotten around.

Ch'ung-ho's position on the textbook selection committee did not last long because the Ministry of Education canceled the project after a year. Ch'ung-ho was not terribly disappointed. She needed to work because, unlike her sisters, she was a single woman on her own. At the same time, she could afford to take some time off while waiting for the next opportunity to come along. The private income from her land in Hofei, which her grandmother had arranged for her long ago, would see her through. It was not a huge amount, but it was enough so that Ch'ung-ho did not have to rush into any decision about work or marriage.

Many men were at her heels by this time. One was Pien Chih-lin, a poet and also a translator of French and British poetry—Verlaine, Valéry, Yeats, and Auden. Pien taught poetry in translation and the art of translation at the Consolidated University in K'un-ming. He was a close friend of Shen Ts'ung-wen; it was he who introduced Shen to the works of Joyce and Freud, which inspired the latter to experiment with a different style of writing during the war. Shen's "nightmare" stories, told as streams of consciousness, were products of this period.

Pien, who died recently at the age of ninety, was in love with Ch'ung-ho all his life. This was open knowledge. He wrote her many letters, long after he realized she would never choose him and after she had married someone else. He collected Ch'ung-ho's poems and stories and had them published in Hong Kong without her knowledge. Even Hu-hu, as a little boy, was aware of Pien's obsession. He told his parents a dream he once had of his aunt coming back from a faraway place, in a "big boat." "The uncle who is the poet was standing on the riverbank. He was clapping his hands, saying 'Good, good.'"

Pien was not writing much poetry after he moved from Peking to K'un-ming. Peking was the city in which he could read the news and still dream of the old. When he left that city, he also left behind the men and women of that city. Even Verlaine and Valéry could not do much for him in K'un-ming. Ch'ung-ho was not drawn to Pien or to his poems. She thought that his poems "lacked depth of meaning" and that he was "a little obvious," "a bit of a show-off." Students and friends of Pien described him as reticent. He wore "extra-thick glasses" and his "thin cheeks" were often "unshaven." Ch'ung-ho thought that his look—even his glasses—was an affectation. But then her judgment of character is often surprising.

Her view of Liu Wen-tien is an example. Liu was her teacher of classical literature at Peking University and also the man who once remarked that Shen Ts'ung-wen's teaching was worth only forty cents a month. Most people understood Liu's bombast merely as an expression of his self-importance. Ch'ung-ho, however, saw hilarity in it. She did not even regard his addiction to opium and his eventual dismissal from Consolidated University as retribution for having excessive pride. Liu was a person who loved excesses, she would say; he lived in an exaggerated way and used extravagant language. He scorned her brother-in-law, but not just him, in fact everyone who wrote in the vernacular, even Hu Shih. Ch'ung-ho insisted that there was no malice in Liu's strong judgment. Liu could not even take himself seriously, she said, so why should the world? She recalled that during the war Liu was separated from his wife, who remained in Peking. "From time to time, this woman would send him money, and in her letter she would specify that he should use it on wine and women. She would tell him: 'How awful that you don't have a wife or a concubine at your side. So go out and have fun.'" Ch'ung-ho did not think that Liu's wife was self-abnegating or just wacky: "It was all affection. This was what he claimed and I believed him. Besides, he was a serious opium addict, so how could he drink or have sex?"

What Ch'ung-ho said and remembered about Liu Wen-tien was not what one would expect, given the hurt Liu had caused Shen Ts'ung-wen. Ch'ung-ho was fond of her brother-in-law but did not think that Liu's comments were meant to wound him. She herself had a similar problem: she was fearsomely honest (people called her "Ironmouth Chang"), and she loved the full comic effect of a sly remark. Her grandmother probably noticed these tendencies in her when she was a young girl, and so warned her not to be cruel. This is not easy when a person is satiric by nature. And for a woman who is also as analytical as Ch'ung-ho, it would almost be impossible to let off a man like Pien Chih-lin, a self-styled poet who sells Valéry and Verlaine and who is also her suitor. But there are reasons she would have respected Liu Wen-tien, even though he was an emaciated addict. Liu had mischief in his blood and could discuss the early philosophers, fourth-century poetry, and *Story of the Stone* with equal prowess and originality.

Among Ch'ung-ho's suitors there was another man with an unkempt appearance, an older brother of Yun-ho's friend Tai Chieh. She called this one "Bookworm." This man, Mr. Tai, was a scholar of oracle-bone and bronze inscriptions, which means that he studied scripts from more than three thousand years ago. When Ch'ung-ho was a student in Peking, he often went to her apartment to see her. She recalls:

Whenever he came over, he was meant to have dinner with me or to have a chat, but he was too shy to do either. He always brought a book. I would ask him to sit down, and he wouldn't sit down. I would offer him tea, and he wouldn't want tea. He just stood in my room and read his book until he was ready to go. On these visits, the two of us often ended up in different corners of the room, he poring over his book and I practicing my calligraphy, with hardly a word exchanged.

Mr. Tai also wrote to Ch'ung-ho, but in oracle-bone scripts, which even Ch'ung-ho with her learning found inscrutable: "I am sure his letters were literary. They went on for pages. But I couldn't understand what he said." After Ch'ung-ho left Peking, Mr. Tai told her brother-in-law Shen Ts'ung-wen in a letter: "The phoenix is gone. The terrace is now empty." Ch'ung-ho did not call this man affected.

There were other men who expressed interest in her, but Ch'ung-ho refused to fall in love with anyone from her circle of friends. She was not afraid of love's risks except for the unpleasant consequences it could have for friendship. Besides, no one had swept her away. She also enjoyed being a single woman. She liked the mobility and freedom, mainly freedom from what society expected of a married woman. Ch'ung-ho did not have the worries her mother or sisters had when they were at her age; she had no appendages and none of the unhappiness of a "housewife." And everyday life was not an aggregate of so many trivialities. Ch'ung-ho was not afraid of spending time alone—her childhood had well prepared her. Nor did she think that she had to marry. Society's pressures in this regard did not mean a thing to her. Yet her strength of character was not the only reason she was able to act alone and decide for herself what to do with her life. Had there not been a war and had she been born even fifty years earlier, things would have been different.

Sometime in 1940, the government in Chungking offered her another job, this time in the department of rites and music, a newly formed division within the Ministry of Education. Chiang Kai-shek himself had sent word that he wanted the head of the ministry to create such an office, to help the government restore proper rites and music. Since the early Chou dynasty, more than three thousand years before, the Chinese had believed that rites and music were a measure of social order. Departures from normative practice signaled that trouble already existed or was in the works. The Chinese also believed rites and music to be instructive. Confucius himself used the *Classic of Rites* and the *Classic of Music* to teach the elements of appropriateness in speech and conduct, and in the arts.

Up to the end of the Ch'ing dynasty, it had always been the ruler's duty to maintain ritual correctness at court. Since his legitimacy and the legitimacy of his dynasty depended on it, a sensible ruler would take ritual matters seriously. He did not—and simply could not—work out everything himself. Rites guided all aspects of his relations with his family, his officials, his people, and even with emissaries from foreign countries, so any form he followed would need historical precedent and theoretical justification. To this end, the ruler would have studied the ritual classics with his tutors when he was young, but on specific questions, he had at his disposal the entire staff of the Ministry of Rites and any scholar he wished to consult.

When Chiang Kai-shek asked the minister of education to gather a group of experts to advise him on rites and music, he probably had in mind some version of the imperial office, only drastically abridged. His decision followed a celebration of Sun Yat-sen's birthday in November 1939. Mourning music was played on this occasion, and Sun had been dead for fourteen years. Chiang regarded this as a gross impropriety because, according to traditional practice, mourning and all rites associated with mourning the deceased should conclude after three years. In the newly formed department, Ch'ung-ho's responsibilities included selecting, from a fifth-century anthology on ritual music, suitable works for public occasions that were to have musical accompaniment. One can imagine her taking a personal interest in this; she would be lending some improvement to ceremonies she had found unbearable in the past. For the reception of foreign visitors, for example, she decided on a poem from the "Minor Odes" section of the *Classic of Odes*:

> *Yu, yu, cry the deer,*
> *Nibbling southwood in the field.*
> *I have fine guests.*
> *Let me play my zither,*
> *Blow my reed organ.*
> *Blow my reed organ,*
> *Trill its tongues.*
> *Take up the baskets of offerings.*
> *The guests are fond of me*
> *And will show me the perfect path.*

It took Ch'ung-ho several months to compile a list of twenty-four works and to produce two copies in her best calligraphy. But these were works whose music scores had long been lost. So as soon as the Ministry of Education approved her list, Ch'ung-ho and her colleagues began to solicit contemporary compositions.

The second half of the project dragged on for two more years. Her department was understaffed, and there were too many submissions. Chiang Kai-shek was given one of the two original drafts in Ch'ung-ho's calligraphy. The anthology had become a favorite read, but he lost his copy on a trip to India, and it was never recovered.

In Chungking, Ch'ung-ho lived in the same building where she had her office. Her situation was comfortable, as comfortable as one could expect in Chungking during the war, and certainly more stable than that of Yun-ho, who, with her little daughter, moved six times in one year. Ch'ung-ho worked with scholars she respected, and she had a wide circle of friends. They might be businessmen or engineers, musicians or novelists, career officials or scholars in official robes—they all loved the arts, and they all were clear-eyed about their relation to whichever political strongmen happened to be in power at the time. Some likened themselves to the utility men in an opera—flag-bearers and pawns, men with walk-on parts. Ch'ung-ho felt that because of their self-awareness these men relished the arts—they played hard at the arts.

She met many of them through the *k'un-ch'ü* theater. They sent poems after they had seen her perform. It was their way of introducing themselves. Even if she knew them through their works, their poems to her could formalize a relationship, making them literary friends if she chose to pursue it.

Two prominent men of letters who made Ch'ung-ho's acquaintance around this time were Chang Shih-chao and Shen Yin-mo. Chang was born in 1881, so was in his sixties when he was living in Chungking. He had studied law and logic in Scotland as a young man. He wrote extensively on constitutional government in the second decade of the twentieth century, but later took a firm position against democracy for his country. He ran political journals and cabinet ministries. He worked with revolutionaries and warlords, crime syndicates and Communist radicals, apparently without internal conflict. Chang was also known for his political theories and syntactic analysis, and was the author of a biography on Sigmund Freud.

Shen Yin-mo was two years younger than Chang, and when they were in Peking in the 1920s they were sometimes political opponents. For example, in 1925 Chang was minister of education under then president Tuan Ch'i-jui when the students at the Women's Normal School went on strike against their new chancellor. Chang took a tough stand, forcing the students to use more and more violent means, and when he finally brought in the municipal police to suppress their activities, the students burned his house to the ground. Shen was a teacher at the school; he stood by his students to the end. When the two saw each other again in Chungking, they probably talked about the 1925 demonstration, but it is difficult to imagine any hard feelings between them. Since their Peking days both men had moved in and out of all sorts of jobs, not because they liked change or felt restless but because the political climate forced them to live peripatetic lives. Now that they were together in Chungking, which could have been their last refuge, they simply had too much to talk about: calligraphy, poetry, opera, or a performance they had seen the night before. Once, in Chungking, Shen wrote a poem that compared his calligraphy with Chang's. This could also be read as a commentary on their relationship: "Ours are two schools, like chicken and duck, so no point in competing / . . . / Each has its strength or the lack of it, too transparent to hide. / Yours has got real spirit, so does mine."

The relationship of such accomplished scholars to Ch'ung-ho resembles their relationship to each other. It began with a recognition of something familiar in each other. But these literary kinsmen had a lot more in common than their literary temperament. They were equals in learning. Most had come to it through the same way: an early start, a lot of time alone with tutors, and few distractions. And when they finally absorbed it all, even their recreation became an expression of their learning. If others could not partake in the fun, it was not because they were deliberately kept out. Scholars had few rules when relaxing with their friends, mainly those that applied to literary contests or the round-robin poetry game they loved to play. Rules that showed off social niceties would have mattered only to those with a merchant's heart and a merchant's susceptibilities.

The scholar and calligrapher Shen Yin-mo, who later became Ch'ung-ho's teacher, described his childhood and youth as a life filled with austere learning— a life that hardly had room for anything else. Shen did not attend any formal schools. He read poetry with a seventy-year-old scholar when he was five and began to practice calligraphy seriously when he was a few years older. His father and grandfather were both skilled in calligraphy, and although he had never known his grandfather, he had been familiar with his brushwork since he was a little boy. Then one day, when he was twelve or thirteen, he learned quite by chance from his father that the style of calligraphy he had been imitating might not be worthy of further pursuit. "After this," he said, years later, "I began to study all the rubbings from stone inscriptions in my father's library when I had some time between my studies, and I would copy from these models."

By the time he was fifteen, he was already known for his calligraphy and would oblige upon request. He remembered that once his father gave him thirty ribbed fans, asking him to fill them with calligraphy. This experience made him realize how unsteady his arm was and "how physically painful it was not being able to write with my arm raised." Still, he resisted starting over again. Ten years later, someone he had just met told him that he had seen Shen's poem at a friend's house. "This poem is excellent," this man said, "but the calligraphy is vulgar. It has no bone."* The smart from this remark convinced Shen to correct his old habits and to learn holding the brush the right way "with solid fingers and an empty palm,"and "wrist and elbow both suspended above the table." Shen said:

> [Every morning] I would copy the rubbings of Han inscriptions on foot-square papers, one character on each sheet. I would use ink so diluted that the writing would leave only a faint trace. I tossed each sheet of paper on the ground as I finished, and when I accumulated a hundred, the ones on the bottom would have dried, so I would start again, this time writing four characters to a sheet. Later, I'd use the same papers to practice cursive writing. I worked like this for over two years.

As soon as Ch'ung-ho met Shen Yin-mo, she asked him for instruction on calligraphy. Shen said that he did not give private lessons but would let her watch him work and would also read and revise any writings that she wished to share. They had no formal arrangement. Every few months, Ch'ung-ho either took the bus or hitched a ride on a kerosene delivery truck for an hour to Mr. Shen's house on Kele Mountain. Many government offices had moved to this place after the Japanese began escalating their air attacks on the Chungking area in 1941. It was safer in the mountains and quieter. The first time Ch'ung-ho was there, Shen asked her to write a few words. He then commented that her calligraphy was like that of a Ming calligrapher imitating the style of the Chin.† Even now Ch'ung-ho does not know if this was meant to be a compliment or criticism.

Shen always got up early in the morning to practice calligraphy from model books. This could take several hours. He would then spend most of the day fulfilling streams of requests from friends and admirers for samples of his calligraphy. He also wrote poems. People at the time considered his compositions technically perfect yet "natural and graceful." Shen thought that nearly all subjects were suitable for poetry—hospital rooms, rickshaws, pigeons, and plough cattle—and was equally at ease writing classical and vernacular verses. By his own account, he nearly had a breakdown at fourteen when he thought that he had a small memory quotient. To make up for it, he steeped himself in T'ang

---

*This person was the radical scholar and early Communist Party member Ch'en Tu-hsiu.

†This would be the fourth century. China's best calligraphers lived during the Han and the Chin dynasties.

poetry until he no longer had to strain to remember the words and phrases. Along the way, he acquired a love for poetry and for writing poetry.

Over the course of their friendship, he wrote Ch'ung-ho many poems, and Ch'ung-ho showed him many of hers, mainly to hear his suggestions about how to make them better. She considered Shen Yin-mo her second teacher, her tutor, Mr. Chu from Hofei, being her first. She was not searching for a teacher when she met Shen Yin-mo. But once she stood in his study and watched him work, she knew that she wanted to emulate him.

At first Shen called her by the polite appellation "Lady Scholar Ch'ung-ho" (Ch'ung-ho *nü-shih*). Then he changed it to "Lady Disciple Ch'ung-ho" (Ch'ung-ho *nü-ti*). Under his influence, Ch'ung-ho was able to build on the habits she had acquired as a child: getting up early in the morning to practice calligraphy from a model book for at least three hours, and more if there was time. She follows this regimen even now, at eighty-eight. Her writing arm is as strong as a young girl's.

Ch'ung-ho says that Shen Yin-mo's work habits were like those of the Han and Chin masters. Of one, Chang Chih, it was said that when he practiced next to a pond, he would blacken the pond with ink. Five hundred years later, another calligrapher wrote, "I kept constant my resolve to practice 'by the pond.'" So in this way, Chang Chih's tradition of working was carried forward until Shen's time. In his own writings, Shen tried to explain the point of it all. "We all know the origin of writing," he said.

> In the beginning our ancestors looked up and down, taking forms and patterns from the stars and clouds, mountains and rivers, the claw prints and footprints of birds and beasts, and they created characters out of what they observed. Thus, the shape of a word can be written on a piece of paper but not its spirit and mood, and not its grace and charm—these things lie outside of paper and ink. Still, every movement in nature has its tally in our own world. So when we see porters, balancing their loads on a shoulder pole and jostling to get ahead of each other on the road, also boats on the water, dancers dancing, grass snakes, and marking-lines, and even when we hear the sound of waves swelling and rushing forward, we know that these things will be of great help to people who are good at calligraphy.

It is, therefore, to catch what one calligrapher called "the postures of wild geese in flight," "the bearing of phoenixes dancing and snakes being surprised," and "the power of sheer cliffs and crumbling peaks" that one would practice until the pond is blackened with ink. It is arduous work to let the brush explore nature's mysteries, and the rewards are quiet and private, almost too subtle to put into words. One fifth-century scholar described it in this way: "The mind has forgotten itself in the brush, and the hand has forgotten itself in the writing. Both mind and hand have reached where their feelings carry them, yet thought is not forgotten in the brushwork."

Ch'ung-ho was also writing her best poems when she was living in Chungking. It is not clear whether this was the consequence of war or the effects of calligraphy and Mr. Shen. Two poems from this period are about a type of freshwater jellyfish found among the rocks near the banks of Chia-ling River. These creatures are much smaller than the ocean variety; their bodies are like translucent parachutes, "glassy with stars imprinted on them." They are called "peach blossom fish."

I

Remember the path along the Wu-ling River:*
In spring breeze, roots and buds are pushing through.

Let them adorn the human world.
I prefer being a butterfly under the waves,
Carried to the world's end by my whims.

Try to describe me: I am but a trace of spring,
with nothing to hold on to.
What I cherish most is having a bubble
and a shadow as body and home.
Like a veil riding in the wind,
I may try to catch the fallen petals.
But my sheer body is nothing but tears
when alighting with mist across the sandbar.

2

Scattered, the hanging pearls are a thousand tears,
Vague, like dreams, imprinted on a gravel bar.
My gauze skirt does not block
the light of of the evening sun.
They are merely translucent shadows

---

*Wu-ling is the river that leads to the Peach Blossom Springs, which is a sort of earthly paradise. See note on p. 200.

When meeting the evening glow.
Shimmering, they reflect the floating clouds.

The scene on the sea surface cannot compete
with the world underneath.
My heart is vast without borders.
So why would I be willing to pull
at the duckweed sprouts with my silk-belt body?
Hardest is to hand over my knowledge of the sea
to the flowers along the road.

In the first poem, Ch'ung-ho begins with an extravagant claim even though the narrator—a phantom of her imagination—is small, almost negligible in the order of things. One can think of other great writers starting off this way. The boldest and smartest of Chinese thinkers, Chuang Tzu, tells us in the opening lines of his book that in Northern Darkness a tiny fish called K'un changes and becomes a bird called P'eng: "The back of the P'eng measures I don't know how many thousands miles across and, when he rises up and flies off, his wings are like clouds all over the sky." Ch'ung-ho's "peach blossom fish" does not transform into something large but remains to the end, large in spirit. In the last line of the second poem, it boasts: "Hardest is to hand over my knowledge of the sea / to the flowers along the road."

This small creature, whose "heart is vast without borders," is, at the same time, aware of its near nonexistence, of hanging somewhere between dream and reality. Yet even this is cause for celebration: "I am but a trace of spring, / with nothing to hang on to. / What I cherish most is having a bubble / and a shadow as body and home." What Ch'ung-ho is pursuing in these poems is the idea of lightness and transparency, of having a body and not having a body, of finding oneself suspended in space between this and that. She calls this *ling-k'ung*. The fish that embodies *ling-k'ung* is but a trace of spring; it is free from the finality of form yet conscious of its limitations and of its mortality. It says of itself: "But my sheer body is nothing but tears / when alighting with mist across the sandbar."

"Peach blossom fish" mean many things to Ch'ung-ho: they are a metaphor for *ling-k'ung*, but also for spring, because they appear when peach trees are in bloom; and for men who parachuted to their death on the sandbars of Chungking, of whom there were many during the war.

The other forms of art Ch'ung-ho loves are also about "being suspended." A calligrapher's wrist is suspended slightly above the table, his palm is empty, his fingers are strong, and his brush has freedom of movement: he can speed up without haste and linger without getting stuck. And when he has mastered speed and lingering and arrested "the bearing of phoenixes dancing" and "the grace of dragons leaping," he has suspended himself—"the mind has forgotten itself in the brush and the hand has forgotten itself in the writing." Performing *k'un-ch'ü* is no different. The best actor lets her singing and her gesturing play the part. She keeps herself distant—suspended—while letting her skills explore her character's motives and moods and manner. Ch'ung-ho feels that the most difficult skill in the *k'un-ch'ü* theater is to be able to represent all that is not shown. Just as a good playwright does not resort to sentimental colloquy, a good actor holds back what she could express. In other words, "she is able to move but does not move"; this is also a kind of suspending, between the apparent and the unapparent, and only strong acting can bring it off.

Ch'ung-ho liked to play at these things, but the war kept her wary: she'd known the death of her niece, the travails of her siblings and friends. Aesthetics did not translate well into real life, and sometimes she found even small things disquieting. The scholar Chang Shih-chao once sent her a poem comparing her to Ts'ai Wen-chi, a female scholar from the second century. Two lines infuriated her: "Who made Wen-chi drift on down to this? / Playing the Tartar's flute, she could only assuage herself." Offended by the older scholar's suggestion that *she* had been wandering about destitute, she called the analogy "farfetched and inappropriate."

Chang Shih-chao probably had his reasons for seeing a likeness between Ch'ung-ho and Wen-chi. Wen-chi had learning, literary talent, and an analytical mind. She also possessed a subtle understanding of musical pitch. She was a young widow when a nomadic chieftain from the north kidnapped her and made him his wife. She bore him two sons and lived in his tent for twelve years. The de facto ruler of China at the time was Ts'ao Ts'ao, who was a close friend of Wen-chi's father. He felt keenly for Wen-chi's misfortunes, so he dispatched an emissary to the north with a sack of gold coins to buy Wen-chi back from her Tartar husband. After Wen-chi returned home, she married one of Ts'ao Ts'ao's lieutenants, a commander of a military settlement. Later, when this man was charged with a capital offense, Wen-chi went to see her benefactor, begging him to pardon her husband. Ts'ao Ts'ao granted her wish but asked a personal favor in return. He said to her: "I understand that in the past, there were many books in your family's library. Can you possibly write down what you have memorized from your readings?" Wen-chi did her best and presented to Ts'ao Ts'ao over four hundred chapters.

Ch'ung-ho knew why Chang Shih-chao compared her with Wen-chi, but simply got hung up on the expression *liu-luo* in the line "Who made Wen-chi drift on down [*liu-luo*] to this?" She pointed out that, unlike Wen-chi, she was not dragged to a Tartar's land and forced to live a Tartar's life. She left home because there was a war. And even under the grimmest conditions, she relied on herself and made the best of what she had.

Ch'ung-ho felt a lot of sadness during the war, but not for herself. Her sadness had to do with knowing that the world she had left behind could never be regained. Even so, she played with the idea of building a country estate after the war was over, on the land her grandmother had given her. She knew how many trees to plant in the garden and whether the garden would be near a stream. She imagined that the place would only be for scholars and friends who loved the arts. They would come whenever they wished and stay as long as they liked. They could work alone or be with a group; they could share a kitchen or not share a kitchen. They could do whatever they pleased. Yet when the time came for her to return home, she wrote:

> Along the Chia-ling River the third month of spring is like wine.
> The boatman's pole enters the emerald water,
> The sail is about to be raised,
> But the willow asks me to stay.
> My best years were spent as a visitor.
> Going home now, I find I yearn only more for home.

She yearned "only more for home" because she was already anticipating the strangeness of being home, of not recognizing a place she had always called home. To long for something from afar, knowing that you cannot get to it, was easier, she thought, than to see it gone and mourn for its loss.

When she returned to her parents' home in Soochow on a visit, remnants of the old world—"broken balustrade" and "battered veranda"—were still visible. "Songs from the past" and "music of mouth organs and flutes" "resounded among the winding roof beams": "Though moths have eaten through the gorgeous costumes, new styles can still be rendered from the old." Ch'ung-ho wrote these words in 1947, after a *k'un-ch'ü* gathering. She still had a wisp of hope then that somehow things could be put together again.

In 1947, Ch'ung-ho was teaching calligraphy and opera at Peking University. Her home was a small room in her sister Chao-ho's modest house on Chung-lao Lane. In September, she met Hans Frankel through her brother-in-law. A year later, they were married.

Hans Frankel came from a family of scholars of German-Jewish descent. He was a refugee during the war. His family had left Germany in 1935, when he was eighteen. They lived in England for a while and then settled in California. Hans's degree was in Spanish literature, but he could easily handle German, French, English, and Italian literature. He came to China for the adventure and to attempt a difficult language. When he met Shen Ts'ung-wen, only a few months after he arrived in China, he must have been relatively fluent, because the two would often have long conversations on Chinese art and architecture and Shen could not speak English or any other European language. Ch'ung-ho knew very little English, so the courtship must have been conducted in Chinese. The wedding took place on November 21, 1948. The Communists were already moving in on Peking. The streets were desolate; most shops were closed. Years later, Hans described the wedding as simple, a Christian wedding, but in the Chinese tradition: "The bride and groom each imprinted their seals on the marriage certificate as proof of their faith in their marriage." The preacher exacted no oath from them. Afterward, everyone had cake. Chao-ho's son Hu-hu said, "Fourth Aunt, I hope you will marry every day, so that I can have cake every day."

One would never ask Ch'ung-ho why she married Hans Frankel. There were no secrets about it, yet one would leave it to her to unravel it or not. It is a curious union: a woman steeped in traditional Chinese learning and art decides to marry a Westerner, an outsider, and then leaves China to go to an unfamiliar place that has no trace of the world she loves. Why did she choose Wen-chi's fate when she did not have to? (Years later, Ch'ung-ho recalled with irony what Chang Shih-chao had predicted in his poem. "He was right," she said, "I did marry a Tartar.") She was self-sufficient, so never felt a need to marry. She also had many friends who shared her interests, and a large family of siblings. When Ch'ung-ho decided to marry Hans, Yun-ho had just returned from America; Yuan-ho would not leave for Taiwan for several months; and Chao-ho and all five of their brothers had firmly decided to stay in China. Why then did she flee? What did she intuit?

At the time of her wedding, Ch'ung-ho did not know that her brother-in-law Shen Ts'ung-wen was on the verge of a mental collapse. Her teacher Shen Yin-mo was living in Shanghai, selling calligraphy to support himself. His misfortunes would unfold slowly. The worst were his last years, from 1966 to 1971. At the beginning of the Cultural Revolution, he tore up all his works, all he had written and thought worth keeping, and all the model calligraphy books and the Ming and Ch'ing scrolls in his collection; he soaked the scraps in water until they became pulp and then carried them in bamboo baskets to the nearby dumps. He erased every trace of his artistic labor to avoid trouble. But the local Communist radicals still did not let him off. Shen was persecuted for five more years, until he was dead.

Ch'ung-ho could not have foreseen these things in 1947. She could not have known all that was in store for those who stayed in China. Although she was disappointed with the world she found upon her return home from Chungking, she could still see vestiges of the world she loved, and she could still dream of rebuilding. But the new world the Chinese Communists had envisioned was bleak and unfamiliar to her; it had no place for the things she cared about, and in this world she could not even dream these things to herself. She felt that she should leave the socialist revolution to others who were more "pliable and adaptable." She knew that if she stayed in China she would have to stop working altogether. In this way, she was closer to her brother-in-law than to her sister Chao-ho, as she readily admits. Like Shen Ts'ung-wen, she grew up without the support of outside beliefs; her private world in Hofei did not encourage her to aim for the big and noble tasks of trying to save China or the world. She learned about compassion through her grandmother's example. That was all the good she needed to know.

When she boarded the *General Gordon* in Shanghai to come to America in January 1949, she brought with her a few changes of clothes, an antique inkstone a friend had given her, her favorite writing brushes, and a box of very old inksticks, some five hundred years old. (Ch'ung-ho had put these inksticks in a bank safe-deposit box in Shanghai just before the war broke out. They survived the bombings, heavy artillery fire, and eight years of enemy occupation.) These writing utensils, along with her clothes, fit into a small case. The rest—books, writing paper, and her collections of Ming and Ch'ing scrolls—she sent by mail. Everything but the Ming and Ch'ing scrolls arrived.

So it was with these few possessions that Ch'ung-ho began to construct a new life, first in Berkeley, California, and then in North Haven, Connecticut. Elderly teachers and old friends came to visit, some after a thirty- or forty-year gap. But once they were together, they played rhyming games as before and wrote verses in turn to amuse themselves. Yun-ho and Chao-ho also had long stays with Ch'ung-ho and Hans when it was possible to see each other again. Everything felt just like before even though they had been universes apart during their separation.

Hans studied Chinese literature after his return from China, and eventually accepted an appointment at Yale as a professor of Chinese poetry. Ch'ung-ho taught calligraphy at the university's School of Art for many years. She never gave up the idea of building a world for herself. This world is much smaller in scale than what she imagined for her scholarly estate in Hofei. It is a patch of garden behind her North Haven house. She planted tree peonies and roses on one side, tall chives, gourds, and cucumbers around the deck, and a pear tree next to the chives. She also created a small bamboo grove in the back, away from the noise of cars and trucks, and there she put a wooden bench. Of her private haven, she writes:

> Travel weary, I return to this nook of earth.
> A squirrel sits on a branch and twitches its head at me.
> "Pinecones cover the ground," I say, "take all you want.
> I just wish to borrow cool shade for a moment of rest."

Ch'ung-ho has few regrets about not realizing her grander ambitions. She writes in another poem:

> In the past, when choosing a scenic spot,
> We went to towering cliffs.
> Now we pass our time anywhere,
> Wherever destiny leads.
> Elegant or common,
> We seek only a place where life stirs.
> Just so, an old man next door
> Peers over the hedge
> And admires my gourds.

In North Haven, Ch'ung-ho also dreamed of home and of going home. Yet in 1979, on the eve of returning to China after three decades of being away, she again wavered:

> The road is long. I remember clearly how it was,
> But only vaguely how things have just been.
> Year after year, dreams of going home supported my translucent shadow.
> But now, just before setting off,
> My dreams themselves need holding up.

She went and came back. Ch'ung-ho hardly leaves her small garden now but carries on her peripatetic life in the manner she knows best, with a brush, moving in and out of the imperceptible.

A Note on Sources

The notes, on the whole, refer to written materials, which include both published and unpublished sources. All other details regarding the Chang family were drawn from interviews.

Notes

Chapter 1: *The Wedding*

1 *Lu Ying's wedding*   Yun-ho learned the details of her mother's wedding from the grandmothers and servants in the family. She recorded them in her diary many years later. The ditty is also found in her diary. In interviews, Ch'ung-ho filled in the background regarding traditional Chinese weddings in gentry households. She had been to several such weddings when she was a child.

2 *people of Huai-pei*   A detailed study of Huai-pei is in Elizabeth Perry's *Rebels and Revolutionaries in North China, 1845–1945*. Her analysis of Huai-pei peasants is found on pp. 43–47.

3 *Anhwei bandits*   The four sisters' sister-in-law, Chou Hsiao-hua, told me this. She was also from a wealthy Hofei family.

3 *Anhwei, 1906*   *Anhwei chin-tai-shih*, pp. 360–61.

4 *worries of bride and groom's families*   A second-century B.C. commentary on the *Classic of Odes* says: "Candles burn for three continuous nights in the bride's home; everyone there broods about the impending separation. The groom's family also does not make mirth; they worry about the question of progeny." (See Han Ying, *Han-shih wai-chuan chi-shih* 2:33, pp. 76–77.)

4 *bride older than the groom*   From interview with Yun-ho. See also the brief biography in Hsaio K'o-fei et al., *Liu Ming-ch'uan tsai Taiwan*, p. 282. Liu Ming-ch'uan, the first governor of Taiwan, was also from Hofei. His wife was six years older than he, and, according to his biographer, it was common practice in this area for the bride to be older than the groom. See pp. 25–28 of the present work for more information about Liu Ming-ch'uan.

5 *Chang Hsüeh-ch'eng on "quiet woman"*   *Wen-shih t'ung-i* 5: 41–43, "Learning for Women."

5 *ode on "quiet woman"*   *Shih-ching* (Classic of Odes), Ode 42; revised from James Legge's translation of "The She King" in his *Chinese Classics*, vol. 4, p. 68. As for the two different readings of this poem, see Chu Hsi, *Shih-ching chi-chu*, pp. 21–22, for the first reading, and Mao Heng, *Mao-shih Cheng-chien* 2: 15b–16a, for the second.

6 *Chang on learning for women*   *Wen-shih t'ung-i*, pp. 40–41.

6 *T'ai-jen and T'ai-ssu*   Ode 240, *Ssu-ch'i* (Great dignity) in the *Ta-ya* (Major odes) section.

7 *Ch'iu Chin*   A moving portrayal of Ch'iu Chin (Qiu Jin) is in Jonathan Spence, *The Gate of Heavenly Peace*, pp. 83–93. See also Fang Chao-ying's biography of Ch'iu in *Eminent Chinese of the Ch'ing Period, 1644–1912*, edited by Arthur W. Hummel, pp. 169–71.

7 *"When it's time to get married ..."*   Translated in Spence, *The Gate of Heavenly Peace*, p. 83.

Chapter 2: Birth

9 *"Changes"*   See hexagram 54, *kuei-mei*, or "Marrying Maiden."

10 *Ch'en Kan-kan*   Interviews with Yuan-ho, who recently also published some of this material regarding her wet nurse and Ch'en Kan-kan in *Shui*, the Chang family journal; see *Shui*, no. 15 (December 31, 2000), p. 9.

12 *Yun-ho's birth*   Drawn from Chang Yun-ho's earlier draft, which is somewhat different from the published version in her *Tsui-hou te kuei-hsiu*, pp. 3–6.

13 *Hofei ditty and wet nurse*   Interviews with Yun-ho. A version of this was later published in her *Tsui-hou te kuei-hsiu*; see pp. 7–10.

Chapter 3: Reasons for Moving

17 *Tax collecting in Anhwei*   *Anhwei chin-tai-shih*, p. 359.

18 *likin goods*   *Anhwei hsien-tai ke-ming-shih tzu-liao ch'ang-pien*, pp. 38–40; *Hsüan-t'ung cheng-chi* (Official records from the Hsüan-t'ung reign), 71 *chüan*, quoted in *Anhwei chin-tai-shih*, p. 359.

18 *lawlessness*   *Anhwei hsien-tai ke-ming-shih*, p. 57.

18 *Patriotic activities in Anhwei*   The *Anhwei chin-tai-shih* has a detailed discussion of activities among the young Anhwei radicals; see pp. 335–51. See also Lee Faigon's biography of Ch'en Tu-hsiu, *Chen Duxiu*, pp. 39–59.

19 *gathering at an An-ch'ing library*   The quote from *Su-pao* is found in *Anhwei hsien-tai ke-ming-shih*, pp. 84–85.

19 *independence and cutting off queues*   *Anhwei chin-tai-shih*, pp. 376–79.

21 *ambiguities in Shanghai culture*   See Gail Hershatter, *Dangerous Pleasures*, pp. 14–20, 165–69; and Yeh Wen-hsin, *The Alienated Academy*, pp. 55–59.

21 *Shanghai newspapers*   See *Anhwei hsien-tai ke-ming-shih*, p. 108.

21 *Ch'en Tu-hsiu statement*   From the first issue of *Anhwei Venacular Paper*, quoted in ibid., p. 84.

Chapter 4: *The Hofei Spirit*

23 *Hofei's early history*   See *Hofei shih-hua*, pp. 5–13.

24 *Chang Shu-sheng*   An official biography of Chang Shu-sheng can be found in the *Ch'ing-shih lieh-chüan* 54:12b–15a. Li Hung-chang also wrote a short biography of Chang, which is included among the prefaces to Chang's collected memorials, *Chang Ching-ta-kung tsou-i* (hereafter, *Tsou-i*).

24 *backgrounds of Hofei generals*   Wang Erh-min discusses this in *Huai-chün-chih*, pp. 137–87. See also *Fei-hsi Huai-chün jen-wu*, pp. 29–30, 109–11, 126–28; and Samuel Chu and Kwang-ching Liu, *Li Hung-chang and China's Early Modernization*, pp. 26–27.

25 *new Hofei gentry in their community*   See *Lu-chou fu-chih*, 13:31–33; and Chang Chung-li, *The Chinese Gentry*, p. 57.

25 *Liu Ming-ch'uan as a youth*   See *Ho-fei wen-shih tzu-liao*, pp.117–18; and *Fei-hsi Huai-chün jen-wu*, pp. 30–31.

26 *Nien in Anhwei*   See Chiang Siang-tseh, *The Nien Rebellion*, pp. 32–44.

27 *flagpole*   See *Fei-hsi Huai-chün jen-wu*, p. 31.

27 *"When the enemies came . . ."*   See Wang Erh-min, *Huai-chün-chih*, p. 118.

27 *Liu's wife . . .*   See *Fei-hsi Huai-chün jen-wu*, p. 31.

27 *"the hood"*   *Hofei shih-hua*, pp. 36–37.

27 *"more talented men . . ."*   See Wang Erh-min, *Huai-chün-chih*, p. 216; see also Wang's discussion of Li as commander of the Huai Army, pp. 216–24.

28 *Liu in Taiwan*   See the biography of Liu Ming-ch'uan in *Eminent Chinese of the Ch'ing Period, 1644–1912* (hereafter, *ECCP*), edited by Arthur W. Hummel, vol. 1, pp. 526–28. See also Hsiao K'o-fei et al., *Liu Ming-ch'uan tsai Taiwan*, pp. 205–40.

28 *"rose to fame . . ."*   See Wang Erh-min, *Huai-chün-chih*, pp. 385–86.

28 *Chang Yin-ku*   Described in the tomb inscription Li Hung-chang wrote for him; see *Fei-hsi Huai-chün jen-wu*, pp. 15–16.

30 *"I have made . . ."*   Chang Shu-sheng, *Tsou-i*, p. 476.

30 *"men who are sloppy . . ."* Ibid., p. 476.

30 *"[Westerners] have a firm . . ."* Ibid., pp. 283–84.

31 *"merely another province"* Ibid., p. 284.

31 *"We constructed . . ."* Ibid., p. 284.

32 *"We have already . . ."* Ibid., p. 306.

32 *"When investigating . . ."* Ibid., pp. 306–7.

33 *on Europeans* See his discussion in *Tsou-i,* pp. 283, 306, and 558.

33 *Chang's reports on the French in Vietnam* *Tsou-i,* pp. 333–38, 431–40, 447–54, and 478–80.

33 *Purists* See Lloyd E. Eastman's discussion in *Throne and Mandarins,* pp. 16–29.

34 *letters from August 1884* See Chang Shu-sheng, *Tsou-i,* pp. 536–39, 542–43, and 546–47.

34 *last letter* Ibid., pp. 558–59.

35 *"It is crucial . . ."* Ibid., p. 560.

36 *Tseng on Hofei men* In Tseng Kuo-fan's diary, *Tseng Wen-cheng kung jih-chi,* pp. 55–56; also quoted in Wang Erh-min's *Huai-chün-chih,* pp. 223–24.

36 *best minds of his generation* Paul A. Cohen's *Between Tradition and Modernity* and Hao Yen-p'ing and Wang Erh-min's essay in *The Cambridge History of China,* vol. 11, part 2, pp. 142–201, throw much light on this subject.

Chapter 5: Grandmother

38 *"perfect travel"* *The Book of Lieh Tzu,* translated by A. C. Graham, pp. 81–82.

38 *Li Yun-chang* Chou Hai-p'ing's schematic summary of the Li family genealogy includes the information regarding Yun-chang's wives and children (*Hofei wen-shih tzu-liao,* pp. 94–95). See also Li Hung-chang, *Li Hung-chang chia-shu* (hereafter, "Family Letters"), pp. 35, 43, and 58.

39 *"Among my nephews . . ."* Li Hung-chang, "Family Letters," p. 60.

40 *Li Hung-chang to Ching-shih* Ibid., pp. 41–42.

40 *"refused to be obstinate . . ."* Confucius, *Analects,* 9:4.

41 *Li Hung-chang on Buddhism* Li Hung-chang, "Family Letters," p. 288.

42 *Li Ch'ing-chao's marriage* Li Ch'ing-chao (1084–ca. 1151) was one of the finest poets in Chinese history. Her moving account of her marriage appeared as an epilogue to her husband's collection of old inscriptions, called *Records on Metal and Stone.* See Stephen Owen's excellent translation of this essay in the collection he edited called *An Anthology of Chinese Literature,* pp. 591–96.

43 *minister and gamekeeper*   The story appears in *Mencius* 5a:2, p. 140 of D. C. Lau's translation.

52 *Chang Tai*   See Chang Tai's essay "Three Generations of Collected Books" *(San-tai ts'ang-shu)* in his *T'ao-an meng-i*, pp. 31–32.

57 *Hsün Tzu on "inwardness"*   This elegant statement is found in chapter 3 of the Hsün Tzu, *Hsün Tzu chi-shih*, p. 47.

Chapter 6: Mother

61 *"It was the perfect year . . ."*   Drawn from Chang Yun-ho's earlier draft of "Wang Chüeh-wu Causing Trouble at School," which was later published in her *Tsui-hou te kuei-hsiu*, pp. 26–27.

61 *Lu Ying's Soochow home*   Ibid., pp. 27–28.

63 *Hofei song*   Yun-ho's diary, 10/22/84.

65 *making Hofei delicacies*   Yuan-ho's essay in *Shui*, no. 9 (December 1998), p. 1.

65 *Kao Kan-kan*   Chao-ho's essay in *Shui*, no. 6 (November 1997), p. 7.

66 *gifts for the elderly*   Yuan-ho's essay in *Shui*, no. 9 (December 1998), pp. 1–2.

66 *Chu Kan-kan and Tou Kan-kan*   Chang Yun-ho, *Tsui-hou te kuei-hsiu*, p. 28.

69 *wedding of Wu-ling's half sister*   From interview with Yuan-ho. She gives a slightly different version in her essay about her mother; see *Shui*, no. 14 (August 2000), pp. 13–14.

70 *baby sister and mother's death*   From interview with Yun-ho. Yun-ho also wrote about her mother's death in *Tsui-hou te kuei-hsiu*, pp. 13–15.

72 *Li Yü and the spirit of a place*   *Li-weng i-chia-yen*, in *Li Yü ch'üan-chi* 2:64a–66a. I have used Patrick Hanan's translation (with romanization altered) in *The Invention of Li Yu*, pp. 192–93.

Chapter 7: Father

74 *books and newspapers*   See Wei Pu's essay in *Shui*, no. 4 (February 1997), p. 2.

75 *a shy man*   Ibid., p. 4.

76 *private academies*   See John Chaffee, *The Thorny Gates of Learning in Sung China*, pp. 89–94, on the Sung academies; Barry Keenan on the late Ch'ing academies in *Education and Society in Late Imperial China, 1600–1900*, edited by Benjamin Elman and Alexander Woodside, pp. 493–524. See also, for example, the biographies of Tsou Yuan-piao and Feng Ts'ung-wu

in *Dictionary of Ming Biography, 1368–1644,* edited by L. Carrington Goodrich and Chaoying Fang, pp. 1312–14; 458–59.

76 *gentry and academies* See Barry Keenan, pp. 498–99.

76 *West Hofei Academy* *Lu-chou fu-chih,* 17:86b.

77 *Kiangsu academies* See Keenan, p. 499.

77 *educators* See Yeh Wen-hsin, *The Alienated Academy,* pp. 102–8. Yeh's book is the best source we have in English on the private schools of the republican period.

77 *China College* Ibid., pp. 106–7.

77 *tuition* Ibid., pp. 195–205.

79 *Ch'üan-fu* See Chia Hsing-yuan's essay in *Shui,* no. 8 (July 1998), p. 3.

81 *servants playing mah-jongg* Yü-ho's essay in *Shui,* no. 11 (August 1999), p. 4.

82 *"Po-chi had another son . . ."* Chang Huai-kuei's letter, dated December 16, 1889, is included in *Shui,* no. 1 (February 1996).

82 Classic of Odes Ode 243, *Hsia-wu* (Footsteps here below), in the "Major odes." See also Huai-kuei's letter in *Shui,* no. 1 (February 1996).

82 *Chi-yu* See Wei Pu's discussion of Wu-ling's name in *Shui,* no. 4 (February 1997), p. 1.

82 *"Only now . . ."* Huai-kuei's letter in *Shui,* no. 1 (February 1996).

83 *Chang Hua-kuei's biography* *Pa-hsien-chih* 9:21–22, pp. 1275–77.

84 *Yen, Feng, and Chiang* See their biographies in *Biographical Dictionary of Republican China,* edited by Howard L. Boorman.

85 *Ting-ho* Chang Tsung-ho's diary from October through December 1932 is a wonderful source on Ting-ho as a young man. In it, Tsung-ho managed to say a lot about his cousin's character and activities in Peking though he never tried to judge Ting-ho. See *Shui,* no. 7 (February 1998). According to Ch'ung-ho, Ting-ho's own children wrote a hagiographic biography of their father, casting him as a Communist martyr.

87 *"It is already a fluke . . ."* Tsung-ho's diary dated 4/5/31, in *Shui,* no. 6 (November 1997), p. 4.

87 *"I believe I have . . ."* Tsung-ho's diary dated 10/22/31, in *Shui,* no. 1 (February 1996).

87 *"Dad is still the best."* Tsung-ho's diary dated 10/25/31, in ibid.

88 *"The moon shines . . ."* Chao-ho's poem is collected in *Shui,* no. 3 (October 1996).

88 *Nara Singde* See Yun-ho's essay in *Shui,* no. 9 (December 1998).

88 *three categories of men* See Confucius, *Analects,* 6:19.

89 *Wu-ling and etymology* *Shui,* no. 11 (August 1999), p. 2.

89 *11/12/30–10/16/31* Tsung-ho's diary, collected in *Shui,* no. 1 (February 1996).

91 *"Courtyard Full of Fragrance"* I have slightly revised James J. Y. Liu's translation of the original poem by Ch'in Kuan, in *Sunflower Splendor*, edited by Wu-chi Liu and Irving Yucheng Lo, p. 360.

92 *Yü-ho* Yü-ho's essay in *Shui*, no. 11 (August 1999), pp. 3–4.

92 *Wei Chün-i* See Kan Lan-ching's biography of Wei Chün-i in *Shui*, no. 15 (December 2000), p. 22; see also Huan-ho's essay in *Shui*, no. 11 (August 1999), p. 6.

94 *Mother and Dad* Tsung-ho's diary dated 2/28/31, in *Shui*, no. 1 (February 1996).

94 *Chün-i's eulogy* In *Shui*, no. 3 (October 1996).

96 *"Funeral Song"* Ibid.

96 *chung-kuei* From the commentary to hexagram 37, *Chou-i*, 4:7b–8a. This is slightly revised from Richard Lynn's translation: see I Ching, *The Classic of Changes*, pp. 363–64.

96 *Tu Fu writes . . .* From the poem "I Hear That the Imperial Army Has Just Recovered the Land North and South of the River," in *Tu Fu shih-hsüan*, p. 149.

97 *Wu-ling's poems* Collected in *Shui*, no. 5 (June 1997).

Chapter 8: The School

98 *the dean's words* Wei Pu's "Foreword #4" in the 1932 *Le-i Yearbook*. A 1932 graduate of Le-i had sent her copy of the yearbook to the sisters' youngest brother, Huan-ho, who in turn shared it with me. This book remains the most important source I have on Le-i Middle School. It includes forewords by Chang Wu-ling, Wei Chün-i (the school's principal and also Wu-ling's wife), and the dean of the school (Wei Chün-i's brother); a short history of the school; the school's song; photos of the nineteen graduates, each with a short biography written by a fellow classmate; sample writings from all the graduates; and posting of the requirements for entrance, the enrollment figures for each year, and the fees and tuition.

98 *Wu-ling's foreword* "Foreword #2" in the 1932 *Le-i Yearbook*.

99 *school song* 1932 *Le-i Yearbook*.

99 *T'ai-po and Yü-chung* Ssu-ma Ch'ien, *Shih-chi*, fourth *chüan*, in Chung-hua edition, p. 115.

100 *Confucius on T'ai-po* *Analects*, 8:1 (revised from Lau's translation, p. 92).

100 *Le-i's history* Yun-ho's account in *Shui*, no. 9 (December 1998).

101 *class of 1932* "Class History," in 1932 *Le-i Yearbook*.

101 *bobbed hair* Yun-ho's essay in *Shui*, no. 9 (December 1998).

101 *Le-i's tuition*   Last page of 1932 *Le-i Yearbook*. Compared with Wen-hsin Yeh's figures in *The Alienated Academy*, this seems a bargain.

101 *Chang children's tuition*   Huan-ho's essay in *Shui*, no. 3 (October 1996), p. 2.

101 *faculty*   1932 *Le-i Yearbook*, p. 70.

102 *Hou and private schools*   See *Chung-kung tang-shih jen-wu-chuan* (Eminent figures in the history of the Chinese Communist Party) (hereafter, *CKTSJWC*), vol. 8, p. 132. *CKTSJWC* gives a detailed account of Hou's life and his activities in education and politics. Yeh also wrote about Hou's talent as a fund-raiser in *The Alienated Academy*, p. 147.

102 *Chou Fo-hai*   See Chou's biography in Boorman, *Biographical Dictionary of Republican China*. See also pp. 147–48, 150 of this book.

102 *Hou's radicalism*   See *CKTSJWC*, pp. 133–39.

103 *Chang Shu-sheng*   *Tsou-i*, p. 559.

103 *Nanyang College*   See Yeh, *The Alienated Academy*, pp. 93–94, 98–100; *CKTSJWC*, p. 135.

103 *expulsion*   See *CKTSJWC*, p. 135.

103 *"How could they . . ."*   Ibid., pp. 139–40.

103 *"free school"*   Ibid., pp. 136–38.

104 *Mao, 1924*   *Mao Tse-tung nien-p'u*, vol. 1, p. 126; *CKTSJWC*, p. 145.

104 *Hou in Shanghai*   See *CKTSJWC*, p. 146; Yeh, *The Alienated Academy*, p. 147.

104 *Chinese Communist Party (CCP) in 1925*   See the documents and analysis of the history of the CCP in *The Rise to Power of the Chinese Communist Party*, edited by Tony Saich, pp. 149–51, 104–5. See also Philip Short, *Mao*, pp. 148–49.

105 *CCP branch unit*   See Saich, *Rise to Power*, pp. 149–50; *CKTSJWC*, pp. 149–50.

105 *alliance and clash*   See Jonathan Spence, *The Search for Modern China*, pp. 334–54; 1932 *Le-i Yearbook*, "School History"; *CKTSJWC*, p. 152.

105 *after leaving Le-i*   See *CKTSJWC*, pp. 153–267.

105 *CCP and girls' schools*   See Short, *Mao*, p. 119.

106 *Soochow authorities*   See *CKTSJWC*, pp. 151–52.

106 *May Thirtieth*   See Short, *Mao*, p. 153.

107 *May Thirtieth and Le-i*   Hou's Communist biographers claimed that it was Hou who helped the Le-i students to organize the benefit concert and that he even performed during it. This contradicts their earlier statement that Hou arrived at Le-i in the fall of 1925. The 1932 *Le-i Yearbook* also places Hou's arrival in the fall. See *CKTSJWC*, pp. 149, 151; 1932 *Le-i Yearbook*, "School History."

107 *"Le-i gave more money"*   Quoted in Chang Huan-ho's essay in *Shui*, no. 3 (October 1996), p. 3.

107 *students' three dramas*   For a translation of *Autumn in the Palace of Han* (*Han-kung-ch'iu*), see *Anthology of Chinese Literature*, compiled and edited by Cyril Birch, pp. 422–48. *The Ruse of an Empty City* (*K'ung-ch'eng-chi*) and *The Story of Hung-fu* (*Hung-fu-chi*) are collected in *Hsi-tian*, vol. 1, pp. 401–16, and vol. 3, pp. 2036–60. *The Story of Hung-fu* was based on an earlier, tenth-century story by Tu Kuang-t'ing. One can find a summary and a history of this drama in English in *The Indiana Companion to Traditional Chinese Literature*, pp. 210–11, 823–24.

108 *Wild Cherry Blossoms*   A translation of this play is found in Kuo Mo-jo, *Five Historical Plays*, pp. 1–86. Kuo himself discussed the writing of this play in *Kuo Mo-jo chü-tsou ch'üan-chi*, vol. 1, pp. 330–32. See also David Roy's discussion in *Kuo Mo-jo*, pp. 96–97.

108 *Kuo and Marxism*   See C. T. Hsia, *A History of Modern Chinese Fiction*, pp. 98–100.

109 *students' writings*   1932 *Le-i Yearbook*, pp. 1–68.

109 *"Rich and Poor"*   Ibid., pp. 13–21.

Chapter 9: Nurse-nannies

112 *Wang Kan-kan*   Yü-ho's essay in *Shui*, no. 2 (June 1996), pp. 7–8. Other than this essay on Wang Kan-kan, most of the stories about the nurse-nannies were drawn from interviews I had with the Chang sisters and brothers.

114 *"Big Sister Kuo"*   Ibid.

115 *"The Destiny of Rebirth"*   See Ch'en Tuan-sheng, *Hsiu-hsiang hui-t'u tsai-sheng-yuan ch'üan-chuan.*

115 *Meng Li-chün and the emperor*   Ibid., 12:19a–b.

116 *Ch'en Tuan-sheng*   *Indiana Companion*, p. 236.

117 *ending of the original story*   See Ch'en Tuan-sheng, *Hsiu-hsiang hui-t'u tsai-sheng-yuan ch'üan-chuan*, 16:14b.

118 *"Kuo, the Lunatic!"*   *Shui*, no. 2 (June 1996), p. 8.

121 *"When Ch'en She . . ."*   Ssu-ma Ch'ien, *Shih-chi*, 48 *chüan* (slightly revised from Watson's translation in *Records of the Grand Historian*, vol. 1, *Han Dynasty*, p. 1).

121 *"like a great wind rising"*   Watson translation, p. 1.

121 *"Ch'en She, born in . . ."*   Watson translation, pp. 12–13 (with romanization changed).

124 *Death of the daughter-in-law*   *Shui*, no. 2 (June 1996), p. 7.

124 *"Kao Kan-kan, standing nearby . . ."*   Ibid., p. 8.

Chapter 10: Yuan-ho

126 *Ling Hai-hsia's family*   Ling Hai-hsia, unpublished memoir, pp. 1–2.

127 *Ling's education*   Ibid., pp. 1–28.

127 *Ling on Yuan-ho*   Ibid., p. 31.

127 *Ling in Le-i*   Ibid., pp. 31–32.

128 *Ling's career*   Ibid., pp. 33–34.

128 *reunion*   Ibid., p. 34.

128 *Haimen Middle School*   Ibid., pp. 32–53.

128 *plans for Yuan-ho's future*   Ibid., pp. 35–44.

129 *1931 to 1935*   From the chronological biography Yun-ho wrote down for her sister based on Yuan-ho's own account, in Yun-ho's diary, 11/27/84.

130 *Chou on Ku*   From Chou Ch'uan-ying's memoir, *K'un-chü sheng-ya liu-shih-nien*, p. 60. Chou's book gives a moving account of the life of a *k'un-ch'ü* actor in the first half of the twentieth century. It is also the most reliable source we have on the history of the Ch'uan-hsi troupe.

131 *"Holding my cup . . ."*   Hung Sheng, *Ch'ang-sheng-tien*, p. 108.

131 *He paces back and forth*   Ibid., pp. 108–9.

131 *"A Mother's Reunion"*   This is a scene from *The Thorn Hairpin* (*Ching-ch'a-chi*), which was one of the most widely performed dramas during the Ming dynasty. Hsü Ling-yun's analysis of this scene is in his book *K'un-chü piao-yen i-te*, pp. 104–20. The quote is on p. 110. For a short summary of this play in English, see *Indiana Companion*, p. 725.

132 *"Written While Plastered"*   Collected in *Liu-shih-chung ch'ü*, the *Tsai-hao* (Variegated brush) volume, pp. 31–34.

133 *Chou on Li Po*   In his memoir, Chou Ch'uan-ying has a chapter on how to bring elegance to Li Po's drunken state when performing this scene. See pp. 144–56. The quote is from pp. 146–47.

133 *entertainment center*   Chou Ch'uan-ying, *K'un-chü sheng-ya*, p. 53.

133 *competition*   Ibid., p. 86.

134 *"In front of the stage . . ."*   *Hsi-chü yüeh-k'an* 1:1, quoted in Lu O-t'ing, *K'un-chü yen-ch'u shih-kao*, pp. 273–74. Lu's book on the history of *k'un-ch'ü* opera performance is simply the best work of its kind. Lu has examined a huge amount of material and made wonderful use of the "minor pieces" (*hsiao-p'in*) tradition, drawing heavily from memoirs and "occasional writings." Few cultural historians could match his range and scholarship.

134 *"Three silver dollars . . ."* Shen-pao, February 22, 1879; quoted in Lu, *K'un-chü yen-ch'u shih-kao*, p. 274.

134 *"family troupes"* Ibid., p. 123. Many Ming authors had written about the "family troupes," the most notable being Chang Tai. Lu gives several examples in his book (pp. 123–32).

134 *reception halls or luxury boats* Quoted in Lu, *K'un-chü yen-ch'u*, pp. 120, 203.

135 *dinner theater* Quoted in ibid., p. 205.

136 *dancers of Ch'i* See *Ch'un-ch'iu ku-liang chuan-chu*, under Duke Ting, tenth year, pp. 458–59. The Han historian Ssu-ma Ch'ien also included a version of this story in his biography of Confucius in *Shih-chi*, 47 *chüan*, pp. 1915–16.

136 *actors as "lowly"* See T'an Fan's discussion in *Yu-ling-shih*, pp. 164–82.

136 *from poor families* See Chou Ch'uan-ying's and Hou Yü-shan's accounts of their childhood and families: Chou, *K'un-chü sheng-ya*, pp. 3–4, 18; Hou, *Wu-t'ai sheng-huo pa-shih-nien*, pp. 162–68. The quotes are from Hou, pp. 165–66.

137 *philosophers' views of entertainers* The writings of the Legalists and the Mohists also reflect a negative view of entertainers. See also Confucius, *Analects*, 18:7.

137 *"Family Instructions"* Quoted in T'an Fan, *Yu-ling-shih*, p. 143.

137 *actors in demand* Lu, *K'un-chü yen-ch'u*, p. 143.

137 *Yuan Mei* David Nivison, *The Life and Thought of Chang Hsüeh-ch'eng*, pp. 262–65; Arthur Waley, *Yuan Mei*, p. 109.

137 *life of an actor* See Chou Ch'uan-ying, *K'un-chü sheng-ya*, p. 74.

138 *guest artists and opera clubs* See Lu, *K'un-chü yen-ch'u*, pp. 81–84, 322–24. Traditional guest artists were different from the amateurs of the last century. They were often men living on the edge of respectability—musicians, painters, calligraphers, seal engravers, doctors, merchants, and writers living off literary commissions. The opera clubs in the 1920s and 1930s were a lot more eclectic; many scholars and officials, and their families, took part in these gatherings.

138 *Nanking opera club* Hou Yü-shan also remembered this occasion in his memoir. See Hou, *Wu-t'ai sheng-huo*, pp. 204–5.

139 *"Seeing one of his . . ."* Quoted in Lu, *K'un-chü yen-ch'u*, p. 348.

139 *Ku playing Emperor Ch'ung-chen* In Chou, *K'un-chü sheng-ya*, p. 60.

139 *boys in Ch'uan-hsi* See Chou, *K'un-chü sheng-ya*, p. 15; also in Yun-ho's diary, 12/4/84. It was Yuan-ho who told Yun-ho about these details of Ku's life during Yun-ho's visit to California in 1984.

140 *"Five-mu Plot"* Chou, *K'un-chü sheng-ya*, p. 15.

140 *Mu Ou-ch'u*   See the biography in Boorman, *Biographical Dictionary of Republican China*, vol. 3, pp. 38–41. Mu Ou-ch'u also wrote a memoir, collected in *Shanghai-t'an, Shanghai-jen*, but most of this work is about his experience in America.

140 *school endowment*   See Chou, *K'un-chü sheng-ya*, pp. 11–12; Lu, p. 345.

141 *origin of name Ch'uan-hsi*   Confucius, *Analects*, 1:4. In the sixteenth century, the Confucian thinker Wang Yang-ming added a lot more meaning to the idea of *ch'uan-hsi*.

141 *"We were all . . ."*   Chou, *K'un-chü sheng-ya*, p. 57.

141 *the "star system"*   Ibid., pp. 57–58.

142 *Yen and partner withdraw support*   Ibid.

142 *"Mu Ou-ch'u and others . . ."*   Lu, *K'un-chü yen-ch'u*, p. 348.

142 *Ch'uan-hsi troupe after Yen and T'ao*   Chou, *K'un-chü sheng-ya*, p. 58.

142 *finding work*   Ibid., pp. 65–66.

143 *actor who played chief eunuch*   Yun-ho's diary, 12/4/84.

143 *the desperate ones*   Chou, *K'un-chü sheng-ya*, pp. 74–76.

143 *Ku's partner*   Yun-ho's diary, 11/2/84.

144 *Yen's scholarship support*   See *Yen Hui-yü chi-nien wen-chi*, pp. 77–79; and *Chen-chiang wen-shih tzu-liao*, p. 165.

144 *actors' work*   See Chou, *K'un-chü sheng-ya*, pp. 42–44.

144 *Miss Yen*   Her name is Yen Chung-wan. See her essay about her growing up and her relationship with her father in *Yen Hui-yü*, pp. 92–101.

144 *Yen Hui-yü's character*   See *Yen Hui-yü*, pp. 93, 96.

145 *Ku's particularities*   Yun-ho's diary, 12/2/84.

145 *"emphasize naturalness . . ."*   See Li Yü's chapter on training women to sing and dance for an opera troupe in *Hsien-ch'ing o-chi*, vol. 1, 7:31b–33a; see also Lu's discussion on this in *K'un-chü yen-ch'u*, pp. 164–65.

147 *prosperity, 1938 to 1939*   See Poshek Fu, *Passivity, Resistance, and Collaboration*, pp. 46–47. See also discussion by Parks Coble in Yeh, *Wartime Shanghai*, p. 64.

147 *after 1939*   Fu, *Passivity, Resistance, and Collaboration*, pp. 46–47.

147 *stock speculation*   Ling Hai-hsia's memoir, pp. 54–55.

147 *Yen and Chou*   See *Yen Hui-yü*, p. 172; *Chen-chiang wen-shih*, pp. 152–53.

148 *end of "solitary island"*   See Fu, *Passivity, Resistance, and Collaboration*, pp. 120–21; Coble, pp. 66–67.

148 *Yen after return from Hong Kong*   See *Yen Hui-yü*, pp. 3, 171–73; *Chen-chiang wen-shih*, pp. 147–67.

148 *Ku Ch'uan-chieh as Yen's student*   *Chen-chiang wen-shih*, p. 165.

149 *theaters closed down*   See Fu, *Passivity, Resistance, and Collaboration*, p. 121.

149 *actors in occupied Shanghai*   See Chou, *K'un-chü sheng-ya*, p. 74.

150 *"Ku-chin"* Yale's Sterling Library has all fifty-seven issues of *Ku-chin*, and they make interesting reading. In his book on occupied Shanghai, Poshek Fu has a whole chapter on this magazine; see *Passivity, Resistance, and Collaboration*, pp. 110–65.

150 *"that nothing is excluded . . ."* *Ku-chin*, no. 29, p. 1106.

150 *food* Ibid., no. 50, pp. 1843–44; no. 49, pp. 1809–10.

151 *"They catch . . ."* Ibid., no. 29, p. 1106.

152 *Chi Fang* See biography in *Biographic Dictionary of Chinese Communism, 1921–1965*, edited by Donald Klein and Anne B. Clark, vol. 1, pp. 163–66.

153 *jasmine flowers* Ling's memoir, p. 63.

153 *"I don't know . . ."* Ibid., pp. 66–67.

154 *Ku's next projects* Yun-ho's diary, 11/28/84.

Chapter 11: *Yun-ho*

My conversations with Chang Yun-ho in the summers of 1996 and 1997 are the main source for this chapter. Some of the materials overlapped with what she had written in her diary, and some appeared in Yun-ho's own autobiographical essays, especially those collected in the two volumes, *Chang-chia chiu-shih* and *Tsui-hou te kuei-hsiu*, that she published in China in 1999.

155 *Lord Kuan* Lo Kuan-chung, *San-kuo yen-i*, p. 4; slightly revised from the translation in *Indiana Companion*, p. 23.

156 *"His manly spirits . . ."* Moss Roberts's translation, *Three Kingdoms*, p. 585.

156 *Death of Lord Kuan* Ibid. (romanization changed).

156 *the abbot P'u-ching* Ibid. (romanization changed). The opera that is based on this scene from the novel is Peking opera, not *k'un-ch'ü*. The script is a condensed version of the novel; it is cruder and less compelling than the original, but it has more popular appeal. For the text of this opera, see *Kuan-kung hsien-sheng* (Lord Kuan has become a divine sage) in *Kuo-chü ta-ch'eng*, pp. 247–53.

156 *conversation of Lord Kuan and the abbot P'u-ching* Lo Kuan-chung, *San-kuo yen-i*, pp. 982–83 (my own translation).

158 *Wang Chüeh-wu* Yun-ho, from a 1979 draft of this story.

160 *a child's eyes* Li-chi chu-shu 47:2a.

162 *"her quick eye . . ."* Chang Yun-ho, *Chang-chia chiu-shih*, p. 62.

163 *Shanghai private colleges* Yeh, *The Alienated Academy*, pp. 102–12, 195–205.

164 *"When Flowers . . ."* Chang Yun-ho, *Chang-chia chiu-shih*, pp. 59, 62.

164 *"arrest the present"* Ibid., pp. 63–65.

166 *"Oblivious of her tumbling hair..."* *Hsi-hsiang-chi* (Western Parlor) in *Liu-shih-chung ch'ü*, pp. 77–78. "A Fine Occasion" is scene 27 of "Western Parlor" (*Hsi-hsiang-chi*). This Ming dynasty opera was adapted from a much superior work Wang Shih-fu had written in the thirteenth century. The later, Ming version, also called the "southern version," was set to *k'un-ch'ü*. The music is beautiful, but the language in the libretto has become obviously sexual and vulgar.

167 *Hangchow papers* I could not find a copy of any local paper of that date, not even in the municipal archives in Hangchow.

170 *"When they bombed the area . . ."* Chang Yun-ho, *Chang-chia chiu-shih*, p. 85.

171 *Yu-kuang's letter* Ibid., pp. 96–97.

172 *Chao-ho wired money* Ibid., p. 98.

173 *ways to borrow money* Chang Yun-ho, *Tsui-hou*, p. 66.

173 *August 13, 1968* Ibid., pp. 82–83.

174 *"Just as I . . ."* Ibid., pp. 83–84.

175 *Chang Fei and Chao Tzu-lung* Ibid., pp. 84–88. The description of Chang Fei in the *Three Kingdoms* is found in Lo Kuang-chung, *San-kuo*, p. 4 (the translation is my own).

178 *"Every person . . ."* Chang Yun-ho, *Tsui-hou*, p. 86.

179 *"stay-at-home tiger"* Chang Yun-ho, *Chang-chia chiu-shih*, pp. 147–52.

179 *home to Soochow* Ibid., p. 153.

179 *"My relationship . . ."* Ibid.

180 *Lieh Tzu* *The Book of Lieh Tzu*, p. 49.

182 *letters* Chang Yun-ho, *Chang-chia chiu-shih*, pp. 151–52.

182 *"My third sister and I . . ."* Chang Yun-ho, *Tsui-hou*, pp. 65–66.

183 *Heart Sutra* *Pan-jo hsin-ching wu-chia chu*, 13b–18a.

183 *"A Fine Occasion"* *Hsi-hsiang-chi* in *Liu-shih-chung ch'ü*, pp. 77–78. (See also note to page 166.)

184 *diary* Yun-ho's diary, 8/2/84.

Chapter 12: Chao-ho

185 *letter of June 1931* Shen Ts'ung-wen and Chang Chao-ho, *Ts'ung-wen chia-shu* (hereafter, *Chia-shu*), pp. 38–39. This collection of "Family Letters" also includes several of Chao-ho's diary entries from July 1930.

186 *childhood in Feng-huang* Shen Ts'ung-wen, *Wo tu i-pen hsiao-shu* (Reading a small book) in *Ts'ung-wen san-wen-hsüan* (hereafter, *San-wen-hsüan*), pp. 7–20. The quotes are from pp. 7, 10, and 12. "Reading a Small

Book" is a lovely essay from Shen's autobiographical collection (*Tzu-chüan*) about life in Feng-huang.

186 *becoming a soldier* *Wo shang hsü-tuo-k'e* (I Have been to many classes) in Shen Ts'ung-wen, *San-wen-hsüan*, p. 40.

187 *"If I can't study . . ."* *I-ke chuan-chi* (A Turning point) in Shen Ts'ung-wen, *San-wen-hsüan*, pp. 122–23.

187 *Hu and Shen* Jeffrey Kinkley, *The Odyssey of Shen Congwen*, p. 83; Chao-ho's diary in Shen and Chang, *Chia-shu*, p. 16.

187 *"Because I love her . . ."* Chao-ho's friend, Miss Wang, included with her letter to Chao-ho a note Shen Ts'ung-wen had given to her, asking her to explain Chao-ho's behavior toward him. Chao-ho copied both letters into her diary. Shen and Chang, *Chia-shu*, pp. 5–6.

187 *Hu Shih* Ibid., p. 6.

187 *Miss Wang on Chao-ho* Wang's letter in ibid., p. 9.

187 *"I have been living . . ."* Chao-ho's diary, 7/4/30, in ibid., pp. 11–12.

188 *Chao-ho and Hu Shih* Chao-ho's diary, 7/8/30, in ibid., pp. 14–16.

189 *Hu Shih's letter* Copied into Chao-ho's diary, in ibid., pp. 22–23.

189 *"Just as I . . ."* Chao-ho's diary, in ibid., p. 16.

189 *stubbornness* Shen's letter, copied into Chao-ho's diary, in ibid., pp. 18–19.

190 *Chao-ho and Yun-ho* Chao-ho's diary, 7/12/30, in ibid., p. 20.

190 *Hu Shih's letter* Copied into Chao-ho's diary, in ibid., pp. 22–23.

190 *"Mr. Hu only . . ."* Chao-ho's diary, 7/14/30, in ibid., pp. 23–24.

191 *"This is a weakness . . ."* Ibid., p. 24.

191 *Chu Kan-kan* Ibid., p. 20.

191 *Yun-ho on Chao-ho* Yun-ho's essay on Le-i, *Shui*, no. 9 (December 1998).

193 *"I am able to see the moon . . ."* In Shen and Chang, *Chia-shu*, pp. 39–41.

193 *two letters* Ibid., pp. 18, 22.

194 *"But nature won't allow it."* Ibid., p. 41.

194 *"Housewife"* Shen Ts'ung-wen, *Shen Ts'ung-wen wen-chi* (hereafter, *Wen-chi*), vol. 6, p. 325.

195 *"After she graduated . . ."* Ibid., p. 329.

196 *dark and plump* See Chang Yun-ho's description in *Chang-chia chiu-shih*, p. 109.

196 *"reciting the classics . . ."* See Chao-ho's essay "I Have Come to Soochow" in *Shui*, no. 5 (June 1997).

197 *destroying dolls* Yun-ho's diary, 10/23/84.

198 *"he had known many women . . ."* Shen Ts'ung-wen, *Wen-chi*, vol. 6, p. 331.

198 *"Let a man of country stock . . ."* Chang Yun-ho, *Tsui-hou*, p. 58.

198 *"disenchanted"* See "Housewife," in Shen Ts'ung-wen, *Wen-chi*, vol. 6, pp. 331–32.

199 *pawnshop receipt*   Kinkley has a somewhat different version of this story. See *Odyssey of Shen Ts'ung-wen*, pp. 317–18, n. 36. Chang Ch'ung-ho also has her version in her essay on Shen Ts'ung-wen in *Hai-nei-wai*, no. 28. In this essay, she also included some charming scenes from the early days of her sister's marriage.

199 *Little Ninth as a child*   Kinkley, *Odyssey of Shen Congwen*, p. 22.

200 *"Everyone needs . . ."*   Shen Ts'ung-wen, *Wen-chi*, vol. 6, p. 327.

200 *"loggy" and "like sandbags"*   Ibid., p. 333.

200 *"has a deeper meaning"*   Ibid., p. 328.

200 *letter of 1/12/34*   Shen and Chang, *Chia-shu*, pp. 47–48.

201 *letter of 1/13/34*   Ibid., p. 49.

201 *letter of 1/16/34*   Ibid., pp. 47–54.

203 *letter of 1/17/34*   Ibid., p. 59.

203 *letter of 1/18/34*   Ibid., p. 62.

204 *"you are in my pocket"*   Ibid., p. 61.

204 *letter of 1/19/34*   Ibid., pp. 63–65.

205 *he composes a self*   These words—and the idea—are borrowed from Wallace Stevens, "The World as Meditation."

205 *letter of 1/9/34*   Shen and Chang, *Chia-shu*, pp. 45–46.

207 like the grapevines . . .   Shen Ts'ung-wen, *Wen-chi*, vol. 6, p. 334.

207 *the "union university"*   John Israel, *Lianda*, pp. 13–14, 19.

208 *"I think that . . ."*   In Shen and Chang, *Chia-shu*, pp. 92–93.

209 *"You understand the temperament . . ."*   Ibid., p. 78.

209 *"You have always blamed me . . ."*   Ibid., pp. 78–79.

210 *"a waste" to use express mail*   Ibid., p. 76.

210 *"You are doing your best . . ."*   Ibid., p. 124.

211 *"life was simpler and happier"*   Ibid., pp. 81–82.

211 *two long letters . . .*   They are dated 11/6/37 and 8/19/38. Ibid., pp. 80–83, 120–26.

211 *"I am someone . . ."*   Ibid., pp. 82–83.

211 *Chao-ho's brisk response*   Ibid., p. 94.

212 *Chao-ho on Shen's writing*   Ibid., pp. 92, 79.

212 *"Your original countenance . . ."*   Ibid., p. 79.

213 *letter from Yuan-ling*   Dated April 13, 1938. Ibid., pp. 114–15.

215 *Shen losing his patience*   Ibid., p. 120.

215 *Chao-ho slow to act*   Ibid., pp. 124, 89, 127.

215 *Shen's letters to his brother Yun-liu*   Quoted in Shen Hu-ch'u's essay, *Tuan-chü* (Reunited), in the appendix to Shen Ts'ung-wen, *Wu-ts'ung hsün-fu te pan-ma*, pp. 175–211. *Tuan-chü* is a charming and moving essay by the younger son, Hu-hu, about his parents and about their life together.

215 *"In the air . . ."* Ibid., p. 176.

216 suggested Chao-ho do some translation Shen and Chang, *Chia-shu,* pp. 107, 95.

216 *Lung-lung and Hu-hu* See appendix to Shen Ts'ung-wen, *Wu-ts'ung,* p. 177.

216 *university moved to K'un-ming* See Israel, *Lianda,* pp. 13–60.

216 *"he jostles his way . . ."* See appendix to Shen Ts'ung-wen, *Wu-ts'ung,* p. 176.

216 *"The old man went to the mountain . . ."* From *Lü-yen* (Green nightmare) in Shen Ts'ung-wen, *Wen-chi,* vol. 10, pp. 92–93. The description of the Ch'eng-kung house appears in one of the three autobiographical stories Shen wrote during the war. I checked with Ch'ung-ho about this, since she had lived in the same house with Shen and Chao-ho for a year. Ch'ung-ho said that this was indeed the house she knew and that the history of the house was accurate.

217 *"My brother and I . . ."* See appendix to Shen Ts'ung-wen, *Wu-ts'ung,* p. 178.

218 *life around the wooden table* Ibid., pp. 178–80.

218 *"When your mom . . ."* Ibid., pp. 180–81.

219 Beat the Drum . . . Ibid., p. 184.

219 *Liu Wen-tien* See Israel, *Lianda,* pp. 143–44.

220 *use of particle* See Shen and Chang, *Chia-shu,* p. 105.

220 *"You have gotten rid of my style."* From interview with Chao-ho.

220 *"This smile should have . . ."* Shen Ts'ung-wen, *Wen-chi,* vol. 10, p. 105.

221 *Shen and "housewife"* Ibid., pp. 105–6.

221 *"The prince had the most beautiful pair of eyes . . ."* Ibid., pp. 116–17.

222 *"Gazing at the Rainbow"* See Kinkley's discussion of this short story in his *Odyssey of Shen Congwen,* pp. 254–56, and also his translation of this story in Shen's *Imperfect Paradise,* pp. 463–81.

224 *"not only lacquer boxes . . ."* Chang Ch'ung-ho, *Wo-san-chieh-fu, Shen-erh-ke,* in *Hai-nei-wai,* no. 28; also quoted in Ling Yü, *Shen Ts'ung-wen chuan,* pp. 439–40.

224 *train ride* Shen Ts'ung-wen, *Wu-ts'ung,* pp. 181–83.

224 *"Although we were reunited"* Ibid., pp. 183–85. For a description of Shen lying on the slope behind his Yunnan house, see Shen Ts'ung-wen, *Wen-chi,* vol. 10, pp. 83–89.

225 *Shen's friend Ting Ling* See appendix to Shen Ts'ung-wen, *Wu-ts'ung,* pp. 185–86.

225 *"At this moment . . ."* In Shen and Chang, *Chia-shu,* p. 132.

226 *"Once I am apart from you . . ."* Ibid., p. 134.

227 *"Young Hu-hu said . . ."* Ibid., pp. 137–38.

227 *Peking during the siege* See appendix to Shen Ts'ung-wen, *Wu-ts'ung,* p. 189.

228 *letter to Mr. Chi-liu* Quoted in ibid., p. 189.

228 *Shen's critics* See Kinkley, *Odyssey of Shen Congwen,* pp. 265–66; Ling Yü, *Shen Ts'ung-wen chuan,* p. 419.

228 *Shen defending his position* See Kinkley, op. cit., pp. 265–66.

228 *the beginning of Shen's illness* See appendix to Shen Ts'ung-wen, *Wu-ts'ung,* pp. 193–94.

229 *"ravings of a madman"* See Shen and Chang, *Chia-shu,* pp. 148–49.

229 *letter with gloss* Ibid., pp. 151–53.

230 *another letter from Chao-ho* Ibid., p. 155.

231 *Ting Ling* See Spence, *The Gate of Heavenly Peace,* pp. 217–19, 250, 240–41. See also Kinkley, *Odyssey of Shen Congwen,* pp. 202–5.

231 *"Let us not say any more . . ."* In Shen and Chang, *Chia-shu,* p. 157.

231 *suicide attempt* See appendix to Shen Ts'ung-wen, *Wu-ts'ung,* p. 198.

231 *visit to Ting Ling* Ibid., p. 196.

232 *why Chao-ho sought reeducation* See the discussions in Kinkley, *Odyssey of Shen Congwen,* p. 267; Spence, *The Gate of Heavenly Peace,* p. 324; and Ling Yü, *Shen Ts'ung-wen chüan,* pp. 423–25.

232 *Chao-ho as an athlete* Chang Yun-ho in *Tsui-hou,* p. 63.

232 *Chao-ho in a cadre suit* See appendix to Shen Ts'ung-wen, *Wu-ts'ung,* p. 197.

233 *"Dad was stricken . . ."* Ibid., p. 201.

233 *Shen and music* See Shen and Chang, *Chia-shu,* pp. 160–64; See appendix to Shen Ts'ung-wen, *Wu-ts'ung,* p. 199.

233 *"looked like Jesse James . . ."* See appendix to Shen Ts'ung-wen, *Wu-ts'ung,* p. 201.

233 *"retired on impulse"* See James Hightower's translation of K'ung Chih-kuei's poem "Proclamation on North Mountain" in Birch, *Anthology of Chinese Literature,* vol. 1, pp. 169–73.

234 *Shen's letter about the author of* Notes In Shen and Chang, *Chia-shu,* p. 255.

235 *"Thank you for sending the essays . . ."* Ibid., p. 235.

236 *an "editor's view" from Chao-ho* Ibid., p. 286.

236 *the letter three days later* Ibid., p. 289.

236 *Shen's letter from his Tsingtao retreat* Ibid., p. 287.

236 *Chao-ho's analysis of Shen* Ibid., p. 315.

237 *Shen's writings on material culture* See Kinkley, *Odyssey of Shen Congwen,* pp. 270–71, 431–35.

237 *coming back to Feng-huang* In Shen and Chang, *Chia-shu,* p. 257.

238 *letter from Ch'ang-sha* Ibid., pp. 259–60.

240 *postscript* Ibid., p. 319.

Chapter 13: Ch'ung-ho

243 *"Outside my window . . ."* Chang Ch'ung-ho, *Ch'iang-feng*, collected in *Ch'iu-shui*, no. 18 (1987), pp. 43–44.

244 *fox spirits and a crack on the wall* Ibid., pp. 44, 45.

244 *the blind nun* Chang Ch'ung-ho, *Shan-mien*, collected in *Hai-wai hua-jen tsou-chia san-wen-hsüan*, pp. 86–89.

245 *airplanes* Chang Ch'ung-ho, *Feng-cheng*, collected in *Ch'iu-shui*, no. 20 (1988), pp. 34–36.

245 *Chang Tsung-chang* See his biography in Boorman, *Biographical Dictionary of Republican China*, vol. 1, pp. 122–27.

246 *"Big Precious"* Ch'ung-ho wrote a version of this story in 1937; it was published in *Hai-wai*, pp. 89–91.

251 *K'un-ch'ü club in Tsingtao* Chang Tsung-ho, *Ch'iu-teng i-yu* (Words recollected under the autumn lamp), collected in *Shui*, no. 14 (August 2000), pp. 15–16.

255 *Pien Chih-lin* See *Twentieth Century Chinese Poetry*, translated and edited by Hsu Kai-yu, pp. 159–160.

255 *aunt in a "big boat"* Shen Ts'ung-wen, *Wen-chi*, vol. 10, p. 116.

256 *Liu's bombast* See Israel, *Lianda*, pp. 143–44.

258 *"Yu, yu, cry the deer . . ."* In *The Book of Songs*, p. 133; slightly revised from Waley's translation.

259 *Chang Shih-chao* See his biography in Boorman, *Biographical Dictionary of Republican China*, vol. 1, pp. 105–9.

259 *Chang and Shen's clash in 1925* See the biography of Chang Shih-chao in ibid.; see also *Shen Yin-mo lun-shu ts'ung-kao*, p. 256.

260 *"Ours are two schools"* *Shen Yin-mo lun-shu ts'ung-kao*, pp. 242–43.

260 *Shen Yin-mo's early learning* Ibid., pp. 146–47.

261 *"with solid fingers and an empty palm"* Ibid., p. 95.

262 *Shen writing poetry* Ibid., pp. 255, 259, 249–50.

262 *"practice 'by the pond'"* In Sun Ch'ien-li (Sun Qian-li)'s *Shu-p'u* (Treatise on calligraphy). See Chang Ch'ung-ho and Hans Frankel's translation in *Two Chinese Treatises on Calligraphy*, pp. 1, 3.

262 *"In the beginning . . ."* *Shen Yin-mo lun-shu ts'ung-kao*, p. 112.

262 *"the postures of wild geese . . ."* See Chang and Frankel, *Two Chinese Treatises on Calligraphy*, p. 3.

263 *"The mind has forgotten itself . . ."* Wang Tseng-ch'ien, quoted in *Shen Yin-mo lun-shu ts'ung-kao*, p. 49.

263 *"Remember the path . . ."* Chang Ch'ung-ho, *T'ao-hua-yu* (Peach Blossom Fish), 1 and 2. Unless otherwise indicated, the translations of Chang

Ch'ung-ho's poems are my own. Hans Frankel also translated these two poems in *Peach Blossom Fish,* which is a collection of Ch'ung-ho's poems published in 1999.

264 *P'eng bird*   In Chuang Tzu, *The Complete Works of Chuang Tzu,* p. 29.

264 *calligrapher's wrist*   See Chang and Frankel, *Two Chinese Treatises on Calligraphy,* p. 13.

266 *"Along the Chia-ling River . . ."*   Chang Ch'ung-ho, "Going Home after the War," slightly revised from Hans Frankel's translation in *Peach Blossom Fish.*

266 *"broken balustrade"* and *"battered veranda"*   From the poem "A K'un-ch'ü Rehearsal in Soochow after the War," by Chang Ch'ung-ho.

267 *wedding cake*   In Hans Frankel's essay about Shen Ts'ung-wen, *Hai-nei-wai,* no. 28 (November–December 1980), p. 33.

269 *"Travel weary . . ."*   Chang Ch'ung-ho, "Small Garden No. 2" (*Hsiao-yuan,* 2), as translated by Hans Frankel in *Peach Blossom Fish.*

269 *"In the past . . ."*   Chang Ch'ung-ho, "Small Garden No. 8" (*Hsiao-yuan,* 8). The last line is Hans Frankel's translation.

269 *"The road is long."*   From Chang Ch'ung-ho's poem *Chiang-kuei* (Just about to return to China).

Bibliography

Anhwei chin-tai-shih (Modern history of Anhwei). Edited by Ong Fei et al. Hofei: Anhwei jen-men ch'u-pan-she, 1990.

Anhwei hsien-tai ke-ming-shih tzu-liao ch'ang-pien (Sources in the modern revolutionary history of Anhwei). Hofei: Anhwei jen-men ch'u-pan-she, 1986.

Birch, Cyril, comp. and ed. *Anthology of Chinese Literature*. New York: Grove Press, 1965.

The Book of Lieh Tzu. Translated by A. C. Graham. New York: Columbia University Press, 1960.

The Book of Songs. Translated by Arthur Waley. Reprint. New York: Grove Press, 1996.

Boorman, Howard L., ed. *Biographical Dictionary of Republican China*. 4 vols. New York: Columbia University Press, 1967.

The Cambridge History of China. Edited by Denis C. Twitchett et al. Vol. 11, part 2. Cambridge: Cambridge University Press, 1980.

Chaffee, John. *The Thorny Gates of Learning in Sung China: A Social History of Examinations*. New ed. Albany, N.Y.: SUNY Press, 1995.

Chang Ch'ung-ho. *Feng-cheng* (Kite). *Ch'iu-shui* (Autumn flood), no. 20 (1988). Hong Kong: Ch'iu-shui wen-i ch'u-pan-she.

———. *Peach Blossom Fish*. Translated by Hans Frankel et al. Walla Walla, Wash.: Crab Quill Press, 1999.

———. *Shan-mien* (Fan). In *Hai-wai hua-jen tsou-chia san-wen-hsüan* (Selected essays of overseas Chinese writers). Hong Kong: San-lian shu-tien, 1983.

———. *Wo-san-chieh-fu, Shen-erh-ke* (My third brother-in-law, Shen Ts'ung-wen). *Hai-nei-wai* (Here and abroad), no. 28 (New York, November–December 1980.)

Chang Ch'ung-ho and Hans H. Frankel, trans. *Two Chinese Treatises on Calligraphy*. New Haven: Yale University Press, 1995.

Chang Chung-li. *The Chinese Gentry: Studies on Their Role in Nineteenth-Century Chinese Society.* Seattle: University of Washington Press, 1955.

Chang Hsüeh-ch'eng. *Wen-shih t'ung-i* (General principles of literature and history). 8 *chüan*. Taipei: Kuang-wen shu-chü, 1967.

Chang Shu-sheng. *Chang Ching-ta-kung (Shu-sheng) tsou-i* (Memorials of Chang Shu-sheng). 8 *chüan*. Reprint. Taipei: Wen-hai ch'u-pan-she, n.d.

Chang Tai. *T'ao-an meng-i* (Dreamlike remembrance of T'ao-an). Reprint. Taipei: Chin-feng ch'u-pan, 1986.

Chang Tsung-ho. Unpublished diary, collected in the Chang family journal, *Shui.*

Chang Yun-ho. *Chang-chia chiu-shih* (Tales from the Chang family). Chinan: Shantung hua-pao ch'u-pan-she, 1999.

———. *Tsui-hou te kuei-hsiu* (The Last of the gentry women). Peking: San-lien shu-tien, 1999.

———. Unpublished diary, 20 vols.

Chen-chiang wen-shih tzu-liao (Sources on history and literature in Chen-chiang), no. 10. Chen-chiang: 1985.

Ch'en Tuan-sheng. *Hsiu-hsiang hui-t'u tsai-sheng-yuan ch'üan-chuan* (Complete works of the *Destiny of Rebirth,* with illustrations). Shanghai: Shanghai kuang-i shu-chü, n.d.

Chiang, Siang-tseh. *The Nien Rebellion.* Seattle: University of Washington Press, 1954.

Ch'ing-shih lieh-chuan (Biographies of figures from the Ch'ing). 80 *chüan*. Reprint. Taipei: Chung-hua shu-chü, 1962.

Chou Ch'uan-ying. *K'un-chü sheng-ya liu-shih-nien* (Sixty years as a *k'un-ch'ü* actor). Shanghai: Shanghai wen-i ch'u-pan-she, 1988.

Chu Hsi. *Shih-ching chi-chu* (Commentary on the *Classic of Odes*). Hong Kong: Kuang-chih shu-chü, n.d.

Chu, Samuel C., and Kwang-ching Liu, eds. *Li Hung-chang and China's Early Modernization.* Armonk, N.Y.: M. E. Sharpe, 1994.

Chuang Tzu. *The Complete Works of Chuang Tzu.* Translated by Burton Watson. New York: Columbia University Press, 1968.

Ch'un-ch'iu ku-liang chuan-chu (Ku-liang commentary on the *Ch'un-ch'iu Chronicle* with Ke Shao-min's subcommentary). 1867 edition. Reprint of 1927 reprint. Taipei: Taiwan Ta-t'ung shu-chü, n.d.

Chung-kung tang-shih jen-wu-chuan (Eminent figures in the history of the Chinese Communist Party). Edited by Hu Hua et al. Hsi-an: Shan-hsi jen-min ch'u-pan-she, 1983.

Coble, Parks. "Chinese Capitalists and the Japanese." In *Wartime Shanghai,* edited by Wen-hsin Yeh. London: Routledge, 1998.

Cohen, Paul A. *Between Tradition and Modernity: Wang T'ao and Reform in Late Ch'ing China*. Cambridge: Harvard University Press, 1974.

Confucius. *The Analects of Confucius*. Translated by D. C. Lau. London: Penguin Books, 1979.

Eastman, Lloyd E. *Throne and Mandarins: China's Search for a Policy during the Sino-French Controversy, 1880–1885*. Cambridge: Harvard University Press, 1967.

Faigon, Lee. *Chen Duxiu: Founder of the Communist Party*. Princeton, N.J.: Princeton University Press, 1983.

Fei-hsi Huai-chün jen-wu (West Hofei figures in the Huai Army). Edited by the Fei-hsi county *wen-shih tzu-liao* editorial board. Hofei: Huang-shan shu-she, 1991.

Frankel, Hans. *Wo he Shen Ts'ung-wen ch'u-tz'u hsiang-shih* (My early encounters with Shen Ts'ung-wen) in *Hai-nei-wai* (Here and abroad), no. 28 (New York, November–December 1980).

Fu, Poshek. *Passivity, Resistance, and Collaboration: Intellectual Choices in Occupied Shanghai, 1937–1945*. Stanford, Calif.: Stanford University Press, 1993.

Goodrich, L. Carrington, ed., and Chaoying Fang, assoc. ed. *Dictionary of Ming Biography, 1368–1644*. 2 vols. New York: Columbia University Press, 1976.

Han Ying. *Han-shih wai-chuan chi-shih* (Han Ying's commentary on the *Classic of Odes*). Peking: Chung-hua shu-chü, 1980.

Hanan, Patrick. *The Invention of Li Yu*. Cambridge: Harvard University Press, 1988.

Hershatter, Gail. *Dangerous Pleasures: Prostitution and Modernity in Twentieth-Century Shanghai*. Berkeley: University of California Press, 1997.

Ho-fei shih-hua (History and stories of Hofei). Hofei: Huang-shan shu-she, 1985.

Ho-fei wen-shih tzu-liao (Sources in Hofei history and literature). Edited by the Research Committee of Hofei *wen-shih tzu-liao*. Hofei: 1985.

Hou Yü-shan. *Wu-t'ai sheng-huo pa-shih-nien* (Eighty years on the stage, an oral account). In *Wen-shih tzu-liao hsüan-pien* (Selected sources in history and literature), no. 25. Peking: Peking ch'u-pan-she, 1985.

Hsia, C. T. *A History of Modern Chinese Fiction, 1917–1957*. New Haven: Yale University Press, 1961.

Hsiao K'o-fei et al. *Liu Ming-ch'uan tsai Taiwan* (Liu Ming-ch'uan in Taiwan). Shanghai: Shanghai She-hui k'o-hsüeh yuan, 1987.

Hsi-tien (Anthology of Chinese drama). 4 vols. Edited by Ling Yin-kuan. Ti-i-wen-hua-she, 1976.

Hsu Kai-yu, trans. and ed. *Twentieth Century Chinese Poetry: An Anthology*. Ithaca, N.Y.: Cornell University Press, 1963.

Hsü Ling-yun. *K'un-chü piao-yen i-te* (From my experiences of performing *k'un-ch'ü* opera). Shanghai: Shanghai wen-i ch'u-pan-she, 1959.

Hsün Tzu. *Hsün Tzu chi-shih* (Collected commentaries on the *Hsün Tzu*). Edited by Li T'iao-sheng. Taipei: Hsüeh-sheng shu-chü, 1979.

Hummel, Arthur W., ed. *Eminent Chinese of the Ch'ing Period, 1644–1912.* 2 vols. Washington, D.C.: Government Printing Office, 1943.

Hung Sheng. *Ch'ang-sheng-tien* (Palace of eternal youth). Peking: Jen-min ch'u-pan-she, 1980.

I Ching. *The Classic of Changes: A New Translation of the I Ching as Interpreted by Wang Bi.* Translated by Richard John Lynn. New York: Columbia University Press, 1994.

The Indiana Companion to Traditional Chinese Literature. Compiled and edited by William H. Nienhauser, Jr., et al. Bloomington: Indiana University Press, 1986.

Israel, John. *Lianda: A Chinese University in War and Revolution.* Stanford, Calif.: Stanford University Press, 1998.

Keenan, Barry. "Lungmen Academy in Shanghai and the Expansion of Kiangsu's Educated Elite, 1865–1911." In *Education and Society in Late Imperial China, 1600–1900,* edited by Benjamin Elman and Alexander Woodside. Berkeley: University of California Press, 1994.

Kinkley, Jeffrey. *The Odyssey of Shen Congwen.* Stanford, Calif.: Stanford University Press, 1987.

Klein, Donald, and Anne B. Clark, eds. *Biographic Dictionary of Chinese Communism, 1921–1965.* 2 vols. Cambridge: Harvard University Press, 1971.

Ku-chin (Past and present). 57 issues (March 1942–October 1944) in 10 bound vols. Reprint. Hong Kong: Lung-men shu-tien, 1968.

Kuo-chü ta-ch'eng (Collected works of traditional Chinese opera). Edited by Chang Po-chin. Taipei: Taiwan Chung-hua shu-chü, 1970.

Kuo Mo-jo [Guo Mo-jo]. *Five Historical Plays.* Translated by Feng Fu-min, Bonnie McDougall, et al. Peking: Foreign Language Press, 1984.

———. *Kuo Mo-jo chü-tsou ch'üan-chi* (Complete plays of Kuo Mo-jo). Vol. 1. Peking: Chung-kuo hsi-chü chu-pan-she, 1953.

Legge, James, trans. *The Chinese Classics.* Vol. 4. Reprint. Taipei: Wen-hsing shu-tien, 1963.

Le-i Yearbook: 1932.

Li Hung-chang. *Li Hung-chang chia-shu* (Family letters of Li Hung-chang). Reprint. Hofei: Huang-shan shu-she, 1996.

Li Yü. *Hsien-ch'ing o-chi* (Casual expressions of idle feelings). 2 vols. Reprint. Taipei: Kuang-wen shu-chü, 1991.

————. *Li-weng i-chia-yen.* Collected in *Li Yü ch'üan-chi.* 15 vols. Reprint. Taipei: Ch'eng-wen chu-pan-she, 1970.

Li-chi chu-shu (*Classic of Rites*). With commentary by Cheng Hsüan. SPPY edition. Reprint. Shanghai: Chung-hua shu-chü, 1936.

Ling Hai-hsia. Unpublished memoir.

Ling Yü. *Shen Ts'ung-wen chuan* (Biography of Shen Ts'ung-wen). Peking: Peking shih-yüeh wen-i ch'u-pan-she, 1988.

Liu, Wu-chi, and Irving Yucheng Lo, eds. *Sunflower Splendor: Three Thousand Years of Chinese Poetry.* Garden City, N.Y.: Anchor Books, 1975.

Liu-shih-chung ch'ü (Sixty operas). 60 vols. Shanghai: K'ai-ming shu-tien, 1935.

Lo Kuan-chung. *San-kuo yen-i* (Romance of the Three Kingdoms). Hong Kong: Kuang-chih shu-chü, 1950.

————. *Three Kingdoms: A Historical Novel.* Translated by Moss Roberts. Berkeley: University of California Press, 1991.

Lu O-t'ing. *K'un-chü yen-ch'u shih-kao* (A History of *k'un-ch'ü* opera performance). Shanghai: Shanghai wen-i ch'u-pan-she, 1980.

Lu-chou fu-chih (Gazetteer of Lu-chou prefecture). 100 *chüan* in 4 vols., 1886 edition. Reprint. Taipei: Wen-ch'eng ch'u-pan-she, 1970.

Mao Heng. *Mao-shih Cheng-chien* (Mao's commentary on the *Classic of Odes* with Cheng Hsüan's subcommentary). 20 vols. Reprint. Shanghai: Chung-hua shu-chü, 1936.

Mao Tse-tung nien-p'u (Chronological biography of Mao Tse-tung). 3 vols. Edited by P'ang Hsien-chih et al. Peking: Jen-min ch'u-pan-she, 1993.

Mencius. *Mencius.* Translated by D. C. Lau. Harmondsworth, England: Penguin Books, 1970.

Mu Ou-ch'u. *Ou-ch'u wu-shih tzu-hsü* (My memoir at fifty). Collected in *Shanghai-t'an, Shanghai-jen.* Shanghai: Ku-chi ch'u-pan-she, 1989.

Nivison, David. *The Life and Thought of Chang Hsüeh-ch'eng (1738–1801).* Stanford, Calif.: Stanford University Press, 1966.

Owen, Stephen, ed. and trans. *An Anthology of Chinese Literature: Beginnings to 1911.* New York: W. W. Norton, 1996.

Pa-hsien-chih (Gazetteer of Pa county). Reprint. Taipei: Hsüeh-sheng shu-chü, 1967.

Pan-jo hsin-ching wu-chia chu (The Heart Sutra with five commentaries). Compiled by Chih Hsü et al. Taipei: Hsin-wen-feng ch'u-pan, 1975.

Perry, Elizabeth J. *Rebels and Revolutionaries in North China, 1845–1945.* Stanford, Calif.: Stanford University Press, 1980.

Rilke, Rainer Maria. *The Selected Poetry of Rainer Maria Rilke.* Edited and translated by Stephen Mitchell. New York: Vintage Books, 1984.

Roy, David Tod. *Kuo Mo-jo: The Early Years*. Cambridge, Mass.: Harvard University Press, 1971.

Saich, Tony, ed. *The Rise to Power of the Chinese Communist Party: Documents and Analysis*. Armonk, N.Y.: M. E. Sharpe, 1996.

Shen Ts'ung-wen (Sheng Congwen). *Imperfect Paradise*. Edited and translated by Jeffrey Kinkley et al. Honolulu: University of Hawaii Press, 1995.

——. *Shen Ts'ung-wen wen-chi* (Literary writings of Shen Ts'ung-wen). Edited by Shao Hua-ch'iang and Ling Yü. 12 vols. Hong Kong: San-lien shu-tien, 1984.

——. *Ts'ung-wen san-wen-hsüan* (Selected essays of Shen Ts'ung-wen). Hong Kong: Shih-tai ch'u-pan, 1980.

——. *Wu-ts'ung hsün-fu te pan-ma* (The Untamable zebra). Peking: Chung-kuo ch'ing-nien ch'u-pan-she, 1996.

Shen Ts'ung-wen and Chang Chao-ho. *Ts'ung-wen chia-shu* (Family letters of Shen Ts'ung-wen and Chang Chao-ho). Shanghai: Shanghai Yuan-tung ch'u-pan-she, 1996.

Shen Yin-mo. *Shen Yin-mo lun-shu ts'ung-kao* (Shen Yin-mo's collected essays on the art of calligraphy). Hong Kong: San-lien shu-tien, 1981.

Short, Philip. *Mao: A Life*. New York: Henry Holt, 2000.

Shui (Water). 17 issues (February 1996 to August 2001). Edited by Chang Yun-ho.

Spector, Stanley. *Li Hung-chang and the Huai Army: A Study in Nineteenth-Century Regionalism*. Seattle: University of Washington Press, 1964.

Spence, Jonathan D. *The Gate of Heavenly Peace: The Chinese and Their Revolution, 1895–1980*. Reprint. New York: Penguin Books, 1982.

——. *The Search for Modern China*. New York: W. W. Norton, 1990.

Ssu-ma Ch'ien (Sima Qian). *Records of the Grand Historian, Han Dynasty I*. Translated by Burton Watson. Rev. ed. Hong Kong and New York: Columbia University Press, 1993.

——. *Shih-chi* (Records of the Grand Historian). 130 *chüan*. Peking: Chung-hua shu-chü, 1959.

T'an Fan. *Yu-ling-shih* (History of actors and performers). Shanghai: Shanghai wen-i chu-pan-she, 1995.

Tseng Kuo-fan. *Tseng Wen-cheng kung jih-chi* (The Diary of Tseng Kuo-fan). Reprint. Taipei: Lao-ku wen-hua, 1985.

Tu Fu. *Tu Fu shih-hsüan* (Selected poems of Tu Fu). Edited by Feng Chih et al. Peking: Tso-chia ch'u-pan-she, 1956.

Waley, Arthur. *Yuan Mei, Eighteenth-Century Chinese Poet*. London: Allen and Unwin, 1956.

Wang Erh-min. *Huai-chün-chih* (History of the Huai Army). Taipei: Shang-wu yin-shu-kuan, 1967.

Wang Pi. *Chou-i Wang-Han-chu* (The *Classic of Changes* as interpreted by Wang Pi and Han K'ang-po). SPPY edition. Reprint. Taipei: Chung-hua shu-chü, 1974.

Yeh, Wen-hsin. *The Alienated Academy: Culture and Politics in Republican China, 1919–1937.* Cambridge, Mass.: Harvard University Press, 1990.

———, ed. *Wartime Shanghai.* London and New York: Routledge, 1998.

Yen Hui-yü chi-nien wen-chi (Essays commemorating the life of Yen Hui-yü). In *Kiangsu wen-shih tzu-liao* (Sources on history and literature in Kiangsu province), no. 74. Nanking: Kiangsu wen-shih tzu-liao pien-chi-pu, 1994.

Index

Academy for Practical Learning, 76
adoption practices, 53–54, 82
Amitabha Buddha, 72
Analects, 51, 100, 141, 245
An-ch'ing, 18–20
Anhwei Advanced Level School, 19
Anhwei Patriotic Society, 19
Anhwei Province, 3, 7, 10, 17–23,
    24–27, 49, 52*n*, 69, 72, 169, 245
Anhwei Vernacular Paper, 21
Anthology of Ancient-style Writings
    (Yao Nai), 52
Anthology of Literature, 81
antiforeign sentiment, 18
art, Western, 114
Auden, W. H., 255
Autumn in the Palace of Han, 107
"Awakening from the Dream," 197, 248
A-yung, 138

Bakunin, Mikhail Aleksandrovich, 102
Beat the Drum and Curse Ts'ao Ts'ao, 219
Beijing K'un-ch'ü Research Institute,
    179
Bibi, 194, 198, 207
"Big Precious," 246
Big Sister Ho, 44, 48
"Big Sister Kuo", 114–18
    as family entertainer, 115–18
"Black Nightmare," 221
Book of Family Names, The, 78
Book of Lieh Tzu, 38

bookshops, 21
Boxer Uprising, 18, 22, 74
bridesmaid in Hofei society, 2
Buddhism, Buddhist practices, 13,
    41–47, 57–58, 62, 68, 72
burial practices, 140
Burma, 34
Burma Road, 252

California, 184, 268
Canton, 107, 168
Central Labor Union, 107
Central News, 255
Chang Chao-ho, 15, 122, 153, 182,
    185–241, 266–68
    attractiveness of, 195–96
    birth of, 15
    Ch'ung-ho and, 216, 250–51, 252–53
    early life of, 65–68, 70, 81, 85, 87–88,
    118, 126, 196–98
    education of, 77–78, 126, 163, 168
    and "Little Ninth," 199–200, 206,
    208, 223
    marriage of, 194–95, 198–200,
    206–16, 220–23, 225–32, 234–41;
    see also Shen Ts'ung-wen
    as mother, 217–18, 223–24
    Yun-ho and, 157, 159, 161, 167–68,
    172–73, 182–83, 190–92, 197,
    198, 215
Chang Chih, 262
Chang Chih-lian, 173, 176

Chang Chong-ho, 230
Chang Ch'uan-fang, 179
Chang Ch'ung-ho (Chang Hsüan), 84,
    218, 223, 242–69
  on the art of *k'un-ch'ü*, 129, 248, 265
  on "Big Sister Kuo," 118
  birth of, 15–16
  as calligrapher, 259–65
  Chao-ho and, 216, 250–51, 252–53
  Chin Ta-chieh and, 120–21
  in Chungking, 257–66
  early years of, 60–61, 120–21, 242,
    246–47
  education of, 50–52, 138–39, 243,
    247, 249–51, 261
  marriage of, 266–67
  mother's death and, 60–62
  in opera club, 138–39, 149, 251–52
  parents as viewed by, 86, 92
  poetry of, 242–43, 263–64, 266, 269
  scholarly pursuits of, 248–49, 258–60
  Shih-hsiu and, 22, 28, 37, 38–39,
    60–61, 68
  Sino-Japanese War and, 110
  in U.S., 153, 182, 184
  on widowhood, 93
  Yuan-ho and, 126, 129
  Yun-ho and, 157–59, 166–67, 170–71
  in Yunnan, 252–55
Chang family:
  daughters' education as organized by,
    80–81
  domestics in, 47–49, 122
  estate in Hofei, 48–49
  holdings and treasures of, 52–53,
    64–65
  members of, listed, xiii–xiv
Chang Fei, 175–76
Chang Hsü, 96
Chang Hsüeh-ch'eng, 5–6, 137
Chang Hua-chen, 42, 46
Chang Hua-kuei, 42, 52–53, 82–83, 97
Chang Huan-ho, 170
Chang Hua-tou, 55
Chang I-lian, 183
Chang Shih-chao, 259–60, 265, 267
Chang Shu-sheng (Cho-yung Brave), 4,
    17, 24–25, 28–37, 38, 40, 48–49,

52, 55, 58, 64, 75–76, 82, 97, 103,
    140, 169
  foreign incursions as viewed by,
    34–35
  as governor-general, 29
  Western knowledge and technology
    as viewed by, 30–33
Chang Tai, 52–53, 150
Chang Ting-ho (Wu-ling's son), 85*n*,
    122, 171–72, 182–83
Chang Ting-ho (Yao-ling's son), 85–86,
    240
Chang Tsung-ch'ang, 245
Chang Tsung-ho, 85, 87, 89–91, 93–94,
    130, 132, 139, 209, 218, 251
Chang Wu-ling (Hsiao-sheng, Sheng-
    ching), 17, 24, 37, 69–71, 73–97,
    120, 127, 161–63, 166, 169, 198
  devoted to his children, 91–92,
    111–12
  dissipation as viewed by, 81–82
  and fall of Ch'ing dynasty, 18–20
  landholdings of, 4
  Lu Ying's relationship with, 61,
    67–68, 73
  military and, 74–75
  modern gadgets collected by, 114
  press and, 21–22
  principles and beliefs of, 86–87
  reasons for move of, 17–22
  scholarly interests of, 73–74, 76–77,
    89
  wedding of, 1–8
  women's education as commitment
    of, 77–81, 98, 102; *see also* Le-i
    Middle School
  Yen Hui-yü compared with, 145–46
Chang Yao-ling, 84–85
Chang Yin-ho, 130, 132
Chang Yin-ku, 28–29
Chang Yuan-ho, 9–12, 67–69, 93,
    125–54, 157, 182, 209, 267
  birth of, 9
  childhood of, 9–10, 120, 122, 161
  Ch'ung-ho and, 126, 129
  education of, 106, 163
  as family beauty, 196
  influence of Ling Hai-hsia on, 127–28

and Ku Ch'uan-chieh, 129–34,
144–46, 151–52, 154
life under the Japanese as viewed by,
146–47
mother's death and, 72, 87
stage performances and, 78–79, 107,
125–54, 248, 129
as university student, 133
in U.S., 184
Yun-ho and, 126, 146, 155
Chang Yü-ho, 89, 92, 112–14, 124
Chang Yun-ho (Erh-mao-tzu), 63, 118,
122–24, 153, 155–84, 188, 248,
259, 267
birth and early years of, 12–15, 61,
65, 88, 123, 126
Chao-ho and, 157, 159, 161, 167–68,
172–73, 182–83, 190–92, 197,
198, 215
Ch'ung-ho and, 157–59, 166–67,
170–71
Cultural Revolution and, 173, 179,
181–83
education of, 67, 88, 106–7, 126, 157,
162–65
as educator, 178–79
interrogated by "special agents,"
173–77
marriage of, 164–67, 172–73,
180–81, 199
as mother, 170–73
mother's death and, 70–72
parents as viewed by, 159
personal qualities of, 157, 159–61
stage performances and, 78, 143
Tai Chieh and, 166–68, 170, 256
in U.S., 184
Yuan-ho and, 126, 146, 155
Chang-ma, 246
Ch'ang-sha, 206–7, 214, 216, 238
Ch'ang-sheng, 45, 244–45
Chao Tzu-lung, 175–76
Chapei district, 109
Chaplin, Charlie, 114
Che-chen, 123
Chekiang province, 3, 7, 104
Ch'en Kan-kan, 10–12, 66
Ch'en She, 121, 143

Ch'en Tuan-sheng, 115–17
Ch'en Tu-hsiu, 19, 21, 261n
Chen Yin-k'e, 220
Ch'en-chou (Yuan-ling), 205
Ch'eng-kung, 182, 216, 223–24, 253–54
Cheng-kuo Temple, 156, 160
Ch'eng-te, 238–39
Ch'eng-tu, 170, 171–73, 182
Chi Fang, 152
Chia-ling River, 263
Chiang Kai-shek, 83–84, 86, 102, 105,
147, 245, 257–59
Chiang-yin, 92–93
Ch'iao-ling, 83–84
Ch'ien Mu, 251
Chihli province, 24, 83
Chi-li, 99
Ch'in dynasty, 121–22
Chin Ta-chieh ("Golden Older Sister,"
Ku-chih), 120–22
China Bank, 55
China College, 77, 163–64, 186–87
China Times, 74
Chin-chou, 203
Chinese City in Shanghai, 21
Chinese Maritime Customs Service, 140
Chinese society:
education in, see education
importance of male progeny in, 1, 4
social status of entertainers in,
135–39, 143–44
traditional marriage customs in, 1–5, 7
unwed mothers in, 166–67
Ch'ing dynasty, 2–4, 29, 77, 98, 257
fall of, 18–20
government of, 17–21, 26–27, 30,
34–35, 75, 102–3
Ch'ing New Army, 19
Ching-hsien Girls' School, 104–5
Ching-men-chou, 156
Ching-pao, 74
Ching-te, 68
Ch'in-huai River, 105
Chinling University, 144
Chinling Women's College, 89
Ch'iu Chin, 7–8, 9
Chou Ch'uan-ying, 129–30, 133, 136,
139, 141, 143

Chou dynasty, 6, 82, 99, 257
Chou En-lai, 240
Chou Fo-hai, 102, 147, 150
Chou Hsiao-ho, 168, 170–72
Chou Hsiao-p'ing, 168, 171–73
Chou Yu-kuang, 164–67, 169–73,
    180–83
Chou-kung Mountain, 169
Ch'u, ancient kingdom of, 24
Chu Kan-kan, 65–66, 68, 118–19, 135,
    191, 196–97, 199, 210, 217
Ch'u Min-i, 138, 149
Chu Mo-ch'ing, 41, 51, 245, 249, 262
Chu Tzu-ch'ing, 220
Ch'ü Yuan, 24, 88
Ch'üan-fu troupe, 79, 140
Chuang Tzu, 24, 36, 264
Ch'uan-hsi opera school, 139–42, 179
Chü-chih, 66, 120
Chu-ke Liang, 108
Chung Han-fu, 201
Ch'ung-chen, Emperor, 139
Chungking, 62, 83, 169–71, 182, 257,
    259–63, 268
Chung-ma, 45–48, 55, 117–18, 246
Chung-shan University, 168
Classic of Changes, 6, 9, 96
Classic of Music, 257
Classic of Odes, 5–6, 51, 82, 249, 258
Classic of Rites, 257
Columbia University, 188
Communications University, see
    Nanyang Public College
Communist History Commission, 179
Communists, Communist Party, 85–86,
    101–2, 104–7, 152–54, 178, 180,
    231, 237, 240, 245, 267–68
    Cultural Revolution and, 173, 179,
        181–83, 239, 267
    First Congress of, 102
    Fourth Congress of, 104–5
Communist Youth League, 104–5
concubines, 46, 54, 69–70, 167
Confucius, 37, 40, 43, 49, 88, 100, 103,
    121, 135–36, 141, 245, 253, 257
Connecticut, 268
Consolidated University, 219, 252,
    254–56

"Courtyard Full of Fragrance," 91
Creation Society, 74
Cultural Ministry, 179–80, 236
Cultural Revolution, 173, 179, 181–83,
    239, 267

"Deed of Sale for My Hill, A," 72
"Destiny of Rebirth, The" (Ch'en Tuan-
    sheng), 115
Doctrine of the Mean, 51
dowries, 4–5, 70–71
"Drinking Water" (Nara Singde), 88

Echo Mountain Academy, 76
education, 98–110
    of Chao-ho, 77–78, 126, 163, 168
    of Ch'ung-ho, 50–52, 138–39, 243,
        247, 249–51, 261
    of Ku Ch'uan-chieh, 144
    in Nanking, 163, 165, 168, 232
    of nurse-nannies, 65–67, 118–19
    as organized by Chang family, 80–81
    private, history of, 76–77
    in Shanghai, 102–9, 127, 128, 133,
        144
    women's, as commitment of Wu-ling,
        77–81, 98, 102; see also Le-i
        Middle School
    of Yuan-ho, 106, 163
    of Yun-ho, 67, 88, 106–7, 126, 157,
        162–65
England, 267
estate management, 49–50

"Family Letters" (Li Hung-chang), 39
Farewell My Concubine, 90
Feng Yü-hsiang, 84
Feng-huang, 186, 204, 231, 237–38
"Finding the Painting and Questioning
    the Painting," 133
"Fine Occasion, A," 166, 183
Firemen's Association of K'un-shan, 130
folk remedies, 113
Foochow, 34–36
fortune-telling, 16, 166
fox spirits, belief in, 62–63, 243–44
France, 31, 33–35, 40, 74, 148
Frankel, Hans, 266–68

French Concession in Shanghai, 15, 21, 105, 146, 148
Freud, Sigmund, 255, 259
funeral rites and practices, 57–59, 69
Fung Yu-lan, 251

Garden of Three Elegances, 134
"Gazing at the Rainbow" (Shen Ts'ung-wen), 222–23
Germany, 74, 148, 266
gift giving, art of, 66, 68–69
Gotanara, Prince, 221
Grandma Number Two, 217, 253–54
Grand World Entertainment Center, 142
Great Britain, 31, 34, 74, 107
Great Learning, 51
"Green Nightmare" (Shen Ts'ung-wen), 220

Hai-hsia Middle School, 129
Haimen county, 126, 128, 151–53
Hainan Island, 168
Han dynasty, 121, 155
Han Kuang-wu, 116
Han Shih-ch'ang, 138, 184
Hangchow, 91, 140, 165, 167–68
Hanlin Academy, 27
Hanoi, 35
Heart Sutra, 183
History of the Former Han, 51
Ho-ch'uan, 170
Hofei, 2, 4, 10–11, 13, 16–17, 22, 23–37, 39, 43–44, 49, 51, 63, 75, 81, 83, 85–86, 96–97, 110, 112, 114, 119, 122–24, 146, 157, 169, 208–9, 217, 243, 245–49, 255, 268
    brides in, 4
    early history of, 23–24
    new gentry in, 25
Hofei Spirit, 23–37
Honan province, 3
Hong Kong, 84, 107, 148, 214–15, 255
Hou Shao-ch'iu, 101–7
"Housewife" (Shen Ts'ung-wen), 194–95, 198, 200, 207, 221, 226–27
Hsiang Yü, 90

Hsin-wen-pao, 74
Hsi-tan, 226
Hsü county, 18
Hsü Hsi-lin, 7
Hsü Ling-yun, 132
Hsü Shu-yin, 177
Hsün Tzu, 57
Hu Shih, 77, 158, 187–91, 194, 219, 251, 256
Hu Yeh-p'ing, 225, 231
Hua Mu-lan, 191
Huai Army, 27–28, 36, 76
Huai River, 2, 23
Huai-nan-tzu, 219
Huai-pei, life in, 2–3
Huang Ching-jen, 90
Hu-hsi, 204, 238
Hui-chou, 3, 22
Hunan province, 207, 215, 231, 233, 237
Hung Hsiu-ch'üan, 79
Hung-fu, 120, 192
Hupei province, 83, 183, 239

I Tun, 121
Illinois, University of, 140
Imperial Museum, 235
India, 34, 259
Inner Mongolia, 180
International Settlement in Shanghai, 21, 107
Italy, 74, 148

Jade Springs Hill, 156–57, 160
Japan, 34, 74, 83, 91, 94, 102, 109–10, 124, 139, 142, 163, 165, 182
    see also Sino-Japanese War
Jesus, 253
"Jolted Back to Reality," 130–32
Joyce, James, 255
Jujube Valley, 170

Kan Ch'en-yü, 81
kan-kan, see nurse-nannies
Kansu province, 84
Kao Kan-kan, 16, 65–66, 70, 120–22, 124, 153, 253–54
Kele Mountain, 261

Kiangsi province, 23, 68–69
Kiangsu province, 3, 24, 77, 102, 104,
    147–48, 152
King Wen, 6–7, 99
Ku Ch'uan-chieh, 125, 130–33, 136,
    139, 141–54
  education of, 139–41, 144
  marriage of, 144–46, 151–55
  as performer, 130–34
  Yen Hui-yü and, 141–45, 148–49,
    152
Ku Chüeh, 151–53
Kuan, Lord, 155–57, 160, 175
Kuang-hsü, Emperor, 30, 33
Kuang-hua Middle School, 163–65,
    170, 173
Kuan-yin, 238, 253
Ku-chin ("Past and Present"), 150–51
k'un-ch'ü opera, 69, 78–80, 90, 114,
    125–54, 160, 171, 179–80, 218,
    248–49, 251, 259, 265
  amateur groups in, 138–39, 149, 179,
    251–52
  history of, 134–35
  in Shanghai theaters, 134
K'ung Chih-kuei, 233
K'un-ming, 207, 214–16, 220, 222–24,
    252, 254–55
K'un-shan, 130
Kuo Mo-jo, 108–9, 228
Kuomintang, see Nationalists,
    Nationalist Party
Kwangsi, 24, 29, 33
Kwangtung province, 24, 29, 32, 34–35,
    37, 40, 76

"Lady Wang Crossing the Border,"
    107–8
Lao She, 119
Lao Tou, see Tou Kan-kan
Lashio, 252
Le-i Middle School, 77, 93–94, 98–110,
    120, 127–28, 162–64, 166, 228,
    232, 247
  early history of, 100–101
  fees and expenses of, 101
  as source of subversive activities, 105–6
Li Ch'ing, 192

Li Ch'ing-chao, 42
Li Ching-shih, 39–40
Li Hung-chang, 24, 27–28, 33–34,
    38–41, 102
Li Po, 88, 132–33
Li Yü, 72, 145, 150
Li Yun-chang, 38–39, 41
Liang-tang Studio, 90
Lieh Tzu, 180
likin, see transit tax
Lin Tai-yü, 160–61
Ling Hai-hsia, 126–29, 146–47, 151–54
Ling Hung, see Ku Chüeh
Ling Yen-ch'ih, 208
Li-niang, 161
literature, nationalistic, 108–10
"Little Ninth Sister," 199–200, 206, 208,
    223
Liu An, 24
Liu Chieh-p'ing, 50
Liu Ming-ch'uan, 25–28
Liu Ts'ui-ying, 113
Liu Wen-tien, 219, 251, 256
Lotus Sutra, 47
Lu Chung-lien, 36
Lu Meng, 156
Lu O-t'ing, 142
Lu Ying, 1–8, 9–10, 12, 15–16, 60–72,
    78, 87–88, 92–93, 118, 121, 159,
    161–62
  clothing and appearance of, 62
  death of, 70–72
  as devoted to nurse-nannies, 65–67,
    71
  dowry of, 2, 4–5
  as family arbiter and financial
    planner, 64–65
  "literacy campaign" of, 65–67,
    118–19
  as "quiet woman," 5–7
  wedding of, 1–8
  Wu-ling's relationship with, 61,
    67–68, 73
Lu-chiang county, 11
Lyrics of Ch'u, 87

Manchuria, 91, 227
Manchus, 7, 18, 24, 147

Mao Tse-tung, 104, 240
Marco Polo Bridge Incident, 182, 207
marriage customs and traditions, 1–5, 119–20
Marxism, 108
    see also Communists, Communist Party
May Fourth movement, 75, 102–3, 164
May Seventh Cadre School, 239
May Thirtieth Incident, 106–8
Mei Lan-fang, 68, 184
Mencius, 36, 43, 51
Mencius, 51, 81
Meng Li-chün, 115–17, 120
Miao tribe, 253–54
midwifery, 12–13
Military Preparatory Academy, 19
Min River, 182
Ming Battalion, 27
Ming dynasty, 53
Ming-huang, Emperor, 130–32, 139, 154
Ministry of Education, 254–55, 257–58
Ministry of Rites, 258
"Misplaced Kite, The," 184
Mo Tzu, 121
"Mother's Reunion, A," 131–32
Mu Ou-ch'u, 140–43
"Multipurpose Scholar, The," 192
"My Life in Middle School," 250

Nankai University, 207, 216
Nanking, 43, 47, 89, 149, 255
    boarding schools in, 163, 165, 168, 232
    celebrities in, 138
Nanyang Public College, 102–3
Nara Singde, 88
Nationalists, Nationalist Party
    (Kuomintang), 84, 86, 92, 102, 104–7, 138, 146–47, 149, 152, 227, 229–31, 240, 245
    see also Chiang Kai-shek
National Revolutionary Army, 84
New Culture movement, 160
New Fourth Army, 152

New York, N.Y., 188
Nien rebels, 3, 17, 24, 26–28, 36, 169
Ninghsia, 180–81, 183, 250
North China University, 232–33
North Haven, 268–69
Notes on a Trip to Hunan (Shen Ts'ung-wen), 207, 234
nurse-nannies, 111–24
    duties and rewards of, 10–12, 65–67, 71
    education of, 65–67, 118–19
    literature as seen by, 114
    modern marriage as seen by, 119–20

opera, see *k'un-ch'ü; Peking Opera
opium addiction, 81–82

Pa Chin, 119
Pa Fortress, 171
Pa Gorge, 97
Palace of Eternal Life, The, 131, 154
Pao-hsing, 44
Pao-ting Military Academy, 83
"Past and Present" (*Ku-chin*), 150–51
Peach Blossom Fan, 248
Peach Blossom Springs, 239
Peking, 18, 22, 24, 34, 52, 75, 83, 119, 126–27, 150, 153, 165, 179–82, 185, 187, 195, 198–99, 205, 207, 210–11, 215–16, 222, 224–25, 227–31, 239–40, 249–51, 255–60, 267
Peking Historical Museum, 233
"Peking Home Cooking," 151
Peking Opera, 68, 78–79, 84, 108, 114, 133, 139, 175, 217–18
Peking Railway Station, 19
Peking University, 173, 207, 216, 224, 228, 233, 249–51, 254, 256, 266
Peony Pavilion, The, 80, 133, 145, 161, 248
People's Daily, 178
People's Education Press, 178
People's Literature, 235
Pien Chih-lin, 255–56
P'u-ching, 156
P'u-i, Emperor, 20
Purists, 33–34, 103

Rangoon, 252
Records of the Grand Historian, 51, 57, 81
Red Guard, 181
Red Pear, The, 130
Revolutionary Alliance, 19
"Rich and Poor" (T'ang Yüeh-hua), 109
Rilke, Rainer Maria, 161*n*
Romance of the Three Kingdoms, 108
"Ruse of an Empty City," 107–8
Russia, 18, 34
Russia-China Airline, 252

St. John's University, 70
St. Mary and McTyeire, 163
Salt Commission, 18, 63
schools, *see* education; *specific schools*
Scotland, 259
Second Sister Ju-i, 44, 48
Shang Hsiao-yun, 68
Shanghai, 11, 38, 47, 58, 61, 67–70, 74, 76, 81, 92, 100, 114, 125–28, 130, 161, 163, 179, 182, 194, 196–97, 224, 235, 248, 251–52, 267–68
    Chinese City in, 21
    courtesans and prostitutes in, 21
    crime in, 177
    education in, 102–9, 127, 128, 133, 144
    energy and edginess of, 20–21, 22
    French Concession in, 15, 21, 105, 146, 148
    Hofei compared with, 17, 22
    International Settlement in, 21, 107
    moral ambiguities of, 21
    Nationalist assault on Communists in, 245
    press of (1890–1910), 21–22
    in Sino-Japanese War, 142–43, 146–52, 165–69
    social history of, 20–22
    theater in, 125, 130, 133–34, 141, 143
Shanghai Art Academy, 93
Shanghai Opera, 78
Shanghai Student Union, 102
Shanghai University, 104
Shantung province, 3, 36, 41, 74, 245–46
Shao-hsing, 7

Shen Ch'uan-chih, 251–52
Shen Hu-ch'u (Hu-hu), 214*n*, 215–16, 218, 221–22, 224, 227, 232, 239, 255, 267
Shen Lung-chu (Lung-lung), 182, 215–16, 218, 221, 223, 226, 232, 239
Shen Ts'ung-wen, 119, 173, 182–83, 185–241, 250–51, 253–57, 267–68
    as father, 218–22
    love letters of, 185–86, 193, 204–5, 213–14, 225–57
    travel letters of, 200–205, 213–14, 237–39
    on writing, 227–28, 234–37
Shen Yin-mo, 259–63, 267
Shen Yüeh-ch'üan, 133, 141
Shen Yun-liu, 205
Sheng Hsüan-huai, 102
Shen-pao, 74, 107
Shih-hsiu, 38–59, 60–61, 62, 68, 86, 243, 247
    Buddhist beliefs and practices of, 42–47
    conservative and liberal qualities of, 40–41, 50–51
    death and funeral rites of, 57–59
    as family mediator, 54–55
    widowhood of, 46, 53, 57
Shou-ning Lane, Soochow, 61, 72, 80
Shu-ch'eng county, 11
Sino-Japanese War (1937–1945), 54, 84, 146–50, 207, 216
    occupation of China in, 94, 109–10, 146–50, 168
    Shanghai in, 142–43, 146–52, 165–69
    see also Japan
"Slanted Cap" (Nara Singde), 88
Soochow, 11, 23, 47, 60–61, 69–70, 72, 74, 77, 79–80, 86, 93–95, 99–101, 105–8, 110, 112, 114, 117, 119–20, 123, 126, 129–30, 135–36, 139–40, 153, 157, 162, 177, 179, 198, 217, 222, 235, 247, 251–52, 255, 266
Soochow Communist Party, 101

Soochow Gazette, 74
Soochow Sports Meet, 90
Southwest Consolidated University, 216
spirit tablet, 23, 37, 59, 103
Ssu River, 156
Ssu-ma Ch'ien, 57, 99, 121
Stone Lotus Pavilion, 238
"Story of Hung-fu, The," 107–8
Story of the Stone (Ts'ao Hsüeh-ch'in),
    53*n*, 160–61, 219, 256
"Stroll in the Garden, A," 80, 184, 197
Su River, 182
Su-chou (Anhwei province), 18
Sun Yat-sen, 19, 104, 147, 247, 258
Sung dynasty, 102
Sung-chiang, 102, 104
Su-pao, 19, 21
Szechwan province, 52, 81, 83, 96, 169,
    182, 215, 235

Ta-ch'ien Mountain, 25–26
Ta-hsia University, 128, 133, 162–63
Tai Chieh, 166–68, 170, 256
Taichung, 154
T'ai-jen, 6–7, 99
Taiping Rebellion, 17–18, 24–29, 37, 48,
    75, 77, 79, 169
T'ai-po, 99–100, 110
T'ai-ssu, 6–7
Taiwan, 28, 35–36, 84, 122, 152–54, 267
T'ang dynasty, 98, 131
T'ang Wei-chih, 103
T'ang Yüeh-hua, 110
Tangyang county, 156
t'an-tz'u, 115
T'ao Chu, 121
T'ao Hsi-ch'üan, 141–43
Tao-ming-shih, 47
T'ao-yuan, 200
Ta-tung Cigarette Company, 148
Temple of Supreme Pureness, 170
"Tetrametrical Classic," 51
Texas A & M, 140
theater, *see k'un-ch'ü;* Peking Opera
Theater Monthly, 90
"Third Party," 152
Thirteen Classics, 248
Three Kingdoms period, 175

Three Knights-Errant, The, 192
Three Principles of the People, 247
Tibet, 34
Tientsin, 207, 214, 224
Times, 74
Ting Ling, 225, 231–32
Tokyo, 149
Tolstoy, Leo, 203, 227
Tou Kan-kan (Lao Tou), 65–67, 123,
    135, 157, 159, 196
transit tax, 18, 83
"Trimetrical Classic," 51
Ts'ai Wen-chi, 265–67
Ts'ao Hsüeh-ch'in, 53*n*, 160–61, 219,
    234, 256
Ts'ao Ts'ao, 156, 265
Ts'ao Tzu-chien, 234
Ts'ao Yü, 109
Ts'ao-hsien, 11
Tseng Kuo-fan, 27, 36–37, 169
Tseng Ts'an, 141
Tsinghua University, 207, 216, 229,
    251
Tsingtao, 198, 224, 236, 251
Tso Commentary, 51, 249
Tu Fu, 88, 96–97
Tuan Ch'i-jui, 75, 259
T'ung-ch'eng Public School, 19
T'ung-meng-hui, 19
Turgenev, Ivan Sergeyevich, 238
Twelve Classics, 90
Tz'u-hsi (empress dowager), 33

United States, 74, 147, 153, 182, 184,
    267–68

Valéry, Paul, 255–56
Variegated Brush, 132
Verlaine, Paul, 255–56
Versailles Peace Conference, 74–75
Vichy French, 148
Vietnam, 33, 40, 214–15
Violent Storm Society, 74
"Visitor from Outer Space," 192

Wan, Miss, 157
Wang Chao-chün, 107–8
Wang Ching-wei, 102, 147, 149–50

310 ❖ INDEX

Wang Kan-kan, 112–14, 117, 124
   folk remedies of, 113
   speech characteristics of, 112, 114
Wang Meng-luan, 80, 120
Wang Shih-p'eng, 131–32
Wei Chün-i, 92–96, 123, 127, 163
Wen Ch'ou, 156
Wen I-tuo, 251
Wen T'ien-hsiang, 102
West Hofei Academy, 25, 76
West Hofei county, 46, 58, 94–95
West Hunan, 119, 186–87, 199–200,
   210, 212, 218, 222, 235
Western art, 114
"When Flowers Shed Their Petals"
   (Chang Yun-ho), 164
White Deer Hollow Academy, 76
widowhood, conditions of, 53, 55–57
Wild Cherry Blossoms (Kuo Mo-jo), 108
Wild Goose Pavilion, 98
women:
   in childbirth, 11
   in Chou dynasty, 6
   education of, as commitment of Wu-
     ling, 77–81, 98, 102; *see also* Le-i
     Middle School
   as midwives, 12–13
   as nurse-nannies, *see* nurse-nannies
   wet nurses, 13–14, 95
   widowhood of, 11
Women's Normal School, 259
"Written While Plastered," 132–33,
   139, 143
Wu, 99
Wu County Daily, 74

Wu Gorge, 97
Wu T'ien-jan, 80
Wuchang, 19
Wuhan, 169, 214
Wuhu, 2–3, 18, 48, 55, 83
Wusung, 187
Wu-wei county, 11

Yale University, 268
Yan Liang, 156
Yang Chen-sheng, 199, 207–9, 219, 225
Yang Pa-chieh, 165
Yang Yü-huan ("Jade Bracelet"),
   131–32
Yang-chou, 1–4, 43–44, 62–63, 71, 80,
   151
Yangtze River, 2, 23, 25, 42, 49, 52, 77,
   126, 142, 170
Yao Nai, 52
Yeats, William Butler, 255
Yellow River, 2
Yen Fu, 77
Yen Hsi-shan, 84
Yen Hui-yü, 141–46, 147–54
Yen Tzu-ling, 116
Yenan, 231
Yin-chou, 22
Yü Ts'ai-yun, 79–80, 129, 141, 184
Yuan Mei, 137
Yuan River, 186, 236
Yuan-ling, 208, 223
Yü-chung, 99, 110
Yüeh Fei, 102
Yunnan province, 34–35, 182, 207, 217,
   220–21, 226

A Note on the Author

Annping Chin was born in Taiwan in 1950 to a family from the mainland, and moved with them to Richmond, Virginia, in 1962. She received her Ph.D. in Chinese Thought from Columbia, and is the author of *Children of China: Voices from Recent Years* and co-author with Jonathan Spence, her husband, of *The Chinese Century: A Photographic History of the Last Hundred Years*. She currently teaches in the History department at Yale, where her fields of study include Confucianism, Taoism, and the early Chinese textual tradition.